SECURITY IN THE
Private Cloud

SECURITY IN THE
Private Cloud

EDITED BY
JOHN R. VACCA

CRC Press
Taylor & Francis Group
Boca Raton   London   New York

CRC Press is an imprint of the
Taylor & Francis Group, an **informa** business

CRC Press
Taylor & Francis Group
6000 Broken Sound Parkway NW, Suite 300
Boca Raton, FL 33487-2742

© 2017 by Taylor & Francis Group, LLC
CRC Press is an imprint of Taylor & Francis Group, an Informa business

No claim to original U.S. Government works

Printed on acid-free paper
Version Date: 20160628

International Standard Book Number-13: 978-1-4822-5955-1 (Hardback)

Library of Congress Cataloging-in-Publication Data

Names: Vacca, John R., editor.
Title: Security in the private cloud / editor, John R. Vacca.
Description: Boca Raton : Taylor & Francis, a CRC title, part of the Taylor &
Francis imprint, a member of the Taylor & Francis Group, the academic
division of T&F Informa, plc, [2017] | Includes bibliographical references
and index.
Identifiers: LCCN 2016024366 | ISBN 9781482259551 (hardback)
Subjects: LCSH: Cloud computing--Security measures. | Computer
networks--Security measures.
Classification: LCC QA76.585 .S4435 2017 | DDC 004.67/82--dc23
LC record available at https://lccn.loc.gov/2016024366

Visit the Taylor & Francis Web site at
http://www.taylorandfrancis.com

and the CRC Press Web site at
http://www.crcpress.com

Printed and bound in the United States of America by Publishers Graphics,
LLC on sustainably sourced paper.

This book is dedicated to my wife, Bee.

Contents

SECTION V **Appendices**

Foreword

Private clouds are very handy to have. An enterprise can load up its private cloud with a wide variety of applications and resources for users to access from almost anywhere. This makes things easier for the user and can simplify the requirements for building a complex network.

However, your private cloud will still require security as a computing environment as a whole, as well as for the individual applications and resources in the cloud. This requires layered security that first provides user access to the cloud, or parts of it, and then specific user rights for various applications. Resources may also need to be segregated in a manner that an unauthorized user may not even know the existence of some applications or data.

In this book, John R. Vacca provides the applicable knowledge and experience to help you secure your private cloud, the applications in your cloud, and the data stored in your cloud. Let's face it: we are in the age of hacks, cracks, and data theft. There are external threats as well as internal threats. You need to protect your cloud-based assets, and this book will help you do that.

Michael Erbschloe
Webster University

Michael Erbschloe teaches information security courses at Webster University in St. Louis, Missouri.

Preface

SCOPE OF COVERAGE

This comprehensive handbook serves as a professional reference as well as a practitioner's guide to today's most complete and concise view of private cloud security. The handbook defines private cloud computing security and establishes a strong working knowledge of the concepts and technologies needed to migrate your data center into a private cloud security solution. The knowledge you gain will enable you to determine whether the private cloud security solution is appropriate for your organization from a business and technical perspective to select the appropriate cloud security model and to plan and implement a cloud security adoption and migration strategy. Furthermore, this handbook will show you how to work with on- and off-premises private cloud computing security technologies and obtain practical experience in implementing security for private clouds. In the handbook, there is an emphasis on the layers of security associated with private cloud security implementations.

The primary audience for this handbook consists of engineers/scientists interested in monitoring and analyzing specific measurable private cloud computing security environments, which may include transportation and/or infrastructure systems, mechanical systems, seismic events, and underwater environments. This book will also be useful for security and related professionals interested in tactical surveillance and mobile private cloud computing security target classification and tracking; other individuals with an interest in using private cloud computing security to understand specific environments; undergraduate and graduate students; members from academia, government, and industry; anyone seeking to exploit the benefits of private cloud computing security technologies, including assessing the architectures, components, operation, and tools of private cloud computing; and anyone involved in the security aspects of private cloud computing who has knowledge at the level of the introduction to private cloud computing or equivalent experience. This comprehensive reference and practitioner's guide will also be of value to students taking upper division undergraduate- and graduate-level courses in private cloud computing security.

ORGANIZATION OF THIS BOOK

The book is organized into five sections composed of 20 contributed chapters by leading experts in their fields and three appendices, including an extensive glossary of cloud security terms and acronyms.

Section I: Introduction to Private Cloud Security

This section discusses private cloud computing essentials, which include cloud computing service models, namely, software as a service (SaaS), platform as a service (PaaS), infrastructure as a service (IaaS), and desktop as a service (DaaS); public, virtual private, and hybrid; and cyber security fundamentals. This section also covers private cloud security baselines and software and data segregation security.

Chapter 1, "Private Cloud Computing Essentials," sets the stage for the rest of the book, by presenting insight into how the cloud market is offering multiple options for businesses to transition their infrastructure, development platform, storage, and software. This chapter also covers how true innovation comes when successfully navigating the cloud space from traditional on-premise models to a recurring revenue model. Finally, it discusses how service providers are offering hybrid, private, and public cloud solutions, which lead to better efficiency, self-service, manipulation, and variety.

Chapter 2, "Integration of Enterprise Content Management and Software as a Service," explores the integration of enterprise content management systems with SaaS applications from the perspective of the user, that is, the enterprise. Terminology is defined, products are examined, security and risk considerations are raised, integration models are discussed, and examples of the integration between ECM systems and SaaS applications are provided.

Chapter 3, "Infrastructure as a Service," reviews the major components of a private cloud infrastructure to help you think about the security of that architecture. Next, it discusses a few high-level conceptual issues. Then, the chapter actually breaks down a cloud infrastructure into its various component pieces.

Chapter 4, "Preservation as a Service for Trust," addresses the difficulty in preserving digital information over the long term with its inherent risks of loss or corruption, and how the ITrust project is generating the theoretical and methodological frameworks necessary to develop local, national, and international policies; procedures; regulations; standards; and legislation that is able to ensure public trust in digital records. In support of this goal, the authors show how ITrust established the preservation as a service for trust (PaaST) project in order to develop a set of requirements that establish a foundation for trusting the preservation of digital information.

Chapter 5, "Software and Data Segregation Security," examines data segregation in cloud landscape, which is dictated through the allocation of a universal nonrepudiated subscribe identity. It also discusses the changes the conventional internal business system concept, because all cloud services subscribers are expected to share a single instance of computing power, database, network, cloud front end, and data resilience.

Section II: Achieving Security in a Private Cloud

This section discusses how to take full responsibility for cyber security by managing the risks of public clouds and identifying and assigning security tasks in each SPI service model: SaaS, PaaS, and IaaS. Next, it shows how to select the appropriate product, by comparing product-specific security features and organizational implementation requirements.

It focuses on the virtual private cloud (VPC) by showing how to simulate a private cloud in the public environment: Google Secure Data Connector and Amazon VPC. It also covers the hybrid cloud alternative by connecting on-premises data with cloud applications, securely bridging with VPC, and expanding capacity to meet business surges. Finally, it explains identification and privacy in the cloud.

Chapter 6, "Taking Full Responsibility for Cyber Security in the Private Cloud," discusses how cyber criminals create an unprecedented challenge to corporate information professionals on critical information asset protection. It also discusses why migration to cloud environments leads to diverse difficulty.

Chapter 7, "Selecting the Appropriate Product," explores the difference between the conventional internal enterprise information evaluation and how the cloud computing environment spans across the internal network and the Internet. It also explores the difference between the conventional internal enterprise information evaluation, how the cloud computing environment spans across the internal network, and the Internet; as well as, how it applies to the hybrid cloud environment. Finally, it focuses on how the selection of cloud computing services starts with a management initiative to take a risk-based approach.

Chapter 8, "Virtual Private Cloud," discusses that with the implementation of the VMware vCloud Suite, the foundation for IaaS will be built, and it is essential for delivering these use cases. It presents the core components of the vCloud Suite: vSphere and vCloud Director (VCD). Then, it specifies the design requirement for two vSphere clusters: an existing production cluster that will be used to host management components and a new two-node cluster that will serve as the initial resource cluster. In addition, it then focuses on the single VCD cell that will be deployed to provide access to the VCD environment. Finally, it shows that by leveraging a vCloud Suite, an IT department will be able to deliver IaaS functionality to the business and increase the overall performance, management efficiency, availability, and recoverability of the test, development, and training infrastructure.

Chapter 9, "Security in the Virtual Private Cloud," explains how VPC evolves naturally in the cloud computing landscape to address risks, vulnerabilities, and business concerns in public and community cloud. It also explains how private cloud attempts to address the security gaps in the emerging cloud computing architecture. Finally, it discusses how more development in VPC can be noted in the following areas: virtual partitioning, fine-grained privacy level, configurable security, and access controls.

Section III: Implementing Security in a Private Cloud

This section discusses the characteristics of private cloud security solutions, such as identifying public and private cloud security technologies and defining a generic public and private cloud security framework. Next, it explores how to transition security to a private cloud, which includes migrating a data center to the cloud by identifying critical performance metrics and autonomic computing with a private cloud. Then, it shows how to secure the management of virtualized resources. It also shows how to improve utilization with virtualization by choosing para- or hardware-assisted virtualization, utilize cores and hyper-threading, calculate the performance of EC2 Compute Units, and compare virtualization and cloud computing. It then presents the deployment of an on-premises system center virtual machine manager (VMM) private cloud through a discussion of virtualizing with Microsoft Hyper-V hypervisor, which includes validating with Microsoft Assessment and Planning Toolkit, creating three types of virtual networks, and matching virtual CPUs to logical CPUs. Next, it covers aggregating virtual cloud resources with VMM (managing the cloud via the VMM Administrator Console, generalizing virtual machine templates and defining profiles, and provisioning users with role-based access control); creating images (performing Physical to virtual (P2V) and Virtual to Virtual (V2V) migrations and organizing VMM library resources); and deploying virtual machines (template-based, shared ISO images, and overwriting a virtual hard drive [VHD]). Then, it presents a description of how to monitor private cloud resources with a system center operations manager, which includes leveraging management packs (monitoring computers, devices, services, and applications, and creating a resource pool) and reporting on the private cloud operation (audit collection services reporting and tracking service levels). Next, it covers continuous private cloud monitoring and shows how to manage a private cloud with a system center service manager, such as leveraging the cloud services process pack (creating a cloud-based pricing chargeback process, automating the deployment of tested Integration as a Service [IASS], and requesting cloud resources with self-service), automating the private cloud (deploying service request catalogs and fulfilling service requests with an orchestrator), and adapting your IT service best practices (incident and problem resolution, change control, asset life cycle management, Microsoft Operations Framework, and Information Technology Infrastructure Library). Next, it shows how to deploy a hosted Amazon VPC, which includes evaluating the benefits of a VPC (creating multiple private and public networks, controlling packets with network access control lists (ACLs), and routing and leveraging elastic network interfaces), and how to deploy a VPC and launch instances (selecting from preset VPC configurations and applying a Classless Inter-Domain Routing address). Then, it describes how to secure a private cloud, such as identifying security weak spots (assessing vulnerabilities and hacking private clouds, and evaluating Amazon Machine Image security) and meeting governance requirements (securing with IT GRC Process Management Pack and protecting users with the Data Protection Manager). This section then discusses cloud security assessment and authorization. It shows a presentation of how to create a hybrid cloud solution, which includes expanding your private cloud (handling excess demand with cloud bursting, connecting your cloud with a virtual private network, and monitoring hybrid cloud with AWS Management Pack) and evolving to hybrid clouds (exploiting the advantages of hybrid clouds and examining hybrid cloud use cases). Finally, it presents an analysis of joint security and privacy aware protocol design.

Chapter 10, "The Hybrid Cloud Alternative," discusses how the hybrid cloud is a promising option to address practical business concerns. It also explains how the current public and private cloud solutions can only handle isolated business situations. It then describes how continuous merger and acquisition complicate business landscape to demand a quick provision and deployment approach. It focuses on why hybrid cloud is a blending of all known cloud technologies. Finally, it explains why OpenStack is an open source to realize this paradigm of hybrid cloud.

Chapter 11, "Identification and Privacy in the Secure Cloud," discusses the concept of identity authentication and its implication for cloud systems. It also discusses the fundamentals of identity in the cloud, the concept of identity assurance, and the considerations for selection of identity authentication technologies and models for the cloud.

Chapter 12, "Private Cloud Security and Identification," examines various identity management and encryption approaches, in order to elaborate the value contribution to the general cloud ecosystem.

Chapter 13, "Secure Management of Virtualized Resources," introduces security issues and solutions. It further delves into virtual resource management. In particular, it deals with real hardware offering virtual resource sharing to cloud hosts, tasks, and services. In order to do that, it further describes the characteristics of the current technology.

Chapter 14, "Designing Cloud Security and Operations Models in the Changed Geopolitical Environment," outlines some of the challenges and developments in the world that could make the usage of cloud more complicated because of newly emerging country specific laws, regulations, and industry standards.

Chapter 15, "Continuous Private Cloud Security Monitoring," outlines some core principles and best practices for security monitoring of IT systems, especially within the context of cloud, and points out the cloud-specific activities that must be considered by a cloud system administrator.

Chapter 16, "Cloud Security Assessment and Authorization," reviews assessment and authorization methods, and activities for cloud-based information systems.

Chapter 17, "Assessment and Authorization in Private Cloud Security," discusses various cloud computing security issues, in particular, those regarding authorization and security assessment. It introduces security challenges and approaches, which result in a broad survey that tries to shed a light on security issues of cloud computing, mainly focusing on the issues related to security assessment and authorization. Based on the survey, this chapter discusses the differences between the various approaches; some are still evolving, and their security has yet to be improved further, whereas others are more technically mature.

Section IV: Advanced Private Cloud Computing Security

This section focuses on advanced private cloud computing security, advanced failure detection and prediction, future directions in private cloud computing security risks and challenges, private cloud computing with advanced security services, and advanced security architectures for private cloud computing.

Chapter 18, "Advanced Security Architectures for Private Cloud Computing," addresses the scope and the nature of privacy and security within the private cloud computing infrastructure.

Chapter 19, "Advanced Private Cloud Computing Security Architectures," shows how security is a process and a mind-set. It also discusses how deploying a private cloud is clearly quite different than on-ramping services to a public cloud. Then, it shows how analyzing every situation from many different angles is the nature of most security professionals, and, when architecting security, a private cloud environment of this quality will be put to the test. Finally, it describes how maintaining a high level of security maturity by performing due diligence and producing strong policies around all your processes will help you lead a successful, robust, and secure private cloud implementation.

Chapter 20, "Privacy Protection in Cloud Computing through Architectural Design," introduces architectural designs for privacy protections in clouds. In this chapter, the authors describe their basic assumptions about the cloud computing environment and discuss what kind of threats are considered in architectural designs. Next, they assume that the swapped pages are encrypted in order to protect the guest VM space. Finally, they describe the privacy protection problem in cloud computing.

John R. Vacca
TechWrite

Acknowledgments

T HERE ARE MANY PEOPLE whose efforts on this book have contributed to its successful completion. I owe each a debt of gratitude and offer my sincere thanks.

I express my very special thanks to my executive editor, Rick Adams, without whose continued interest and support this book would not have been possible, and to my editorial assistant, Sherry Thomas, who provided staunch support and encouragement when it was most needed. I thank my production editor, Cynthia Klivecka; project coordinator, Marsha Pronin; and copyeditor, Indumathi, S., whose fine editorial work has been invaluable. I also thank my marketing manager, Joanna Knight, whose efforts on this book have been greatly appreciated. Finally, I thank all of the other people at CRC Press (Taylor & Francis Group), whose many talents and skills are essential to a finished book.

I thank my wife, Bee Vacca, for her love, help, and understanding of my long work hours. Also, I express my very very special thanks to Michael Erbschloe for writing the foreword. Finally, I thank all the following authors who contributed chapters that were necessary for the completion of this book: Lauren Collins, Patricia C. Franks, Mario Santana, Luciana Duranti, Adam Jansen, Giovanni Michetti, Courtney Mumma, Daryll Prescott, Corinne Rogers, Kenneth Thibodeau, Daniel Ching Wa, Sarbari Gupta, Roberto Di Pietro, Flavio Lombardi, Matteo Signorini, Thorsten Herre, Pramod Pandya, Riad Rahmo, Albert Caballero, Wanyu Zang, Meng Yu, and Peng Liu.

Editor

John R. Vacca is an information technology consultant, professional writer, editor, reviewer, and internationally known, best-selling author based in Pomeroy, Ohio. Since 1982, Vacca has authored/edited 77 books; some of his most recent books include the following:

- *Handbook of Sensor Networking: Advanced Technologies and Applications* [Publisher: CRC Press (an imprint of Taylor & Francis Group, LLC) (January 14, 2015)]

- *Network and System Security,* second edition [Publisher: Syngress (an imprint of Elsevier, Inc.) (September 23, 2013)]

- *Cyber Security and IT Infrastructure Protection* [Publisher: Syngress (an imprint of Elsevier, Inc.) (September 23, 2013)]

- *Managing Information Security,* second edition [Publisher: Syngress (an imprint of Elsevier, Inc.) (September 23, 2013)]

- *Computer and Information Security Handbook,* second edition [Publisher: Morgan Kaufmann (an imprint of Elsevier, Inc.) (May 31, 2013)]

- *Identity Theft (Cybersafety)* [Publisher: Chelsea House Pub (April 1, 2012)]

- *System Forensics, Investigation, and Response* [Publisher: Jones & Bartlett Learning (September 24, 2010)]

- *Managing Information Security* [Publisher: Syngress (an imprint of Elsevier, Inc.) (March 29, 2010)]

- *Network and Systems Security* [Publisher: Syngress (an imprint of Elsevier, Inc.) (March 29, 2010)]

- *Computer and Information Security Handbook, 1E* [Publisher: Morgan Kaufmann (an imprint of Elsevier, Inc.) (June 2, 2009)]

- *Biometric Technologies and Verification Systems* [Publisher: Elsevier Science & Technology Books (March 16, 2007)]

- *Practical Internet Security* (Hardcover) [Publisher: Springer (October 18, 2006)]

- *Optical Networking Best Practices Handbook* (Hardcover) [Publisher: Wiley-Interscience (November 28, 2006)]

- *Guide to Wireless Network Security* [Publisher: Springer (August 19, 2006)]

- *Computer Forensics: Computer Crime Scene Investigation* (with CD-ROM), 2nd Edition [Publisher: Charles River Media (May 26, 2005)]

He has published more than 600 articles in the areas of advanced storage, computer security, and aerospace technology (copies of articles and books are available upon request). He was also a configuration management specialist, computer specialist, and the computer security official for the National Aeronautics and Space Administration (NASA)'s space station program (Freedom) and the International Space Station Program, from 1988 until his retirement from the NASA in 1995.

In addition, Vacca is also an independent online book reviewer and was one of the security consultants for the MGM movie titled *AntiTrust*, which was released on January 12, 2001. A detailed copy of his biography can be viewed at http://www.johnvacca.com. He can be reached at john2164@windstream.net.

Contributors

Albert Caballero
HBO Latin America Group
Caracas, Venezuela

Daniel Ching Wa
Kun Hang Group
and
HK University of Science and Technology
and
HK Polytechnic University
and
University of Hong Kong
Hong Kong, China

and

Jiangxi University of Finance and
    Economics
Nanchang, China

Lauren Collins
Winning Edge Communications
New Lennox, Illinois

Roberto Di Pietro
Alcatel Lucent Bell Labs
Boulogne-Billancourt, France

Luciana Duranti
Archival Studies
School of Library, Archival and
    Information Studies
The Irving K. Barber Learning Centre
University of British Columbia
Vancouver, British Columbia, Canada

Patricia C. Franks
School of Information
San Jose State University
San Jose, California

Sarbari Gupta
Electrosoft Services, Inc.
Reston, Virginia

Thorsten Herre
Security and Compliance Office
Cloud and Infrastructure Delivery
SAP SE
Walldorf, Germany

Adam Jansen
School of Library, Archival and
    Information Studies
University of British Columbia
Vancouver, British Columbia, Canada

Peng Liu
Pennsylvania State University
University Park, Pennsylvania

Flavio Lombardi
Istituto per le Applicazioni del Calcolo,
    IAC-CNR
Rome, Italy

Giovanni Michetti
Department of Document Studies,
    Linguistics and Geography
Sapienza University of Rome
Rome, Italy

Courtney Mumma
The Internet Archive
San Francisco, California

Pramod Pandya
Department of Information Systems and
    Decision Sciences
Mihaylo College of Business and
    Economics
California State University
Fullerton, California

Daryll Prescott
Independent Consultant
Government Domain Task Force
Dickinson, North Dakota

Riad Rahmo
Independent Researcher and Consultant
California State University, Fullerton
Mission Viejo, California

Corinne Rogers
School of Library, Archival and
    Information Studies
University of British Columbia
Vancouver, British Columbia, Canada

Mario Santana
Terremark Worldwide, Inc.
Miami, Florida

Matteo Signorini
Pompeu Fabra University
Barcelona, Spain

Kenneth Thibodeau
Independent Researcher
Centre for the International Study of
    Contemporary Records and Archives
Evergreen, Colorado

Meng Yu
University of Texas at San Antonio
San Antonio, Texas

Wanyu Zang
Texas A&M at San Antonio
San Antonio, Texas

I

Introduction to Private Cloud Security

CHAPTER 1

Private Cloud Computing Essentials

Lauren Collins

CONTENTS

1.1 INTRODUCTION

Cloud computing is a service model delivering on-demand computing resources over the Internet. This cloud model is composed of five essential characteristics, three service models, and four deployment models [1]. Cloud computing features all aspects of modern-day technology and affects the users, process, and technology of an enterprise; cloud infrastructures are scalable, readily available, accessible, and elastic. There are several tools at our disposal for consuming data across thousands of machines. Businesses are able to run an entire development environment, even an entire company, without procuring or housing a physical enterprise grid of hardware and resources. Today, virtually all businesses are using cloud services and may not even be aware of it. There are countless benefits derived from cloud infrastructures addressing business needs and delivering simplicity in order to accelerate growth and innovation.

Although there are numerous characteristics defining cloud computing, the following list summarizes the scope of cloud data, applications, services, and infrastructure:

- *Hosting*: platform, services, or data accessed are hosted on remote infrastructure.

- *Ubiquitous*: platform, services, or data are accessible from any location at anytime.

- *Commodity*: pay by use, customizable, and scalable.

Cloud computing characteristics can be further divided into two groups: essential characteristics and common characteristics, as shown in Figure 1.1.

The National Institute of Standards and Technology (NIST) lists five essential characteristics of cloud computing: on-demand self-service, broad network access, resource pooling, rapid elasticity or expansion, and measured service. It also lists three "service models" (software, platform, and infrastructure) and four "deployment models" (private, community, public, and hybrid) that together categorize ways to deliver cloud services. The definition is intended to serve as a means for broad comparisons of cloud services and deployment strategies, and to provide a baseline for discussion from what is cloud computing to how to best use cloud computing [2]. A consumer is able to unilaterally provision computing capabilities, referred to as on-demand self-service, and is customarily done through a web-based portal or management console. Server up-time and allocation of network storage can be predefined and increased automatically without the need for human interaction from each service provider ("service provider refers to departments of information technology [IT]: server team, storage team, etc."). Broad network access provides competencies available over the network, accessed through typical mechanisms, which promote use by assorted client platforms (laptop, mobile devices, etc.). Resource pooling refers to the independence and availability of resources, such as processing power, memory allocation, storage, network bandwidth, and virtual machines (VMs). Usually, a

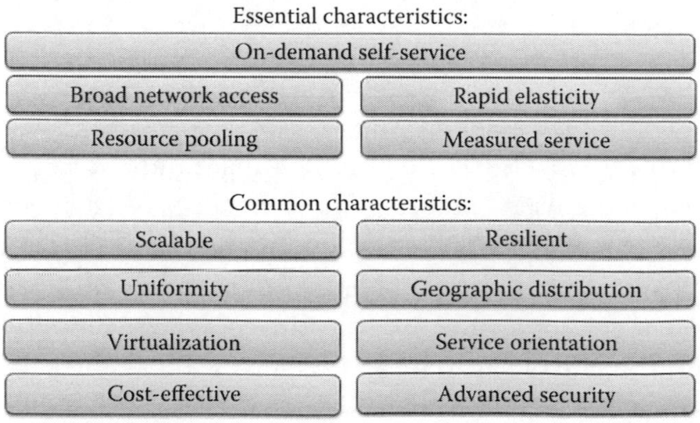

Essential characteristics:

On-demand self-service	
Broad network access	Rapid elasticity
Resource pooling	Measured service

Common characteristics:

Scalable	Resilient
Uniformity	Geographic distribution
Virtualization	Service orientation
Cost-effective	Advanced security

FIGURE 1.1 Cloud computing composed of five essential characteristics and eight common characteristics.

consumer is unaware (and has no control) of the exact location of resources provided to their platform. Resource pooling effectively establishes the concept for presenting and consuming resources in a consistent and transparent manner. Subsequently, capabilities can be rapidly and elastically provisioned instantaneously and automatically. To the consumer, the capabilities available for provisioning resources appear to be limitless and therefore can be purchased and allocated in any quantity at any time. With that being said, cloud platforms regulate and augment resources by gauging some level of abstraction appropriate to the service type (e.g., processing, memory, bandwidth, storage) by user group and account. Service providers such as Amazon, Google, Microsoft, and Rackspace provide numerous infrastructures spatially located in segregate grids, allowing for robust capacity and minimal downtime. Their cloud solutions entertain mirrored solutions, offering a resilience that gives businesses the necessary sustainability during unforeseen events. Regardless of the chosen provider, the cloud model makes it easy for businesses to work with clients, even if they use an entirely different service provider. Further elaboration of the five essential features of cloud computing is as follows:

1. *On-demand self-service*: IT provisions VMs for their internal customers, departments. Users have the ability to provision cloud computing resources using either a web portal or management console, all without human interaction.

2. *Broad network access*: Connectivity is only for internal customers, departments, accomplished by either local network access or connection to a virtual private network (VPN). Many client platforms are supported, such as the use of mobile devices, laptops, and workstations.

3. *Resource pooling*: Multiple customers are able to use the same physical resources, by segregating logical resources in a secure environment.

4. *Rapid elasticity*: IT provisions VMs by selecting the operating system (OS) and software, but now resources can be provisioned and released based on predefined parameters. Environments do not outgrow themselves too quickly and starve for resources, and an application will have the amount of necessary capacity at any point in time.

5. *Measured service*: The use of resources is monitored and then reported, or billed transparently back to a business unit based on utilization. Chargeback is accomplished by allocating budgets by department, rather than measuring actual usage.

Separately, these platforms conceal the complexity and level of specificity of the underlying infrastructure from the user and their applications by providing an easy-to-use graphical interface or applications programming interface. In addition, such a platform provides on-demand services that are always accessible from anywhere at anytime. Cloud service offerings have irrevocably changed the way software is deployed. Yet, the majority of organizations are slow to adopt cloud-based architectures; therefore, security concerns steer enterprises toward a private cloud deployment. Services are accessed via an interface that requires thorough design from an architect.

1.2 CLOUD COMPUTING SERVICE MODELS

In effort to appreciate the business value of cloud computing, it is essential to first identify the components, and then determine the capacity in which it can be utilized. Cloud computing describes such a broad range of services but is ultimately a model for facilitating accessible, on-demand access to a shared pool of resources that can quickly be provisioned with minimal user or administration interaction. The three service models of cloud computing are infrastructure as a service (IaaS), platform as a service (PaaS), and software as a service (SaaS). Table 1.1 illustrates the comparison of service and sourcing models of cloud computing.

The core concepts and configurations of cloud computing are used throughout most service providers and implementations. Robust architecture is of the utmost importance in which service delivery is referenced; the methodology, sourcing, and regulation of a cloud computing environment will extend an available, scalable, and agile solution. IT must adjust their logic from individual, specific deployment models to delivering a predetermined and standard deployment. This strategy will become the norm as more organizations choose the cloud to meet their specific needs.

1.2.1 Infrastructure as a Service

IaaS incorporates vendor-managed network appliances, storage, servers, and virtualization layers in which consumers run their application and store data. Countless benefits are present when using IaaS, but every service provider offers a little different platform. Most have heard of Amazon's offering of cloud services; QualiSystems' CloudShell is unique in which they are based on the model of mixed infrastructure environments that can support any variety of infrastructures connected in any manner. For instance, CloudShell is able to support both on-premise and public cloud servers along with mainframe sessions

TABLE 1.1 The Cloud Computing Model Incorporating IaaS, PaaS, and SaaS

Type	Consumer	Service Provided	Service-Level Coverage	Customization
IaaS	• Application owner of IT provides OS • Application and middleware support	• Virtual server • Cloud storage	• Virtual server availability • Provisioning time • No platform or application coverage	• Minimal constraints on application installed on standardized virtual OS builds
PaaS	• Application owner	• Runtime environment for application • Cloud storage • Additional cloud services such as integration	• Environment availability • Environment performance • No application coverage	• Robust application level of customization available within constraints of services offered
SaaS	• End user	• Finished application	• Application uptime • Application performance	• Minimal to no customization • Capabilities dictated by market or service provider

connected along with legacy Unix servers. Various networking topologies are also supported; whether using virtual switches, software-defined networking switches, or conventional layer 2 switches, seamless connectivity is present.

Consider the infrastructure requirements of a proprietary trading firm: the headquarter, and 35 of the desk traders, is located in Chicago, Illinois. A second, smaller office is located in Manhattan, New York, with only four desk traders. The traders from both offices actively trade on Singapore, Dubai, London, New York, and Chicago markets. Prior to cloud computing, the game of speed was played in which the pricing and order matching servers needed to be collocated in proximity to the respective markets. Figure 1.2 illustrates a network diagram relative to the infrastructure requirements described above.

Each market location requires collocated servers and a dedicated circuit for connectivity. The costs involved in this infrastructure are extraordinary; a dark fiber circuit, providing low-latency, high-frequency speed, could cost US$10,000, on average. Then, consider the cost of the actual space leased from the collocation along with the cost of physical servers and networking hardware, such as firewalls and switch gear. Figure 1.3 shows the required infrastructure in a typical collocation cabinet. Located at the top of the rack are network switches, establishing both site-to-site connectivity for each trading firm office location and cross-connects to respective market infrastructures, possibly located in the same room or another floor in the same building. Local server connections pictured in this figure also tie into the switches within the cabinet. The average cost for hardware pictured in this diagram is about US$200,000. Add in the time to design, configure, ship, and install this infrastructure and the total cost could near half a million dollars.

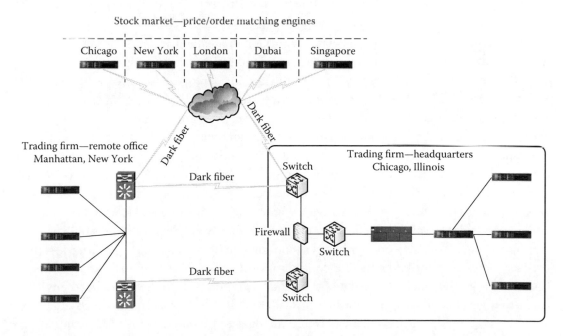

FIGURE 1.2 Infrastructure requirements prior to cloud computing architectures for a proprietary trading firm.

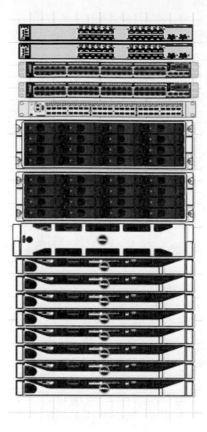

FIGURE 1.3   Typical collocated infrastructure for connectivity at one proprietary trading site.

The saying "time is money" resonates with IT management when deciding to move to a cloud infrastructure. The days of configuring equipment and shipping it all over the world are over. Not only does the amount of time for deployment decrease considerably, but resources can be allocated to other service areas as needs change or grow. And if a particular product is not traded any longer, the server does not sit in the cabinet collecting dust, using electricity, and cooling. Infrastructure engineers are able to focus on innovation and agility, and organizations can reallocate a substantial percentage of their budget on providing real value to clients rather than simply keeping the lights on. In an IaaS environment, the resources can be allocated to another deployment or can be turned off, saving money in a usage-based or pay-as-you-go program, which is discussed later in this chapter.

Now, consider the above physical requirements of hardware deployed into a pool of computing, storage, and network connectivity options delivered as a service. The consumer, or user, takes responsibility for the configuration of the OS and the necessary software and database. The goal is to create and provide a standard, flexible, virtualized environment that will become the foundation for PaaS and SaaS. IaaS has transformed organizations from being decidedly logistic driven to being vastly cloud driven, and businesses are appreciating pronounced payoffs from the transformation. Automation and self-service are the buzz words associated with cloud computing. When an infrastructure is carefully architected and orchestrated, customers and business are able to operate in an agile manner, gaining efficiency and productivity. The industry moving toward cloud computing incorporates IaaS with its current, legacy infrastructure. Most IT and development teams are conflicted with their on-premise mixture of legacy and virtual hardware and applications infrastructure. An IaaS environment mitigates the risk of legacy application and server migrations, and sets the stage for effective cross-team collaboration, testing, and seamless integration and provisioning of products and services.

1.2.2 Platform as a Service

PaaS builds on top of IaaS, utilizing vendor-managed middleware applications, databases, and most commonly web portal software. It offers an agile approach to run scalable applications in a predictable, cost-effective fashion. Service levels and operational risks are now shared because the user accepts the responsibility for the configuration and operation of the application, and the provider delivers the platform resources (operational functionality and infrastructure). Figure 1.4 compares the process of delivering an application. On the legacy platform, once an application is requested by a development team, IT has to procure and build the server OS, install updates and service packs, then install relative software for developers to use the server, along with a bunch of other minor access details such as setting up user accounts and adding security groups. A cloud computing environment delivers an application in the matter of time it takes to open a browser. Furthermore,

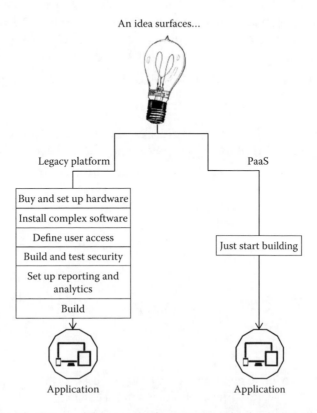

FIGURE 1.4   Compare the time to deliver an application using both a legacy platform (left) to PaaS.

PaaS applications have the latest features excluding the pain of constant upgrades and troubleshooting of those updates.

The legacy model of building and running on-premise applications is too complex, expensive, and slow. One application needs a lot of hardware, an OS, a database, and web servers, and may even require additional software. An entire application, network, systems, and server team were needed to keep everything running smoothly. Once a change or upgrade to the application was requested, another cycle of lengthy development, planning, testing, and deployment results; these cycles are a part of everyday business across all organizations. Aside from the painful, lengthy process to deploy an environment, applications built on this complex framework do not scale for usage demands nor business changes.

1.2.3 Software as a Service

SaaS provides substantial efficiencies in which cost and time to deployment are concerned, just as IaaS and PaaS. It is an innovative approach to distributing software, in which instead of selling to clients or businesses it is made available over the Internet using cloud computing methodology. Subsequently, providers host the software remotely, saving the additional investment in hardware and then charging the users with respect to the time spent using it or by paying a monthly fee. Access to applications is simplified, and no installation, deployment, or maintenance costs are incurred. Similar to IaaS and PaaS, a shift in operational risk is now on the provider rather than the client in a SaaS environment.

SaaS employs applications such as customer relationship management (CRM) (e.g., SalesForce), social performance management tools (e.g., SuccessFactors), tracking and monitoring solutions (e.g., Google Analytics), Professional Services Automation (e.g., Riverbed), and cloud integration applications. Figure 1.5 illustrates a SaaS deployment in which software is delivered as a service, primarily over a uniform resource locator.

1.2.4 Other Cloud Service Models

Organizations have expanded their horizons of cloud service offerings to further simplify the deployment of desktops, servers, storage, and even entire environments. Centralized management and rapid deployment save time and money when considering

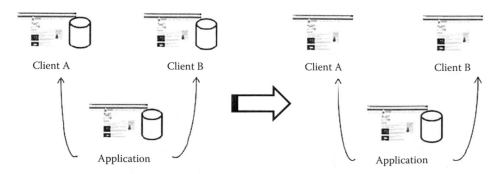

FIGURE 1.5 SaaS employing applications relevant to the user, such as e-mail, social analytics, document management, or CRM. The application database remains in the same location as the application (right) in a SaaS environment.

the management of devices as well as the physical footprint. The additional cloud services are as follows:

- Desktop as a service

- Hardware as a service

- Disaster recovery as a service

- Business process as a service

- Big data as a service

Data analytics and business intelligence have become an integral piece of organizations; therefore, consulting firms have added a fourth service model, business process as a service (BPaaS). Just as the other service models, BPaaS builds on top of all the other cloud service models and considers an entire spectrum of vertical or horizontal business process. In addition to all the service models, big data as a service is on the horizon.

1.3 PUBLIC CLOUD

The public cloud is defined as a multitenant environment, where a service provider makes resources, such as applications and storage, available to multiple users, known as the general public, over the Internet. Services available in the public cloud are usually free or use a pay-as-you-go model. Cloud service providers in this arena are Amazon Web Services, Google, SalesForce, and so forth. One use case of an organization's choice for a public cloud environment is when they desire to implement global or large-scale solutions, which would typically be out of reach without utilizing the cloud due to incurring significant costs or their IT staff lacks the expertise. Public cloud services deliver flexible, cost-effective implementations and facilitate access to cutting-edge technologies.

1.4 VIRTUAL PRIVATE CLOUD DESIGN

Generally, when discussing a "private cloud" environment, some are under the assumption that privacy and security are accomplished only by deploying physical hardware in private data center space. There are also some who believe cloud deployments only consist of virtualizing servers, implementation of management tools for provisioning of virtualization, and all connectivity and management happens on the local network. Those who make either or both assumptions will be enlightened to learn that you are on the right track; but, there is more. Virtualization can be a core component of cloud deployments, whether public or private.

1.4.1 Case 1: Virtualization

IT departments seem to be chasing their tails and finding the need for more resources as soon as they finish a deployment. They implement a virtualization solution, so they can quickly provision an infrastructure and consolidate servers. Not only are they able to provision storage space based on departmental needs, but they can also configure machines with the hypervisor of choice and ample processing power and memory using management tools. Image files are created and uploaded to the management software, so a new OS can be installed on a VM. The environment must be connected to its local network for machine and resource management. Table 1.2 illustrates a key theory of cloud architecture, resource pooling, and abstraction of virtualized resources from an underlying virtual infrastructure. A number of constructs allocate capacity and resources by department, and are then charged back to internal department or client budgets, or the cost can be split between groups or locations, or simply track the number of machines deployed for each department.

1.4.2 Case 2: Private Cloud

A global software company's headquarters in Manhattan, New York, employ a central IT department that supports proprietary company-wide and department-specific applications. There are several additional locations each with a handful of local IT staff that focus on level 1 and 2 support of desktops or network tasks. Occasionally, a site may place an order for a server, then set it up on the domain itself, including all service packs, software, and network configuration. However, process could be streamlined by IT staff located

TABLE 1.2   A Number of Principles for Cloud Architecture Map to Virtual Data Centers for Resources

Virtualization Concept	Description
Provider virtual data center	Logical grouping of computing resources (attached virtual cluster of or more datastores) to provide cloud resources to consumers
Organization	Unit of administration that represents a logical collection of users, groups, and computing resources. Also serves as a security boundary from which only users of a particular organization can deploy workloads and have visibility into such workloads in the cloud. An organization is an association of related end users
Organization virtual data center	Subset allocation of provider virtual data center resources assigned to an organization, automatically backed by resource pool • Allocation • Reservation • Pay as you go
External network	Network that connects to the outside using an existing virtual network port group
Organization network	Network visible within an organization. External organization has connectivity to an external network using a direct or routed connection, or an internal network visible to apps within the organization
Network pool	Set of preallocated networks that can be allocated as needed to create private networks and network address translation (NAT)-routed networks
Virtual application	Preconfigured container of one or more VMs and virtual application networks
Virtual application network	Network visible within a virtual application, connected to other virtual application networks within an organization using a direct or routed connection, or internal network visible only to VMs within the virtual application
Virtual application templates and catalogs	Collection of available services for consumption. Catalogs contain virtual application template (preconfigured containers of one or more VMs) and/or media (images of operating systems)

in Manhattan procuring and implementing servers or applications. Given that not only can they provide better centralized support for remote branches, but they also have the ability to deliver servers with predefined, benchmark-tested specifications, and deploy storage in their preferred manner. IT headquarters also possess the image file for server or VMs, complete with preinstalled and configured OS and drivers. Furthermore, management software permits various users of distinctive access levels to perform tasks such as launching VMs, installing VMs from images, rebooting machines or tweaking memory or processing specifications, and configuring virtual networks between VMs.

Instantaneously, the remote sales department is able to login to a portal, spin up a new VM with the latest release of their proprietary software, and use it for a few days for testing. If something breaks or has to be redone, the VM can be turned off, reconfigured, or deleted without impacting the production version of the current software. Engineering and development teams will usually deploy several VMs to test the new software and act as a staging environment, having several more on hand in case a need arises. The company no longer has to store old workstations and repurpose them as a need arises, which is always an immediate need.

Case 2 utilizes virtualization but has also incorporated the remaining components of cloud functionality. The services can be accessed either by VPN connection via the Internet or by an secure socket layer (SSL)/transport layer security (TLS) web-based portal. Management and IT are able to monitor and track the actual usage of each service by department or as granular as a monthly or hourly basis. Most importantly, upper-level IT resources are freed up as local IT staff, and delegated employees are able to add capacity as well as turn off machines. Once virtualization is paired with the five essential features listed earlier, true cloud services provide specific benefits to both the IT departments and consumers alike.

1.5 PRIVATE CLOUD AND VIRTUALIZATION

Case 1 displays the use of automation, server consolidation, and a service-oriented architecture. Although case 1 alone does not represent a cloud deployment, it necessitates some of the core impressions of cloud computing. Therefore, not all virtualized environments are private clouds.

When an organization requires a secure environment due to regulatory governance, private cloud addresses security concerns by accessing VPNs, having physical environments, or incorporating both types within the firewall. Health care and pharmaceutical companies require their data and applications to conform to a mixture of regulatory standards. Therefore, transferring sensitive data to the cloud violates privacy specifications. Private cloud deployments are desirable in such cases as both a segregated and physical location has the flexibility and capability to be fluid with workloads among servers as usage increases or as new applications are deployed.

1.6 COMMUNITY CLOUD

Community clouds offer similar advantages of a private cloud deployment, but at a lower cost and greater flexibility. The infrastructure can reside either on- or off-premise and can be managed either by the organization or by a service provider. As shown in Figure 1.6 [3],

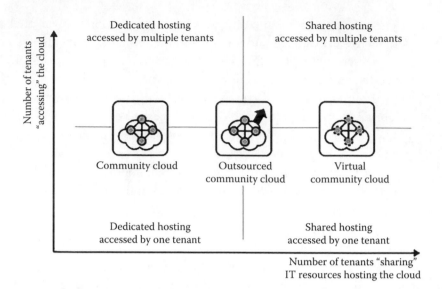

FIGURE 1.6   Whenever companies collaborate, they commonly have access to shared application and data to do business. Even though the companies have mutual relationships and agreements in place, the data and application functionality may be sensitive and critical to their business needs.

multitenancy is the key attribute to community cloud; it shares multiple services of the cloud service models: IaaS, PaaS, and SaaS. Technology organizations and their clients often collaborate and work on shared projects and applications. A central cloud computing service is essential when executing this type of project; thus, community cloud is an ideal solution. Data security, compliance, and policy considerations are all taken into consideration and accounted for when data are shared with others in the community and controlled in a secure fashion. Even though a community cloud is a more secure option than the public cloud, exercise discretion when storing data because it is accessible to everyone in the community. Proper allocation of governance and security must be instituted and still poses challenges in community cloud deployments.

1.7 HYBRID CLOUD

Hybrid cloud computing can be used as a stepping stone to mainstream cloud computing, as it involves the aggregation of cloud services utilizing two or more clouds, (private, community, and public). Of all service models, hybrid cloud features the most efficiency, best performance, reduced risk, and most granular customization. Organizations have the most control of their data even though this is a cloud model. Most businesses adopting the hybrid cloud model continue to run a business critical core application in-house; and, are running all other applications in the cloud, all the while in control of their secret sauce. Figure 1.7 shows a hybrid cloud environment.

Companies who are not ready to store their applications or files in the cloud for access can back up data to the cloud. One of the most popular uses of hybrid cloud computing is disaster recovery. Business continuity planning minimizes downtime with the ability to have an entire working environment operational in a very short period of time.

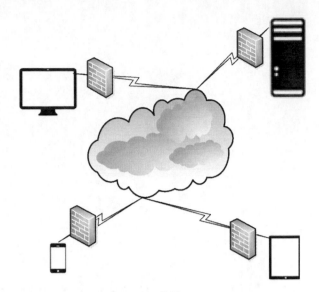

FIGURE 1.7 Hybrid cloud computing environments are device agnostic and all connect to the cloud securely.

1.8 SUMMARY

The cloud market is offering multiple options for businesses to transition their infrastructure, development platform, storage, and software. True innovation comes when successfully navigating the cloud space from traditional on-premise models to a recurring revenue model. Service providers are offering hybrid, private, and public cloud solutions, which lead to better efficiency, self-service, manipulation, and variety.

REFERENCES

1. Mell, Peter M., and Timothy Grance. *Publication Citation: The NIST Definition of Cloud Computing*. The National Institute of Standards and Technology, December 19, 2013. Web. April 23, 2015.
2. Brown, Evelyn. *Final Version of NIST Cloud Computing Definition Published*. Web. May 9, 2015.
3. "Community Cloud." *Cloud Computing Patterns*, n.d. Web. June 30, 2015.

CHAPTER 2

Integration of Enterprise Content Management and Software as a Service

Patricia C. Franks

CONTENTS

2.1 INTRODUCTION

Organizations today face unprecedented challenges in capturing, managing, making available, and preserving information. In addition to the increased volume and velocity of information created, difficulties arise from the use of mobile technology, social media, and cloud computing. What began as a solution to control information in both paper and digital formats, enterprise content management (ECM) is rapidly transforming into a vehicle to derive value from the information managed to meet a range of business needs such as improved customer service and case management.

In an attempt to meet diverse and growing expectations on the part of customers, vendors of ECM systems integrate modular components they have created or acquired into their basic ECM offerings and collaborate with partners to provide integration between the ECM and third-party systems with a major focus on software as a service (SaaS).

This chapter explores the integration of ECM systems with SaaS applications from the perspective of the user, the enterprise. Terminology is defined, products are examined, security and risk considerations are raised, integration models are discussed, and examples of the integration between ECM systems and SaaS applications are provided.

2.2 TERMINOLOGY

Carefully defined terminology enables individuals within a particular industry to communicate clearly with one another and to communicate a consistent message with those outside of the industry. However, definitions may differ for professionals depending on their perspectives (e.g., information technology, business unit, risk management, security, privacy, legal, records management). The following definitions provide a common frame of reference for the major concepts explored in this chapter:

- *ECM*: The strategies, methods, and tools used to capture, manage, store, preserve, and deliver content and documents related to organizational processes [1] and workflows throughout the content life cycle, from creation to disposition. The term "content" refers to a wide range of unstructured information, including documents, spreadsheets, records, web content, and digital assets.

- *Integration platform as a service (iPaaS)*: A suite of cloud services aimed at addressing a wide range of cloud, business to business (B2B), and on-premise integration and governance scenarios [2].

- *Internet of things platform as a service (IoT PaaS)*: A platform to coordinate and manage the connectivity and security of networked devices and their data to drive intelligent business decisions based upon an analysis of large volumes of data in real time.

- *SaaS*: The capability provided to the consumer to use the provider's applications running on a cloud infrastructure. The applications are accessible from various client devices through either a thin client interface, such as a web browser (e.g., web-based e-mail), or a program interface [3].

Central to any discussion of the integration of ECM with SaaS is an understanding of the cloud deployment models available and the ways in which cloud providers can assist the organization in their use of cloud-based solutions. Therefore, four additional terms referred to in this chapter need clarification; they are as follows:

- *Cloud provider*: An entity offering management and support to cloud consumers for access to a range of ubiquitous, convenient services, including infrastructure, platform, and applications, that can be rapidly provisioned with minimal effort by the consumer [4].

- *Hybrid cloud*: A deployment model in which two or more clouds (private, community, or public) remain unique entities but are connected by standardized or proprietary technology that enables data and application portability [4].

- *Private cloud*: The cloud infrastructure is provisioned for exclusive use by a single organization comprising multiple consumers (e.g., business units). It may be owned, managed, and operated by the organization, a third party, or some combination of them, and it may exist on- or off-premise) [3].

- *Public cloud*: The cloud infrastructure is provisioned for open use by the general public. It may be owned, managed, and operated by a business, academic, or government organization, or some combination of them. It exists on the premise of the cloud provider [3].

2.3 ENTERPRISE CONTENT MANAGEMENT

ECM is both a strategic framework and a technical architecture to capture, manage, store, preserve, and deliver all types of content and documents (in all formats) related to business processes throughout the content life cycle [2]. Both the concept of ECM and the systems that enable the management of enterprise content have evolved over the years.

2.3.1 ECM—Concept and Early Systems

ECM is a mature concept, having been introduced in 2000 by the Association for Information and Image Management (AIIM) to describe solutions to manage an explosion of information in both paper and digital forms.

At the time of the development of the first ECM system, two other systems now considered components of ECM were most in demand by organizations seeking to control content: electronic document management systems (EDMSs) and electronic records management systems (ERMSs). The term "document" was referred to all recorded information that could be treated as a unit, including information in text formats, databases, technical drawings, audio and video objects, and other information content saved by a computer [5]. The EDM and ERM systems were hosted within the enterprise, and the level of control and security was high.

A task force was formed in 2000 to develop a framework for integrating EDMS and ERMS based on three key areas—metadata management, functionality, and implementation approaches. The first version of the Technical Report, "Framework for the Integration of Electronic Document Management Systems and Electronic Records Management Systems, ANSI/AIIM/ARMA TR 48-2004," was published in 2004 with a revised version released in 2006. Subsequent efforts by the AIIM were devoted to the broader concept of ECM, which subsumed both EDMS and ERMS as well as the following key components: imaging, workflow, collaboration, web publishing, digital asset management (DAM), and electronic forms management.

Although research was being conducted into the integration of EDMS and ERMS, vendors were already developing early ECM systems. Microsoft launched the first version of SharePoint in 2001; Alfresco launched their ECM system in 2005. InfoSys [6] describes the early focus of ECM in this way:

> Historically, the key focus of ECM projects was to provide organizations with a content storage repository. It provided secured access and better management of all types of documents and content. Even product vendors focused on ensuring content storage and accessibility in a secure manner. Through imaging systems, paper documents created as a part of different business processes were scanned into the ECM system for future reference. The system also provided basic features such as document routing, approval, and publishing via workflow. For faster retrieval of information, advanced search functionality was made available. Implementation of ECM projects changed the method in which information was managed and handled in organizations. It helped in removing silos of information and in implementing enterprise-wide strategies.

Although records management functionality might be integrated into an ECM system, early systems were independent of other systems used within the organization, such as enterprise resource planning (ERP) and customer relationship management (CRM) systems. Therefore, information silos still existed, but not to the extent they had before the implementation of ECM systems.

2.3.2 Enterprise Content Management

As used in this chapter, an "enterprise" is a business or government entity, regardless of its size. Today's enterprises realize the value of the content stored within the ECM system as well as locations external to it. The driving force behind the use of ECM systems regardless of size of the enterprise or industry in which it operates is the active use of stored content to improve business operations and increase productivity. Those who require information can access it through a shared repository as needed using assorted devices. Updated information is instantly available across departments and locations.

Hullavard et al. [7] state that the primary goal of ECM is "to enable transparent content sharing by making different and incongruent applications (for example, web content management and records management) interoperable." Most ECM systems integrate two or more sets of applications. An annual report of ECM systems prepared by Gartner, Inc., Stamford,

Connecticut is based on an evaluation of seven core components most often integrated into the ECM product or suite of products: document management, web content management, records management, image processing applications, social content, content workflow, and extended services (e.g., search features). These components are described as follows:

- Document management functionality includes check-in/checkout capabilities, version control, security, and library services for business documents.

- Web content management functionality offers control over website content through the use of tools based on a core repository, including content creation and content deployment functions.

- Records management provides, at a minimum, the capability to enforce the retention and disposition of content according to the organization's records retention schedule.

- Image processing applications allow for the capture of paper documents, their transformation into digital surrogates, and the management of those digital images in a repository as another content type that can be routed through an electronic process.

- Social content functionality allows for document sharing and collaboration support for project teams using tools such as newsfeeds, blogs, wikis, and video channels.

- Content workflow supports business processes by providing the routing of content, assigning workflow tasks and states (including approval), and creating audit trails.

- Extended components can include one or more of a number of services, such as mobile applications, DAM, advanced search, data analytics, and packaged integration capabilities [8].

Organizations must determine their needs before deciding upon an ECM system. This involves determining their own needs and gathering information on available options to ensure they meet the organization's requirements, which may include integration with existing on-premise and cloud-based systems. When reporting the results of an annual survey of vendors in the ECM market, Gartner [8] classifies vendors into four quadrants based on their completeness of vision and ability to execute: Leaders, Visionaries, Niche Players, and Challengers. The 2014 *Magic Quadrant for Enterprise Content Management* recognized IBM, Open Text, EMC, Hyland, Perceptive Software, Oracle, and Microsoft as Leaders in this field. Visionaries included Xerox, Alfresco, and Newgen Software. Only one was considered a Challenger, HP. However, a number of Niche Players were identified: Laserfiche, Fabasoft, Objective, M-Files, Ever Team, Systemware, Upland Software, Software Innovation, Siav, SunGuard, and Unisys.

A similar value matrix of ECM systems is published by Nucleus Research [9]. Nucleus evaluates ECM solutions on the basis of usability and functionality rather than completeness of vision and ability to execute. Most of the ECM products in the Leader quadrant of the "ECM Value Matrix 2014" are found in Gartner's as well, but there are some differences. Microsoft is omitted from this category by Nucleus, and SpringCM, HP Autonomy, and M-files are included. Nucleus' ECM Matrix identified Leaders as those that provide products that are easily deployed on-premise, in the cloud, or in hybrid solutions. The three remaining Nucleus quadrants are Expert, Facilitator, and Core Provider. Experts include Alfresco, Kofax, OnBase, and Xerox; Facilitators include Digitec, DocSTAR, Fabasoft, Intralinks, Microsoft, Newgen, and Software Innovation. Five products are identified as Core Providers: EverTeam, Laserfiche, Objective, Systemware, and Unisys.

From a customer perspective, more than a quarter of the respondents to a recent study reported using cloud-based ECM systems already, and three-quarters (total more than 100%) said that they are likely to use some form of cloud ECM within the next 4 years [10]. Vendors, who once offered only on-premise versions of their ECM systems, are now integrating cloud features into their ECM system and/or are offering cloud-based alternatives to retain current customers and attract new ones. They are enhancing their ECM systems by adding features to existing products, acquiring firms that offer software to complement theirs, or establishing partnerships with third-party vendors.

As new products are offered and existing content management and cloud storage services add core content management functionality to their offerings, ECM vendors are pressured to differentiate their offerings to maintain or increase their market share. Differentiation can take the form of added advanced functionality, such as metadata search, process and content archiving, text mining, and mobile technology. It can be accomplished through the integration of additional features, such as microblogs and instant messaging capability to improve collaboration or add a "like" commenting feature to increase social engagement. Increasingly, ECM vendors, trying to simplify the user experience, are developing strategic partnerships to integrate their software and systems with those of other vendors. For example, SpringCM integrates its ECM system with Oracle Fusion CRM and Oracle Sales Cloud.

2.3.3 ECM: A Look to the Future

There has been a shift in recent years from building ECM solutions to manage documents to build ECM solutions to meet user needs in response to bring-your-own-device policies and the use of mobile technologies. ECM will continue to expand to include the concept of "content in context," in which content will be delivered in a personalized fashion—to the right people, at the right time, on the right device, and in the context of particular business processes or needs [8].

SaaS ECM offerings will continue to emerge, whereas on-premise ECM systems will morph into hybrid systems. Hybrid systems will be the choice of organizations seeking to take advantage of the cloud for noncritical data but uncomfortable moving critical or confidential information off premise.

According to the AIIM President John Mancini, "The ECM industry is in need of a new label and organizations are desperate for best practices to deal with the technology disruption that is occurring" [11]. However, merely renaming today's systems is not enough. The most disruptive force on the horizon is the IoT. Just as early enterprise document management systems evolved into ECM systems to handle more data in new formats, today's ECM's musty evolves to remain relevant in the world of big data, sensors, and the IoT.

2.4 SOFTWARE AS A SERVICE

SaaS applications are hosted by a vendor or service provider and made available to customers over a network, typically the Internet. These can be hosted on private or public clouds, and the risks presented range on a continuum from low to high depending on the cloud deployment model, with the private enterprise cloud hosted on-site offering the least risk. SaaS is an overall term that includes a variety of types of products and services.

2.4.1 Public SaaS

Consumers are most familiar with public SaaS in the form of cloud-based applications such as Facebook, Twitter, Flickr, Snapchat, and Google Apps that they can access for personal use through Internet-enabled devices, such as smartphones and tablets. Most public SaaS applications are free, but enhanced versions of some can be obtained for a fee. Examples of free services that provide additional features at a cost include Dropbox's Dropbox Pro option and LinkedIn's Premium account. In addition to enhanced features for personal use, business versions of some of these SaaS solutions are also available and used by employees conducting official business. Employees within organizations, at times without the approval of supervisors, use cloud services such as Box.com and Dropbox to store, synchronize, and share files. Dropbox, for example, claims that more than 35 billion Microsoft Office files are stored in Dropbox for Business (https://www.dropbox.com/business/tour).

2.4.2 Enterprise

Office productivity suites, such as "Microsoft Office 365" and Google Apps for Business, provide the best example of the use of SaaS within an enterprise. By 2022, the proportion of business users provisioned, in whole or in part, with office system capabilities from the cloud will grow to 60%, or approximately 700 million users, up from 15% in 2015 [12].

Enterprise SaaS includes collaborative tools such as the private social networks Yammer and Socialcast. In addition, departments and business units employ applications for a range of core business needs, such as accounting and invoicing, tracking sales, planning, performance monitoring, and communications (e.g., webmail, instant messaging). Examples of cloud services meeting core business needs are Salesforce's CRM software and Workday's Human Capital Management (HRC) software.

A recent entry to the SaaS market is known as long-term digital preservation as a service (LTDPaaS). LTDPaaS is designed to store documents in secure, trusted digital repositories to meet long-term retention requirements. Two services in this space are ArchivesDirect and Preservica. These categories and examples, as summarized in Table 2.1, deserve further explanation.

2.4.3 SaaS and Office Productivity

Today's office suites are composed of browser-based applications and hosted services that replace local software and servers. The leading products are leased on a monthly and per-user-fee basis, and can potentially result in lower costs and lower demand for IT support. Applications are updated automatically when there is a new feature or upgrade.

TABLE 2.1   SaaS: Examples of Categories and Vendor Offerings

SaaS Category	SaaS Example 1	SaaS Example 2
Office productivity	Microsoft Office	Google Apps for Work
Social computing	Yammer	Socialcast
File synchronization and sharing	Box.com	Dropbox for Business
Core business needs	Salesforce's Sales Cloud	SAP Cloud for Sales
Long-term preservation	ArchivesDirect	Preservica

Collaboration is improved, because documents are stored in a central cloud repository. Authorized users have access to the most recent versions, and team members can work on the same document in real time. The use of Microsoft's Office 365 can make the transition to the cloud easier for employees who use Microsoft products such as Word, Excel, and PowerPoint on-site; a hybrid approach is also an option that allows employees to work offline and synchronize their documents with the online versions. Google took advantage of its standalone products to build Google Apps for Work, including integration with online personal, shared, and public calendars and video conferencing using Google Hangouts and a telephone. Google Apps for Work is simple to use, especially for employees who have used Google's free versions for personal use.

Employees who create documents daily may experience a slower response rate with software in the cloud than if it were stored on-premise. This may result in frustration and a loss of productivity. A fundamental concern when opting for online office productivity suites is a reliable, secure Internet connection. In addition, both the vendor's uptime guarantee and track record should be investigated before making a decision. Not all suites offer the same features in the online and on-premise versions, and the features that are offered may not be integrated seamlessly into the overall online suite. Office 365, for example, includes a newsfeed feature that can be enabled easily for users, but the administrator must take a number of additional steps in order to provide access to Yammer, a private social network owned by Microsoft and advertised as part of the Office 365 suite.

Office 365 offers a number of options at different prices. However, all include Active Directory integration to manage user credentials and permissions. It provides security and privacy features such as encryption of data both at rest and via the network when transmitted between the user and the data center, regular backup of data, and hosting of customer data in-region. Office 365 complies with a number of standards, including the Health Insurance Portability and Accountability Act, the Federal Information Security Management Act, the US–EU Safe Harbor framework, and ISO 27001:2013, "Information technology—Security techniques—Information security management systems—Requirements" [13].

Security and control features vary not only among vendors but also according to the plan selected for the products. Google Apps for Work, for example, offers two options. The lower priced product allows up to 30 GB of storage per user and the more expensive version allows unlimited storage per user (limited to 1 TB if fewer than five users). However, from a security aspect, a more important distinction is that only the more expensive option offers security features that may be necessary from the organization's point of view, such as the following [14]:

- Advanced administrative controls for Drive

- Audit and reporting insights for Google Drive content and sharing

- Google Vault for eDiscovery, covering e-mails, chats, docs, and files

- Archive of all e-mails sent by the company

- Set message retention policies

2.4.4 SaaS and Social Computing

Social computing is an approach to IT whereby individuals tailor information-based and collaborative technologies to support interactions with relatively large and often loosely defined groups [2]. Public social media tools provide a means for organizations to interact with prospective and current customers. Social media hosted on public platforms can be used to provide superior customer service.

Enterprise social networks (ESNs) are private social networks that can be hosted on-premise or in the cloud. A key difference between ESNs and public social networks is that ESNs offer the organization complete control of the community. This includes features, policies, security levels, and management of data produced. The goal of employing ESNs is to tap into the expertise and creativity of employees, increase employee satisfaction, and improve speed to market. Groups can be created for employees and clients to access the network with their own devices and collaborate with one another regardless of time or location. Yammer and Socialcast are two products promoted as ESNs to create community and facilitate collaboration.

Yammer was acquired by Microsoft in 2012 and is available for free, but it is also offered for integration with Office 365/SharePoint Online and Microsoft Office and SharePoint on-premise. As a private social networking tool, it can be used to organize conversations, decrease the volume of e-mail sent and stored, and keep project documents together so that team members can track progress.

Socialcast was acquired by VMware in 2011 and has transformed into a product that enables a common social experience across all business applications. Collaboration is in the form of discussions and instant messages and takes place around activities, files, and projects. Organizations can use a full-featured version of the product hosted in a multitenant cloud for up to 50 users for free. Organizations needing more than 50 seats must enter into a paid subscription. The subscription with the lowest fee is hosted on a multitenant public cloud. If additional security is required, organizations can select from two private cloud options: a single-tenant environment hosted in a US or a European data center certified as SOC 2, type II compliant or a private cloud deployed on-site for maximum enterprise control.

A serious concern, especially for enterprises in highly regulated industries, is data privacy. Careful consideration of the type of content shared though social networking tools and training is required so that employees understand what can and cannot be shared through ESNs. In addition, storage options for content shared through ESNs must be understood.

2.4.5 SaaS and File Synchronization and Sharing

The benefits of enterprise file synchronization and sharing (EFSS) solutions include protecting and synchronizing files across computers, tablets, and smartphones, and providing unlimited version history and deletion recovery. Files or folders can easily be shared with others within or outside of the organization, including partners, consultants, subcontractors, and customers. Access to files in the repository regardless of the location of the employee promotes worker productivity and efficiency.

Although file sharing and synchronization is integrated into other cloud products, both Box.com and Dropbox for Business were designed for this purpose and operate in a public cloud. According to a recent survey [15], public cloud sharing tools present a primary security risk to organizations. Respondents to this survey expressed fear that the organization would be vulnerable to malware and viruses, exposure of sensitive or confidential information, and cyberattacks. A major concern was that data breaches would go undetected and sensitive, and confidential information would be exposed [15].

Security and control features vary among vendors and cloud services. Security features for data protection on devices may include password protection, remote wipe, data encryption, data loss prevention, digital rights management, document protection, encryption key management, and access tracking. Controls to verify access may include sharing and permissions rules such as expiration dates and passwords for sharing sensitive information within the organization and with people outside of the organization and two-step verification to add an extra layer of protection to user accounts.

2.4.6 SaaS and Sales Force Automation

SaaS is available to meet core business needs, including accounting and finance, HCM, and CRM. CRM is a component of Sales Force Automation (SFA) and includes the core functionalities of account, contact, and opportunity management. However, additional capabilities, such as sales configuration, guided selling, proposal generation and content management, and sales performance management support, may be included. According to Gartner, Leaders in the CRM field include Salesforce and Microsoft Dynamics CRM Online; Visionaries include Oracle, SugarCRM, and SAP Cloud for Sales; Challengers include SAP CRM and NetSuite; and Niche Players include Base, CRMnext, Aptean, Zoho, Sage, Infor, Bulhorn, and Tour de Force [16].

The adoption of SFA for CRM delivers the following benefits: increased productivity and improved customer service, more accurate sales forecasting, increased sales through upselling and cross-selling, improved sales team management, and automated lead conversions. Cloud SFA software offers access to customer and product information through any web-enabled device from any location.

Salesforce's Sales Cloud includes customer management and opportunity management features. Additional components can be added to facilitate anticipation of customer needs, personalize sales campaigns designed by marketing, tap the expertise of coworkers with social collaboration, and set metrics-based goals to drive team performance. Sales Cloud integrates with e-mail applications; files can be synchronized and shared; workflows and approvals can be designed and run; and a real-time picture of the business can be viewed through a dashboard. Sales Cloud can be integrated with Salesforce's Social Studio to allow a social service team to handle the customer care requests using public channels such as Facebook, LinkedIn, and Twitter.

SAP Cloud for Sales is built specifically for salespeople. It offers basic customer management and opportunity management features as well as user-friendly features such as message feeds and tagging and flagging of information for fast access. SAP Cloud for Sales integrates with SAP ERP software for access to back-office systems, such as sales orders or invoices. It provides a dashboard to view sales information, allows users to create reports, and supports a wide range of mobile devices. SAP took a proactive approach to foster integration by introducing SAP HANA Cloud Integration (HCI), a cloud integration platform for SAP Cloud customers. SAP HCI connects SAP Cloud Applications with SAP on-premise, third-party on-premise, and third-party cloud solutions to achieve real-time process integration and data integration.

SFA software presents challenges to those for whom it is intended, the sales force and management. Training is required to ensure that the sales team understands how to use the software to support the sales process and that management understands how to create reports. Vendor lock-in may be a concern. Understanding the business needs to be satisfied with the SFA and carefully evaluating the options available before selecting SFA software can mitigate the risk.

2.4.7 SaaS and Long-Term Preservation

As the technology to create, manage, and store digital information increases, the ability to preserve and make that information accessible for the long term decreases. However, government regulations and user expectations for access to information indefinitely can only be met by implementing long-term digital preservation solutions. Digital preservation on-premise is costly in terms of initial investment in technology and expertise to implement as well as ongoing costs to operate, maintain, and upgrade as necessary based on emerging technology, new file formats, and increased volume. Cloud solutions for digital preservation offer similar benefits and risks as other cloud solutions but present additional challenges.

Storage in the cloud does not meet the functional requirements necessary for long-term digital preservation. The same is true of digital archives, which are described in the Storage Networking Industry Association Glossary as follows [17]:

> A storage repository or service used to secure, retain, and protect digital information and data for periods of time less than that of long-term data retention. A digital archive can be an infrastructure component of a complete digital preservation service, but is not sufficient by itself to accomplish digital preservation, i.e., long-term data retention.

Cloud digital preservation service is a natural progression from cloud storage and archiving services. But preservation services must include management and curation functions that will accomplish digital preservation goals, including long-term preservation [18].

ISO standard 14721: 2012, Space data and information transfer systems—Open archival information system (OAIS)—Reference model, [19] describes "a full range of archival information preservation functions including ingest, archival storage, data management, access, and dissemination." It also addresses "the migration of digital information to new media and forms, the data models used to represent the information, the role of software in information preservation, and the exchange of digital information among archives."

"Few long-term digital preservation cloud services exist at this time; however, there are two that enable OAIS-based digital preservation workflows through a fully hosted, web-based application: Preservica and ArchivesDirect" [20]. Preservica offers cloud-hosted and on-premise editions of its suite comprising OAIS compliant workflows, a hosted public access module, and an active preservation technology that allows management and migration of content to newer file formats overtime rather than only at ingest (i.e., normalization). Metadata is held in fast Amazon RDS storage, and data is held in Amazon S3 and/or lower-cost Amazon Glacier cloud storage for content infrequently accessed. This solution provides out-of-the-box connectors that enable synchronization and automation of ingest of content from other systems, including digital asset libraries, content/records management systems, and e-mail systems. To date, this solution has been adopted by archives, libraries, government organizations, and businesses, including major State Archives, the UK National Archives, and HSBC bank.

ArchivesDirect is a more recent entry to the hosted digital preservation field, the result of a partnership between DuraSpace and Artefactual Systems. It uses an open-source software, so vendor lock-in is avoided; organizations can download and run Archivematica and/or DuraCloud software locally and move their cloud content to those local servers at any time. ArchivesDirect provides a framework for normalizing ingested digital objects into preservation-friendly formats while preserving the original objects. ArchivesDirect supports the key aspects of preservation and archiving. Two copies of content are stored, a primary copy in Amazon S3 and a secondary copy in Amazon Glacier. Archivematica, the digital preservation microservices engine behind ArchivesDirect, allows integration with several content management and public access systems, including ArchivesSpace, Islandora, and CONTENTdm.

Barriers to adoption of cloud digital preservation services are similar to those for other cloud services (e.g., handing over sensitive data to a third party, threat of data breach or loss, uptime/business continuity, and financial strength of the cloud computing provider) [18]. The success of long-term digital preservation initiatives rests upon the techniques employed to identify and manage the content before it is transferred to a trusted digital repository. Research in the area of digital preservation is ongoing, and it is conceivable that in the future consideration of long-term digital preservation requirements may be built into systems at every stage of the content life cycle.

2.5 INTEGRATION OF ECM WITH OTHER SYSTEMS

Integration can be thought of as interoperation via an interface specification or standard. In software systems, the mediation component is commonly a bridge or an adapter; they mediate between the interfaces of the disparate systems that you wish to integrate [21].

Unfortunately, more enterprise content sits outside of an ECM system than inside: for 61% of organizations, half or more of their content is held in non-ECM/Document Management systems such as ERP, HR, and Finance. However, 61% of workers have no connection between their ECM system and their other business systems [22].

The growth in adoption of cloud services and the fact that most enterprises use different combinations of public and private cloud deployment models, including hybrid and multiple, and various combinations of cloud services within those clouds, necessitates identifying and managing content residing in cloud-based SaaS systems within the information governance strategy. This can be accomplished through the integration of ECM solutions, whether located on-premise and in the clouds, with content residing in other cloud-based applications (see Figure 2.1).

A brief introduction to the integration approaches taken by two ECM vendors is provided to underscore how complex the issue of integration is. One vendor is recognized as a Leader in Gartner's *2014* "Magic Quadrant for Enterprise Content Management" but as a Facilitator in Nucleus Research's "ECM Value Matrix 2014": Microsoft [8]. The second vendor is recognized as a Leader by both Gartner and Nucleus Research: EMC [9].

2.5.1 Microsoft SharePoint Online, Office 365, and Yammer

Integration can take place between an ECM system and applications the vendor of the ECM system already offers, creates specifically for the system, or acquires in order to differentiate its product from others on the market. Microsoft has many opportunities to integrate SharePoint with other Microsoft SaaS products, including Office 365 and Yammer.

SharePoint is offered on-premise and in the cloud. Both versions integrate with Office 365 and Yammer. The subscription plans for the current version of Office 365 allow the

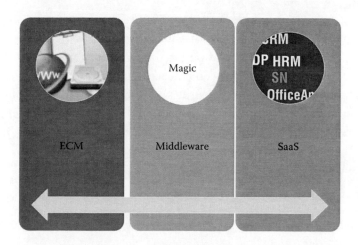

FIGURE 2.1   Enterprise expectations: ECM integration with SaaS applications.

user to work in the cloud and download and install the following Office applications for use within the enterprise: Word, Excel, PowerPoint, OneNote, InfoPath, Outlook, Publisher, and Access. Publisher and Access are available on PC only. Office 365 can be installed across multiple devices, including PCs, Macs, tablets, and smartphones.

Organizations employing SaaS products must be aware that features can be added or removed with short notice; for example, a feature that allowed public-facing websites to be designed and published through SharePoint Online was discontinued in early 2015. New subscribers are now encouraged to use an Office 365 web-hosting partner for their public-facing website; only two are on the list at this time.

Users logging into Office 365 will see icons for each of the components of Office 365 on their dashboard. However, Yammer, a product recently acquired by Microsoft but also available as a stand-alone social network, is not included and must be added later. The integration of Yammer requires involvement of the user, because Yammer must be set up using a company domain. If a domain is not available for use, one must be purchased from a domain name registrar. Organizations that do not choose to use Yammer for social communication can still engage socially through the default feature: newsfeeds.

SharePoint's latest release, SharePoint 2016, takes a hybrid approach to search by enabling Office 365 users with hybrid SharePoint Server architectures to search across premise and cloud for unified search results. Microsoft cautions users that "Office 365 doesn't support interoperability with any software that isn't supported by its manufacturer" [23]. Due to the popularity of this product, however, a number of SaaS vendors provide connectors to SharePoint.

2.5.2 EMC Documentum, SharePoint, and SAP

Documentum [24], originally a document management solution, was acquired by EMC in 2003 and is offered in the cloud, on-premise, or as a hybrid ECM suite. Documentum EMC is considered a leader in this field based on its extensive content management stack that includes most ECM elements: capture (Captiva), document management (Documentum), process management (Documentum xCP), and records management (Documentum Records Manager).

When offered in the cloud, both EMC Documentum and SharePoint Online are considered SaaS solutions. EMC recognizes that many users may prefer SharePoint as a portal for team collaboration and information document management, but they also believe that Documentum features—including advanced security, business process management, information rights management, and records and retention management—can better satisfy the users' needs for information governance and control. EMC, therefore, offers the "Documentum Connector for Microsoft SharePoint" to allow SharePoint users to [25]

- Access Documentum repositories via the SharePoint interface.

- Transfer Documents that need to be archived from SharePoint to Documentum.

- Use the extended document management functions from Documentum in SharePoint.

- Perform cross-platform search options.

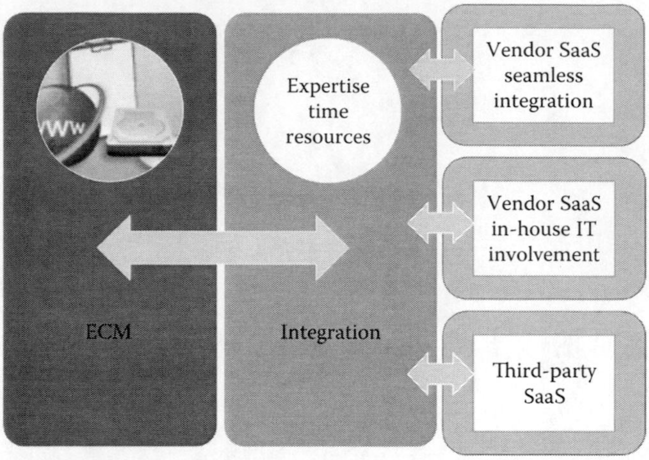

FIGURE 2.2   ECM integration viewpoint—Multiple requirements based on the SaaS model.

The integration between two ECM systems allows the enterprise to leverage the strengths of each.

EMC Documentum integrates with SaaS Business Productivity applications as well. EMC Documentum Archive Services for SAP has been in existence since 1996. Current features include applying SAP-defined retention to business content in the SAP Archive and augmenting retention with additional services such as workflows and storage policies (see Figure 2.2).

2.6 INTEGRATION PLATFORM AS A SERVICE

In the two examples of ECM integration with SaaS, various approaches were taken. In one instance the vendor, Microsoft, developed an Office Productivity Suite and an ECM system, and then integrated the two in order to create an attractive option for clients who want to take advantage of the benefits of working in the cloud (e.g., access 24/7, mobility, pay-as-you go model). Access through a dashboard allows users to log in once to use all of the components. The vendor further enhanced the options for organizations who wish to retain critical and confidential content on-premise by integrating the SaaS Office Productivity suite with a cloud version of the ECM system and offering the Office Suite for Office 365 customers within the enterprise if desired.

In the second example, EMC promoted the value their ECM system could add to SharePoint and SAP through integration. The integration allowed the ECM system to augment SharePoint's functionality with its own features that were missing from or not as mature in SharePoint (e.g., imaging). Following the same premise, EMC Documentum added the value to SAP's applications by integrating content management capabilities within the secure SAP archiving platform.

A third approach to integration was mentioned in the discussion of SaaS and SFA. In that case, the SaaS Business process provider, SAP, took the initiative by creating an integration platform and making it available to customers who wanted to develop connectors

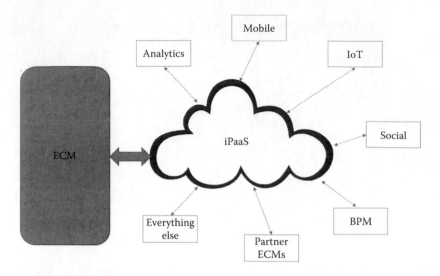

FIGURE 2.3   Integration platforms facilitate connectivity between ECM, SaaS, and devices.

to integrate the vendor's own cloud offering with its on-premise version but also with third-party on-premise and cloud applications. EMC is one of the vendors who took advantage of the offer. A term has emerged to describe the approach SAP took, iPaaS (see Figure 2.3).

2.6.1 Gartner's 2015 Magic Quadrant for Enterprise iPaaS

The March 2015 version of the "Enterprise iPaaS Quadrant" [26] categorizes 16 vendors into four quadrants. Leaders are Dell Boomi, Informatica, and MuleSoft. Visionaries include IBM, SnapLogic, Youredi, SAP, and Microsoft. Challengers include Fujitsu and Adaptris. Niche players are Jitterbit, Celigo, Cloud Elements, Flowgear, TerraSky, and Attunity. Each of these vendors has specific goals, strengths, and weaknesses.

The desired outcome of the use of iPaaS is [the development of] a cloud service, not a software product [26]. The requirement for inclusion in this group is that the company provide integration platforms in the form of public cloud services. Examples of iPaaS functionality are support for and bridging between a variety of connectivity protocols and data/message delivery styles, integration flow development and lifecycle management tools, and reusable integration templates [26].

Two vendors considered Leaders in this field were discussed previously in this chapter, Microsoft and SAP. SAP's iPaaS offering is the HCI platform described earlier. Microsoft was included for its Azure BizTalk Services platform that focuses primarily on integrating SaaS offerings to on-premise applications and supporting B2B integration.

2.6.2 On the Horizon: IoT PaaS

Cisco [27] estimates that 50 billion devices will be connected to the Internet by 2020. Services to control data generated by these devices that comprise the IoT are emerging. The massive amounts of data must be processed and analyzed in real time for maximum value when making decisions. Cloud service providers, IBM, Google, and Amazon, provide platforms for IoT applications to collect, ingest, process, and analyze big data.

Microsoft announced its Azure IoT Suite in 2015 [28]. It is bundling existing applications into a preconfigured solution built on Microsoft's cloud platform. Because the solution is designed to work with the organization's existing devices and IoT systems, they also announced the "Azure Certified for IoT" program to help customers identify hardware and software verified to work with Azure IoT services [28].

General Electric, a technology and financial services company, developed a software platform to store, analyze, and manage machine's internal data for better and faster decision making. The iPaaS, Predix Cloud, will be commercially available in 2016 [29].

As with early ECM systems, the impetus for iPaaS is a growing volume of data. Unlike early the corporate customers who invested in ECM systems to manage data, the main goal of enterprises investing in iPaaS is to derive value from big data in real time. The commercial literature describing and promoting iPaaS does not "yet" touch on compliance or retention and disposition requirements that may be applicable to some of these data. Take, for example, data gathered in real time from an automobile, airliner, or train involved in an incident that costs lives. What would the sensor information sent to an iPaaS application reveal if it were stored and could be accessed? How long would it be available? Would the firm be wise to dispose of it as soon as it no longer has business value or must it be retained to meet regulatory requirements? Would destruction be possible? These are the types of questions that resulted in the inclusion of records centers and compliance workflows in a number of current electronic content management systems.

2.7 SUMMARY

Disruptive technologies—for example, mobile devices, wearable devices, social media, sensors, and the cloud—have changed the way we live and work. Users expect to have access to information when they need it, on any device, from any location, and in context. Business and government institutions are seeking ways to utilize information to help them make wise decisions and provide superior customer service. They view information as a valuable asset, but one that is difficult to control.

Adoption of ECM systems has grown, as organizations view them as a means to capture, manage, and control content. Organizations can select from a number of products now on the market. Many of those products are offered as SaaS applications. Vendors seeking to differentiate their products from others to gain economic advantage not only provide core functions within their offerings but also enhance their products with additional features, such as unified search capabilities and content analytics.

Integration is now seen as a business strategy for the user and the vendor. ECM systems are often integrated with on-premise products, other ECM systems, and SaaS applications. Integration facilitates collaboration, supports decision making, and enhances productivity for the user. Vendors develop custom integrations to connect their product to other SaaS or enterprise products, or they employ integration specialists to do it for them. iPaaSs are provided by organizations or vendors who specialize in integration to assist organizations that create connectors.

As a result of perceived benefits of moving content and applications to the cloud, an increasing number of organizations are taking advantage of cloud-based ECM systems, utilizing public, private, or hybrid deployment models. A look to the future reveals new challenges to be overcome. The massive amount of data generated by devices connected to the Internet calls for a different approach to managing information. Recent efforts to capture, manage, and analyze these data in real time have resulted in the development of another "as-a-service" option: IoT PaaS. IoT cloud services are offered by several large cloud vendors, including IBM, Amazon, and Microsoft. One industry giant, General Electric, developed a solution for in-house use and will soon enter the cloud service market by offering it commercially. The goal of developing IoT solutions is to capture and manage data so the organization can make better business decisions.

Questions related to retention, disposition, and compliance with government regulations must be addressed in relation to the adoption of IoT platforms and applications. Whether current ECM systems evolve to play a role in managing big data generated through SaaS running on IoT platforms is yet to be determined.

REFERENCES

1. AIIM Glossary. *What Is Enterprise Content Management (ECM)?* Association for Information and Image Management, Silver Spring, MD, 2015.
2. Gartner IT Glossary. Integration Platform as a Service (iPaaS). Gartner, Stamford, CT, 2015.
3. Badger, Lee, Tim Grance, Robert Patt-Comer, and Jeff Voas. *Cloud Computing Synopsis and Recommendations.* Gathersburg, MD: National Institute of Standards and Technology, 2012.
4. InterPARES Trust. Terminology Database [Restricted access]. interparestrust.org, 2015.
5. ANSI/AIIM/ARMA. *Revised Framework for the Integration of Electronic Document Management Systems and Electronic Records Management Systems.* Silver Springs, MD: AIIM®, 2006.
6. Infosys. *An ECM Journey* [White paper]. infosys.com, 2014.
7. Hullavard, Shiva, Russell O'Hare, and Ashok K. Roy. Enterprise Content Management solutions—Roadmap strategy and implementation challenges. *International Journal of Information Management*, 35: 260–265, 2015.
8. Gilbert, Mark R., Karen M. Shegda, Kenneth Chin, Gavin Tay, and Hanns Koehler-Kruener. *Gartner: Magic Quadrant for Enterprise Content Management.* Gartner.com., 2015.
9. Nucleus Research. *Technology Value Matrix 2015: ECM*, 2015.
10. DATAMARK. *Organizations Struggling to Implement Mobile Enterprise Content Management (ECM).* DATAMARK, 2015.
11. DATAMARK. AIIM: The Era of Enterprise Content Management (ECM) is coming to an end. *Outsourcing News*, 2015.
12. Mann, Jeffrey and Bill Pray. *Office 365, Google Apps for Work and Other Cloud Office Key Initiative Overview.* Gartner, Stamford, CT, 2015.
13. Microsoft. *Office 365 Trust Center.* Microsoft Office 365, 2015.
14. Google. *Google Apps for Work. Get Email for Your Business.* Google, n.d.
15. Ponemon Institute. *Achieving Security in Workplace File Sharing.* Ponemon Institute LLC, 2014.
16. Desisto, Robert P. and Tad Travis. *Magic Quadrant for Sales Force Automation.* Gartner, 2015.
17. SNIA. *The 2015 SNIA Dictionary.* SNIA, 2015.
18. Franks, Patricia. *Records and Information Management*, pp. 280–282. Chicago, IL: ALA-Neal-Schuman, 2013.

19. International Organization for Standardization (ISO). ISO standard 14721: 2012, Space data and information transfer systems—Open archival information system (OAIS)—International Organization for Standardization (ISO). Reference model, 2nd edition, pp. 1–2. Geneva, Switzerland: ISO, 2012.
20. Franks, Patricia C. Government Use of cloud-based long term digital preservation as a service: An exploratory study. *Proceedings of the 2nd Digital Heritage International Congress*, 2015.
21. Association for Information and Image Management (AIIM). *ECM at the Crossroads*, p. 4. AIIM, 2013.
22. Trebaol, Lacey. Integration vs. interoperation. *Real-Time Innovations Blog*, 2013.
23. Microsoft. System requirements for Office. *Microsoft Office*, 2015.
24. EMC. Documentum by EMC. *EMC²*, 2015.
25. EMC. Documentum Connector for Microsoft SharePoint. *EMC²*, 2015.
26. Pezzini, Massimo, Yefim V. Natis, Paolo Malinverno, Kimihiko Iijima, Jess Thompson, Eric Thoo, and Keith Guttridge. *Magic Quadrant for Enterprise Integration Platform as a Service, Worldwide*. Gartner, 2015.
27. Cisco. *Seize New IoT Opportunities with the Cisco IoT System*. Cisco, n.d.
28. Microsoft. Azure IoT Suite now available. *Microsoft, Internet of Things*, 2015.
29. General Electric. *GE Announces Predix Cloud—The World's First Cloud Service Built for Industrial Data and Analytics* [Press release], 2015.

CHAPTER 3

Infrastructure as a Service

Mario Santana

CONTENTS

IN THIS CHAPTER, I will review the major components of a private cloud infrastructure (PCI) to help us think about the security of that architecture. Whether a cloud environment performs business-critical tasks or supports peripheral activities or houses important data, we must understand the mechanics that make a cloud work before we can secure it.

We'll begin our discussion by touching on a few high-level conceptual issues. Then we'll actually break down a cloud infrastructure into its various component pieces. These components include the compute nodes that actually encapsulate the computational capability of a cloud infrastructure and make it fractionally available to several users for sharing; the network connectivity that allows several compute nodes to communicate with each other and with the outside world while maintaining network layer isolation between unrelated users of the cloud infrastructure; the storage services that provide functionality for applications in the cloud environment to maintain state, usually in the form of virtualized hard drives, that can be used and manipulated by compute nodes and potentially shared over the network capability; and the management layer that lets us manage all the rest. As we look at these component pieces of an infrastructure-as-a-service (IaaS) cloud infrastructure, we'll take a look at some underlying approaches used by various cloud technologies to deliver each component, and we'll review some of the key security considerations that pertain to each component. Let's get started!

3.1 CONTEXTUAL CONSIDERATIONS

Cloud infrastructure is appealing for many reasons. However, fundamentally, the value proposition is very simple: We use it to optimize resource utilization by sharing those resources among multiple users. As we consider security from the perspective of a user of a cloud infrastructure, it will be valuable to consider the bigger picture of how the operation of the cloud infrastructure as a whole can potentially impact us as a single user of that cloud. We'll review three important concepts [1].

3.1.1 Greatest Common Denominator

One important concept is that of "greatest common denominator." In operating a cloud environment in support of multiple users, the cloud operator must meet the security requirements of all users of the environment. These various users will generally have various security requirements as well. In a simplistic understanding of this concept, it's clear the some users will have more rigorous security requirements than others. This understanding actually holds true much of the time, especially to the extent that some users must meet a more stringent set of compliance requirements than others. For example, users running their payment processing or point of sale (POS) backends in the cloud will need to meet PCI and probably additional requirements, compared to a training tool that only hosts nonsensitive corporate training content. In this situation, the concept of greatest common denominator dictates that the cloud environment must meet the needs of the user with the most stringent set of requirements, because this will also meet the needs of all users with less stringent requirements.

However, the mass of requirements gets more complicated when there are users with different requirements, where one set of requirements isn't necessarily more stringent than another. An example of this situation is when one user runs a POS backend in the cloud environment, whereas another user hosts medical information. One user may need to meet PCI requirements, whereas the other user must comply with Health Insurance Portability and Accountability Act (HIPAA) standards. Both of these standards are stringent in their own ways, but it's not always possible to say that one standard is more stringent than the other. Therefore, there is no single set of requirements that will meet the needs of both users. Instead, in this situation, we must meet the superset of all requirements demanded by all users, understanding that there is no user that needs all of these requirements.

3.1.2 User Communities

Managing a cloud environment in accordance with the greatest common denominator principle can be a daunting task, because meeting multiple overlapping sets of complex security requirements and managing the audits and certifications around those requirements require a great deal of overhead in terms of planning and governance. One way to reduce the governance overhead in this kind of circumstance is to isolate different groups of tenants or applications into various "communities," according to their various security needs. The key to this approach is to find users with similar security requirements and group them together. Therefore, any users or applications that deal with credit card or payment information are grouped together into, say, a PCI group. Likewise, all users that deal with medical information are grouped together in a HIPAA group, all users that deal with corporate finance information are grouped together into a Sarbanes–Oxley Act (SOX) group, and so on. We can even have a community of users or applications with minimal security requirements, perhaps called the "out in the cold" group.

Once the various communities have been identified, and if they've been well sorted into groups with similar sets of security requirements, the task of managing in accordance with the principle of greatest common denominator is greatly simplified. There is still a need to manage diverse security requirements, but these requirements can be compartmentalized, reducing their impact on each other, the complexity of the overall operational, governance, and management overhead, and ultimately reducing the cost of providing a cloud environment that meets all the users' needs. In turn, the users enjoy a simpler relationship with their cloud environment, needing only to understand the ways in which the environment meets their security needs without the distraction and confusion of superfluous requirements that don't apply to their situation. And, of course, if a user's or application's needs evolve slightly, the security configuration of their existing community could be evolved to meet the new requirement. Alternatively, if the new requirements represent a more drastic change, the user or application could be migrated to a different community that more closely matches their new set of needs.

3.1.3 Shared Impact

One more overarching concept that is important to keep in mind is the idea of "shared impacts." There are obvious shared impacts, of course, related to attacks on or failures of the shared infrastructure. Clearly, if an attacker targets any of the users on a shared cloud environment with any kind of successful resource exhaustion attack, then all the other users of that shared cloud environment are likely to feel the effects of resource exhaustion. The best cloud infrastructures are configured in ways that minimize these effects—for example, by minimizing the types and amounts of shared resources that can be exhausted by any one user of the environment.

However, there are other shared impacts that are less obvious, though no less critical. For example, consider the effects of a court-issued subpoena to seize the servers of one user in a multitenant cloud environment. Even if the subpoena is only concerned with the data related to one user or application, law enforcement may judge that the subpoena calls for physical hardware rather than virtual. In that scenario, law enforcement may shut down and seize hardware that supports multiple users—not just the target user!—and therefore cause an outage that impacts all users of the environment.

Now, this particular scenario was once very common. The best and largest cloud operators have relationships with local law enforcement agencies, and the local offices of regional and national law enforcement agencies, specifically to mitigate the shared impact of evidence seizure activities. Moreover, law enforcement is increasingly educated about the high and unnecessary impact of brute-force seizures, and thus, this specific issue is much less prevalent now than it was 5 years ago. However, it's a great example of the kinds of nonobvious shared impacts that can make one user's actions and interactions have a significant effect on other cloud users that have nothing to do with the action or interaction that caused the impact.

3.2 COMPONENTS OF A PRIVATE CLOUD INFRASTRUCTURE

Cloud infrastructures are built to manage various kinds of resources and distribute those resources efficiently among workloads and applications. In the following sections, we'll take a look at what kinds of resources are managed and distributed by a cloud infrastructure [2].

3.2.1 Compute

The compute component of a cloud infrastructure is the workhorse of that infrastructure (see Figure 3.1). In the context of an IaaS cloud, a workload typically we'll call a compute instance. The physical hardware that provides compute resources we'll call compute nodes. One compute node may run multiple compute instances. The compute instances actually encapsulate the computational capability, in the form of CPU processing time and RAM memory working space, of the compute nodes in the cloud infrastructure and make it fractionally available to several users for sharing [3]. There are three underlying approaches to implementing compute instances: hypervisor, container, and bare metal.

3.2.1.1 Hypervisors

In practice, most cloud infrastructure designs leverage virtualization to implement the compute component. That's because virtualization defines hardware as software—a virtualized compute instance is essentially a file, like a program or a configuration file or the file I'm editing as I write this chapter. It is much easier to copy a file to a new location than to move a physical server. It is much easier to reconfigure a server by editing a file than by opening a physical piece of hardware, and add or remove CPUs, RAM memory, storage, and so on. To that end, there are two main kinds of virtualization in use for cloud infrastructures today.

Perhaps the most common kind of virtualization is a hypervisor. A hypervisor creates virtual machines, complete with virtual CPUs, memory, network cards, peripheral busses, disks, even a complete virtual basic input/output system (BIOS). It isolates compute instances by keeping their kernel space separate, while allowing to share a single physical CPU, RAM, and storage space—this is the chief security concern when considering hypervisor implementations. With a hypervisor, each compute instance is running an entirely distinct and isolated operating system.

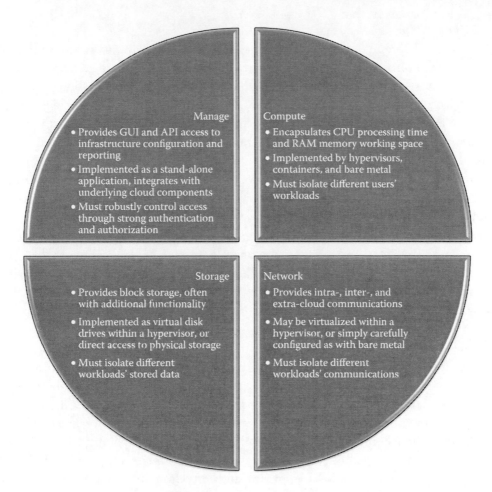

Manage
- Provides GUI and API access to infrastructure configuration and reporting
- Implemented as a stand-alone application, integrates with underlying cloud components
- Must robustly control access through strong authentication and authorization

Compute
- Encapsulates CPU processing time and RAM memory working space
- Implemented by hypervisors, containers, and bare metal
- Must isolate different users' workloads

Storage
- Provides block storage, often with additional functionality
- Implemented as virtual disk drives within a hypervisor, or direct access to physical storage
- Must isolate different workloads' stored data

Network
- Provides intra-, inter-, and extra-cloud communications
- May be virtualized within a hypervisor, or simply carefully configured as with bare metal
- Must isolate different workloads' communications

FIGURE 3.1 Components of a cloud infrastructure.

3.2.1.2 Containers

In contrast to the hypervisor approach, a container virtualizes the operating system. The same operating system kernel is shared among multiple applications or workloads, which represent the compute instance in the container model. Each virtualized environment in this approach, what we generically call a compute instance, is called a container in the context of this approach. The container functionality is actually part of the host operating system that runs on the host compute node. This approach is much more lightweight than the hypervisor approach.

A container isolates applications by keeping their user space separate, while allowing them to share a single kernel space. It's the job of the container software to ensure that one container is not accessible in any way by a different container. The maintenance of that strict isolation, a thorough reworking of every operating system facility that might expose one container to another, is the chief isolation challenge of a container implementation, making it more complex to isolate workloads in a container model compared to a hypervisor.

3.2.1.3 Bare Metal

A "bare metal" compute component manages workloads without virtualization. Each workload is run on a separate piece of physical hardware. In the bare metal approach, the distinction between compute node and compute instance is eliminated—they are one and the same. The benefit of including bare metal compute in a cloud architecture is the ability to monitor and report on the bare metal node in ways that are compatible with the monitoring and reporting of the rest of the cloud infrastructure.

And the reason why bare metal compute nodes are valuable is because there are certain workloads and applications that do not lend themselves to efficient virtualization. Performance-intensive applications—especially applications that require fast, low-latency disk I/O performance, such as large and high-performance databases—are the prime example of applications that don't lend themselves to effective virtualization. For this reason, many cloud infrastructure support bare metal nodes where these kinds of applications can run, while still allowing the management of the overall infrastructure using a cloud-oriented management model.

3.2.2 Network

The network component of a cloud infrastructure allows for connectivity among the compute, storage, and other elements of that infrastructure, as well as with the broader environment outside that infrastructure. At a minimum, the network component connects the network facilities of the compute component to the edge of the cloud environment and manages the kind of access that the compute instances have between each other and to the broader environment. Beyond that minimum required capability, there are several techniques to manage the network topology in a cloud infrastructure: virtual switching, management of physical network equipment, and software-defined networking.

3.2.2.1 Underlying Approaches

Virtual switching enables a compute node to define virtual networks that only exist inside the hypervisor or container. This allows the creation of a virtual subnet by connecting the virtual network interfaces of several virtual machines to this virtual switch. This virtual subnet is totally isolated from the physical network, but the virtual workloads and applications on that virtual subnet can communicate as if they were physical machines connected to the same physical network switch.

More advanced versions of this technology allow for "ports" on the virtual switch to exist on separate physical compute nodes, so that workloads on different physical compute nodes can connect to the same virtual switch. This makes it possible to configure the network so that compute instances can operate as if they were on the same switch, regardless of which physical compute node is running that instance, and regardless of whether that workload is migrated to different compute nodes over time.

To support these advanced operations, the network component of a cloud infrastructure must often manage physical network equipment—nonvirtualized switches, firewalls, and so on—to create the network topology that has been configured. By coopting physical network equipment, the network component can manage communications between compute instances across separate compute nodes when those compute nodes are connected to separate physical switches and even when those compute nodes are in different data centers across the world.

A "software-defined network" technology takes these concepts even further. In software-defined networking, the network topology definition is abstracted and completely virtualized. This allows for switch ports, virtual local area networks (VLANs), firewall rules, and other advanced network configurations of a cloud infrastructure to be managed by the network component through management interfaces or configuration files. The network component then configures the details of each physical and virtual network device in the infrastructure, to implement the topology as defined in the abstraction. The main benefits of a software-defined network are centralized network management of diverse devices; more flexible configuration options; and seamless disaster recovery, load balancing, and other typical cloud operations.

3.2.2.2 Security Implications

The most security-critical responsibility of the network component is isolation. The network component must keep separate compute instances from communicating to each other in unauthorized ways. For example, the network component must prevent malicious workloads from accessing unauthorized VLANs and subnets that may be accessible by authorized workloads sharing the same physical hardware. The virtualization of the network component also makes it possible to implement a wide variety of monitoring schemes for network traffic in the cloud infrastructure.

3.2.3 Storage

The storage component of a cloud infrastructure provides data storage services to that infrastructure. At a minimum, the storage component stores cloud management information, such as virtual machine and virtual network definitions, and provides working space to applications and workloads running in the cloud environment. Beyond that minimum required capability, there are several techniques to provide workload migration, automated backups, integrated version control, and optimized application-specific storage mechanisms.

3.2.3.1 Underlying Approaches

The fundamental capabilities of the storage component involve managing the storage required by the cloud infrastructure management functions. The details of this depend on the specific technology and approach of the compute component. For compute nodes running a hypervisor, the storage component must provide storage for the hypervisor, which then virtualizes that storage for the virtual machines under its control. For compute nodes running containers, the storage component can be nothing more than the file system drivers built into the operating system kernel shared among the host compute node and the compute instances running in the containers on that host. For compute nodes running on bare metals, the compute instance being indistinguishable from the host compute node, the workload typically has direct access to the host's storage hardware—indeed, this is the primary reason for running bare metal compute nodes in the first place, because this allows the workload to operate without the performance overhead of virtualized storage I/O for applications such as high-performance databases.

Beyond the minimum requirement to run a workload in a cloud environment, the storage component as implemented by most modern cloud infrastructure technologies can provide various additional capabilities for advanced operational capabilities, or simply to improve management convenience. For example, most hypervisor implementations support so-called snapshots. These snapshots capture the state of a virtual machine at a moment in time, allowing the user to revert to that state at any time in the future. A modern storage component can implement automated backups by working with the hypervisors to create a snapshot at regular intervals and storing them according to the configured backup scheme. These backups capture everything about the state of the machine at the time of the backup, so that if the backup ever needs to be restored, the workload can begin working right where it left off. Closely related to this is integrated version control, for example, to enable multiple versions of an application to be run at any time in support of development or support efforts.

Another way that the storage component can collaborate with the hypervisor or container is to allow for workload migration among host compute nodes. The storage component enables this by providing some mechanism for different compute nodes to access the storage related to a given workload. This may be accomplished through network file systems (NFSs), shared storage fabrics such as internet small computer system interface (iSCSI) or fiber channel storage area network, or some copy-on-demand mechanism. Although it is managed, it allows the compute component to shuffle workloads among the various compute nodes.

There is a fine line between advanced storage component functionality and functionality more properly attributed to the database component. For example, we'll discuss key-value stores in the database section, but these may be implemented by the same component that provides more traditional storage mechanisms. Cloud infrastructure technology is developing quickly and gray areas like this abound.

3.2.3.2 Security Implications
As with other components of a cloud architecture, perhaps the most critical security-related consideration involves the enforcement of complete isolation between compute instances, workloads, and applications. In the case of storage, the compute component plays an important role in enforcing that isolation; however, the storage component must also ensure that compute instances can access only authorized storage areas, for example, by configuring robust NFS permissions and iSCSI authentication. Malicious code on one compute instance should not be able to access another workload's data by manipulating the storage infrastructure.

3.2.4 Management
The management component of a cloud infrastructure provides the means by which users and administrators can configure and operate all the managed aspects of that infrastructure.

Ideally, all other components of the infrastructure can be managed via the management component. The functionality of the management component may be exposed via graphical user interface for manual operation or via application program interface for automated operation and integration with other tools and technologies. The introspection functionality of a cloud architecture exposes various aspects of the internal operating state of the various components that make up that architecture. This allows application running outside the component to view and possibly modify the running state of the cloud component in question.

3.2.4.1 Underlying Approaches

The management component must provide a mechanism for managing the cloud infrastructure components under its control. This includes the following:

- Defining specific workloads or applications as virtual machines, containers, or bare metal nodes, and providing a means to provision CPU and memory resources to these workloads

- Defining network access mechanisms as appropriate for the network components being managed and allocating these network resources to defined workloads or applications

- Defining storage and database units as appropriate for the underlying storage component being managed and making them available to workloads on compute nodes

- Coordinating migration of all these resources for various use cases, including load balancing and outage resiliency

The management component may also manage the introspection capabilities of the cloud infrastructure. These capabilities expose the information about the state of the various components in the cloud infrastructure and enable operations that manipulate or record that state. These capabilities support tools, for example, that can make forensically sound recordings of raw disk blocks used by a virtual machine, or record network traffic generated by that virtual machine. For some use cases that only leverage introspection sporadically, such as digital forensics and incident response, it may be feasible to manage the introspective mechanisms manually on a case-by-case basis. However, for security use cases that depend heavily on routine introspection, such as antivirus and intrusion detection system (IDS), the management component provides critical support for scaling and automating introspective activities.

3.2.4.2 Security Implications

Securing the management component is a critical part of securing a cloud infrastructure deployment. It is also arguably the most complex part of a cloud infrastructure to properly secure. That is both because of the complexity of the operations performed by the management component and because of the many interface points the management component must support.

3.3 SUMMARY

PCIs can be extremely complex, yet it's important to understand it intimately in order to secure private clouds properly. It's impossible to cover the topic thoroughly in one chapter, but this information will get you started and help you determine what knowledge gaps to fill in more detail.

REFERENCES

1. Gurkok, Cem. Securing Cloud Computing Systems. In Vacca, J. R., ed. *Computer and Information Security Handbook*. 2nd Edition. Elsevier: Boston, MA, 2013, pp. 97–123.
2. National Institute of Standards and Technology. *The NIST Definition of Cloud Computing*. NIST Special Publication Gaithersburg, MD, 2011, 800-145.
3. Yeluri, Raghu and Enrique Castro-Leon. *Building the Infrastructure for Cloud Security*. Apress Media: New York, 2014, pp. 160–163.

CHAPTER 4

Preservation as a Service for Trust

Luciana Duranti, Adam Jansen, Giovanni Michetti,
Courtney Mumma, Daryll Prescott,
Corinne Rogers, and Kenneth Thibodeau[*]

CONTENTS

4.1 INTRODUCTION

Preserving recorded information for long periods of time may be required by practical considerations; for example, medical records are kept for the life of individuals, and possibly their descendants, to ensure continuing health care; design, engineering, and manufacturing data are kept to enable reproduction of piece parts for physical systems, such as ships or aircraft, that are in service for decades; and records of myriad administrative activities are kept to enable audits, management analyses, and data analytics to identify relationships, trends, and anomalies. In addition, recorded information is maintained over the long term

---

[*] The names are listed in alphabetical order. However, it is important to note that the InterPARES Trust working group which is developing the preservation as a service for trust model is chaired by Kenneth Thibodeau, and its members are Adam Jansen, Giovanni Michetti, Courtney Mumma, and Daryll Prescott. Luciana Duranti and Corinne Rogers are ex-officio members, being, respectively, the director of the InterPARES Trust project and its coordinator, and take active part in the modeling effort. This chapter has been primarily drafted by the working group chair, Kenneth Thibodeau, and reviewed as to content and form by all the individuals named in this footnote.

to fulfill more general societal interests; for example, data on natural phenomena are kept to improve understanding of the processes that generate them; government records are kept to enable citizens to hold their governments accountable; and socioeconomic and cultural information is kept to enrich our understanding of human history. By greatly expanding our ability to generate information, digital information technology increases the amount of data eligible for preservation. The technology also provides additional motivations for keeping information by augmenting and improving capabilities for combining data from disparate sources and for mining and analyzing the data, thus enabling the generation of new knowledge (NIST 2009).

At the same time, digital technology increases the difficulty of preserving information and the risks that it will be lost or corrupted. Three inherent problems plague the preservation of digitally encoded information. First, unlike information in traditional, hard copy forms, such as that affixed to paper, parchment, or clay tablets, digital information is not permanently inscribed on physical media. This is not due to any physical or chemical limitations of digital media. Extremely durable media have been proposed and developed to store bits, but they have not proven to be economically competitive in the face of continuing improvements in data densities and read/write speeds in newer storage media.*

Second, for information produced by humans, and in many cases also for that generated by systems or applications, the information is not saved in the physical form in which it was created either as rendered on a display device for human perception or in computer memory. Data saved to digital storage media necessarily differ from the way they are inscribed on any rendering device or in computer memory. Because the media are different physical substances, inscription of data on them necessarily differs substantively. Thus, in the digital realm, we do not preserve the recorded information in its original materialization, but rather copies of it, because the original inscription, both on a screen and in computer memory, disappears when it is saved to a storage medium and closed. When we recall it, we generate a copy, and we produce still different manifestations of the same data when we retrieve information on different devices or even on the same device using different display settings. Moving recorded information from the application in which it is made or received to storage, memory, or display devices changes its physical instantiation and may introduce substantial alterations. The success of the Internet has reified both of these factors because data are transformed from inscription to signal every time they are transmitted and to a new inscription when they are received. The Internet has also introduced a new variation whereby parties that exchange information regularly agree to an interchange format that may vary significantly from the way the same data are represented within the parties' systems. A widespread example of this is the eXtensible Business Reporting Language (XBRL), a voluntary international standard that enables businesses to communicate and exchange information, especially financial data, between systems

---

* For example, Norsam's HD-Rosetta is described as an "archival preservation technology," capable of lasting 10,000 years, but only the publicized use of technology is in jewelry making (Norsam Technologies 2015; Schiff 2008).

without requiring conformity in the way that data are represented internally in different systems (XBRL International 2013).

Third, continuing improvements in information and communications technologies entail a twofold complication: the hardware and software originally used to create the information become obsolete, and, even if they remain available, people often want to use more advanced current technology to access and use preserved information. The cloud increases the problem of digital preservation because those responsible for preserving recorded information relinquish control to cloud service providers (CSPs) and may not even have direct knowledge of how the data are preserved. Thus, preserving information in the cloud may be a black box process in which we know, at least ideally, what we put in for preservation, and we know what we want to access and retrieve—essentially the same things we put in—but often we do not know what technology is used by the CSPs to manage, store, or process our information. With commercial CSPs, those responsible for preservation may not even know where the information objects are. CSPs can and do subcontract some of the capabilities they offer to other service providers, potentially maintaining servers or being registered as providers in different countries. Even if a CSP is willing to inform those entrusting them with preserving their information objects about the technology it does or can use, those responsible for the information cannot expect that the same hardware and software will remain in service for as long as the information objects must be preserved, or even that the technologies replacing them will be compatible with the previous ones.

In this respect, however, preservation in the cloud is not fundamentally different from in-house preservation. Even in-house preservation often relies on a service provider, such as an organization's IT division, that makes decisions concerning implementation or operation of hardware or software independently of those responsible for the information. Moreover, it is unlikely that those who either want to preserve digital information or have legal or moral responsibility for its preservation are experts in all or even most of the technologies required for or used in digital preservation. Even experts who have extensive and deep knowledge of all the hardware and software they use to preserve digital information cannot know what technology will be used for preservation in the future, for the simple reason that no one knows how information and communications technologies will evolve over sizable time frames. To address these issues, InterPARES Trust, an international multidisciplinary research project on the authentic preservation of digital records, is developing a set of requirements for Preservation as a Service for Trust (PaaST).

4.2 PaaST

InterPARES Trust (ITrust 2013–2018) is a research partnership that comprises over 50 universities and organizations, national and multinational, public and private, in North America, Latin America, Europe, Africa, Australasia, and Asia. Leadership and coordination of the partnership is provided by the School of Library, Archival and Information Studies at the University of British Columbia, British Columbia, Canada, under a grant funded by the Social Sciences and Humanities Research Council of Canada, Ottawa,

Ontario, Canada.* ITrust explores issues concerning digital records entrusted to the Internet, specifically those within a multitenancy, multijurisdictional, third-party Internet-based storage system, that is, the cloud. The project's goal is to generate the theoretical and methodological frameworks to develop local, national, and international policies, procedures, regulations, standards, and legislation, in order to ensure public trust grounded on evidence of good governance, a strong digital economy, and a persistent digital memory. Its researchers are experts in archival science, records management, diplomatics, law, information technology, communication and media, journalism, e-commerce, health informatics, cybersecurity, information governance and assurance, digital forensics, computer engineering, and information policy. ITrust has defined five broad topic domain areas of research of particular importance to the creation, management, access, or storage of digital records within Internet-based environments:

- *Infrastructure*: Relating to system architecture as it affects those records that are created, managed, or stored in Internet-based environments. Examples of areas studied under this domain include types of Internet-based environments and their reliability (e.g., public and private clouds); types of contract agreements (e.g., service-level agreements) and their coverage, flexibility, and modification; and the cost of services, both upfront and hidden.

- *Security*: Relating to the protection of Internet-based records. Examples of areas studied under this domain include security technologies (e.g., encryption, sharding, obfuscation); data breaches, prevention, and handling; cybercrime; risks associated with shared tenancy and third-party providers; information assurance; auditability and conduct of audits; and backup policies.

- *Control*: Relating to the management of Internet-based record environments. Examples of areas studied under this domain include authenticity, reliability and accuracy of online records; integrity metadata; chain of custody through social and technological barriers; retention and disposition of records within an online environment; transfer to and retrieval from online environments; and intellectual and access controls provided by online systems.

---

* InterPARES Trust (www.interparestrust.org) is the fourth phase of the International Research on Permanent Authentic Records in Electronic Systems (InterPARES) (www.interpares.org), which has developed the knowledge essential to the long-term preservation of authentic records created and/or maintained in digital form and provided the basis for standards, policies, strategies, and plans of action capable of ensuring the longevity of such material and the ability of its users to trust its authenticity. InterPARES 1 (1998–2001) focused on the development of theory and methods ensuring the preservation of the authenticity of records created and/or maintained in databases and document management systems in the course of administrative activities. Its findings present the perspective of the records preserver. InterPARES 2 (2002–2006) continued to research issues of authenticity and examined the issues of reliability and accuracy during the entire life cycle of records, from creation to permanent preservation. It focused on records produced in dynamic and interactive digital environments in the course of artistic, scientific, and governmental activities. InterPARES 3 (2007–2012) was built upon the findings of InterPARES 1 and 2, as well as other digital preservation projects worldwide and put theory into practice, working with archives and archival and/or records units within organizations of limited financial and/or human resources to implement sound records management and preservation programs.

- *Access*: Relating to open access and/or open data stored online. Examples of areas studied under this domain include balancing and enforcing the right to know versus right to be forgotten, ensuring privacy, accountability, and transparency of actions and services.

- *Legal*: Relating to juridical issues that arise from the creation, storage, management, and use of records online. Examples of areas studied under this domain include the application of legal privilege (including the issue of extraterritoriality), documenting and enforcing legal holds, providing a chain of evidence, authentication of Internet-based materials provided as evidence at trial, certification of records stored online, and those soft laws (e.g., UN standard-setting instruments) that have an impact on records.

This delineation of domains and the corresponding division of labor among and within the various cultural teams (i.e., Team North-America, Team Europe, Team Africa, Team Asia, Team Australasia, and Transnational Team, this latter involving organizations that do not have a national juridical context, such as the United Nations Educational, Scientific and Cultural Organization, the North Atlantic Treaty Organization, the Red Cross, the World Bank, the International Monetary Fund, and the International Atomic Energy Agency) facilitates targeted research and analysis of specific areas of study, with each working group concentrating on specific areas of research that leverage their collective expertise and geopolitical environment.

To address the pitfalls of preserving information in the cloud, in 2014, ITrust established a study within the North American team, under the Control Domain, named PaaST. The reason for this was to explore what would be required to enable digital recorded information to be reliably preserved in the cloud. In other words, to make it possible to entrust digital data objects designated for long-term preservation to one or more CSPs; as well as, to be able to retrieve those objects. And most important, having the knowledge that the retrieved objects are identical to those transferred to the provider in all essential respects; or, knowing any differences between the submitted and the retrieved objects with sufficient accuracy and precision, in order to be able to judge whether they are suitable for any intended use.

In order to increase the potential for implementation of the requirements articulated in the PaaST project, and to enrich the formulation of these requirements by augmenting the technical expertise contributing to their development, ITrust approached the Object Management Group (OMG), an international, open membership, not-for-profit technology standards consortium, with a proposal to use the PaaST requirements as the basis for an OMG standard for preservation. OMG standards are driven by vendors, end users, academic institutions, and government agencies. OMG Task Forces develop standards for a wide range of technologies and industries. Among the many standards established by the OMG, two are especially relevant to the PaaST initiative: the Unified Modeling Language (UML), which ITrust had already decided to use to model preservation requirements in PaaST, and the Records Management Services (RMS) specification, which defines a technologically agnostic approach for managing digital records that are maintained within business systems or other applications. The records management domain has substantial requirements for digital preservation of both current records that have long retention requirements and historical records that are kept for posterity. For the former, a preservation standard is complementary to the OMG RMS specification. For the latter, it is essential to ensure that future generations will have a memory of our times. The ITrust focus on records and their reliability, accuracy, and authenticity enables the articulation of functional requirements to benefit from centuries of understanding of what it takes to preserve trustworthy records in general and extensive experience in the preservation of digital records in a variety of settings.

OMG accepted the ITrust proposal and established a working group, under the aegis of the Government Information Sharing and Services Domain Task Force, to shepherd the development of the preservation standard. The OMG and the ITrust working groups have overlapping membership and are proceeding in parallel. The ITrust team is articulating requirements for preservation in the cloud by applying the knowledge gained from archival science, records management, and related disciplines for the preservation of authentic records, whereas the OMG team is translating these requirements into a form that supports production of software to implement them.

The OMG working group intends to generalize the preservation requirements to all types of digital information objects, without diminishing their applicability to records and maintaining compatibility with the OMG RMS specification. The OMG specification is being elaborated as a platform-independent model, giving developers freedom to choose the approach and the technologies they use in developing implementations. Thus, the OMG specification will define a well-grounded approach for preserving information in the cloud, but it will also be broadly applicable in other contexts, such as in-house preservation or when current records are maintained for lengths of time that span several generations of technology and thus require preservation actions to counteract obsolescence. For example, architectural and engineering records may be kept for as long as the physical things to which they relate, such as buildings, bridges, ships, or aircraft, in order to support maintenance or to enable production of replacement parts. If a business that maintains such records decided to replace the computer-assisted manufacturing system it uses to produce replacement parts with one that required data in a different format, it might contract with an external firm for the format conversion. The OMG preservation specification is being articulated so that a business can maintain unbroken control over its current records, when managed in a system that implements the OMG RMS standard, even when the business sends records to a service bureau for format conversion or other specialized services, such as recovery from damaged or deteriorated digital media.

Figure 4.1 presents a summary view of the parallel paths being pursued by the ITrust and OMG teams.

The PaaST project builds on earlier products, notably those developed in the course of the three preceding InterPARES projects and the ISO Open Archival Information System (OAIS) standard (International Organization for Standardization 2015). PaaST diverges from the OAIS standard in that OAIS is a reference model that defines the functions and information necessary for preservation but does not address how they might be

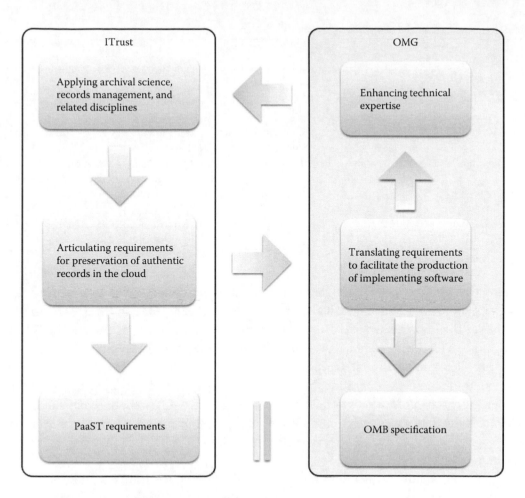

FIGURE 4.1   Overview of ITrust/OMG collaboration.

implemented. Although PaaST is neutral with respect to what methods and technologies may be used for implementation, it is being developed to facilitate the production of implementing software. Accordingly, the scope of PaaST is narrower than that of the OAIS standard, specifically excluding functions whose fulfilment is not automated, such as soliciting and negotiating submission agreements in the OAIS Administrative Functional Entity and the production of recommendations and plans in the OAIS Preservation Planning Functional Entity. Table 4.1 summarizes major differences between the two approaches.

4.3 DIGITAL PRESERVATION

PaaST is concerned with the preservation of information that is encoded as binary bits. Any string of binary bits that a computer could treat as a distinct object is called a "data object." The boundaries of data objects are defined by the software that is used to create or process them, as well as by the bits that comprise them. One type of data object is a digital file in a wrapper or archive or file format, such as zip and tar, but each of these files may contain many other data objects in a variety of other formats. In e-mail applications, each message

TABLE 4.1   Comparison of OAIS and PaaST

	OAIS	PaaST
Scope	Any type of information object	Only digital information objects, focusing on digital records
Intent	A reference model	Intended to guide and facilitate implementation
Functionality	Comprehensive functions both for and related to preservation	Only functions specific to preservation
Solution approach	Envisions a coherent system for preservation	Assumes that preservation is achieved through a set of services that may be designed and implemented independently
Implementation	Neutral	Platform independent, but designed for optimal automation

is treated as a distinct data object, but some e-mail applications, such as Microsoft Outlook, routinely store all the messages in an e-mail account in a single file, in this case an Outlook Data File. The file is treated as a data object by the software that writes and reads bits to and from storage media. Many database applications integrate data from multiple sources into what is called an operational data store that is optimized for querying or reporting. Each distinct source and the operational data store are separate data objects. Similarly, a map rendered on a screen by a geographic information system (GIS) is a data object, but the map may combine data extracted from multiple "layers" in the system, where each layer stores data of only one type, such as waterways, roads, or buildings. Each of these layers is treated as a data object by the GIS.

The PaaST requirements adopt the OAIS distinction between information objects and data objects. An information object is a persistent, objectified (i.e., materialized outside of the mind such as on a screen or a digital storage medium) piece of information. It may be any type of information, such as a letter, book, tweet, database, image, design, audio recording, or GIS. An information object is materialized in one or more data objects. An information object may be instantiated in multiple copies and different ways. The same information object may be instantiated in different digital encodings, each of which could be materialized in one or more data objects. For example, a letter might be recorded in different files in Microsoft Word, Apple Pages, or other character-encoded formats. A single letter might be encoded in several different digital files, for example, with the content in an Extensible Markup Language (XML) file linked to an XML schema and displayed using an XPath specification and style sheet. It might also be encoded as a pixel image of a printed document or a screen display. In some cases, the different encodings might be considered as equivalent or substitutable. In other cases, substitution of one format for another would be unacceptable, for example, if the original format had features that are not available in another.

Although the scope of the OAIS reference model is intended to cover any type of information, the scope of PaaST is limited to information in digital form. Information objects that are, or are designated to be, preserved may more precisely be termed preservation objects. Digital preservation inevitably involves other types of information objects, notably

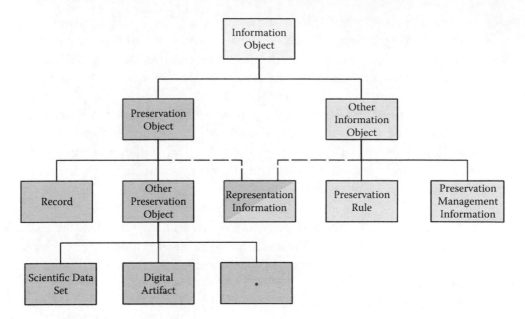

FIGURE 4.2 The PaaST information model.

the business rules applied in preservation and information that is used to manage preservation. Figure 4.2 depicts the main types of information objects involved in the PaaST requirements.

The two main types of information objects shown in Figure 4.2 are Preservation Objects and Other Information Objects. The main focus of PaaST is on the preservation of digital Records, but the scope extends to Other Preservation Objects, which might be Scientific Data Sets, Digital Artifacts, or Others. A Preservation Object comprises both content and Representation Information. Representation Information is described in the OAIS standard as information that is used to interpret content data. Some Representation Information may be contained in the same data object that stores content data. For example, many file formats include in each file an internal signature that identifies the format. Other Representation Information that is needed to process or interpret a data object may be external to it. Common types of external Representation Information include data models, schemas, namespaces, style sheets, and thesauri. The PaaST information model includes Representation Information as a distinct subtype of Preservation Object to provide for external Representation Information. Some external Representation Information Objects, such as the data model for a database, may be associated with a single or a few Preservation Objects. However, some Representation Information Objects may have very broad, even worldwide, applicability, such as standards established and owned by external entities, for example, XML standards in the technical realm (Health Level Seven International 2015), XBRL in the financial realm, or HL7 standards in the health care domain (World Wide Web Consortium 2015). In such cases, the external Representation Information, although used in preservation, is not itself a target of preservation. Hence, the PaaST information model depicts Representation Information as either a Preservation

Object or a subtype of Other Information Objects. The discrimination between Representation Information as either a Preservation Object or Other Information Object is based on ownership or control. If a Representation Information object relates to one or a set of Preservation Objects and is controlled by the same entity that controls that set, then the Representation Information should be considered as a related Preservation Object. However, if the Representation Information is controlled by another entity and has not been designated by that entity for preservation, then it should be treated as an Other Information Object. The model includes two other subtypes of Other Information Objects: Preservation Rules and Preservation Management Information. There can be many types of Preservation Rules, including those governing submission of objects for preservation, designation of the specific properties of Preservation Objects that must remain unchanged, criteria for implementing changes in preservation techniques, provisions for assessing authenticity, and access restrictions. Preservation Management Information encompasses the information that is needed in or produced by preservation processes to ensure that the objectives of preservation are met.

Given continuing and often unpredictable changes in digital technologies, it is often necessary to change the encoding of preservation objects in data objects so that they remain accessible. Other strategies for preservation keep Preservation Objects in their original encodings but counteract obsolescence by using different software, including not only newer versions of the original ones but also mediators such as emulation software. Digital preservation requires understanding the differences in alternate formats or the differential impacts of different software.

4.4 CRITERIA FOR DIGITAL PRESERVATION

Preservation comprises the activities and controls that enable preservation objects to persist over time in the face of changes in technology and possibly administrative control, so that they remain accessible and usable, and their critical properties do not change. The focus of ITrust is on the preservation of digital records. The key difference between records and other types of information objects is that records are produced or acquired as a means of carrying out an activity or as a by-product of it and are kept for further action or reference. Thus, a record has a known connection to the entity that keeps it and the activity in which it participated.

Since its beginning in 1998, InterPARES has emphasized the importance of preserving authentic records. Archival science defines authenticity as "The trustworthiness of a record as a record; i.e., the quality of a record that is what it purports to be and that is free from tampering or corruption" (InterPARES 2015). Operationally, this means that an authentic record is one that is capable of communicating the message it originally conveyed. This is complicated in the case of digital records because, as discussed previously, we cannot preserve the original manifestation of a digital record; therefore, preserving a digital record requires maintaining the data object or objects that embody it, along with the ability to produce authentic copies of the record in its original form. Given that the original is not available for comparison with copies, digital preservation relies on information about the record and about its preservation in order to assess the authenticity of copies. This information enables us to assess whether any copy is identical to the original in all essential respects and free from corruption.

Two types of information about digital records are needed for their preservation: (1) the permanent properties of records and (2) contextual information. The permanent properties of records are those that must be preserved unchanged for as long as the records are preserved. Obviously, properties considered to be permanent differ according to the type of information object, and in some cases, they depend on particularities of the individual data objects that instantiate the preservation objects. Examples of permanent properties derived from the type of preservation objects for the class of textual documents are all the words they contain, in their original order and grammatical structures, as well as the separation of different parts of text, such as headings, paragraphs, and footnotes. Some objects of this type may also require preserving other properties, such as type face and size, capitalization, underlining, and other presentation features. All of these textual properties might be maintained when the instantiation of a textual document is exported from one format of data object to another; for example, from Microsoft Word format to Hypertext Markup Language. However, not all conversions between digital formats for text preserve all necessary textual properties unchanged. Identification of the permanent textual properties, then, establishes a baseline control that should be applied to determine whether a particular format conversion would retain the ability to produce authentic copies.

A broad category of permanent properties that depend on how preservation objects are instantiated in data objects comprises those that depend on software for their realization. Digital texts, for example, may contain hyperlinks both to other parts of a document and to other files. The ability to execute hyperlinks might be essential to maintaining the integrity of a record, as is the case for a website that consists of multiple files. Preservation of properties that depend on software is especially important, and even critical, for types of preservation objects that can only exist in digital form, such as interactive, dynamic, and experiential records (Duranti and Thibodeau 2006).

The permanent properties of preservation objects are not necessarily expressed in or directly derivable from the objects themselves. The relationship between records and activities is expressed in the way an actor accumulates and organizes records. In preserving records, it is essential to preserve their relationships to other records. Often relationships among records are explicitly expressed on the face of the records, through registration, classification or filing codes that identify their place in a procedure, or a recordkeeping system. However, records may be aggregated with other records without being annotated. With physical records, the aggregation is ordinarily materialized by collocation in filing units. Similarly, relationships among digital records may be expressed by assignment to virtual folders without any indication of this assignment in the data objects themselves. Relationships can also be established by virtue of the fact that related records are kept under the control of a particular system or application, such as an inventory database, a sales application, or a financial management system. In such cases, preserving the records requires preserving the relationships expressed in the file allocations or the structure of the system or application.

Preserving records entails not only preserving the records themselves and their inter-relationships but also preserving contextual information about them. One of the most fundamental types of contextual information about records is their provenance, that is, the organizational and functional context in which they were created and used. Other types of contextual information that can enhance understanding of records include information about business processes, documentation practices, and, specifically for digital records, system design and implementation.

Many of the criteria for preservation of digital records are also valid in other domains. A draft international standard on the preservation of multimedia lists authenticity as a core concern. Its definition of authenticity is consistent with that of archival science:

> "Authenticity encompasses information to enable an Agent to verify that an object is correctly identified and free from (intentional or accidental) corruption (i.e., capable of delivering its original message). The Agents that issue statements about authenticity must also be correctly identified. Authenticity encompasses identity and integrity. Identity comprises all those attributes necessary to determine what a thing is (e.g., the original recording of a Work). Integrity asserts that none of those essential attributes have changed, i.e. there are no significant differences neither in the same resource over time nor between two resources thought to be copies of the same asset" (ISO/IEC Joint Technical Committee 2015).

The terms "asset" and "resource" in this standard correspond to preservation object and data object in PaaST, and "essential properties" is another term for permanent properties.

Both the identification of permanent properties of preservation objects and the contextual information about them can be valuable in the preservation of other types of preservation objects besides records (Hockx-Yu and Knight 2008). A proposed framework for preservation of software includes a general model of digital software objects that identifies four components of every software system: product, version, variant, and instance. The model defines permanent properties of each component; for example, a product has a functional purpose, an owner, a history, and an overall conceptual architecture (Matthews et al. 2009). The Long-Term Archiving and Retrieval (LOTAR) project, an international collaborative project primarily supported by the aerospace industry, stipulates that the preservation of digital product and technical information requires the demonstration of the equivalence of product aerospace models across successive generations of computer-assisted design (CAD) applications by verification of the preservation of "Key Characteristics" (Delauney 2012). Key Characteristics are a type of permanent properties. In the LOTAR standards, product data models are the preservation objects. They are instantiated in CAD and Product Data Model data objects. Information about provenance of data preserved for scientific research is widely recognized as essential for determining if a given data set is appropriate for a specific research purpose and for becoming aware of peculiarities in the way the data were defined, generated, or processed that affect their use (Simmhan et al. 2005). The information about data provenance needed for scientific use is much more extensive than that usually kept in preserving records. Data provenance information encompasses traces of all transformations, selections, and combinations of data from different sources, from the time the data were originally generated or collected to the point of access. Certain data sets may be preserved to enable reuse for purposes identical to the original, such as the reproduction of piece parts of physical systems. In such cases, the permanent properties will be much more exacting than if the purpose of preserving them were only to enable later users to visualize what the original design was.

Differences in the identification of permanent properties and of the contextual information needed for preservation entail variations in the particular terms, conditions, and practices for preserving different types of preservation objects for different purposes; nevertheless, all depend on a general and explicit foundation justifying trust that information has been preserved appropriately. The building blocks of that foundation consist of the following:

- Knowledge of what is to be preserved and of its permanent properties

- Knowledge of how preservation objects are encoded in data objects

- Knowledge of how the data objects have been stored

- The ability to apply specific preservation requirements, especially those related to permanent properties, in any changes to the data objects, the hardware and/or software on which they depend, or both, in order to maintain authenticity

- Knowledge that any changes in storage, encoding, or the technologies used to process the data have neither corrupted the preservation objects nor impeded the possibility for rendering the data objects appropriately

- Maintenance of complete and correct links among related preservation objects and between preservation objects and contextual information and related representation information

- Knowledge of how to output authentic copies of the preserved information

These building blocks form the basis for the PaaST functional requirements. These requirements define not only the capabilities but also the metadata and other information necessary to preserve digital records and to reproduce authentic copies of them.

4.5 THE PaaST APPROACH

The PaaST project is defining the data that are necessary to provide the types of knowledge identified previously. These data should be used to control preservation processes being articulated by the project. Some of the required data should be acquired with the preservation objects that are to be preserved and even before any preservation processes begin. Additional data elements should be produced in or derived from preservation processes. Both types of data can be used to determine targets and set criteria for preservation processes and to assess whether these processes achieve outcomes appropriate for the purposes of preservation.

Although the core motivation for developing PaaST is to provide a comprehensive and detailed set of requirements for trustworthy preservation in the cloud, given that there are several commonalities between preservation in the cloud and other digital preservation scenarios, the requirements produced by PaaST will be applicable across a range of situations, allowing both the allocation of different preservation tasks to different agents and the execution of these tasks, by one or more agents, using different methods and technologies. Thus, preservation requirements are being articulated as services, that is, sets of related capabilities that could be executed using different and potentially unrelated technologies, under separate and independent administrative or operational control. This flexibility in the orchestration of capabilities means that the PaaST requirements neither assume nor require that preservation activities or controls are implemented in an integrated system. Hence, the overall context in which PaaST preservation processes are carried out is called the Preservation Environment rather than a preservation system. A Preservation Environment is the ensemble of technological infrastructures and tools used in digital preservation of a given set of preservation objects. It may include separate, different, and independently managed hardware and software used by different entities. The flexible orchestration of capabilities does not exclude the possibility of utilizing a single, comprehensive system for preservation. That is one option for implementing PaaST requirements. Other options include dividing preservation responsibilities so that some tasks are performed in-house, whereas others are executed externally under contract. There could be more than one contract; for example, one contract might provide for basic, ongoing preservation services, such as storage and data management, and others for specialized services, such as media migration or data conversion, on an as-needed basis.

PaaST defines four primary roles involved in digital preservation: The first three are on the supply (preservation) side and the fourth on the demand (access) side. The first of these roles is the Initial Holder, that is, the party that, at least at the start of activities related to preservation, holds, owns, or controls digital preservation objects that are candidates for preservation. The Initial Holder may complete its role long before preservation processes start. For example, the Initial Holder may be an individual writer or scientist who arranges for his or her personal papers to be preserved in a university archives after his or her death. The individual would negotiate a deed of gift or other legal agreement to this effect with the university archives. Once the agreement is finalized and accepted by both parties, the individual might not take any additional action related to the preservation of the papers and, after his or her death, the role of the Initial Holder may be fulfilled by the executor of his or her estate. The second defined role is that of the Preservation Director, the party that has responsibility for the preservation of preservation objects. In the example of individual papers, the Preservation Director would be the university archives or its designated agent, most likely the university archivist. The Preservation Director is in essence the manager who decides what preservation processes are executed and by whom and who evaluates the results. The third role is the Preservation Service Provider, the party that provides technological resources and services to carry out digital preservation. The fourth role, the Access Client, is a party that wishes to obtain, or actually obtains, access to preserved information. There is also a secondary role, the Submitter, the party that actually sends preservation objects for preservation to a Preservation Service Provider and is the default respondent for any questions or issues the Service Provider has with the submission. The Initial Holder will often act as the Submitter, but not necessarily. When an organization that maintains the current records on a system operated by an external technology service provider, the external entity will probably submit those records selected for long-term preservation directly to the Preservation Service Provider, if different. In the case of an individual who provides for the eventual preservation of personal papers by a university archives, the Submitter might be someone employed by the executor of the individual's estate to collect, package, and physically transmit the preservation objects. The activities of the Submitter are also, obviously, on the supply side. The four supply side roles and their relationships are illustrated in Figure 4.3.

Roles could be fulfilled by an individual, an organization, or a position within an organization. It is important to emphasize that these are roles, not entities. The same entity could fulfill more than one role or different roles at different times. Moreover, PaaST roles are defined not with respect to objects but in relation to participation in fulfilling PaaST requirements. Commonly, the Initial Holder of records would be the human or legal person who created the records; however, this is not necessarily the case. Many government archives acquire full legal authority over the records of other agencies that they accept for preservation. The originating agency would fulfill the role of the Initial Holder in negotiating terms and conditions for transferring records to the archives. After acquiring legal custody, however, the archives might act as an Initial Holder; for example, it might decide to contract an external body for the preservation of digital records that it had been

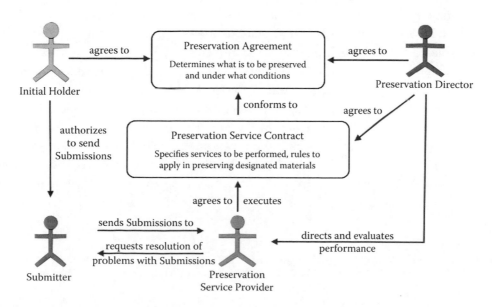

FIGURE 4.3   Preservation roles and relationships.

preserving in-house. The archives might also have legal authority to override the access policies of the originating agency.* In this example, the archives fulfills multiple roles at different times. It acts a Preservation Director in arranging for the transfer of records from originating agencies and in contracting for preservation of digital records. When it preserves records in-house, it acts as a Preservation Service Provider. It acts as an Initial Holder in making access decisions that are not consistent with the originating agency's policies and in stipulating provisions in a preservation contract that deviate from its agreements with originating agencies.

Specific terms and conditions for the preservation of any particular set of preservation objects may be grouped under two headings: a Preservation Agreement and a Preservation Service Contract. The Preservation Agreement and the Preservation Service Contract may be embodied in one or more documents, depending on how many distinct entities are involved in fulfilling the supply side roles. A Preservation Agreement is an accord between an Initial Holder and a Preservation Director designating what preservation objects are to be preserved and setting out terms and conditions for their preservation. Terms and conditions would specify when the Preservation Director will assume responsibility; how long the preservation objects should be preserved; what rights and constraints govern their access and use; and so forth. A Preservation Agreement may not be explicitly identified as such, and it may be embodied in one or more documents. For example, in government organizations where retention and disposition of records is under the authority of an independent archival entity, the determination of what records should be preserved after the originating agency's need for them has expired is usually included in records retention schedules, whereas stipulations for the means of transfer to a Preservation Environment, the formats allowed, and so on might be set out in directives issued by the archival entity or in IT policies, and provisions governing access and use may be encoded in law or regulations. By contrast, in the case of a university that accepts donations of the personal papers of prominent individuals, provisions for what is to be preserved, when it is to be transferred, and so on are usually defined in a deed of gift or deposit agreement negotiated between the donor and the university. A Preservation Service Contract is an agreement between a Preservation Service Provider and a Preservation Director for one or more preservation services. The Preservation Service Contract should translate the terms and conditions of applicable Preservation Agreements into operational business rules, which can be implemented in the preservation environment. The provisions for preservation services may not have the form of a legal contract between two parties. For example, if the service provider is an officer or unit within a larger organization, the responsibilities of the service provider may be set out in an organizational policy or delegation of authority.

---

* See, for example, the authorities of the National Archives of the United States set out in the Federal Records Act and the Presidential Records Act, 44 US Code, 2107–2108, 2202, 2203(g)(1), and 2204–2205 (Office of the Law Revision Counsel 2015).

ITrust intends to provide guidance on the elaboration of Preservation Agreements and Preservation Service Contracts. This guidance will be derived from other, relevant ITrust studies, including, but not limited to, the following:

- Developing Model Cloud Computing Contracts, which is developing boilerplate provisions for cloud computing model contracts (for common law and civil law use) that will provide insight and guidance to fair and balanced contracts for those who entrust records to the Internet and those who provide Internet services for records

- Retention and Disposition in a Cloud Environment, which is elaborating a checklist for determining if service providers and systems that store records in the cloud, ensuring that the records will be retained and disposed of in accordance with the applicable requirements governing retention and disposition of the records

- Metadata, Mutatis Mutandis—Design Requirements for Authenticity in the Cloud and Across Contexts, which intends to generate ideal design requirements for the assessment of records' authenticity

- Ensuring Trust in Storage in Infrastructure as a Service (IaaS), which is analyzing policies and standards related to IaaS within regulatory environments in order to establish a test bed within a financial institution

- Trusted Certification Based on Long-Term Preservation of Digital Archival Resources, which aims at articulating strategies, using both technology and management methods, that Preservation Directors could apply to certify that long-term preservation requirements are satisfied

- Standard of Practice for Trust in Protection of Authoritative Records in Government Archives, which will create a standard of practice and corresponding certification process for risk management regarding the preservation of reliable digital records of legal value

The PaaST requirements and the corresponding OMG specification will support the implementation of as wide a variety as possible rules set out in Preservation Agreements and Preservation Service Contracts. Most of these rules will relate to what is to be preserved, the services to be provided, and the terms and conditions for both. One type of preservation rule identifies permanent properties that are either inherent in the preservation objects or the aspects of the creation or evolution of the objects, such as in the aggregation and arrangement of records. A preservation rule might define permanent properties that would not be obvious or reasonably inferred from any other source. For example, if an artist gave digital works to a cultural institution for preservation, but stipulated that the institution must maintain the ability to present the artworks using the same hardware and software that the artist used, their use would be a permanent property. Other rules established in Preservation Agreements and Preservation Service Contracts might include access and exploitation restrictions that have no expiration date, so that the restrictions should be imposed any time the object is requested or accessed.

4.5.1 Preservation Services

As mentioned earlier, PaaST groups preservation requirements under the heading of "Services," that is, sets of related capabilities. Ideally, each service, and even particular capabilities within a service, could be executed using different and potentially unrelated technologies under separate and independent operational control. The preservation services elaborated in PaaST are Submission, which ingests preservation objects into a Preservation Environment; Characterization, which inspects the technical, archival, and representational properties of the preservation objects; Authenticity, which captures and reports information about the identity and integrity of the preservation objects, and the application of authentication methods; Preservation Storage, which controls storage of the data objects that encode the preservation objects to maintain identity, prevent corruption, and satisfy other preservation requirements; Preservation Change, which governs technological changes, such as format migration or replacement of software, to ensure survival and usability; and Access, which provides the ability to deliver copies of data or preservation objects. The services are not necessarily independent. For example, Characterization will often be invoked by Submission in order to decide whether to accept a set of preservation objects submitted for preservation. Similarly, if required by an Access Client, Authenticity could be invoked to enable assessment of copies delivered to the client. Figure 4.4 lists the major capabilities in each service and indicates where a service, or a particular capability within a service, calls another one.

PaaST does not include services that are not specifically devoted to digital preservation, even though they may be closely related, or general services that a service provider could be expected to offer regardless of whether preservation objects were designated for long-term preservation. General services would include telecommunications, data management, system logging, security, generic search facilities, storage subsystems, and file transfer capabilities. Preservation services will often make use of such general services, but the presumption of availability means that they do not have to be articulated within the PaaST requirements. A common example of a related service that is not included in PaaST is the holdings management system often used by institutions such as archives and libraries to manage the inventories of materials for which they are responsible. Figure 4.5 depicts two different scenarios in which an access client obtains copies of preservation objects.

In the first scenario at the top of Figure 4.5, the Preservation Director contracts with a Preservation Service Provider for Preservation Access Service. The client queries the Preservation Access Service to identify preservation objects of interest. On receiving a positive response, the client orders a copy of one or more preservation objects and the Preservation Access Service outputs the copies. In the lower portion of Figure 4.5, the Preservation Director also contracts with a Preservation Service Provider for Preservation Access Service, but in addition operates its own Catalog of Holdings, which may include materials not held by the Preservation Service Provider, such as hard copy documents. In this scenario, the Access Client has the same interactions, but with the Catalog application

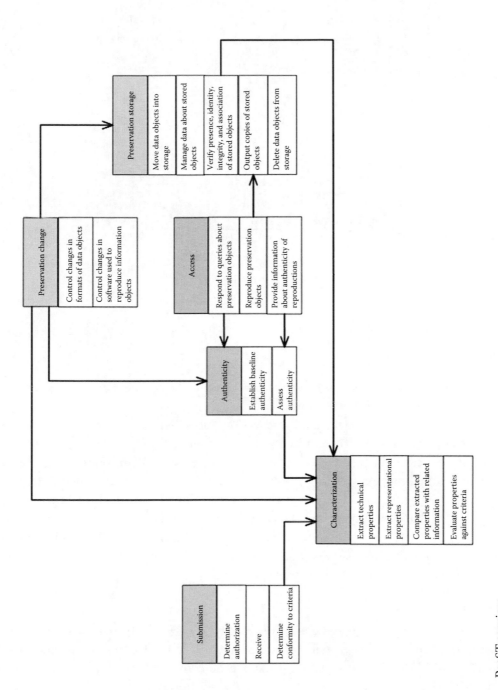

FIGURE 4.4 PaaST services.

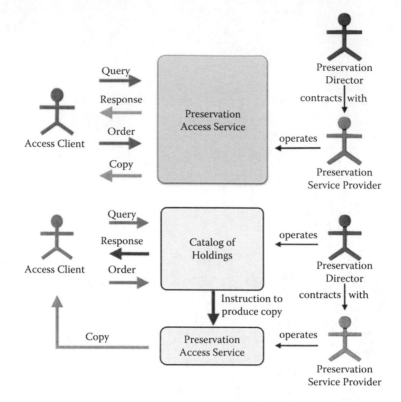

FIGURE 4.5   Access paths.

rather than the Preservation Access Service. When the client orders copies, the Catalog application sends a copy instruction to the Preservation Access Service, which then outputs the copy. In the first scenario, the Preservation Access Service includes dissemination capabilities beyond those strictly required for production of copies of preservation objects. Those additional capabilities are outside the scope of the PaaST Requirements. In the second scenario, one would expect the Preservation Service Contract to stipulate that the provider must deliver to the Preservation Director data about the preservation objects held by the provider that would serve the needs of the holdings management system. Similar scenarios would apply for other related services not specifically devoted to digital preservation, such as applications used to manage relationships between a Preservation Director and Initial Holders, or an institution's web portal.

4.5.2 Basic Scenario

The following scenario describes a complete set of preservation processes from entry into a Preservation Environment, through changes in preservation technology, to delivery to Access Clients. The scenario focuses on positive outcomes, where things work as they should and desired outcomes are produced. Obviously, however, the PaaST requirements include provisions for addressing problems that might occur in service execution.

The PaaST requirements assume that certain preconditions have been met. The fundamental preconditions are that there is a Preservation Agreement between an Initial

Holder and a Preservation Director, and that, when preservation requirements are fulfilled by third-party providers, such as CSPs, one or more Preservation Service Contracts are in place.

The active process of preserving specific preservation objects begins when data objects that encode the preservation objects are ingested into a Preservation Environment. Consistent with the OAIS standard, ingest includes the transfer of preservation objects to a Preservation Service Provider; inspection of the Submission to verify that the transfer process was successful; review of the Submission to determine if it contains everything it should and nothing extraneous; evaluation and, if needed, production or collection of information about the preservation objects in the Submission to determine their permanent properties; comparison of this information with the data objects that embody the preservation objects; and, if the outcome of these activities is positive, capture of the data objects in a Preservation Storage system. Thus, the process of ingest will involve several PaaST services, including at least Submission, Characterization, and Preservation Storage. Depending on applicable rules, the Preservation Service provider might also be required to establish a baseline assessment of authenticity on ingest, and it might be tasked with migrating some data objects to different formats, involving the Authenticity and Preservation Change services as well. The ideal case would start with a Submitter informing the Preservation Service Provider of its intent to submit preservation objects for preservation. The Provider would then determine if the Submitter is authorized to send the proposed materials and check to see if the proposal satisfies provisions of the applicable Preservation Service Contract. If so, the Provider would approve sending the submission. Once the submission is received, the Provider would determine if the transmission was successful. If the transmission was made using physical media, that determination would include whether each unit of physical media was intact and undamaged. Whether on media or online, the Provider would also need to determine if each file in the submission is readable and free from unrecoverable read errors. The Provider would also need to examine information about the submission, whether it was transmitted with the data objects or obtained in some other manner, to see if it was appropriate and capable of enabling the Provider to preserve the materials and meet other contractual requirements. This information should enable the Preservation Service Provider to identify which data objects in the submission encode which preservation objects and to determine if the correspondence between the two sets is complete and correct. Information about the submission is also important to enable the Preservation Director to evaluate whether the set of data objects that should represent an preservation object does so appropriately. Precisely what is appropriate will vary depending on the records and the terms of the preservation agreement. Common criteria for evaluation include chronological, geographical, and organizational scope of the records; for example, if the records were to be transferred in 5-year blocks, does the Submission include records for the whole time? If the records were to cover an entire nation, are there significant areas with no records? Alternatively, for structured data, do the data in the Submission match the applicable data model and are all data values found in coded fields defined in the data dictionary? Making such determinations and evaluations would involve the Characterization service.

Problems can occur with the data objects, the information about them, or during the process of transmission. One common transmission problem is when the Submitter sends backup copies of files that are mirror images of physical storage devices and thus can only be restored to the same devices from which they were copied and not read on any other system. This problem can be solved by asking for retransmission in an exportable file format, which will often be the native format of the application used to create the file. A common problem that spans both the data and the information about them in the case of structured data is a mismatch between the data and the corresponding technical specifications, such as data models, data element dictionaries, and code books. Characterization serves to identify such problems and, when performed in conjunction with Submission, can enable their timely resolution.

The Characterization service supports discovery, comparison, and evaluation of properties of a set of preservation objects as instantiated in a set of data objects both in terms of their technical characteristics and with respect to what they are supposed to represent in the real world. In the discovery mode, the Characterization service examines data objects and/or metadata about them to identify and record the presence, value, or state of a specified set of either technical properties or properties of the physical or notional phenomena the preservation objects represent. In the comparison mode, the Characterization service compares the properties found in the data objects with other information about the corresponding properties of the preservation objects they instantiate and the real-world phenomena they represent. In the evaluation mode, the service applies criteria to the discovered or compared data to determine if they conform to those criteria. For example, the Characterization service may be used to determine that a set of data objects properly instantiates a set of preservation objects. The criteria for evaluation should be set out in the Preservation Service Contract. Figure 4.6 depicts the three modes of operation of the service, including examples of both technical and representational characteristics and sources of information of both types that can be used to compare to what is found in the data objects.

The Characterization service may also be used to identify properties of the preservation objects that are of interest to a community of Access Clients for whom the preservation objects are being preserved. Community interests could determine the criteria for evaluating whether the preservation objects would satisfy the purposes for which they are being preserved. For example, both the legal community and climatologists are interested in weather records, but lawyers are interested in records describing conditions at specific times and locations, and they are concerned with whether the particular records are admissible in court and the weight they would carry in judicial decisions, whereas climatologists are interested in long and consistent time series of data that can be used for analysis of climatic trends. The interests of access clients can also be impacted by how preservation objects are embodied in data objects. Weather records that suit litigation needs might contain data valuable for climatological analysis; however, if the records were digitally scanned images of handwritten documents, reliably extracting the data for scientific research might entail substantial technical or economic challenges.

The Characterization service may also be invoked after a submission has been accepted, for example, in order to determine that no inappropriate change has occurred

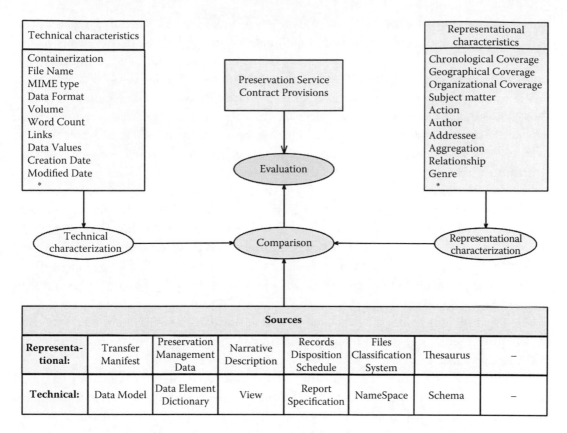

FIGURE 4.6 PaaST characterization service.

in storage. Characterization might be invoked by the Authenticity service, for example, to verify that a Preservation Change has not affected permanent properties, or to verify the authenticity of a copy of a preservation object made for an Access Client. Some Characterization capabilities might be used after transfer of a set of data objects from one Preservation Environment to another to determine if any inappropriate changes have occurred in the transfer.

If a submission is free of problems, or all significant problems are resolved, the Preservation Service Provider would accept it and move the data objects into a storage environment where they would be managed to guard against loss or corruption. The Preservation Storage service puts data objects into storage, retrieves them on demand, and, if appropriate, removes them from storage. It also provides the capability for verifying that the objects remain in storage with their identity and integrity (i.e., authenticity) intact. For this purpose, it invokes the Characterization service and/or the Authenticity service.

The Preservation Storage service does not assume that special storage technologies are required for long-term preservation, but identifies testable and reportable parameters to enable determination of whether records remain correctly identified, intact, and uncorrupted both within a given storage system and when there are changes in storage technology or media. Given the frequent replacement of storage subsystem infrastructure (e.g., hard drives, network switches, storage enclosures) due to scheduled replacement or unplanned failure, and the nature of automated resource balancing, the Preservation Storage service captures, reports, and makes available those attributes of the storage environment within which the data objects are being kept as key storage-related events occur. For example, a large cloud-based environment is typically composed of multiple storage subsystems that are expanded once disk space utilization exceeds a certain percentage. As new subsystems are brought online, existing data objects may be moved in whole or part over to the new systems. As these movement events occur, the Preservation Storage service will capture these events along with other relevant data (i.e., name of authorizing party, name, and version of software used to perform the migration, quality assurance process used to confirm results of migration, etc.). In the event of a hardware failure in any storage subsystem (such as a drive failure), the Preservation Storage service will record the mitigation process used to ensure the integrity of the data objects stored within that particular subsystem (such as results of the recreation of the redundant array of independent disks (RAID) array upon disk replacement), as well as the location and extent of any permanent data loss in a data object. Furthermore, this service will provide the ability to periodically validate that the bits comprising the data objects are readable and maintain their integrity on whatever media they are written upon (hard disk, solid-state memory, magnetic tape, etc.) through a standardized, regular process of verification.

The Preservation Change service defines comparable capabilities for evaluating whether preservation objects remain authentic in the face of other technological changes, such as when data are migrated to new formats or when new software is used to manage or provide access to preserved collections. This service also generates data about such changes to maintain a complete preservation audit trail and also to guarantee that each preservation object is correctly associated with all versions of data objects that instantiate it, and that all data objects are associated with the software needed to process them.

The Access service provides for output of preserved preservation objects, including replication, and provides support for assessing authenticity. It uses capabilities provided by Preservation Storage to locate and retrieve data objects, ensuring that the data objects are those that are needed to reproduce the desired preservation objects, and that they are appropriately combined or otherwise processed to generate the requested output. The Access service invokes the Authenticity service both to provide information to Access Clients about the authenticity of preserved preservation objects and to assess the authenticity of copies.

The Authenticity service has two subservices: Baseline Authentication and Assessment of Authenticity. Baseline Authentication imports data about the authenticity of one or more preservation objects generated before they were ingested into the Preservation Environment, preserves the data linked with the related preservation objects, and makes the data available for comparison with the results of subsequent assessments of authenticity. Assessment of Authenticity subservice provides capabilities comparable to those related to authenticity in the OMG Records Management Specification by providing assurance that what is retrieved from a preservation environment is identical to that which was put there (Object Management Group 2011). This subservice provides for the application of an automated authentication method as specified by the Preservation Director or potentially by an Access Client, collects the results of such application, and associates them with the preservation objects to which the method was applied. For long-term preservation, it is further desirable to retain information that describes applied authentication methods with sufficient detail to enable Access Clients to understand the methods employed even if the software products that implemented them are no longer operative.

4.6 SUMMARY

To address the difficulty of preserving digital information over the long term with its inherent risks of loss or corruption, the ITrust project is generating the theoretical and methodological frameworks necessary to develop local, national and international policies, procedures, regulations, standards, and legislation able to ensure public trust in digital records. In support of this goal, ITrust established the PaaST project in order to develop a set of requirements that establish a foundation for trusting the preservation of digital information. The core of this foundation comprises data that enable both those who are responsible for the preserved information objects and those who wish to derive knowledge from them to assess their authenticity; that is, to identify the properties of the preservation objects that have remained unchanged, to assess the import of technological changes in either the way the preservation objects are digitally encoded or in the software used to process them, and to learn whether any corruption has occurred. The data are collected, generated, managed, and applied in the execution of preservation services that implement the PaaST functional requirements. While targeting preservation in the cloud, the PaaST requirements are applicable to any approach to digital preservation and in essence to any type of information object. PaaST services articulate the actions that must be performed by one or more identified roles either within or outside the organization in order to confirm and document that the authenticity of preservation objects over time. To ensure the implementability of the proposed Preservation Services, PaaST is working with the OMG to transform archival science-based functional requirements into software-centric UML models in order to develop a working prototype for evaluation and eventual release as a publicly available specification. Thus, the preservation services produced by PaaST are articulated in a technology neutral format that enables multiple organizations with dissimilar technology environments to collaborate seamlessly on the execution of the services. Additionally, the Preservation Services defined by PaaST will work both as stand-alone requirements that can be implemented in cloud-based Preservation Environments and as an extension to the existing OMG RMS.

REFERENCES

Delauney, Jean-Yves. 2012. "Overview of the LOTAR Project and LOTAR Standards, Status of Implementation in Europe." Presented at the GIFAS, Paris, France, May 29. http://www.lotar-international.org/fileadmin/user_upload/documents/2_2012-05-29_GIFAS_LOTAR_Overview_Final_V5.pdf#page=30&zoom=auto,-106,30.

Duranti, Luciana, and Kenneth Thibodeau. 2006. "The Concept of Record in Interactive, Experiential and Dynamic Environments: The View of InterPARES." *Archival Science* 6 (1): 13–68.

Health Level Seven International. 2015. "Introduction to HL7 Standards." Accessed September 13, 2015. http://www.hl7.org/implement/standards/.

Hockx-Yu, Helen, and Gareth Knight. 2008. "What to Preserve?: Significant Properties of Digital Objects." *The International Journal of Digital Curation* 3 (1): 141–153.

International Organization for Standardization. 2015. "ISO 14721:2012—Space Data and Information Transfer Systems—Open Archival Information System (OAIS)—Reference Model." Accessed September 13, 2015. http://www.iso.org/iso/catalogue_detail.htm?csnumber=57284.

InterPARES. 2015. "InterPARES 2 Project: Terminology Database." Accessed September 13, 2015. http://interpares.org/ip2/ip2_terminology_db.cfm.

ISO/IEC Joint Technical Committee. 2015. "Text of ISO/IEC DIS 23000-15 Multimedia Preservation Application Format | MPEG." February 20. http://mpeg.chiariglione.org/standards/mpeg-a/multimedia-preservation-application-format/text-isoiec-dis-23000-15-multimedia.

Matthews, Brian, Juan Bicarregui, Arif Shaon, and Catherine Jones. 2009. "Framework for Software Preservation." Report. Accessed September 13, 2015. https://epubs.stfc.ac.uk/work/51076.

NIST, Interagency Working Group on Digital Data. 2009. "Harnessing the Power of Digital Data for Science and Society." Report of the Interagency Working Group on Digital Data to the Committee on Science of the National Science and Technology Council. Accessed September 13, 2015. https://www.whitehouse.gov/files/documents/ostp/opengov_inbox/harnessing_power_web.pdf.

Norsam Technologies. 2015. "HD-Rosetta™ and Related Processes." Accessed September 13, 2015. http://www.norsam.com/rosetta.html.

Object Management Group. 2011. "Records Management Services (RMS), Version 1.0." Accessed September 13, 2015. http://www.omg.org/spec/RMS/1.0.

Office of the Law Revision Counsel. 2015. "United States Code, Title 44." Accessed September 13, 2015. http://uscode.house.gov/browse/prelim@title44&edition=prelim.

Schiff, Jennifer. 2008. "Storage That Really Lasts." September 11. Accessed September 13, 2015. http://www.enterprisestorageforum.com/technology/features/article.php/3771001/Storage-That-Really-Lasts.htm.

Simmhan, Yogesh L, Beth Plale, and Dennis Gannon. 2005. "A Survey of Data Provenance in E-Science." *SIGMOD Record* 34 (3): 31–36.

World Wide Web Consortium. 2015. "Extensible Markup Language (XML)." September 5. Accessed September 13, 2015. http://www.w3.org/XML/.

XBRL International. 2013. "Extensible Business Reporting Language (XBRL) 2.1." February 20. Accessed September 13, 2015. http://www.xbrl.org/Specification/XBRL-2.1/REC-2003-12-31/XBRL-2.1-REC-2003-12-31+corrected-errata-2013-02-20.html.

CHAPTER 5

Software and Data Segregation Security

Daniel Ching Wa

CONTENTS

5.1 INTRODUCTION

Cloud computing has been perceived as a striking technology and management system since the turn of twenty-first century. It changes the business operation landscape, which is dominated in physical building. Cloud computing offers a scalable and global ecosystem of computing resources, storage arrays, and instant provision (Figure 5.1). It is worthwhile to revisit the definition and architecture in cloud computing. Architecture and weakness of the cloud computing environment is walked through and leading to the issue of security, access control, audit measurement, authentication, and authority. Aggregately, the segregation of duties applies in software and data conventionally. The innate characteristic of multitenancy in the cloud system relies extensively on the subscriber identity as the master framework of data segregation. This applies to cloud computing resources, cloud storage, access control, change control, software development, backup and restore, global data replication, and business continuity.

• Connect devices
• Connect data
• Connect apps and services
• Connect people
• Connect businesses
• Connect everything...

Cloud platform

FIGURE 5.1   Cloud ecosystem.

5.2 ORIGINS OF CLOUD COMPUTING

Cloud computing carries a main goal of maximizing the value of distributed resources (Figure 5.2) through combining disparate components to achieve a higher transaction rate. This enables a high capability to solve bigger scale of computational issues. Under the hood of cloud computing spanning private, public, and hybrid deployment, key ingredients are quality of services, virtualization, interoperability, and scalability. John McCarthy was the first one to quote the concept of cloud computing in 1960s (Foster et al., 2008). According to this seminal opinion, computation was organized as a public utility similar to water, gas, and electricity. The associated characteristics were depicted in the book of Douglas Parkhill, *The Challenge of the Computer Utility*, in 1966 (Zhang et al., 2010).

Historically, the paradigm of cloud emerges from the telecommunications industry. This is where operators commonly offer virtual private network (VPN) services, which bear similar services quality in term of engineering (see Figure 5.3), but charge a very low cost of execution. This averts the former situation in telecommunication in which dedicated point-to-point telecommunication circuits show a high degree of resources redundancy. Cloud computing provokes a more balanced utilization of network and computing resources in servers (Wood et al., 2011). Users can access data, applications, and other resources plainly through a computer browser. This is independent of the devices used and available at any location where users stay. Cloud infrastructure is supported through the latest state of art of internet infrastructure offering high resiliency in throughput and reliability such that more intensive computing jobs can be handled.

Sophisticated technology skills are demanded in cloud computing installation. High-level reliable services (Figure 5.4) in cloud computing are obtained through sharing over multiple work sites (Popa et al., 2012). This is good for better action in business continuity and a good provision for disaster recovery in case of infrastructure outage. Metropolitan sharing of computing resources and infrastructure drives a higher efficient utilization of the infrastructure. This facilitates a simpler maintenance for cloud-based applications

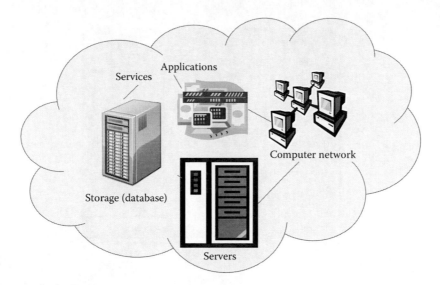

FIGURE 5.2   Distributed resources.

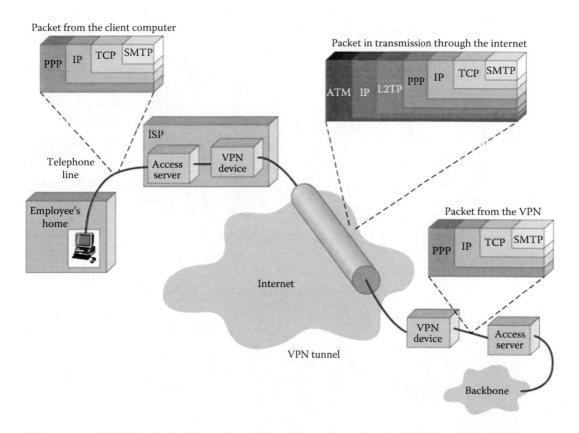

FIGURE 5.3   VPN for cloud computing. PPP, point-to-point protocol; IP, internet protocol; TCP, transmission control protocol; SMTP, simple mail transfer protocol; ATM, asynchronous transfer mode; and L2TP, layer 2 tunneling protocol.

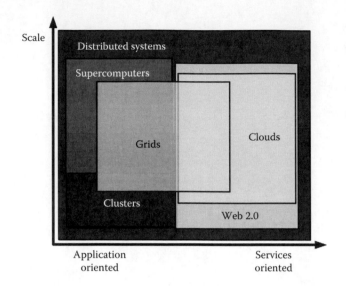

FIGURE 5.4   Cloud services.

since the actual installation happens in shared cloud data center. Nothing is installed in the front-end system. This increases the business agility in cloud computing.

"Pay as use go" is a core characteristic of cloud computing (Sotola, 2011). This is a two-sided sword (Figure 5.5). Cloud computing subscribers can minimize huge amount of prepayment and capital expenses as in a conventional internal technology platform, and this can measure the usage of cloud computing through a granular control of metering. Thus, performance is carefully monitored because the meter payment is scalable in cloud computing investment.

The centralization nature (Mather et al., 2009) in cloud computing renders a high position of information security in enterprise subscribers. Providers can devote more time and effort to mitigate technology security issues, which is not possible in an individual enterprise user.

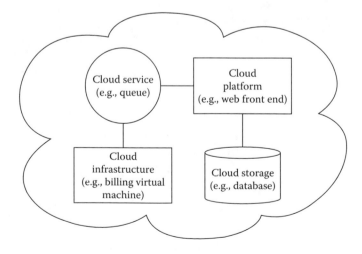

FIGURE 5.5   Pay-as-you-go cloud architecture.

5.3 ARCHITECTURE OF CLOUD SYSTEMS

Architecturally speaking, cloud computing system has two core components: front end and back end. They are integrated through a high-speed network infrastructure (Figure 5.6). Cloud is a public object, and thus, the connectivity is mostly Internet (Malathi, 2011). Users interact with the front end to perceive the response from back-end computing resources. Nonetheless, the front end is the client's office computer and business applications demanding access to the back-end computing services, such as computers, servers, and data storage. Traffic monitoring (Chaves et al., 2011) is critical in the cloud architecture. All administration work is performed in the back-end central computing server. A piece of software in the middle, or middleware, is used to conduct all communication rules, protocols, and rules to orchestrate all components in the cloud computing landscape.

Technically speaking, a cloud client is a blend of computing hardware and software, aiming to serve the purpose of application delivery (Figure 5.7). It is a presentation device possessing no much computing power. In a cloud computing paradigm, a cloud delivery model calls "software-as-a-service (SaaS)" surfing over high-speed internal or external Internet. SaaS eliminates the requirement for installing and running application programs in the cloud front-end system. In this perspective, one critical characteristic is the conduit of network-based access and management being managed from a centralized location somewhere in the cloud infrastructure spanning across the globe. This facilitates all subscribers to use those business and system applications remotely through either internal or

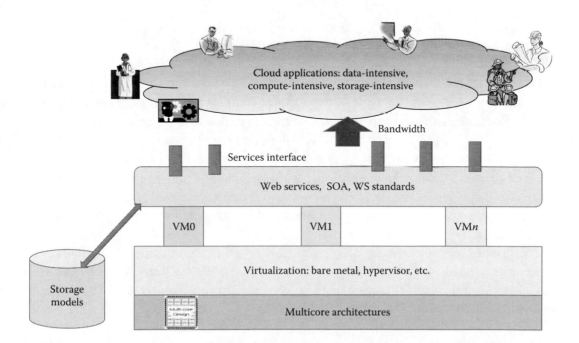

FIGURE 5.6 Cloud architecture: SOA, service-oriented architecture; and WS, web services.

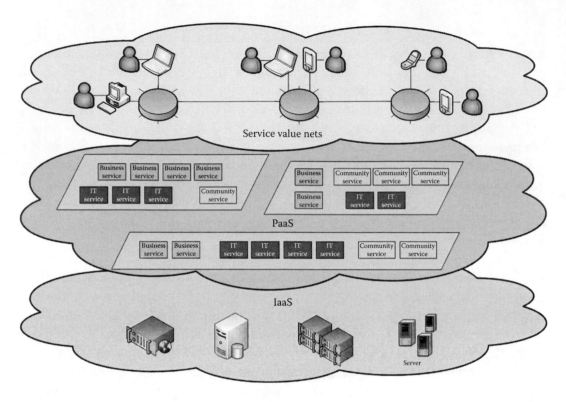

FIGURE 5.7   IaaS, PaaS, and SaaS in cloud computing.

external Internet. To name a few, the key providers of this kind of SaaS providers in this writing are SalesForce, NetSuite, Oracle, IBM, Microsoft, and Google Apps (Doelitzscher et al., 2011).

Another delivery channel is known as "platform as a service (PaaS)", in which cloud computing providers offer a computing platform to users and subscribers in the form of tools as services. Inside, all applications tactically expected by the clients are deployed and run. Therefore, users do not have to face the pain points of acquiring and setting up the necessary software and hardware. Internal developers of subscribing user companies can access all preinstalled computing resources in PaaS cloud deployment such that full life cycle of system developments can be performed on tasks of developing, testing, deploying, and hosting of user-specific cloud system and business applications. A key example is Microsoft Azure.

"Infrastructure as a service (IaaS)" is the last resort in cloud computing's delivery. In this category, subscribers do not require to buy any particular software or hardware before enjoying cloud services. This extends to no procurement need on servers, data center, or connectivity resources. The core objective of IaaS is for customers paying only for the time duration of their subscription, which is meter based. A fast service delivery can be achieved at minimal cost. Good examples are GoGrid, Flexiscale, IBM SoftLayer, Joyent, and Rackspace (Doelitzscher et al., 2011).

5.4 CLOUD COMPUTING BENEFITS

There are numerous market-perceived commercial and technical advantages, which are impeccable in the cloud system (Dillon et al., 2010):

- *Simple landscape management*: All infrastructures in cloud computing systems are simplified, and this creates fewer headaches for internal technology support team. Most systems and business applications demand huge amount of expensive storage, and this is now easily catered for in an Internet-based cloud-based system. All cloud-based architectures rely solely on a simple web browser and high-speed internal and external network connectivity.

- *Cost minimization*: Small and medium enterprises shall enjoy more benefits of cloud computing than big enterprises. Through the nature of resources sharing in cloud computing, both capital and operational expenses on technology are drastically reduced. Information technology installation demands a huge upfront cost of procurement and installation. In cloud systems, all expensive equipment and facilities are shared across all subscribers of cloud systems. Further, there could be idle resources in conventional internal information technology systems, and cloud computing can release untapped computing resources in the technology platform of small and medium enterprises. This can minimize the idle cost in case of occasional use of intensive computing resources. Technology human resources can be minimized at the same time.

- *Nonstop services*: Outage prevention is a top priority in all cloud computing service providers. Nonetheless, there are several service interruption in some big cloud computing companies, such as Gmail outage in 2009 and Amazon EC2. Continuous improvement is being done in this perspective.

- *Business continuity*: Disaster recovery is a native construction in cloud computing providers. On-site and offsite backups are turned on by default. Subscribers' critical data backups are conducted through cloud-based storage services. This can ensure a full system restore available either on-site or offsite.

- *Sustainability*: There are many greenhouse gas emission and electronic waste accumulated in case of individual companies building up internal information technology systems. Centralization through cloud computing landscape maximizes the use of back-end computing resources to minimize the release of carbon dioxide and the consumption of electricity. Less hardware is procurement to reduce the accumulated of electronic wastes.

5.5 CONCERNS IN CLOUD COMPUTING

In view of many appealing advantages in cloud computing, there are substantial weaknesses inherited (Hashizume et al., 2013). The biggest ones are security and privacy. Both of them could bring in disastrous consequences. Big companies and small and medium enterprises show concern in locating crucial confidential data, such as customer information, financial data, trade information, design, and patents into the cloud environment. A cloud is a shared-based approach; and, there should be some sort of preventive measures to ensure zero leakage in company confidentiality.

Reputation risk is another critical issue in cloud computing. Data leakage and outage are key drivers in this enterprise risk. Cloud computing subscribers lose customers in case of breaching security controls; and cloud providers face massive lawsuits for offering low degree of security measurements.

Privacy is a twin concern to security concerns. Cloud subscribers colocate their data in the same physical cloud computing data centers. A top priority is to prevent compromise in client's privacy. Proper authentication must be installed to mitigate this risk. Authorization should be tightened to restrict and monitor data access by subscribers or delegated agents.

Most cloud data centers are spanned across the globe. The time of replication and amount of execution cost must be minimized to give a better profit margin in cloud operator's financial ledgers. High data resiliency should be established through a mesh-like global cloud infrastructure. This can enhance reliability at large.

5.6 MULTITENANCY IN CLOUD

Multitenancy (Domingo et al., 2010) is an instantiation of the software architecture in which one software instance serves multiple cloud computing subscribers over a cluster of computing servers (Figure 5.8). The administrator of cloud computing resources could

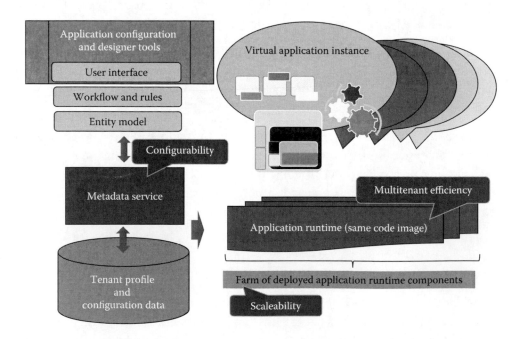

FIGURE 5.8 Multitenancy.

find one single piece of database or application system hosting computing images owned by different and competing clients.

The definition of a tenant means a group of subscribers sharing a common access, but configured with dedicated and specific privileges, against that particular cloud computing instance. In a multitenancy model, systems and business applications are constructed and executed to enable each subscriber, or tenant, a dedicated portion of the shared system instance. This contains data, configuration, user management, personalized functionality, and other nonfunctional characteristics. Customers of multitenancy do not share or see others' data. Different clients share the same piece of systems and business applications running on the same piece of operating system, hardware, and data storage. This is totally different from the multiinstance system structure in which separate system instances are running for individual subscribers. When contrasted against the technology of software and hardware virtualization, multitenancy is different because there is no dedicated virtual machine created for each subscriber. It is the system and business application architecture designed to allow different clients sharing the same computing and storage resources purely on the subscriber identity.

One upfront benefit in multitenancy is cost savings. Economy of scale is solicited in consolidating different clients' technology requests onto a single instance of software operation. Technically speaking, a system and business application incurs substantially a high degree of memory and computing overhead. In case of single tenancy in which one user rides on a single instance of system and business application, back-end computing resources will be exhausted very quickly. Multitenancy trims out this unnecessary wastage through amortization of computing and storage resources over multiple customers. Additional cost savings come from licensing in operating systems and database.

Data aggregation and mining is simpler in multitenancy. In single tenancy, data are collected from different and multiple data sources, and there are different schemas to make the data consolidation very clumsy. When a customer wants to run queries across multiple data sources in order to perform data mining and trend analysis, tremendous effort is needed. Multitenancy makes use of single schema for all subscribed customers such that fast query and data analysis can be performed instantly.

Release management is simple in multitenancy. All subscribers share the same instance of hardware and software. Once a thorough testing and validation is done, the same piece of new software or hardware can be released to benefit all subscribers.

5.7 CUSTOMIZATION IN CLOUD COMPUTING

Sharing of computing resources is a key characteristic in the cloud architecture, and a high degree of customization (Mehrsai et al., 2013) is deemed to cater for an individual subscriber's needs. Customization normally spans the following perspectives:

- *Branding*: This enables an individual client of a cloud system to the tailor-made look and feel of system and business applications, in order to fit into the respective corporate branding.

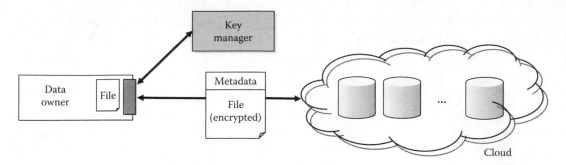

FIGURE 5.9   Access control in cloud computing.

- *Workflow*: Different companies bear an individual wishlist on operation flow for business. Cloud computing should bear the flexibility to cater for the workflow for a wide range of potential customers.

- *Data schema expansion*: Cloud computing system should be provisioned with high scalability for subscribers to extend the information structure easily at will.

- *Access control* (Figure 5.9): Each cloud computing user should be able to customize access rights and restrictions for each user independently.

- *Quality of service*: Cloud computing applications should be provisioned with adequate isolation of security, robustness, and performance among cloud subscribers.

5.8 SEGREGATION OF DUTIES

Fraud happens when there is collusion. A classical security approach is to install separation of duties (Carroll et al., 2011; Chen and Zhao, 2012). This can contain well the issues of conflict of interest, the appearance of conflict of interest, and fraud. Structurally, it minimizes the amount of power, bestowed on any individual, vulnerable to corruption and other unethical acts. Separation of duties acts as a barrier in workplace, including cloud computing landscape, to mitigate fraud perpetrated through users.

An information flow diagram should be created for each function in a business and the implementation in cloud computing ecosystem. This can identify which situations are good for separation of duties. Then preventive, detective, and avoiding controls can be installed. There is no single rule of separation of duties applicable to all organizations. Cloud computing environment is share oriented and multitenancy; risk assessment is deemed to determine which compensating controls are adequate. Risk assessment of segregation of data and system can be in the form of self-assessment. Cloud Security Alliance develops a template, which will be discussed in Chapter 7.

5.9 SEPARATION OF DUTIES IN CLOUD COMPUTING

Cloud computing is made up of a virtualization technology to enable computing resources sharing. The multitenancy nature in all deployments of cloud computing ecosystem posts data security concerns. The fundamental question is how to keep cloud-based data safe in a shared ecosystem. All computing and data resources of cloud services subscribers are placed in multitenant cloud infrastructures to maximize cost-effectiveness and efficiency. All cloud services providers should address the issues of data separation and geolocation (Dustin Owens, 2010) in view of increasing complex international legal and political landscape. There are two factors of data separation in the cloud environment: tenancy and geolocation:

- Cloud ecosystem is always multitenant. This might not be a big issue to private cloud users because most computing and storage resources are housed within a company's premise. The sharing of memory space, disk space, and processor cycles running the same piece of physical hardware posts a data separation concern in hybrid, public, and community clouds. Nonetheless, full data separation is impossible. It is inevitable to face a fact that cloud computing users' data space and virtual machines are shared among other subscribers. Virtualization is good for containing workloads and avoiding cross-interference. Nonetheless, a very high level of data encryption is needed to protect system and business data from unauthorized access and retrieval. Some cloud providers for governmental works build a fully walled-over operation zone to bound sensitive workloads. Stringent regulations and security requirements are implemented at the same time.

- Another perspective in data separation is geolocation, that is, the actual physical locations of those cloud data. Geolocation sorts out the issue of data separation in two perspectives. First, cloud computing users should use cloud providers able to manage workload, computing resources, and data storage with trusted physical geolocation. Second, cloud providers should provide assurance to address client's concerns on platform security and geographically workload management. Some sort of service-level agreements should be developed.

Software development (Géczy et al., 2013) is a key area employing separation of duties. Owing to the versatility of the cloud computing ecosystem, a strong control must be installed when developers configure and program cloud systems for business needs. System and software developers are not allowed to access production systems directly. A configuration management mechanism should be installed to transfer program codes from the development and testing environment to the production landscape environment. No source code is allowed in the cloud's production environment. Software and system developers are not provisioned access and authorization on production systems. In addition, a secure channel must be installed for system operator when managing production environments. This is close to multitenancy such that the system operator is treated as a cloud system subscriber. Their authentication and authorization rights prevent any access to other users' systems and data. All network activities are logged with auditing and fraud detection. VPN is enabled in this system operator access.

In most cloud providers, production environments are encrypted. This can avoid any data leakage in case of disaster recovery. In case of an emergency fix, cloud providers should activate an automated data and systems change mechanism, in order to isolate problematic data and programs into a quarantine for later troubleshooting. Still customer data are encrypted such that developers can do program troubleshooting using a native development tool without peering over confidential data. As such, change control is a mandate requirement in cloud computing landscape in order to enable separation of duties.

Cloud computing consists of three deployment models: IaaS, PaaS, and SaaS. Customization is encouraged in the cloud environment, because numerous computing resources are present and high scalability is around. There will be many developer source codes tailored for cloud instances. They are intellectual properties of either cloud operators or subscribers. A strong control should be installed into regular source code repositories with tight version control, tracking, and lifetime monitoring. In case of disaster recovery and new feature releases, this can avoid substantial amounts of revalidation.

Backup in the cloud environment shall carry the principle of data segregation as well. All customer data are profiled in multitenancy. Some of the label-based security classifies all system business data as per subscribers' identity. Content of label-based data can be revealed only with subscribers' convoluted identity. At the moment of backup, all label-based security attributes are carried over to backup media, such as hard drive and tapes. In case of normal data restore or disaster recovery, all resuming works are executed as per subscribers' identity. This is designed into the cloud computing back system. This offers a thorough data protection in case of restore and business continuity.

Data segregation is not a pure technology issue (Figure 5.10). People's accountability must be enforced to deliver a compensative control. All generic administrative accounts must be disabled and removed permanently so as to restrict only authenticated and well-labeled access that are running. The traditional role-based security should be enhanced

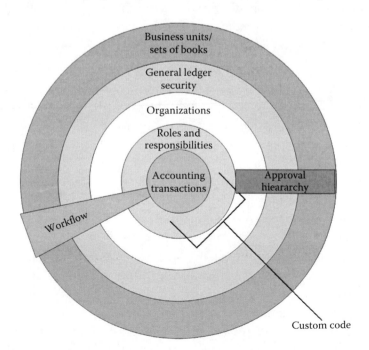

FIGURE 5.10   Segregation of duties.

to incorporate the subscriber's identity as the ultimate data partition. This is the master framework in data segregation.

Data segregation must be supplemented with a mature system logging in all computing resources, network equipment, databases, and cloud front-end devices. This master logger must be single directional and write only. Preferably, this master logging system is administered by a third-party professional firm to assure no chance of internal compromise. It functions more like an external flight recorder used in today's jet planes. This kind of escrow-like arrangement enhances the creditability of cloud computing's data segregation management.

5.10 SUMMARY

Data segregation in the cloud landscape is dictated through the allocation of a universal nonrepudiated subscriber's identity. This changes the conventional internal business system concept, because all cloud services subscribers are expected to share single instance of computing power, database, network, cloud front end, and data resilience. This subscriber's identity is more than virtualization. It manages the fundamental structure of cloud systems and data. Nonetheless, detective, preventive, and compensating controls can be installed in the cloud system to enhance the ability of data segregation.

REFERENCES

Carroll, M., Van Der Merwe, A., and Kotze, P. (2011). *Secure Cloud Computing: Benefits, Risks and Controls*. Paper presented at the Information Security South Africa (ISSA).

Chaves, D., Aparecida, S., Uriarte, R. B., and Westphall, C. B. (2011). Toward an architecture for monitoring private clouds. *Communications Magazine, IEEE, 49*(12), 130–137.

Chen, D., and Zhao, H. (2012). *Data Security and Privacy Protection Issues in Cloud Computing*. Paper presented at the International Conference on Computer Science and Electronics Engineering (ICCSEE).

Dillon, T., Wu, C., and Chang, E. (2010). *Cloud Computing: Issues and Challenges*. Paper presented at the 24th IEEE International Conference on Advanced Information Networking and Applications (AINA).

Doelitzscher, F., Sulistio, A., Reich, C., Kuijs, H., and Wolf, D. (2011). Private cloud for collaboration and e-learning services: From IaaS to SaaS. *Computing, 91*(1), 23–42.

Domingo, E. J., Niño, J. T., Lemos, A. L., Lemos, M. L., Palacios, R. C., and Berbís, J. M. G. (2010). *CLOUDIO: A Cloud Computing-Oriented Multi-Tenant Architecture for Business Information Systems*. Paper presented at the IEEE 3rd International Conference on Cloud Computing (Cloud).

Dustin Owens, B. (2010). Securing elasticity in the cloud. *Communications of the ACM, 53*(6).

Foster, I., Zhao, Y., Raicu, I., and Lu, S. (2008). *Cloud Computing and Grid Computing 360-Degree Compared*. Paper presented at the Grid Computing Environments Workshop.

Géczy, P., Izumi, N., and Hasida, K. (2013). Hybrid cloud management: Foundations and strategies. *Review of Business and Finance Studies, 4*(1), 37–50.

Hashizume, K., Rosado, D. G., Fernández-Medina, E., and Fernandez, E. B. (2013). An analysis of security issues for cloud computing. *Journal of Internet Services and Applications, 4*(1), 1–13.

Malathi, M. (2011). *Cloud Computing Concepts*. Paper presented at the 3rd International Conference on Electronics Computer Technology.

Mather, T., Kumaraswamy, S., and Latif, S. (2009). *Cloud Security and Privacy: An Enterprise Perspective on Risks and Compliance*. O'Reilly Media.

Mehrsai, A., Karimi, H. R., and Thoben, K.-D. (2013). Integration of supply networks for customization with modularity in cloud and make-to-upgrade strategy. *Systems Science and Control Engineering: An Open Access Journal*, *1*(1), 28–42.

Popa, L., Kumar, G., Chowdhury, M., Krishnamurthy, A., Ratnasamy, S., and Stoica, I. (2012). *FairCloud: Sharing the Network in Cloud Computing*. Paper presented at the Proceedings of the ACM SIGCOMM 2012 Conference on Applications, Technologies, Architectures, and Protocols for Computer Communication.

Sotola, R. (2011). Billing in the cloud: The missing link for cloud providers. *Journal of Telecommunications Management*, *3*(4).

Wood, T., Ramakrishnan, K., Shenoy, P., and Van der Merwe, J. (2011). *CloudNet: Dynamic Pooling of Cloud Resources by Live WAN Migration of Virtual Machines*. Paper presented at the ACM SIGPLAN Notices.

Zhang, Q., Cheng, L., and Boutaba, R. (2010). Cloud computing: state-of-the-art and research challenges. *Journal of Internet Services and Applications*, *1*(1), 7–18.

II

Achieving Security in a Private Cloud

CHAPTER 6

Taking Full Responsibility for Cyber Security in the Private Cloud

Daniel Ching Wa

CONTENTS

6.1 INTRODUCTION

One very striking instance in corporate information technology leaders happens when their associated organizations are illegally broken into suffer big loss in data theft and reputation damage. Cybercrime is a matter of top priority item (Yang and Hoffstadt, 2006) in small and large enterprises. Internet in business brings both the layman world and commercial sectors closer and closer. Other than normal users making their living through cyber world, there are groups of technical competent and diligent people

FIGURE 6.1   FBI (https://www.fbi.gov/about-us/investigate/cyber).

who spend long hours surfing the Internet for covert income. This behavior is known as "cybercrime."

Law enforcement agencies, such as Interpol and the Federal Bureau of Investigation (FBI) (Figure 6.1) (Broadhurst, 2006), are stepping up efforts to preempt this technology-based crime. Nonetheless, more and more people and organizations become victims of hacking, theft, identity theft, and malicious software. The leakage of cozy photos owned by celebrities is a typical case. The solid way to avoid being a cybercrime target is to protect sensitive information offline and in the cloud. Impenetrable security built on a unified system composed of software, hardware, and security policy can authenticate information traversing over the Internet.

A list of generalized recognized instances of cyber crimes in the FBI (Chen et al., 2004) is as follows:

- *Hacking*: This means an illegal break-in a person's computer without acknowledge (Figure 6.2) and aims accessing personal or sensitive information. US jurisdiction takes as a felony and punishable. In commercial world, there is activity called ethical (white) hacking which companies employed to validate and verify Internet security level.

- *Theft*: This involves downloading music, movies, games, and software illegally and infringes copyrights. Peer-sharing software, such as BitTorrent, is used to share copyright protection files. This is a serious piracy issue, and the FBI takes this seriously.

- *Cyber stalking*: It is the name for online harassment and causes sustainable mental damage. Victim is barred from online messages and e-mails. Normally, stalkers may know victims beforehand. Sometimes, offline stalking follows to render victims' lives more miserable.

- *Identity theft*: This is a very popular type of cybercrime these days. The end goal is to steal money through the use of stolen cloud identity for cash. Cybercriminal accesses

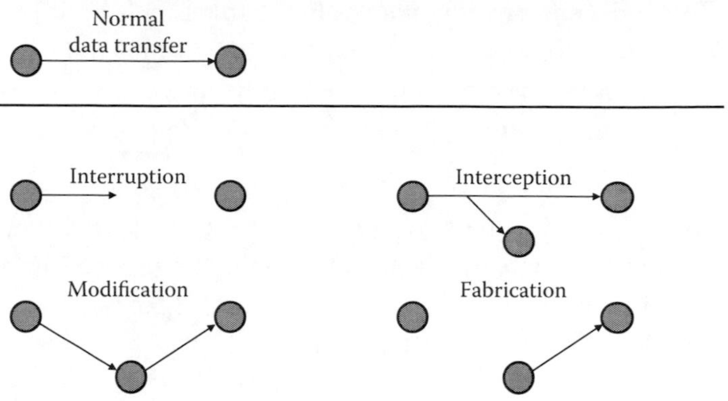

FIGURE 6.2 Meaning of hacking.

a victim's bank account, credit cards, Social Security ID, debit card, and other financial sensitive information. The key goal is to collect money directly or perform online shopping using victim's identity online.

- *Malicious software*: They are used to spoil an Internet network operation. Through gain access to a system, owners of malicious software steal sensitive information and cause damage to the infected companies.

- *Child soliciting and abuse*: This is a kind of cybercrime on child pornography and pedophile. The FBI patrols chat rooms to reduce and prevent child abuse and soliciting.

6.2 CYBERCRIME TODAY

Since 1990s, massive quantity of personal computers and networks has roll out to form a new industry called information technology. Cybercriminals find that the rate of return on illegal break-ins is high and the associated risk is low. More and more hackers make use of self-developed tools to access sensitive information and personal data hoping to harvest big returns. This happens remotely (Cache et al., 2010) to render difficult to catch cybercriminals. Hackers sometimes launch competition (Håpnes and Sørensen, 1995) to identify the best hacking skill. Initially, hackers' attempts are brushed off as a simple nuisance. After the popularity of malicious software, hackers drag down networks and systems performance.

The objective of contemporary cybercriminals is no longer driven purely out of ego or expertise. On the contrary, they wish to gain benefits through stealing, deceiving, and exploitation. This makes cybercrime a real threat, which is totally different from old-school situations, robbing, mugging, or stealing.

Cybercriminals can perform malicious actions single handedly and not requiring any physical presence.

The following malicious actions can be activated from a remote- or even a cross country location:

- *Individual perspective*: This includes cyber stalking, distributing pornography, trafficking, and "grooming."

- *Property*: This indicates stealing of a victim's bank details and siphoning off money, misusing credit card for online purchases, running scams to lure naïve people to do money laundry, using malicious software to solicit access to companies' websites, or paralyzing computer systems. Malicious software can damage the physical property as well.

- *Government*: This is a rare perspective. The most commonly known instantiation is cyber terrorism. It can wreak havoc and cause panic in a country. Cyber criminals could be terrorists or unfriendly governments, aiming to hack government websites, military websites, or circulate propaganda.

One interesting attribute of cybercriminals is loosening connection, in which casual collaboration and cooperation are noted. In contrast to other real-world crimes (Florêncio and Herley, 2013), cybercriminals intend not to fight among themselves for supremacy or control. Instead, Internet-based syndication is used to improve hacking skills. Mutual compliment is noted to help each other when new tough hacking target is noted. One investigation method to fight cybercrime is cross-domain solutions (Marshall et al., 2004). Organizations can deploy cross-domain cyber security solutions to protect exchange of information using classified protocols. The framework enables companies to deploy an integrated environment comprising software and hardware authenticating both manual and automatic remittance of security data and accessing confidential information through various security classifications. This facilitates seamless exchange, sharing, and execution of security credentials within a specific security classification not intercepted by, or advertently revealed to, malicious hackers.

6.3 CASES OF CYBERCRIME OUTBREAKS

There are several major and influential cyber security outbreaks worthy of studying. The first case is about a top-tier supermarket chain in the United States suffering from data theft and leading to step-down of the respective chief executive officer (CEO). The second case is about a massive internal data theft of a Korean credit bureau. The last one is about a US–Europe Internet hacker taking advantage of vulnerability in legacy Internet protocol.

6.3.1 Target CEO Step-Down for Data Breach

In May 2014, Gregg Steinhafel, Target CEO, President, and Chairman, made an immediate resignation (Walters, 2014). It was mutually decided between the then CEO and company's board of directors a right moment for Target to find a new leadership. Commercially, the company's board of directors was not satisfied with Steinhafel's strategies and performance due to slipping sales. The most critical consideration was the massive data breach in the United States in 2013. Few Target staff acknowledged certain computer hacking warning signs ignored right before the massive data breach. Cybercriminals hacked into Target's customer database and extracted all consumers' information. The massive data breach involved personal information, with credit/debit card details, close to 110 million individuals. This outbreak drove Target less visiting those shops as they all felt that their credit card/debit card security is weak. After the disclosure of the disaster, Target hired a top-notched cyber security company to do investigation. The consulting report concluded that Target's shortcomings are on cyber security awareness and no specific procedures are on cyber security. Target planned to enhance security enhancements through incorporating the new MasterCard chip-and-PIN technology. Further, partner financial institutions of Target replaced most of consumer credit cards involved in this data breach at free of charge. The company enhanced fraud detection for all consumers on one hand, and offered close credit monitoring and identity theft protection on the other hand.

6.3.2 Korean Credit Card Data Theft

In 2014, half portion of South Korea citizens had their credit card details stolen (Broadhurst et al., 2014). The end buyer was local marketing firms. It was a computer contractor employed in Korea Credit Bureau. That insider thief copied 20 million sets of consumer names, social security numbers, and credit card details. Luckily, that subcontractor and marketing firm's manager were arrested promptly. Stolen data came from top-tier South Korean credit card firms, that is, KB Kookmin Card, Lotte Card, and NH Nonghyup Card.

Interestingly, this data theft was carried out using a universal serial bus (USB) stick. All credit data were unencrypted, and there was no surveillance to detect illegal and massive data movement. Top managements of three South Korean credit card firms gave public apology with regard to this massive data breach.

6.3.3 Esthost Takedown

In 2011, Esthost, the world's biggest cybercrime robotic network (BOTNET), was taken down by the FBI, Estonian police, Trend Micro, and few other industry partners (Alrwais et al., 2012). This marked an end to more than 4,000,000 infected machines in the BOTNET history. The operation code name was "Operation Ghost Click." The FBI raided and seized two data centers in New York City and Chicago where a command and control infrastructure was composed of more than 100 servers. Estonian police arrested core operational personnel Tartu, Estonia.

The functioning of this BOTNET (Abu Rajab et al., 2006) was through Domain Name Server (DNS) settings pointing toward foreign Internet protocol (IP) addresses. DNS reads human-readable domain names and translates to Internet addresses allocated to computer servers on the Internet. Esthost BOTNET installed DNS-changing Trojans silently onto infected computers and modified network settings in searching DNS servers, which contain malicious software. Cybercriminals made money through replacing online advertisements, hijacking search results, and selling additional malware to blackmail users.

6.4 CYBER THREATS TO CLOUD LANDSCAPE

Cybercrime is a growing menace impairing the proper functions of Internet, e-commerce, and cloud services operation. More sophisticated attacks are approaching normal cloud service users. Here are some emerging threats and risks in cloud computing, including all deployment modes (Choo, 2011):

- *Zero-day attack*: Cybercriminals are very inventive and innovative. They keep on exploiting new vulnerability in Internet and cloud systems to steal data and master control cloud back-end systems. New and sophisticated attack appears every second. Interesting, hackers make use of cloud services, in particular, public and community cloud ecosystems, to ally and form a global syndicate of hacker research network.

- *Cloud for hackers*: Many big companies are migrating core data, systems, and applications to the cloud ecosystem at full speed so as to take advantage of cloud computing's promises in cost savings, flexibility, and highly scalable computing resources. Cybercriminals can earn more through staying anonymity. Hacking is launched from infected cloud systems. They can evade from detection on one hand and using the superfast global computing systems on the other hand. Their data theft can be completed quite in shorter time. Cloud computing environment actually gives cybercriminals a perfect platform to launch large-scale and coordinated attacks. This is impossible in conventional local area networks.

- *Misconception on hacker landscape*: Earlier, cybercrime attack was presumed to come from computers located and hosted in countries such as Russia, China, and Brazil. Security Engineering Research Team Quarterly Threat Intelligence Report (Gad, 2014), from Solutionary security group, ran an investigation in 2013 on 100 countries about the distribution of hosting malware. Surprisingly, half of the malware hosting sites are located in the United States (50%), Germany (5%), the Netherlands (5%), Russia (5%), and China (5%). Three top hosting providers found in this malware distribution investigation are Amazon, GoDaddy, and LeaseWeb. This indicates cybercriminals moving onto cloud computing landscapes as well. Cybercrime involves millions of computers. Cloud services offers computing processing power not able to achieve in in-house technical systems. Scalability in cloud services provides instant solution to massive cyberattack requirements from cybercriminals. Provisioning and implementation can happen in few seconds and full automation.

Cybercriminals compromise legitimate domains first, and then use for later malicious purposes. The hopping from one domain to another domain thwarts law enforcement's efforts to track down the root sources. Some hackers even misuse free-of-charge trial periods in cloud services providers, such as Microsoft Azure, such that fake websites are built in relative anonymity for later massive cyberattacks. In order to bypass account creation authentication, cybercriminals exchange stolen credentials from phishing campaigns or buy open black market. Hackers are able to write programs to automate signup processes to create large numbers of fake accounts.

An interesting question is: How deep is the cybercrime arena in the Internet? It is estimated that only 5% of the Internet is visible to common search engines, such as Google. The rest of the Internet is enormously large to give cybercriminals plenty of room to develop and hang out, but remaining in obscurity. This enables hackers to access the Internet in complete anonymity. There are networks of servers routing traffic so as to prevent associated IP addresses from tracking by authority. Those servers conceal traffic details and senders' information so as to resist monitoring and surveillance. The Online Routing (TOR) (McCoy et al., 2008) is such a tool. It is originated from the TOR project by the US Naval Research Laboratory in 2002. This system encrypts data packets many times before directing through multiple network nodes. Each router then peels away a layer of encryption to read the next routing instructions. Packets are sent to the next node. Such intermediary nodes have no capability to read the packets' contents. A special browser is needed to access the TOR network to ensure operating anonymously. TOR is open sourced on the Internet, and hackers can modify to ensure their malicious traffic traversing safely on the Internet and skip the monitoring from law enforcement. It acts as a safe haven for cybercriminals with nefarious intentions, such as terrorists, anarchists, and global criminals. Through TOR, cybercriminals can exchange drug deals, human trafficking, child pornography, arms deals, financial fraud, human experimentation, and other illegal and underhanded activity.

Cloud computing environment sits on the Internet. Public and community cloud expose to cybercriminal checking every moment. Hybrid cloud actually connects private cloud with a company's premise to external Internet world. This posts a hassle of how to protect cloud-based information object.

Cybercrime as a service (Wall, 2007) is a new trend. It employs a concept as in software as a service, platform as a service, database as a service, and other as a service. It allows individuals and gangs to buy malicious products or services to commit a cybercrime instantly. One example is to break into cloud computing landscape and steal information. According to the 2014 Internet Organized Crime Threat Assessment report (Duijn et al.), this cybercrime-as-a-service allows nontechnical people to acquire the hacking skills in a short moment. This posts a big threat to cloud users.

6.5 INSIDER THREATS

Internet hackers hide in the dark side of the Internet, in order to perform break-in experiments in a cloud computing ecosystem. They are still externals and there are firewalls and intrusion detectors to defend. Many widely advertised risks to cloud systems falls on vulnerability to external attackers. Corporate security teams, on the contrary, frequently express concern over threats from within. Some insiders intend to do some headline-grabbing actions. It could be a whistle-blowing exposure to public media, and one good example of Edward Snowden's disclosure on the US National Security Agency's works (Greenwald et al., 2013). Disastrous effect comes after this. Nonetheless, insider threats could be well intentioned, mistakes from careless employees, and rogue insiders aiming for personal gain. In Skyhigh's latest Cloud Adoption and Risk Report (Mera, 2015), there is a strong tendency of insider threat in 85% of surveyed companies. Cloud computing enjoys rapid expansion for the last decade, and there are six harrowing and layman perspectives on insider threats (Kasar, 2006), which are described in Sections 6.5.1 through 6.5.6.

6.5.1 Leaving Salespersons

It is a common concern in corporate management for top sales representatives leaving for competitor along with good sales leads. Stealing leads is hard to detect, but the end effect is adversely affecting business at large. Cloud system intensifies this sales embezzlement because all customer information is kept out on the Internet. Leaving employees can copy confidential data to cloud storage for later retrieval.

6.5.2 Rogue System Administrator

In the cloud environment, all company employees rely on cloud computing services. There are privileged administrators to perform data management on the cloud service, which are accountable for controlling users' permissions and security policies. It is possible for rogue administrators to access executive-only financial information and do insider trading.

6.5.3 Cloud Employee

Insider threat conventionally comes from company internals. In the cloud computing arena, confidential data and applications are moved over to the cloud system, and this creates a security exposure in the context of cloud employees. Rogue cloud employees can trick subscribers to expose security token and steal confidential information.

6.5.4 Globetrotter

Outsourcing involves global collaboration, and it is a common practice in the cloud environment to have companies working in Europe and the United States with their contracting parties in India and China. Security vulnerability appears in the form of low-wage contractor ghost employee. Globetrotters can steal information through short-term human memory.

6.5.5 Intellectual Property

Cloud computing drives a global flat operation. One software developer creates propriety software for his or her company. Related intellectual property belongs to the company. This careless user uploads those software codes to the code-sharing site, which infringes the copyright law immediately.

6.5.6 Employee Careless Mistakes

Employees are human beings. There could be careless mistakes, such as a financial services staff accidentally uploading sensitive customer data to social media.

6.6 CLOUD SECURITY GOVERNANCE

Corporate management expects a structural and systematic approach to handle cyber security for cloud computing systems. A governance framework is deemed to apply policies regarding the deployment and operation of cloud services. Security governance framework for cloud computing can be examined from an opposite angle, that is, walking through free-for-all chaos on cloud landscapes without any oversight installed. Then, security policies are installed to control the information leakage and access to confidential and private information stored in cloud systems.

Cloud governance (Rebollo et al., 2012) has two components. One is design-time governance, which defines policies to cloud services; and the other one is runtime governance, which actually executes security policies in real time.

FIGURE 6.3   Cloud security governance general framework.

Cloud security governance (Figure 6.3) involves the presence of a registry, which is the central location for both subscribers and cloud administrators to check and monitor services running in the cloud computing environment. This cloud registry controls the mapping and operation between cloud services and security policies.

In the cloud governance framework, life cycle management (Ko et al., 2011) in cloud computing resources is critical. This is the ability to check, monitor, and track changes to cloud systems. Through this mechanism, cloud operators and subscribers can keep track of who creating a cloud service, making changes to the cloud service and when the changes occur. Virtual machine and hypervisor controls are critical elements in cloud governance. This can avoid operation chaos in virtual machines competing for cloud resources. Virtual machine and hypervisor governance are part of life cycle cloud governance.

Client-side governance is another area within the cloud security governance framework. Client front end is a core component in all deployment models in cloud computing, and therefore, it is naturally part of cloud security governance. Proper secret access key should be deployed in cloud security governance for strong authentication and authorization.

Hybrid cloud system (Figure 6.4) involves both public cloud infrastructures on the Internet and private cloud systems within the subscriber's office. Dedicated consideration should be placed in cloud governance regarding the traversing of confidential information across public and private data.

6.7 SUMMARY

Cybercriminals create an unprecedented challenge to corporate information professionals on critical information asset protection (Figure 6.5). The migration to cloud environments leads to diverse difficulty. Public cloud usage demands a strong control on access,

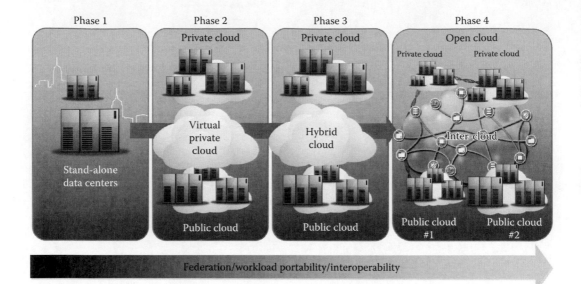

FIGURE 6.4   Hybrid cloud development.

FIGURE 6.5   Protecting critical information asset.

authentication, and authorization. The emerging of hybrid cloud connects highly secure private cloud with Internet-based public cloud. This exposes the whole corporate information systems on the cloud to huge amount of risk.

External threats are from hackers, and they are aiming at stealing confidential information, such as credit card and patents for profits. It is insider threats to exert most pressure. Careless employees can leak highly confidential information to social media. Cloud security governance framework should cover back-end cloud resources, network infrastructure, and front-end devices.

REFERENCES

Abu Rajab, M., Zarfoss, J., Monrose, F., and Terzis, A. (2006). A multifaceted approach to understanding the botnet phenomenon. Paper presented at the Proceedings of the 6th ACM SIGCOMM conference on Internet measurement.

Alrwais, S. A., Gerber, A., Dunn, C. W., Spatscheck, O., Gupta, M., and Osterweil, E. (2012). Dissecting ghost clicks: Ad fraud via misdirected human clicks. Paper presented at the Proceedings of the 28th Annual Computer Security Applications Conference.

Broadhurst, R. (2006). Developments in the global law enforcement of cyber-crime. *Policing: An International Journal of Police Strategies and Management*, 29(3), 408–433.

Broadhurst, R., Grabosky, P., Alazab, M., Bouhours, B., and Chon, S. (2014). An analysis of the nature of groups engaged in cyber crime. *International Journal of Cyber Criminology*, 8(1), 1–20.

Cache, J., Wright, J., Liu, V., Scott, E., Antoniewiecz, B., and Wang, C. (2010). *Hacking Exposed Wireless*. McGraw-Hill.

Chen, H., Chung, W., Xu, J. J., Wang, G., Qin, Y., and Chau, M. (2004). Crime data mining: A general framework and some examples. *Computer*, 37(4), 50–56.

Choo, K.-K. R. (2011). The cyber threat landscape: Challenges and future research directions. *Computers and Security*, 30(8), 719–731.

Duijn, P. A., Kashirin, V., and Sloot, P. M. (2014). The relative ineffectiveness of criminal network disruption. *Scientific reports*, 4.

Florêncio, D., and Herley, C. (2013). Sex, lies and cyber-crime surveys. In *Economics of Information Security and Privacy III* (pp. 35–53). Springer.

Gad, M. (2014). Crimeware marketplaces and their facilitating technologies. *Technology Innovation Management Review*, 4(11).

Greenwald, G., MacAskill, E., and Poitras, L. (2013). Edward Snowden: The whistleblower behind the NSA surveillance revelations. *The Guardian*, 9.

Håpnes, T., and Sørensen, K. H. (1995). Competition and collaboration in male shaping of computing: A study of a Norwegian hacker culture. *The Gender-Technology Relation: Contemporary Theory and Research*, 174–191.

Kasar, S. (2006). Legal issues alone are not enough to manage computer fraud committed by employees. *Journal of International Commercial Law and Technolgy*, 1, 25.

Ko, R. K., Jagadpramana, P., Mowbray, M., Pearson, S., Kirchberg, M., Liang, Q., and Lee, B. S. (2011). TrustCloud: A framework for accountability and trust in cloud computing. Paper presented at the 2011 IEEE World Congress on Services (SERVICES).

Marshall, B., Kaza, S., Xu, J., Atabakhsh, H., Petersen, T., Violette, C., and Chen, H. (2004). Cross-jurisdictional criminal activity networks to support border and transportation security. Paper presented at the Proceedings of the 7th International IEEE Conference on Intelligent Transportation Systems.

McCoy, D., Bauer, K., Grunwald, D., Kohno, T., and Sicker, D. (2008). Shining light in dark places: Understanding the Tor network. Paper presented at the Privacy Enhancing Technologies.

Mera, A. (2015). Unintentional insider threat: Policy, training and technologies to mitigate end user risk.

Rebollo, O., Mellado, D., and Fernández-Medina, E. (2012). A systematic review of information security governance frameworks in the cloud computing environment. *Jouranl of Universal Computer Science*, 18(6), 798–815.

Wall, D. (2007). *Cybercrime: The Transformation of Crime in the Information Age* (Vol. 4). Polity.

Walters, R. (2014). Cyber attacks on US companies in 2014. *Heritage Foundation Issue Brief* (4289).

Yang, D. W., and Hoffstadt, B. M. (2006). Countering the cyber-crime threat. *American Criminal Law Review*, 43, 201.

CHAPTER 7

Selecting the Appropriate Product

Daniel Ching Wa

CONTENTS

7.1 INTRODUCTION

Enterprise information system is costly, and it takes long time to build. It has to align with user expectation and custom documented in the IT business alignment model (Figure 7.1) (De Haes and Van Grembergen, 2005). The surface of cloud computing ecosystem bears the mission to scale up the computing power of internal technology landscape, providing a dynamic provision and commission mechanism such that small to large companies can address business needs instantly with no hassle. System migration and extension always come from additional costs. Users face delays and compatibility issues. Ernst & Young's IT security survey (Stanton et al., 2005) discovers a drastic downturn in the corporate security

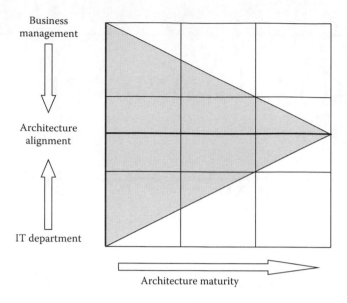

Business
management

Architecture
alignment

IT department

Architecture maturity

FIGURE 7.1 IT business alignment model.

if a cloud computing environment is not evaluated well. KPMG International's cloud survey (Feuerlicht et al., 2011) says that some cloud providers only offer lip services when selling cloud solutions to small and large companies. Moreover, one-half of respondents are using cloud for business processes. Users say that it is far easier to get new markets and driving process transformation in the cloud environment. Unfortunately, one-third of respondents say that the relocation cost is higher than expected. The cause is the new changes in their existing business and technology architectures. Further, there are a substantial number of entities complaining cloud computing that cause concerns in security, operation, and daunting costs.

Business process redesign is a common failure detected in cloud computing migration (Marston et al., 2011). This includes business process redesign, IT management capabilities, systems integration, infrastructure and other technology configuration surfacing in transition process, and reporting notes.

7.2 PREQUESTIONING ON CLOUD SERVICES

Cloud computing services can be as simple as the online e-mail system or document storage. It can be a full-blown enterprise resources planning. The goal of cloud computing is to streamline business workflow and reduce the reliance on internal technology resources. Cloud systems enjoy a shared, low-cost remote support from cloud providers' employees. Company users can use a simple cloud front end, such as browsers, or a dedicated small program, to clock-in daily attendance, access company's and customer's confidential information, and collaborates online. Another striking benefit of cloud services is the auto backup, which is expensive to install and run for small- and medium-sized companies. Before jumping on the cloud computing wagon, 10 questions should be walked through among corporate management, which are discussed in Sections 7.2.1 through 7.2.10.

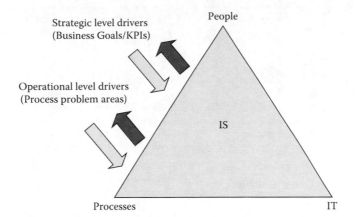

FIGURE 7.2   Prequestioning.

7.2.1 Cloud Services Expectation

The very first question to query (Figure 7.2) is which particular cloud services are expected (Durkee, 2010) in a company's operation. This is critical for small, medium, and large enterprises. Some niche cloud software providers deliver single function offering. Good examples are Dropbox (www.dropbox.com) for online document, photo, and video storage; Intuit and QuickBooks (www.intuit.com) for online accounting; and Salesforce (www.salesforce.com) for online customer relationship management. If the company expects more than the basic data function, some cloud services providers offer a range of general-purpose features, such as information technology networking infrastructure, on-demand access to virtual servers, applications, and software. Good examples are IBM SmartCloud (www.ibm.com), Amazon Web Services (www.amazon.com), and GoGrid (www.gogrid.com). This first assessment question is to perform an expectation evaluation of bare requirement in cloud services.

7.2.2 Pricing Structure

Cloud computing ecosystem advocates the pay-as-use-go approach (Walker et al., 2010). Unlike conventional internal technology setup in which a huge upfront capital investment is found, cloud services providers should bear a pay-as-services-go pricing scheme. Fees are charged hourly, monthly, semiannually, or annually.

7.2.3 Security Level

This is a major evaluative criterion when assessing cloud services to store company's confidential and critical data. It is expected in cloud services operators to exert various standard security measures and followed up with constant review and update. Security measures include firewalls, antivirus detection, multifactor authentication, data encryption, and regular security audits. A critical question is whether staff of cloud providers can access and read company's confidential data (Kandukuri et al., 2009) kept in cloud objects. Preferably, cloud companies should perform employee background checks to reject potential cybercriminals or identity hackers. Industry security standards should be followed. One example is health

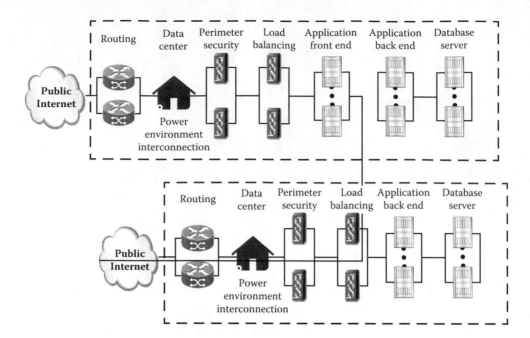

FIGURE 7.3 Complexity in the cloud data center.

care companies to comply with the Health Insurance Portability and Accountability Act on patient data privacy and security (Ness and Joint Policy Committee, 2007).

7.2.4 Location and Security Level of Cloud Data Center

There is a need to record locations (Sądowski, 2013) and security level of subscribed cloud data centers and servers (Figure 7.3). This applies to small, medium, and large enterprises. This prechecking can reveal any opportunity of compromise and misuse. Cloud services providers should present measures against natural disasters, such as fires, floods, earthquakes, and storms. For employee security, there should be vetting process to spot out staff and guest having the chance to take sensitive data out of office physically or through Internet and cloud. Certain certifications are recommended, and one such is the Statement on Standards for Attestation Engagements 16. They focus on customer access and privacy, data center physical security, and data redundancy.

7.2.5 Remediation in Case of Data Leakage

Murphy's law (Buhalis and Law, 2008) states that things will go wrong, if it goes wrong. There are chances for cloud providers to accidentally damage or lose subscribers' data. A service-level agreement (SLA) should present to subscribers with remediation, in handling potential data losses. Financial compensation and data store redundancies are recommended. Further, there should be a risk mitigation framework to reduce the chance of data damage and loss.

7.2.6 Expected Customer Support Services

Cloud providers should state the availability of technical support (Mell and Grance, 2011). Preferably, it should be online through web and Internet, and by phone 24 hours a day and

365 days annually. In additional, the average reaction time should be within 1 minute, and the time of problem and the time of resolution should be within 2 hours. All customer engineers should have access to automated knowledge systems to track issues and problem identification.

7.2.7 Scalability of Cloud Services

One of the cloud computing promises is to expand functional capability instantly to meet the swift market demand (Zhao et al., 2010). This should be cascaded to cloud services (Figure 7.4); and thus, there has to be an assurance from cloud providers, to offer a validated cloud infrastructure, that is able to support an expanding business operation.

7.2.8 Downtime

Downtime (Armbrust et al., 2010) is a disaster to both cloud operators and subscribers. Cloud-based systems and data are inaccessible over a substantial time period. Cloud outages are disruptive and costly for both cloud providers and users. Performance records must be tracked to locate a cloud provider showing close-to-zero downtime.

7.2.9 Ease of User Configuration

Simple interfaces and dashboard features are expected to give user a straightforward experience (Kégl et al., 2000). There should be zero learning time. It will be good, if there is artificial intelligence supporting the user configuration tasks.

7.2.10 Medium of Cloud Access

Cloud computing users are debriefed to access the cloud system anywhere and through any device (Sistanizadeh et al., 2002). This is supplemented by sophisticated security controls. It is preferable to conduct a comprehensive examination on cloud service providers before sealing contracts on cloud services.

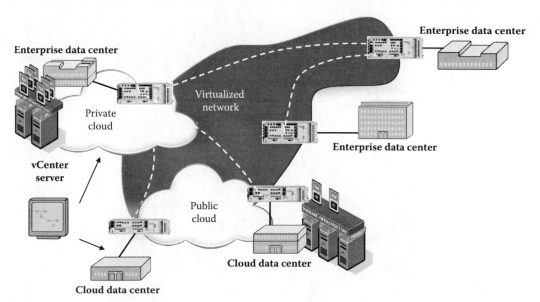

FIGURE 7.4   Scalability in the cloud data center.

7.3 CONTROLS FOR EVALUATION WHEN SELECTING CLOUD SERVICES

In the course of cloud services supplier assessment, there are certain controls worthy of attentions. Upcoming cloud subscribers should consider an evaluation plan (Wan et al., 2012):

- *Internal trust*: This could sound not quantitative and objective. In reality, there could be strong resistance from internal staff fearing about losing jobs after migrating to cloud systems. It will be corporate management's mission to bring in the core business of cloud computing to all staff in the company. Retrenchment is not an option in cloud computing initiative.

- *Expertise*: Plainly, all cloud service providers are assumed to be proficient in technology level and business sense. A pure technical cloud provider cannot understand the business process well. Cloud services suppliers have to balance both technology and business.

- *Third-party audit*: Standing from the cloud governance point of view, an external independent assessment is the best (Figure 7.5). Cloud services providers have to demonstrate that all promises are delivered. One audit standard is the Unified Certification Standard dedicated toward cloud and managed service sector. This audit standard contains 11 control objectives to validate cloud services.

- *Risk management*: All cloud services providers have to demonstrate a mature and formal management structure. There should be organizational charts, risk assessment policies, formalized processes, controls for third parties, and adequate segregation of duties.

- *Policies and procedures*: All cloud services companies should be able to show documented policies and procedures on request. All documents are subject to frequent review and update. Cloud services providers' employees are required to attest and adhere to practicing policies and procedures. Formal training methodology must be installed.

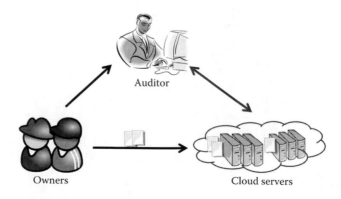

FIGURE 7.5　Third-party audit architecture.

- *Change management*: A structural and formal change management framework should be installed under formalized change controls. This includes capacity planning and modification for client configurations. Further, standardized and well-informed change workflow should be established to update enterprise information systems. This covers formal processes for requesting, logging, approval, testing, and acceptance of change requests.

- *Event management*: All cloud services companies should equip the Network Operations Center (NOC) with well-trained personnel able to monitor, identify, and resolve cloud issues. This is a safeguard for the agreed SLA between the cloud services vendor and subscribers. A central help desk should be installed to coordinate all cloud issues and events.

- *Logical security*: This governs all access to cloud services providers' and subscribers' information systems and data. This must comply with sets of well-established policies and procedures. Well-documented controls for user authentication should be maintained, including password policies and upper management review. This applies to both internal and remote access. A good track record should exist on administrator IDs and vendor and third-party access policies.

- *Data and process integrity*: There should be adequate and sufficient information security policies and procedures to ensure good data backup and retention policies. Data integrity should be reviewed, updated, approved, and communicated within cloud services vendors frequently.

- *Physical and environmental security*: Cloud systems run in a physical data center. There are instances of cybercriminals overriding conventional physical protection. All cloud providers should demonstrate documented policies governing physical access and visitor and guest logs. Strict security controls in physical facility include card key, closed-circuit television (CCTV), and on-site security guards. Cloud security control should document controls on access to facilities. Terminated cloud providers' employees should be reported and tracked within cloud facility. The NOC and data centers should be protected from disruptive events. Effective redundancy should be shown on connectivity and power. Disaster recovery and business continuity plan should be rehearsed frequently.

- *SLA*: This is the baseline concurred between cloud providers and clients to track and monitor subscribed services. It is the control for tracking service modification.

- *Financial status*: All cloud providers should report a stable and healthy financial status. Good profitability should be maintained for six previous months. This can ensure sufficient capital in cloud providers to attain financial sustainability.

7.4 CLOUD SECURITY ALLIANCE

Prequestioning and controls are predominating procedural matters. They are formed through the experience of practicing security professional on cloud services (Bardin et al., 2009). In the industry, there is an international organization dedicated to cloud security control, and it is the Cloud Security Alliance (CSA) (www.cloudsecurityalliance.org). The organization is voluntary with representatives from big conglomerates. Under this cloud security initiative, a special Cloud Controls Matrix Working Group is designated to build an evaluative assessment matrix on cloud services providers.

CSA's Cloud Controls Matrix (CCM) is constructed to offer fundamental security principles for cloud vendors to follow (Guo et al., 2010). This can assist prospective cloud subscribers to assess security vulnerability in cloud providers. The CSA's CCM matrix is a set of controls specially entailed for understanding security concepts and principles tailored for cloud computing security. There are thirteen domains in the CCM. Its foundations rely on the customized relationship with respective industry-accepted security standards, regulations, and controls frameworks, which are ISO 27001/27002, Information Systems Audit and Control Association (ISACA) Control Objectives for Information and Related Technology (COBIT), payment card industry (PCI), National Institute of Standards & Technology (NIST), Jericho Forum, and NERC CIP. Each of them augments the internal control direction in service organization. All controls attest all offered cloud services.

The CSA's CCM is a framework to facilitate all cloud users with the needed structure and detail, for the sake of clarifying information security checking for the cloud industry. It strengthens the security control through emphasizing business information security control requirements; reducing and identifying consistent security threats and vulnerabilities; providing standardized security and operational risk management; seeking normalization on security expectations, cloud taxonomy, and terminology; and finally performing successful security implementation in cloud computing landscape.

This CCM is a key component of CSA's Governance, Risk Management and Compliance (GRC) stack, the end goal of which requires appropriate assessment criteria, relevant control objectives, and timely access to necessary supporting data. This CSA's GRC can apply to private, public, community, or hybrid clouds. In short, this stack is a universal toolkit for enterprises, cloud providers, security specialists, and IT auditors to instrument and assess all cloud deployment to meet security best practices, standards, and critical compliance requirements.

Cloud audit (Wang et al., 2010) is a critical process in the CCM. Its end goal is to establish a common interface and namespace such that cloud computing vendors can automate the process of audit, assertion, assessment, and assurance of cloud's infrastructure as a service, platform as a service, and application as a service. Authorized cloud subscribers can run their respective cloud services via an open, extensible, and secure interface. Therefore, cloud audit takes the role of technical foundation to enable transparency and trust in all cloud deployment models. Under the CSA, there is a Cloud Audit Working Group. Following the convention in the CSA, the Cloud Audit Working Group is a volunteer-based, cross-industry effort consolidating experts in cloud technology, networking ability, security experts, audit professional, assurance personnel, and architecture professional. The key benefit of cloud auditing is to enable the automation of one-off labor-intensive, repetitive and costly auditing, assurance and compliance functions such that a controlled set of interfaces evolves to simplify security assessments demanded in cloud services providers and clients.

In additional to the CCM and cloud audit, another critical contribution of the CSA is the Consensus Assessments Initiative Questionnaire. This is a powerful tool of the CSA's

Consensus Assessments Working Group to address the issue of lack of security control transparency, which is a prime inhibitor to cloud computing adoption. This performs research, creates tools, and creates industry partnerships to provoke global cloud computing assessments. This questionnaire is available in a spreadsheet format for cloud consumers, cloud auditors, and cloud providers to evaluate.

The final offering from the CSA is the Cloud Trust Protocol (CTP). It is a mechanism by which cloud subscribers can ask for and receive information about the issue of transparency. The CTP aims to generate evidence-based confidence. The CTP tactical implementation offers well-defined and measurable SLAs and continuous security monitoring. This is a classic application of digital trust and assurance of collected evidence. CTP cloud users are offered a way to identify important pieces of information concerning the compliance, security, privacy, integrity, and operational security history. The CTP builds confidence in cloud subscribers' market in order to accelerate secure adoption of cloud services and promote collaboration between international standards organizations and global regulatory authorities. Ultimately, it raises trust in cloud providers and users so as to promote broader adoption of safe cloud landscape.

7.5 WHITE HACKING (PROS AND CONS)

In normal trading and manufacturing situation, pilot test and sampling are the standard approach to dry run a product for safety, functionality, price performance, and marketability. In the cloud computing environment, this trial effort can be fulfilled in the form of white hacking. Companies can hire white hackers (Kaminsky, 2006) to test and implement the best practices on the cloud infrastructure so as to make it less vulnerable to malicious hacking attempts in the future.

In terms of technical levels, white hackers are similar to hackers. They are proficient in computing kernels and network protocols. They can detect vulnerability and weakness in information systems swiftly. Thus, a white hat hacker is classified as a computer security specialist able to break into protected systems and networks to test and evaluate the security of the cloud computing infrastructure. Therefore, white hackers utilize professional skills to enhance the security through finding vulnerabilities right before being detected and exploited by malicious hackers, also known as black hackers.

One key prerequisite of a white hacker is to seek permission from employed companies of cloud services and subscribers first, before starting white hacking work. White hackers are somewhat considered to recontribute their top-notched skills to benefit the society in return.

The most common approach of a white hacker is penetration test. This is normally called "pentesting," "pen testing," or "security testing" (Harris et al., 2011). It is a practice of attacking a company's own or clients' information technology systems more or less the same way as a normal hacker (Figure 7.6). The aim of a white hacker is to identify security loopholes. The person conducting penetration test is known as pentester. Before doing a penetration testing, the fundamental requirement is to get permission from a hiring company or a subcontractor. Otherwise, illegal white hacking becomes a cybercrime.

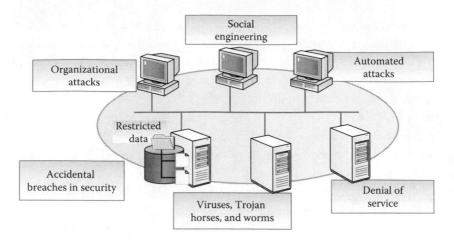

FIGURE 7.6   Scope of white hacking.

7.6 SUMMARY

Unlike conventional internal enterprise information evaluation, cloud computing environment spans across internal network and Internet. This applies to a hybrid cloud environment. The selection of cloud computing services starts with a management initiative to take a risk-based approach. A questionnaire walkthrough with focused controls is a good standard. The CSA develops several standard procedures and frameworks to standardize the evaluation of cloud services.

REFERENCES

Armbrust, M., Fox, A., Griffith, R., Joseph, A. D., Katz, R., Konwinski, A., … Stoica, I. (2010). A view of cloud computing. *Communications of the ACM, 53*(4), 50–58.

Bardin, J., Callas, J., Chaput, S., Fusco, P., Gilbert, F., Hoff, C., … Matsumoto, S. (2009). Security guidance for critical areas of focus in cloud computing. *Cloud Security Alliance,* 0–176.

Buhalis, D., and Law, R. (2008). Progress in information technology and tourism management: 20 years on and 10 years after the Internet—The state of eTourism research. *Tourism Management, 29*(4), 609–623.

De Haes, S., and Van Grembergen, W. (2005). IT governance structures, processes and relational mechanisms: Achieving IT/business alignment in a major Belgian financial group. Paper presented at the Proceedings of the 38th Annual Hawaii International Conference on System Sciences, 2005.

Durkee, D. (2010). Why cloud computing will never be free. *Queue, 8*(4), 20.

Feuerlicht, G., Burkon, L., and Sebesta, M. (2011). Cloud computing adoption: What are the issues. *Systémová Integrace,* 187–192.

Guo, Z., Song, M., and Song, J. (2010). Notice of retraction a governance model for cloud computing. Paper presented at the 2010 International Conference on Management and Service Science (MASS).

Harris, S., Harper, A., Ness, J., Williams, T., and Lenkey, G. (2011). Gray hat hacking.

Kaminsky, D. (2006). Explorations in namespace: White-hat hacking across the domain name system. *Communications of the ACM, 49*(6), 62–69.

Kandukuri, B. R., Paturi, V. R., and Rakshit, A. (2009). Cloud security issues. Paper presented at the IEEE International Conference on Services Computing, 2009.

Kégl, B., Krzyzak, A., Linder, T., and Zeger, K. (2000). Learning and design of principal curves. *IEEE Transactions on Pattern Analysis and Machine Intelligence, 22*(3), 281–297.

Marston, S., Li, Z., Bandyopadhyay, S., Zhang, J., and Ghalsasi, A. (2011). Cloud computing—The business perspective. *Decision Support Systems, 51*(1), 176–189.

Mell, P., and Grance, T. (2011). The NIST definition of cloud computing.

Ness, R. B., and Joint Policy Committee (2007). Influence of the HIPAA privacy rule on health research. *JAMA, 298*(18), 2164–2170.

Sądowski, A., Narayan, R., Sironi, L., and Özel, F. (2013). Location of the bow shock ahead of cloud G2 at the Galactic Centre. *Monthly Notices of the Royal Astronomical Society, 433*(3), 2165–2171.

Sistanizadeh, K., Amin-Salehi, B., Ghafari, E., and Sims, W. (2002). Universal access multimedia data network. Google Patents.

Stanton, J. M., Stam, K. R., Mastrangelo, P., and Jolton, J. (2005). Analysis of end user security behaviors. *Computers and Security, 24*(2), 124–133.

Walker, E., Brisken, W., and Romney, J. (2010). To lease or not to lease from storage clouds. *Computer, 43*(4), 44–50.

Wan, Z., Liu, J. E., and Deng, R. H. (2012). HASBE: A hierarchical attribute-based solution for flexible and scalable access control in cloud computing. *IEEE Transactions on Information Forensics and Security, 7*(2), 743–754.

Wang, C., Wang, Q., Ren, K., and Lou, W. (2010). Privacy-preserving public auditing for data storage security in cloud computing. Paper presented at the 2010 Proceedings IEEE on INFOCOM.

Zhao, G.-S., Rong, C.-M., Liu, J.-L., Liu, H., Zhang, F., Ye, X.-P., … Tang, Y. (2010). Modeling user growth for cloud scalability and availability. *Journal of Internet Technology, 11*(3), 395–405.

CHAPTER 8

Virtual Private Cloud

Lauren Collins

CONTENTS

8.1 INTRODUCTION

A virtual private cloud (VPC) deployment allows companies to use equipment in data centers and provide global accessibility. The access is based on the identified detailed design requirements, defined use cases, and definitions for integration conditions for a new environment. A VPC deployment can be more secure than most office networks. Each device will have a connection to the Internet, thereby accessing the cloud. There are many disparate devices that will need to access a centrally located set of data, all connected via a secure connection. This chapter covers its user base as delivery drivers, work-from-home employees, and project teams. Note that all of these users can be located anywhere but will have a connection to the Internet, accessing centrally located data with nothing being stored on their local device. Each connection to the remote server can host a remote connection of a hosted application, which is running on a server in the cloud. Although the appearance is that the application runs locally on the tablet, laptop, or mobile device, it is running from a server in the cloud, as shown in Figure 8.1. A VPC

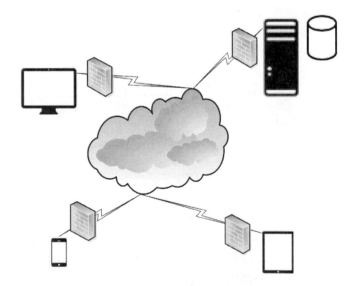

FIGURE 8.1   Cloud computing environment in a VPC. A cloud user securely connects and accesses a hosted environment.

carves out a private network that gives access to a predefined set of users, whether it is vendors, employees, or project teams. Each group can have its own access roles, differentiating the files and applications available to them.

Applications can range from Microsoft applications to industry-specific, proprietary applications. Because the application is running from a server in the cloud, any type of device can be used (e.g., iPad). Various devices are compatible running applications through the cloud, which would not ordinarily support an application when it is locally installed. After connecting securely, usually a virtual private network, a device can either utilize a remote desktop connection or a shortcut pointing to the application housed on the cloud server. Each user will only be able to view and access files and applications they have permissions for. When data are securely stored in the cloud, accessible from anywhere will give businesses a strategic advantage.

8.2 SIMULATING A PRIVATE CLOUD IN A PUBLIC ENVIRONMENT

Although developers will lean toward a public cloud, IT professionals lean toward a VPC, whether it be hosted or on-premise. Resources are better utilized in a VPC and can use private clouds as a testing ground to test out deployments and use cases of each of the service models. Because use cases can be utilized by both internal customers and external customers, a VPC is best designed in a public environment. The core components of VPC are as follows:

- Standardized service offering

- Shared

- Automated

- Self-service

- Pay per use

The cloud cannot be customized for every type of user who is going to access the application. By offering a small subset of standardized services, there is a predefined user base that is proven to be successful in accessing the cloud with a limited set of proven services. When a team articulates business needs and technology objectives, the respective design is addressed accordingly. The following are the best practices for private cloud success:

- Identify core business need.

- Standardize your virtual machine (VM) catalog.

- Automate VM deployment and retirement.

- Utilize VM-aware monitoring and management tools.

- Track business unit and catalog utilization and costs.

When sharing cloud services, there are different business units and different use cases. The design of a VPC should take both the business unit needs and their specific use cases into consideration, keeping in mind the first component (standardized service offering). Therefore, with the preceding in mind, the following are the business and technology objectives:

- Define use cases.

- Provide access to test environments for support and development teams.

- Allow self-provisioning demonstration and training environments.

- Host multiple versions of software code.

- Design all components of a VPC environment.

- Determine the base infrastructure: compute, storage, and network needs.

- Define integration points.

- Require transition support.

- Define consistent service across the entire organization.

Infrastructure is generally shared in a VPC deployment, so theoretically it is a shared use case. The most important component of a VPC should be the automation; there is no such thing as a manual cloud deployment. The provisioning of resources should be automated from the beginning when a user requests access, to when the resources are allocated based on the capacity and performance management, all the way through to when the user is taken offline. Self-service is the key to VPC access. As much as possible, users should have an experience similar to if they were shopping online. When browsing a catalog online, the users should know how much they have to spend, just as one does when shopping in a store. It is important for users to understand what it costs to use the resources they demand and consume, which is the process of charge-back or pay per use. The foundation is then built for transparent pricing of all resources allocated across business units and use cases. The most important item when designing and deploying a VPC is to ensure that its maturity is comparable to that of the behavior of a public cloud deployment. When users try to compare their experiences when using a VPC, they will look to how the machines are managed. VMs are typically provisioned by the actual infrastructure that a company owns (in a noncloud environment). Subsequently, policy-based automation allocates resources automatically based on demand. When resources of VMs are not tracked by policy-based automation based on changing demand, a user will have to manually interact with IT and wait for necessary resources, or their application will be negatively impacted. Resources should move around automatically; there should be chargeback and most importantly should offer self-service portal so a user can select his or her machine from a catalog, shown in Table 8.1.

8.2.1 Cloud Component Architecture

The cloud solution used in the remainder of this chapter will be based on VMware's vCloud. These products, solutions, and related technologies deliver an elastic, on-demand, self-service infrastructure, which forms a vCloud solution. Table 8.2 provides a high-level summary of the vCloud components used in this chapter's VPC solution:

8.2.2 vSphere Design

To support a vCloud solution, vSphere is deployed to provide the compute resource. vSphere resources are organized and separated into the management cluster and one or more resource clusters. This establishes a base for use of provider virtual data centers with vCloud Director (VCD), illustrated in Figure 8.2. The management cluster is a VMware ESXi cluster. It is used for running the servers required to manage a vCloud infrastructure. A resource cluster is a cluster dedicated to running end-user virtual applications, referred to as vApps.

TABLE 8.1 Use Cases for vCloud Suite

Use Case	Description	Attributes
Base environment	Single VM vApp providing all software components installed on Windows Server VM	Direct connectivity to an external network
Training environment	Single VM vApp providing all software components installed on Windows Server VM	Direct connectivity to an external network, with firewall rules in place to allow access from outside the organization, and to restrict access to any other private, company-owned resources
Large environment	Four VM application environment, providing a distributed installation of proprietary software	Isolated back-end network to allow for consistent component IP addressing, and direct connectivity to an external network to allow for communication between virtual application VMs and other organization resources

TABLE 8.2   vCloud Component Summary

vCloud Component	Description

VMware VCD	Primary coordination tool and user interface for abstracting vSphere resources.
	• The VCD deployment includes the following:
	  • VCD servers (referred to as VCD cells)
	  • VCD database (MS SQL or Oracle)
	  • vCloud API (application interface)

VMware vSphere	Underlying virtual compute resources that are further abstracted by VCD.
	• The vSphere deployment includes the following:
	  • vCenter Server
	  • vCenter Server databases
	  • ESXi hosts (clusters)
	  • VMware vCenter Update Manager
	  • vCenter Update Manager databases

VMware vCloud Networking and Security	Provides the capability to offer secure network services.
	• vCNS deployment includes the following:
	  • VMware vCNS Manager virtual appliance
	  • vCloud Edge devices (deployed by VCD)

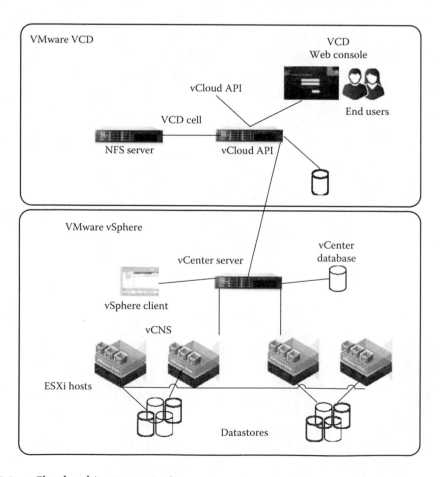

FIGURE 8.2   vCloud architecture overview.

TABLE 8.3   vCloud Definition—Clusters

vCloud Pod	Description
Management cluster	A dedicated vSphere cluster for running management servers is preferred, including the following: • vCenter Server and associated database servers • ESXi hosts • VCD cells and disassociated database schemas • vCNS Manager for VCD
Resource cluster	Cluster dedicated to running end-user servers: • ESXi hosts • User-created VMs

The separation of resources for management functions and end-user functions achieves the following:

• Management components are separated from the resources they are managing.

• Overhead for cloud consumer resources is minimized. Resources allocated for cloud use have little overhead reserved. For example, cloud resource groups do not host VMware vCenter VMs.

• Resources are dedicated to the cloud. They are consistently and transparently managed and allocated to cloud consumers and scaled horizontally.

• Troubleshooting and problem resolution are performed quickly, as management components are strictly contained in a modestly sized and manageable cluster.

This design requires two clusters: an existing production cluster will be used to host management components and a new two-node cluster will serve as the initial resource cluster. Table 8.3 shows an overview of the management and resource clusters to be implemented to the vCloud environment.

8.3 VMware vSPHERE ARCHITECTURE DESIGN—MANAGEMENT CLUSTER

vCenter Server, vCenter Update Manager Server, and vCenter Server Databases are the components of the vCenter Server design. vCenter Server is deployed as a VM within the management cluster as opposed to a stand-alone physical server. This allows for the vSphere high-availability (HA) feature to protect the vCenter Server VM in the event of hardware failure. The specification and configuration of the vCenter Server VM are detailed in Table 8.4.

8.3.1 vCenter Update Manager Server

vCenter Update Manager is implemented as a component part of this solution for monitoring and managing the patch levels solely of the ESXi hosts, with VMs updated according to the existing processes of physical servers. Although patch levels of VMs are not managed by vCenter Update Manager, the exceptions are versions of VMware Tools.

TABLE 8.4   vCenter Server Specifications—Management Cluster

Attribute	Specification
Vendor model	VMware Virtual Hardware 8
Number of video compression processor units	2
Memory	8 GB
Number of virtual network interface card ports	1
Number of local drives	2
Total useable capacity	20 GB (C:\) and 40 GB (E:\)
vCenter Server version	vCenter 5.1
Operating system	Microsoft Windows Server 2008 R2 64-bit

The specification and configuration for the vCenter Update Manager Server VM are detailed in Table 8.5.

8.3.2 vCenter Server Databases

vCenter Server and vCenter Update Manager require access to a database for which the database server (Oracle Database 11 g or Microsoft SQL Server 2008) server (provided for VCD) is used. Table 8.6 summarizes the configuration requirements for the vCenter and vCenter Update Manager databases. Table 8.7 identifies the required databases and provides details regarding the associated server accounts and database privileges. To use the databases, the vCenter Server VM must be configured with a number of appropriate Open

TABLE 8.5   vCenter Update Manager Server Specifications—Management Cluster

Attribute	Specification
Vendor model	VMware Virtual Hardware 8
Number of video compression processor units	1
Memory	2 GB
Number of virtual network interface card ports	1
Number of local drives	2
Total useable capacity	20 GB (C:\) and 40 GB (D:\)
vCenter Update Manager Server version	vCenter Update Manager 5.1
Operating system	Microsoft Windows Server 2008 R2 64-bit

TABLE 8.6   vCenter and vCenter Update Manager Server Schema Specifications—Management Center

Attribute	Specification
Vendor and version	MS SQL 2008 R2
Database instance name	Default
Authentication method	Local database user
Auto extend	On, in 10 MB increments
vCenter statistics level	3
Estimated database size (vCenter, vCenter Update Manager)	10 GB, 150 MB initial + 49–61 MB per month

TABLE 8.7   vCenter Server and vCenter Update Manager Schema—Management Cluster

Database Name	Account Name	Database Role	Function
VCD-VC	VCD_VC	Connect, resource, create, view	vCenter Server database
VCD-UPD	VCD_UPD	Connect, resource, create, view	vCenter Update Manager Database
VCD-SSO	RSA_USER RSA_DBA	(set via script)	vCenter SSO database

TABLE 8.8   vCenter Server System DSN Configuration—Management Cluster

Data Source Name	Server	ODBC Driver	Authentication	Account
vCloud vCenter Server DB	VCD-MGMT-SQL-01	SQL Native Client	Database user	DB_User
vCloud vCenter Update Manager DB	VCD-MGMT-SQL-01	SQL Native Client	Database user	DB_User

Database Connectivity (ODBC) System database source names (DSNs). Table 8.8 summarizes the required system DSNs and provides configuration details.

8.3.3 Management Components

The management components are the server components, deployed as VMs, which are required to operate a vCloud solution. Table 8.9 summarizes the management components and how they are deployed as VMs within the management cluster. Although it is not shown in the table, vCNS Edge appliances are deployed automatically by VCD, through vCNS Manager, as required. These appliances are deployed in the resource cluster, not in the management cluster.

8.3.4 VCD Design

VMware VCD cells are stateless in operation with all information stored in the database. There is some caching that happens at the VCD cell level, such as secure socket layer session data, but all refreshes and updates are done to information stored in the database. In a production environment, VMware recommends that the database be housed in a cluster configuration or at the very least have a hot standby available. The specifications for the VCD servers are detailed in Table 8.10. Table 8.11 provides a summary of the configuration requirements for the VCD databases. Table 8.12 identifies the required databases and provides details regarding the associated server accounts and database privileges.

TABLE 8.9   Management Component Workloads

Cluster	Name	Purpose
BackOffice	VCD-MGMT-PROD	Existing vCenter Server managing production cluster used to host management components
BackOffice	VCD-MGMT-VCTR	New vCenter Server (including SSO) managing the resource cluster
BackOffice	VCD-MGMT-VUM	New VUM Server managing the resource cluster
BackOffice	VCD-MGMT-CELL01	VCD cell
BackOffice	VCD-MGMT-SQL01	vCenter, VUM, SSO, and vCloud databases (SQL server)
BackOffice	VCD-VCNS-01	vCNS Manager appliance

VUM, vCenter Update Manager.

TABLE 8.10   VCD Server Specifications

Attribute	Specification
Vendor model	VMware Virtual Machine Virtual hardware version 8
Number of video compression processor units	2
Memory	4 GB
Number of virtual network interface card ports	2 (VMXNET3)
Number of local drives	1
Total useable capacity	40 GB
VCD version	vCloud Director 5.1
Operating system	Red Hat Enterprise Linux 6, Update 2

TABLE 8.11   VCD Schema Specifications

Attribute	Specification
Vendor and version	MS SQL 2008 R2
Database instance name	Default
Authentication method	Local database user
Auto extend	On, in 10 MB increments
vCenter statistics level	3
Estimated database size	100 MB initial, 30–50 GB

TABLE 8.12   VCD Database Specifications

Database Name	Account Name	Database Role	Function
VCD-SQL	VCD_SQL	Connect, resource, create, view	VCD database

vCD has a number of specific requirements with respect to network connections. The first of these requirements is to provide dedicated connections and Internet Protocol (IP) addresses for the hypertext transfer protocol (HTTP) and Console Proxy services. In addition, it is common to have supplementary connections for dedicated storage networks for access to network file system (NFS) storage. As only a single vCD cell will be deployed in this design, NFS storage will not be used and only two network adapters are required. Table 8.13 provides a summary of the VCD cells that are deployed for this design and their associated network connections.

8.3.5 vCNS Manager Design

Every resource pod vCenter Server has a vCNS Manager deployed and associated with it. The vCNS Manager is used to manage all the vCNS service VMs that are created. This includes pushing out configuration changes to the vCNS Edge devices.

TABLE 8.13   VCD Networking Specifications

VCD Cell	HTTP Service/ Management	Console Proxy	Subnet Mask	Gateway	DNS Servers
VCD-MGMT-CELL01	172.1.1.30	172.1.1.31	255.255.252.0	172.1.1.1	172.1.1.10 172.1.1.11

TABLE 8.14   Management Component Workload Resilience Utilizing HA

Cluster	Name	Purpose	Resiliency (HA/FT)
BackOffice	VCD-MGMT-VCTR	vCenter Server	HA
BackOffice	VCD-MGMT-CELL01	VCD cell	HA
BackOffice	VCD-MGMT-SQL01	Microsoft SQL Server databases	HA
BackOffice	VCD-VCNS-01	vCNS Manager appliance	HA

vCNS Manager is a virtual appliance deployed from an open virtualization format (OVF) package whose hardware does not need any customization. You must configure the VM with an IP address and hostname to integrate it into a vCenter Server. vCNS Edge devices are used for fenced networks. These networks sit behind vCNS devices, and therefore, specific services, such as network address translation (NAT) or the firewall, can be used.

8.3.6 Management Component Resilience Considerations

Unlike traditional vSphere environments, where admins are the primary users of the management components, VCD is dependent on these components for handling all VM provisioning requests. The vCenter Server that manages the resource clusters is a prime example, as an outage with this component instantly impacts end-user self-service provisioning capabilities. It is therefore recommended that management components are made highly available. Table 8.14 summarizes the management components deployed in the management cluster and the proposed solution for HA.

8.3.7 vCNS Manager

vCNS Manager, in conjunction with vCNS Edge, is a critical component of the VCD stack as it protects VMs in a vCloud environment from attacks and enables the end user to have multiple similar networks within their vCloud environment, for example, for testing purposes. Although HA provides resiliency on an ESXi host level, VMware recommends using fault tolerance (FT) to offer an additional level of protection. Although VMware recommends enabling FT on vCNS Manager to increase resiliency of the vCNS management layer, host hardware limitations may make this recommendation impractical. Spare network adapters are necessary to dedicate to FT.

8.4 VMware vSPHERE ARCHITECTURE DESIGN—RESOURCE CLUSTERS

The compute logical design encompasses the resources provided by the underlying ESXi clusters. The resource clusters are ESXi clusters that are dedicated to running the servers required to host vCloud workloads. These resources are carved up by VCD. The level of detail defined in this section is limited to the extent of the information required to deploy a vCloud solution and does not constitute a full vSphere design.

8.4.1 Data Center

For this design, there is a single site, with no secondary sites or decision resources (DR) sites in scope. Within the vSphere inventory, the data center is the highest-level logical boundary and is typically used to delineate separate physical sites or locations, or potentially an

TABLE 8.15   vSphere Data Center—Resource Clusters

Data Center Name	vCenter Server Name	Description
vCloud	VCD-MGMT-VCTR	Data center for resource cluster resources

additional vSphere infrastructure with completely independent purposes. In the case of this design, a single data center is created to logically encapsulate the data center and the resource clusters detailed in Section 8.4.2. Table 8.15 summarizes the data centers to be created for this design and their purpose.

This design is defined under the context of a single physical site, and the data centers listed are located in the same site as the management data center. The current version of VCD is not supported in multisite deployments.

8.4.2 vSphere Cluster

The resource clusters are vSphere clusters dedicated to running end-user vCloud workload infrastructure. Table 8.16 summarizes the management cluster in use, its purpose, and its high-level configuration.

Expanding on the previous information, Table 8.17 provides details of the IP addresses in use for the management cluster. Tables 8.1 through 8.17 provide details of the management, vMotion, iSCSI, and remote management. Table 8.18 provides additional details regarding default gateway interfaces, subnet masks, and Domain Name Service (DNS). HA is configured on the resource clusters to recover VMs in the event of an ESXi host failure. If a host fails, the VMs running on that server go down but are restarted on another host within a few minutes. Although the service interruption is perceivable to users, the automatic restarting of these VMs on other ESXi hosts minimizes the impact.

The HA percentage-based admission control policy is used in an $n + 1$ fashion instead of dedicating a single ESX host or defining a given number of ESX host failures to tolerate. This avoids reduced consolidation ratios due to the overly conservative approach when using slot-sized calculations. In configuring a cluster for HA, there are a number of additional properties to define. Table 8.19 details the HA configuration of the Management Pod

TABLE 8.16   vSphere Cluster—Resource Clusters

Cluster Name	vCenter Server Name	Purpose	Number of Servers	HA (%)
vCloud	VCD-MGMT-VCTR	Resource cluster	2	50

TABLE 8.17   ESXi Host IP Address Information—Resource Cluster (vCloud)

Host Name	Mgmt IP	vMotion IP Address	iSCSI IP Addresses
VCD-RES-ESX01	172.16.1.50	Shared management	vmk2: 192.168.200.126 vmk3: 192.168.200.127 vmk4: 192.168.200.128 vmk5: 192.168.200.129
VCD-RES-ESX02	172.16.1.51	Shared management	vmk2: 192.168.200.130 vmk3: 192.168.200.131 vmk4: 192.168.200.132 vmk5: 192.168.200.133

TABLE 8.18   ESXi Host Additional IP Address Information—
Resource Clusters

Description	IP Address
Management gateway	172.16.1.1
Management subnet mask	255.255.252.0
vMotion gateway	172.16.10.1
vMotion subnet mask	255.255.252.0
Remote management gateway	172.16.2.1
Remote management subnet mask	255.255.252.0
DNS1	172.16.1.10
DNS2	172.16.1.11

TABLE 8.19   HA Cluster Configuration—Resource Clusters

Attribute	Specification
Enable host monitoring	Yes
Admission control	Disable: power on VMs that violate availability constraints
Admission control policy	50% resources reserved
Default VM restart priority	Medium
Host isolation response	Leave VMs powered on
Enable VM monitoring	Yes
VM monitoring sensitivity	Medium
Advanced settings	None

cluster. In the initial vCloud deployment, only two hosts will be provided. HA Admission Control will be disabled initially to allow for the full commitment of these hosts' resources to vApp workloads. As workloads are moved from the existing vSphere clusters to vCloud, additional hosts will be added to the resource cluster and HA will be configured per standard practices.

VMware distributed resource scheduler (DRS) must be configured, as it is mandatory for use with VCD such that it can continuously balance workloads evenly across available ESXi hosts to maximize performance and scalability. In configuring a cluster for DRS, there are a number of additional properties to define. Table 8.20 details the DRS configuration of the Management Pod cluster.

TABLE 8.20   DRS Cluster Configuration—Resource Clusters

DRS Cluster Setting	Configuration Value
VMware DRS	Enabled
Automation level	Fully automated
Migration threshold	Three or more stars
Rules	n/a
VM options	n/a
Power management	Off

TABLE 8.21   ESXi Host Platform Specifications—Resource Clusters

Attribute	Specification
Vendor model	Dell PowerEdge R810
Total CPU cores	20
Processor speed	E7-8800
Memory	256 GB
Number of NIC ports	8
Local storage	Local
Shared storage	Shared: Gold—2 × 2 TB Silver—2 × 2 TB
ESX version	ESXi 5.1 build

8.4.3 Host Logical Design

The Dell PowerEdge R810 has been selected as the hardware platform for hosting the resource cluster. The specifications and configuration for this hardware platform are detailed in Table 8.21.

It is assumed that the assembly and configuration process for each system is standardized, with all components installed identically for all ESXi hosts. Standardizing the model and also the physical configuration of the ESXi hosts is critical to providing a manageable and supportable infrastructure by eliminating vulnerability.

8.4.4 Network Logical Design

This section provides details about networking and networking security configuration for the ESXi hosts supporting the resource clusters. In keeping with the network design methodology described in Section 8.3, the resource cluster logical network design leverages vSphere Distributed Switches and incorporates further best practices as follows:

- The default Maximum Transmission Unit (MTU) on virtual disk service (vDS) will remain at the default of 1500, as VCD Network Isolation (VCD-NI) will not be used. Instead, very large area network (VLAN)-backed pools will be used to provide isolated vApp networks. For this purpose, a specific range of VLANs will be allocated and trunked to host uplinks designated for VM guest connectivity.

- The vDS ports per host are increased from the default value of 128 to the maximum of 4096 to allow for VCD to dynamically create port groups.

Table 8.22 describes the vDSs that are configured across the ESXi hosts within the resource cluster.

TABLE 8.22   Virtual Switch Summary—Resource Cluster

Virtual Switch	Function	Switch Type
dvSwitch0	Management network, vMotion, and internal consumer networks	vDS
dvSwitch1	iSCSI connectivity	vDS

8.4.4.1 Virtual Network Distributed Switch

Table 8.23 defines the standard vnetwork distributed switch (dvSwitch) switches that are created and configured within the management cluster. There are a number of additional properties regarding security, traffic shaping, and network interface card (NIC) teaming that can be defined on a dvSwitch. Table 8.24 lists these properties, their default values, and any changes to these values associated with this design.

Connections to a vDS are configured through Distributed Virtual Port Groups (Distributed Port Group), in a similar manner as a volume shadow copy service (vSS). To support the VM connections described previously, a number of Distributed Port Groups must be configured, shown in Table 8.25.

TABLE 8.23   Distributed Virtual Switch Configuration—Resource Cluster

Virtual Switch	Function	Number of Network Adapters per Host
dvSwitch0	Management network, vMotion, and internal consumer networks	4
dvSwitch1	iSCSI connectivity	4

TABLE 8.24   Common vNetwork Distributed Switch Properties—Resource Cluster

Properties	Default Setting	Revised Setting
Security: promiscuous mode	Reject	
Security: MAC address change	Accept	Reject
Security: forged transits	Accept	Reject
Ingress traffic shaping. status	Disabled	
Egress traffic shaping	Disabled	
VLAN	VLAN trunking	
Teaming and failover: load balancing	Route based on originating virtual port ID	Route based on physical NIC load
Teaming and failover: failover detection	Link status only	
Teaming and failover: notify switches	Yes	
Teaming and failover: failback	Yes	
Teaming and failover: failover order	All active	
Advanced: maximum MTU	1500	

TABLE 8.25   vNetwork Distributed Switch Port Groups—Resource Cluster

Virtual Switch	Port Group Name	Binding	VLAN Description
dvSwitch0	Management	Dynamic	Internet VM connections
dvSwitch0	vMotion	Dynamic	Internet VM connections
dvSwitch0	(VLANs)	Dynamic	Guest external networks
dvSwitch1	iSCSI_1		IP storage network
dvSwitch1	iSCSI_2		IP storage network
dvSwitch1	iSCSI_3		IP storage network
dvSwitch1	iSCSI_4		IP storage network

There are a number of additional properties regarding security, traffic shaping, and NIC teaming that can be defined on a port group. By default, a vDS port group inherits settings for these properties from its parent vDS. You can override and customize these settings on a per-port group basis. Tables 8.26 and 8.27 list these properties, their inherited values, and any changes to these values associated with this design.

8.4.5 Network Physical Design

This section expands on the logical network design in the corresponding Section 8.4.4.1 by providing details of the physical NIC layout and physical network attributes. Table 8.28 summarizes the physical NICs and their function in relation to the logical virtual networking design.

TABLE 8.26   vNetwork Distributed Switch Port Group Properties—dvSwitch0

Properties	Default Setting	Revised Setting
Security: promiscuous mode	Reject	
Security: MAC address changes	Accept	Reject
Security: forged transmits	Accept	Reject
Ingress traffic shaping: status	Disabled	
Egress traffic shaping: status	Disabled	
VLAN	VLAN trunking	<VLAN ID>
Teaming and failover: load balancing	Route based on originating virtual port ID	Route based on physical NIC load
Teaming and failover: failover detection	Link status only	
Teaming and failover: notify switches	Yes	
Teaming and failover: failback	Yes	No
Teaming and failover: failover order	All active	

TABLE 8.27   vNetwork Distributed Switch Port Group Properties—dvSwitch1

Properties	Default Setting	Revised Setting
Security: promiscuous mode	Reject	
Security: MAC address changes	Accept	Reject
Security: forged transmits	Accept	Reject
Ingress traffic shaping: status	Disabled	
Egress traffic shaping: status	Disabled	
VLAN	VLAN trunking	<VLAN ID>
Teaming and failover: load balancing	Route based on originating virtual port ID	
Teaming and failover: failover detection	Link status only	
Teaming and failover: notify switches	Yes	
Teaming and failover: failback	Yes	No
Teaming and failover: failover order	All active	

TABLE 8.28   Network Adapter Assignments

Adapter	Physical Adapter	vSS/vDS	Speed	Function
VMNIC0	On-board adapter 1 Port 1	dvSwitch0	1000 Auto	Management (active) VMkernel vMotion (standby) VM Guest (active)
VMNIC1	On-board adapter 1 Port 2	dvSwitch1	1000 Auto	iSCSI vmk2
VMNIC2	On-board adapter 2 Port 1	dvSwitch0	1000 Auto	VM Guest (active)
VMNIC3	On-board adapter 2 Port 2	dvSwitch1	1000 Auto	iSCSI vmk3
VMNIC4	PCI adapter 1 Port 1	dvSwitch0	1000 Auto	Management (active) VMkernel vMotion (standby) VM Guest (active)
VMNIC5	PCI adapter 1 Port 2	dvSwitch1	1000 Auto	iSCSI vmk4
VMNIC6	PCI adapter 2 Port 1	dvSwitch0	1000 Auto	VM Guest (active)
VMNIC7	PCI adapter 2 Port 2	dvSwitch1	1000 Auto	iSCSI vmk5

8.4.6 Shared Storage Logical Design

Datastore sizing and storage array configuration structure the shared storage logical design. Let's take a look at how that is happening.

8.4.6.1 Datastore Sizing

A Dell Compellent storage array will host the datastores used by VCD. To provide flexibility in this initial deployment, a small number of standard-sized logical unit numbers (LUNs) will be allocated. With Compellent, storage profiles are managed through data tiering among redundant array of independent disk (RAID) and drive types. This can be applied to LUNs, allowing configuration of storage performance grades within VCD, shown in Table 8.29.

8.4.6.2 Storage Array Configuration

The chosen storage array for the purpose of this chapter will use the resource clusters in the Dell Compellent. Table 8.30 summarizes the specifications of this array. Table 8.31 provides additional details of the datastores that are available to the management cluster and provides details of the name, size, and purpose of the datastore.

TABLE 8.29   Datastore Profiles and Sizing—Resource Cluster

Profile	Description	Number of Datastores	Size
Gold	Untiered, default to RAID 10	2	2 TB
Silver	Default Compellent tiered profile	2	2 TB

TABLE 8.30   Storage Array Specifications—Resource Cluster

Attribute	Specification
Storage vendors	Dell Compellent
Storage models	
Storage type	iSCSI storage area network
Array type	Active–Active (Path policy: Round-Robin)
Firmware	
Number of switches	2 (redundant)
Number of ports per host per switch	4
Storage area network zoning	Single initiator zoning
LUN masking	Available to all hosts within a given cluster
LUN sizes	Gold: 2 TB, silver: 2 TB
LUN quantities	Gold: 2, silver: 2

TABLE 8.31   Shared Storage Datastore Summary—Resource Cluster

Cluster	Datastore Name	Size	Purpose
vCloud	BASS-PROD_VCD-Gold01	2 TB	RAID10 Storage Profile
vCloud	BASS-PROD_VCD-Gold02	2 TB	RAID10 Storage Profile Auto
vCloud	BASS-PROD_VCD-Silver01	2 TB	Default Tiered Storage Profile
vCloud	BASS-PROD_VCD-Silver02	2 TB	Default Tiered Storage Profile

8.5 VMware vCLOUD PROVIDER DESIGN

A key tenet of the cloud architecture is resource pooling and abstraction of virtualized resources from an underlying vSphere infrastructure. VCD provides a number of constructs that map to vSphere resources, shown in Table 8.32. Figure 8.3 illustrates the VCD relationships.

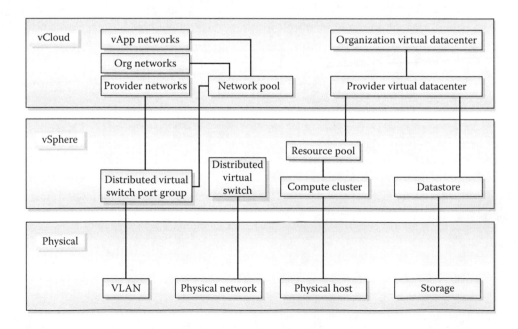

FIGURE 8.3   VCD abstract layer diagram.

TABLE 8.32   VCD Constructs—Overview

VCD Construct	Description
Provider virtual data center	Logical group of vSphere compute resources (attached vSphere cluster and one or more datastores) to provide cloud resources to consumers
Organization	A unit of administration that represents a logical collection of users, groups, and computing resources. It also serves as a security boundary from which only users of a particular organization can deploy workloads and have visibility into such workloads in the cloud. In the simplest term, an organization is an association of related end consumers
Organization virtual data center	Subset allocation of a provider virtual data center's resources assigned to an organization, backed by a vCenter resource pool automatically created by VCD. An organization virtual data center allocates resources using one of three models: • Pay as you go • Reservation • Allocation
External network	A network that connects to the outside using an existing vSphere network port group
Organization network	A network visible within an organization—an external organization network with connectivity to an external network using a direct or routed connection, or an internal network visible only to vApps within the organization
Network pool	Set of preallocated networks that VCD can draw upon as needed to create private networks and NAT-routed networks
vApp	Preconfigured container of one or more VMs and vApp networks
vApp network	Network visible within a vApp—connected to other vApp networks within an organization using a direct or routed connection, or an internal network visible only to VMs within the vApp
vApp templates and media catalogs	Collection of available services for consumption. Catalogs contain vApp templates (preconfigured containers of one or more VMs) and/or media (independent system operator images of operating systems)

8.5.1 Provider Virtual Data Centers

A provider virtual data center is a construct in VCD that maps to a vSphere cluster or resource pool and one or more datastores. Table 8.33 summarizes the provider virtual data centers that are created.

To access vSphere compute resources from within VCD, there is a requirement to allocate one or more vCenter Servers to VCD. In conjunction with vCenter Server, there is a requirement to allocate a corresponding vCNS Manager that provides the enhanced virtual networking capabilities of VCD. Table 8.34 provides the details of the vCenter Server and vCNS Manager instances allocated to VCD for this design.

TABLE 8.33   Provider Virtual Data Center Summary

Virtual Data Center	Purpose
vCloud01	Initial vSphere cluster

TABLE 8.34   VCD Allocated vCenter Server and vCNS Manager

vCenter Server	vCNS Edge	Description
VCD-MGMT-VCTR	VCD-VCNS01	Dedicated vCenter Server and vCNS Manager for resources

TABLE 8.35   Provider Virtual Data Center Configuration

Virtual Data Center	vCenter Server	Cluster	Datastores
vCloud01	VCD-MGMT-VCTR	vCloud	BASS-PROD_VCD-Gold01 BASS-PROD_VCD-Gold02 BASS-PROD_VCD-Silver01 BASS-PROD_VCD-Silver02

Provider virtual data centers comprise central processing unit (CPU), memory, and storage resources in the form of a vSphere cluster or resource pool. Table 8.35 details the configuration of each of the provider virtual data centers previously listed.

8.5.2 Organizations

An organization represents a collection of end consumers, groups, and computing resources. Users authenticate at the organization level, using credentials established by an organization administrator locally within VCD or lightweight directory access protocol (LDAP). LDAP integration is performed at the cloud system level or per organization. Table 8.36 provides a summary of the organizations that are created. Tables 8.37 through 8.39 provide detailed information regarding the configuration of each of the previously listed organizations.

8.5.3 Organization Virtual Data Centers

An organization virtual data center allocates resources from a provider virtual data center and makes it available for use by a given organization. Multiple organization virtual data centers can consume resources from the same provider virtual data center. An organization can have multiple organization virtual data centers. Resources are allocated from a provider virtual data center and to an organization virtual data center using one of three resource allocation models:

TABLE 8.36   Summary of the Organizations

Organization Name	Full Name	Publish Catalogs	Description
General	General-purpose vApps	Yes	General purpose for application
Education	Training	Yes	Training and certification
ExternalLab	External lab access	Yes	External access to single VM lab vApps

TABLE 8.37   Organization Specifics—General

Attribute	Value
Organization name	General
Organization full name	General-purpose vApps
Description	
LDAP option	VCD system LDAP service
Local users (name/role)	Administrator (org admin)
Catalog publishing	Yes
E-mail preferences	Use system default simple mail transfer protocol server
Notification settings	Customer product group
Policies (leases)	
vApp maximum runtime/storage lease	14 days/21 days
vApp storage cleanup	Move to expired items
vApp template maximum storage lease	Never expire
vApp template storage cleanup	Move to expired items
Policies (quotas)	
Running VM quota	Unlimited
Stored VM quota	Unlimited
Policies (limits)	
Resource-intensive operations per user	Unlimited
Resource-intensive operations per organization	Unlimited
Simultaneous connections per VM	Unlimited

TABLE 8.38   Organization Specifics—Education

Attribute	Value
Organization name	Education
Organization full name	Training and certification
Description	
LDAP option	VCD system LDAP service
Local users (name/role)	Administrator (org admin)
Catalog publishing	Yes
E-mail preferences	Use system default simple mail transfer protocol server
Notification settings	Customer product group
Policies (leases)	
vApp maximum runtime/storage lease	7 days/10 days
vApp storage cleanup	Move to expired items
vApp template maximum storage lease	Never expire
vApp template storage cleanup	Move to expired items
Policies (quotas)	
Running VM quota	Unlimited
Stored VM quota	Unlimited
Policies (limits)	
Resource-intensive operations per user	Unlimited
Resource-intensive operations per organization	Unlimited
Simultaneous connections per VM	Unlimited

TABLE 8.39   Organization Specifics—ExternalLab

Attribute	Value
Organization name	ExternalLab
Organization full name	External lab access
Description	
LDAP option	VCD system LDAP service
Local users (name/role)	Administrator (org admin)
Catalog publishing	Yes
E-mail preferences	Use system default simple mail transfer protocol server
Notification settings	Customer product group
Policies (leases)	
vApp maximum runtime/storage lease	14 days/21 days
vApp storage cleanup	Move to expired items
vApp template maximum storage lease	Never expire
vApp template storage cleanup	Move to expired items
Policies (quotas)	
Running VM quota	Unlimited
Stored VM quota	Unlimited
Policies (limits)	
Resource-intensive operations per user	Unlimited
Resource-intensive operations per organization	Unlimited
Simultaneous connections per VM	Unlimited

- *Pay as you go*: Resources are reserved and committed for vApps only as vApps are created. There is no upfront reservation of resources.

- *Allocation*: A baseline amount (guaranteed) of resources from the provider virtual data center is reserved for the organization virtual data center's exclusive use. Additional resources are available to oversubscribe CPU and memory, but this taps into compute resources that are shared by other organization virtual data centers, drawing from the provider virtual data center.

- *Reservation*: All resources assigned to the organization virtual data center are reserved exclusively for its use.

It is common practice that the first organization virtual data center to be created is an administration organization virtual data center for use by the administration organization. The allocation model is set to pay as you go to avoid taking resources from other organization virtual data centers until they are needed. Subsequent organization virtual data centers are created to provide resources for consumers, illustrated in Table 8.40.

Organization virtual data centers comprise CPU, memory, and storage resources in the form of an allocated subset of the resources available from an underlying provider virtual data center. Tables 8.41 and 8.42 provide details of the configuration of each of the organization virtual data centers previously listed. Table 8.41 provides details of the compute resources to

TABLE 8.40   Organization Virtual Data Center Summary

Organization Virtual Data Center	Organization	Provider VDC	Allocation Model	Additional Information
External Lab-Gold	ExternalLab	vCloud01	Pay-as-you-go	Gold storage profile
EDU-Silver	Education	vCloud01	Reservation	Silver storage profile
General-Silver	General	vCloud01	Pay-as-you-go	On-demand general-purpose vApps, silver storage profile

TABLE 8.41   Organization Virtual Data Center Configuration (Compute Resource)

tbd-Organization Virtual Data Center	CPU Allocation (GHz)	CPU Speed (GHz)	CPU (%)	Memory (GB)	Memory (%)
External Lab-Gold	tbd	tbd	50	tbd	50
EDU-Silver	tbd	tbd	100	tbd	100
General-Silver	tbd	tbd	50	tbd	50

TABLE 8.42   Organization Virtual Data Center Configuration (Disk and Network Resource)

Organization Virtual Data Center	Disk Limit (TB)	Thin	Network Pool	Network Quota	Enabled
External Lab-Gold	Unlimited	Yes	netpool_01	50	Yes
EDU-Silver	Unlimited	Yes	netpool_01	50	Yes
General-Silver	Unlimited	Yes	netpool_01	50	Yes

be allocated to each organization virtual data center in the form of CPU allocation (GHz), CPU speed and guarantee (%), memory allocation (GB) and guarantee (%), and VM quota.

In addition to the allocation of compute resources (CPU and memory), the configuration of an organization virtual data center also dictates the storage and network resources available to an organization. Table 8.42 expands the information provided in Table 8.41 to provide details of the storage and network resources to be allocated to each organization virtual data center as a storage limit (TB), thin provisioning support, network pool, network quota, and whether the organization is initially enabled or disabled.

8.5.4 Networks

External networks provide connectivity to networks outside an organization with an existing preconfigured vSphere port group.

8.5.4.1 Network Pools

VCD creates a private network as needed from a pool of networks to facilitate communication between VMs and NAT-routed networks. VCD supports one of three methods to back network pools:

- vSphere port group backed
- VLAN backed
- VCD-NI backed

TABLE 8.43   Network Pool Summary

Network Pool Name	Number of VLANs	Backing Type	Description
netpool_01	200	VLAN	Network pool to be leveraged for all customers

TABLE 8.44   Network Pools (VLAN Backed)

Network Pool	vDS	Description
netpool_01	dvSwitch0	Network pool shared by all organizations

vSphere port group-backed network pools use one or more existing, preconfigured vSphere networks to create virtual organization or vApp networks. The networks themselves can have VLAN tagging for additional security. VLAN-backed network pools are similar to port group-backed networks, with the exception that the vSphere port groups are dynamically created using a preallocated set of VLANs. VCD-NI-backed network pools automatically create internal networks using MAC-in-MAC encapsulation.

As port group-backed pools require additional manual configuration effort, and VCD-NI pools require upstream switch MTU changes. The alternative is to use VLAN-backed pools, shown in this design. Table 8.43 provides a summary of the network pools that are created for this design. Table 8.44 provides a detailed information regarding the configuration of each of the previously listed network pools.

8.6 vCLOUD DIRECTOR

Section 8.6 composes VCD setup, standardization, monitoring, and logging. For this design, we will leverage a kick start-based Red Hat installation processes to maintain consistency of the installation and configuration processes for VCD cells and, following the installation of the first VCD cell, the responses; the properties file is used during the installation process to help enforce further consistency.

Monitoring is performed with custom queries to VCD using the Admin API to get the consumption data on the different components. Some of the components in VCD can also be monitored by log aggregating the Syslog-generated logs from the different VCD cells found on the centralized log server. Table 8.45 summarizes the VCD items to monitor.

Logging is a key component in any infrastructure. It provides audit trails for user log-in and log-out events among other important functions. Logging records various events happening in the servers and helps to diagnose problems, detect unauthorized access, and identify other issues. In some cases, regular log analysis should be conducted proactively to discover problems that might turn out to be critical to the business.

Each VCD cell logs audit messages to the database in which they are retained for 90 days by default. If logs must be retained longer than 90 days, centralized logging

TABLE 8.45   VCD Monitoring—Items Summary

Scope	Item
System	Leases
	Quotas
	Limits
vSphere resources	CPU
	Memory
	Network IP address pool
	Storage free space
VMs/vApps	Scope defined in later chapter

is required. To address this requirement, the VCD cells are configured to forward messages to an existing Syslog server.

8.7 MAINTENANCE TASKS

To perform VCD database maintenance, all VCD cells must be gracefully shut down before bringing the database down. This flushes all in-flight transactions and writes changes to the database. VCD cells are stateless in nature; hence, there is little maintenance required, other than ensuring that the underlying Red Hat Enterprise Linux installation is correctly patched and maintained. To handle maintenance cycles in the management clusters and resource groups, it is critical to maintain all clusters provisioned for at least one host failure. This allows vCenter Update Manager to keep the ESX hosts updated and to handle host maintenance.

8.7.1 VMware vCloud Recovery Considerations

To evaluate component resiliency, consider the total component failure and how to recover from it. VCD has redundancy built into it that makes it resilient to individual component failure. If a total site failure occurs, these steps must be taken to be able to recover. The VCD database is the single most critical component in the system. Recovery of other failed components is pointless if the database cannot be recovered. Consequently, it is critical that a high service level agreement be associated with the hardware supporting the database. It is also critical that regular backups be taken to reduce recovery point objective (RPO) as VCD is a very dynamic system.

Unlike the VCD database, VCD cells are stateless and interchangeable. Encryption keys, passwords, and certificates are used by the cells that must be stored safely. The main files that must be protected are the certificates associated with the HTTP and Proxy interfaces as well as the responses, the properties file created during the installation of the first cell.

Each vCenter Server managing resource clusters has an associated vCNS Manager. vCNS Manager is responsible for storing and pushing out configuration changes to all the vCNS Edge devices that it deploys on behalf of VCD. To recover a failed vCNS Manager, restore a saved configuration back into a newly deployed vCNS Manager.

To enable automatic backups, log in to the vCNS Manager Web interface. Under Settings and Reports, enter the required data under Configuration > Backups. A daily backup might suffice depending on the RPO organizations for vCNS but consider an hourly backup to capture changes in a highly dynamic VCD environment.

Active Directory is used as the authentication repository. Therefore, an lightweight directory interchange format backup of the schema must be taken often to be able to recover user authentication data.

The vCenter single sign-on (SSO) service must be available to authenticate VCD users. Should the configuration of this service become corrupted and permanently unavailable, VCD may be unrecoverable. The vCenter SSO service can be protected by making regular backups of the SSO database and by generating a backup bundle using the "sso-backup.wsf" script file.

8.8 SUMMARY

With the implementation of VMware vCloud Suite, the foundation for IaaS will be built, and it is essential for delivering these use cases. Deploying vCloud Suite will drastically improve the operational efficiency of those environments, in addition to streamlining their ongoing support and management.

The core components of the vCloud Suite are vSphere and VCD. These components create pools of servers, storage, and networking with dynamically configurable security, availability, and management services, which help realize the agility, efficiency, and intelligent operations management of cloud computing. The vCloud Suite of software will allow an organization to provide a highly automated and scalable service that will permit users to self-provision and manage their own systems. It also reduces the burden of an IT organization for managing those systems.

This design specifies the requirement for two vSphere clusters: an existing production cluster that will be used to host management components and a new two-node cluster that will serve as the initial resource cluster. For this design, there will be a single vSphere site, with no secondary or DR sites in scope. In addition, the vCenter Server will be deployed as a VM within the management cluster to isolate it from the resource cluster it will be managing.

A single VCD cell will be deployed to provide access to the VCD environment. A single provider VDC will also be created in VCD to manage all resources in the cluster. Three organizations will be created to control access to vCloud environment and allocate resources to the use cases. In addition, three organization VDCs will be created to segregate the various resource allocation models being used.

By leveraging vCloud Suite, an IT department will be able to deliver IaaS functionality to the business and increase the overall performance, management efficiency, availability, and recoverability of the test, development, and training infrastructure. Don't just collect all metrics; use the analytics to make informed decisions. What machines haven't been powered on in the last 30, 60, 90 days? Tools and alarms will help an admin sort through all the data to continually reengineer the VPC environment. Encourage good behavior by instituting a variable for how long a user can have access to a resource before it is taken offline. A VPC must remain as elastic as a public cloud and reclaim as often as new resources are being provisioned. Make informed decisions so that users realize the cost of resources they use in an effort to continue to expend and utilize a VPC environment.

CHAPTER 9

Security in the Virtual Private Cloud

Daniel Ching Wa

CONTENTS

9.1 INTRODUCTION

Cloud computing is perceived as a breakthrough in service delivery through information technology (IT). It is a paradox (Ahmed et al., 2012) such that computers become exponentially more powerful every quarter on one hand, whereas the unit cost of computing continues to drop materially in terms of manufacturing and operation rapidly on the other hand. Computing power is largely a commodity and utility resembling the supply of water, electricity, and gas (Durkee, 2010). Structurally, computing resources are pervasive within and outside companies. The increasing complexity of provision and executing the infrastructure of disparate information architectures and distributed data and software renders the cost of computing more expensive than ever before. Cloud computing is expected to provide the functionality of contemporary IT services. It could dramatically eliminate the upfront costs of computing so that medium-sized organizations can install cutting-edge IT services in a shared manner (Jadeja & Modi, 2012). The impetus for this change is perceived predominantly from a costs perspective, instead of functionality and performance.

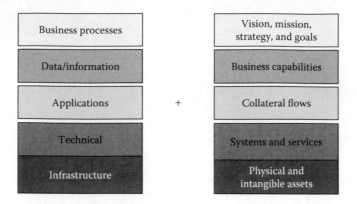

FIGURE 9.1   Merging of IT efficiency and business agility.

Many small- and medium-sized companies shortly discover a situation of underutilization of bygone capital investments in IT. Even, similar situation is pertinent in the maintenance and service costs of paid internal IT infrastructure as well. This overconsumes scarce corporate resources.

The benefit of cloud computing is a convergence of two major trends in IT (Keahey et al., 2008; Marston et al., 2011). The first is IT efficiency such that the power of modern computers is utilized more efficiently through highly scalable hardware and software resources; and the second is business agility through a better instantiation of IT to act as a competitive tool through rapid deployment, parallel batch processing, use of compute-intensive business analytics, and interactive mobile applications that respond in real time to user requirements (Figure 9.1). IT efficiency takes hold of ideas encapsulated in green computing and long-distance internet. Computing resources are executed more efficiently so that the physical computers are physically located in geographical areas able to access to electricity of lower cost. Renewal energy is employed. Business agility expects more than just cheap computing. It facilitates a commercial operation through configurable computational tools able to be deployed and scaled rapidly. Small upfront investment in IT is a key feature in this perspective.

9.2 EVOLVING VIRTUAL PRIVATE CLOUD

It is observed that a widespread adoption of cloud computing is noted in public web services and general batch-style applications, such as those instant messaging tools and social media. Many enterprises are skeptical in accepting cloud computing as a viable choice to maintain mission critical processes. Here are many reasons behind and a case study can illustrate the problem area. One good example is to consider an enterprise grade's accounting information application composed of a client program in desktop personal computing, an intermediate business logic processing layer, and a back-end enterprise database (Lee, 2012). There are private and sensitive business data, which are regulated under a public authority from a local government. Traditionally, this sensitive accounting control business application runs in a secure private computing environment encapsulated within the boundary of the prescribed enterprise physically. A high cost of installation, implementation, and maintenance is attached, and this hinders small companies to buy in.

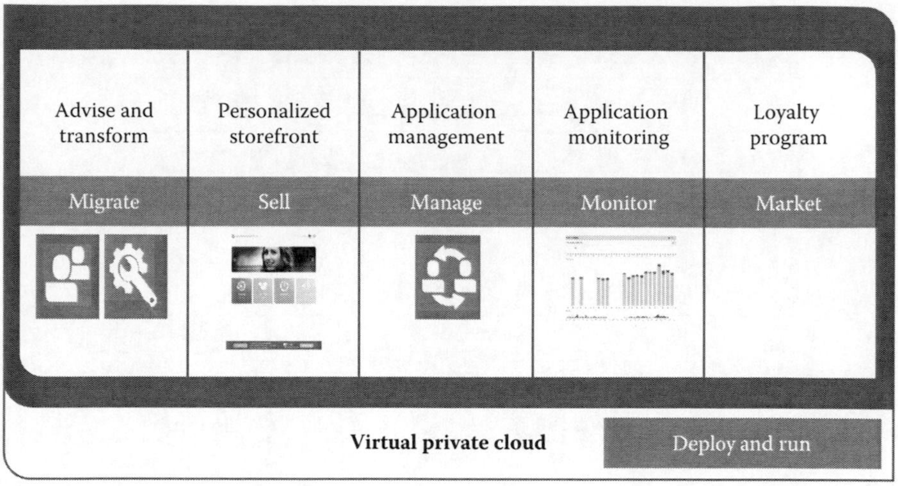

Advise and transform	Personalized storefront	Application management	Application monitoring	Loyalty program
Migrate	Sell	Manage	Monitor	Market

Virtual private cloud — Deploy and run

FIGURE 9.2   Virtual private cloud.

If organizations now relocate this critical information processing component to a cloud computing data center, which is situated outside a company's physical boundary, for the sake of higher scalability in functionality, better efficiency and performance, and a drastic reduction in provision and running IT costs, two immediate questions surface (Porwal et al., 2012; Sabahi, 2011). One is the level of data security in external cloud computing data center, and the other one is how to fulfill stringent local regulatory compliance.

An innovation breakthrough is private cloud (Chaves et al., 2011), which colocates all cloud computing equipment in a company's premise (Figure 9.2). Virtual private cloud is a substantiation of virtualization technology in cloud computing such that every single piece of internal computing resources is shared instantly. It is branded with automated provisioning and self-services. Key features of virtual private clouds are mentioned as follows:

- *High transparency in resources provisioning*: Companies could easily provision and deploy self-created virtual machines in the virtual private cloud (Beach, 2014; Krautheim, 2009) to run mission-critical applications. All virtual machines in the virtual private cloud and the associated components are running within the boundaries of enterprises. All of them are allocated public Internet Protocol addresses for establishing dedicated network connectivity with internal systems and external counterparts. Virtual private cloud is deemed to have an automated provisioning capability to install necessary and bare minimum changes against existing information infrastructure to facilitate a seamless connectivity between external access and private internal resources. No modification is needed for those business application codes to cater for this new virtual private cloud topology.

- *High security awareness*: The auto-provisioning and deployment of virtual private cloud resources demand more than just attaching computing resources to a company's internal network. This vulnerability is mitigated through the use of dedicated

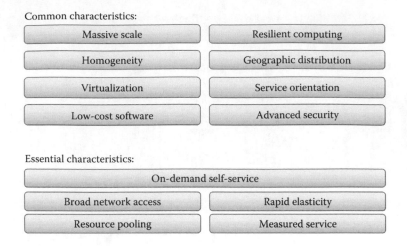

Common characteristics:

Massive scale	Resilient computing
Homogeneity	Geographic distribution
Virtualization	Service orientation
Low-cost software	Advanced security

Essential characteristics:

On-demand self-service	
Broad network access	Rapid elasticity
Resource pooling	Measured service

FIGURE 9.3   Configurable cloud resources.

secure channels webbing authorized virtual private cloud nodes to both internal counterparts and external parties. Firewall rules and router switching rules are configured dynamically when virtual private cloud components are created. Fine-grained access controls are expected in firewall and network switching equipment. Dynamicity in the virtual private cloud system (Chaves et al., 2011; Doelitzscher et al., 2011; Moghaddam et al., 2011) could expose security holes in internal networks if misconfigured. Therefore, a strong self-checking mechanism is expected in the virtual private cloud framework.

- *Flexible and highly configurable computing resources*: A major drive to migrate business critical applications from an internal network to a virtual private cloud is the simple configuration (Figure 9.3) and reallocation (Sotomayor et al., 2009; Wood et al., 2009) of computing resources in a company's infrastructures. Corporates can transfer any processing computing components from fixed internal networks to the virtual private cloud. New replicas can be built on demand. Common Internet Protocol address is a key winning capability in the virtual private cloud. Nonetheless, special network traffic labeling is embedded to facilitate a fine-grained traffic control.

9.3 TECHNOLOGY BEHIND THE VIRTUAL PRIVATE CLOUD

There is not a single and consistent definition of the virtual private cloud. It is naturally resorting to the authoritative sources on cloud computing. The US National Institute of Standards and Technology (NIST) offers a solid and self-improving framework for cloud computing in general (Jansen & Grance, 2011; Mell & Grance, 2011). It includes the associated service-oriented models, such as infrastructure as a service (IaaS), platform as a service (PaaS), and software as a service (SaaS). There are the deployment models of private, community, public, and hybrid clouds.

Private cloud (Beach, 2014; Krautheim, 2009; Moghaddam et al., 2011; Sotomayor et al., 2009; Wood et al., 2009) describes the cloud infrastructure dedicated for a company such that all cloud management is performed on-premise; community cloud is shared by several companies belonging to a particular community having shared concerns, such as security requirements, policy, or compliance mandates; public cloud is bestowed toward general public or a mega industry group; hybrid cloud comprises two or more cloud deployment models, such as private, community, or public clouds, bundled through a standardized or proprietary technology to facilitate a high portability of data and business applications. Cloud bursting is advocated.

Unfortunately, there is no formal description on the virtual private cloud. In current cloud provider marketplaces, two companies officially offer virtual private cloud services: Amazon Virtual Private Cloud and IBM SoftLayer (Beach, 2014; Wood et al., 2009). Ideally, virtual private cloud describes a cloud infrastructure being executed solely for an enterprise, and it could be a subset of another larger cloud infrastructure coming from private, community, or public cloud resources.

A virtual private cloud involves a virtual partition (Figure 9.4), instead of being physically separated from another set of larger cloud deployment. Both Amazon VPC and OpSource present respective virtual private clouds through the foundation of virtual private network (VPN) (Doelitzscher et al., 2011; Krautheim, 2009; Wood et al., 2009). Shifting encryption is adopted at the network traffic layer to facilitate a strong mechanism in implementing this virtual cloud partitioning. In addition to VPN, virtual local area network provides an additional virtualization capability to construct the VPN. Virtual machines from various virtual private clouds are not running on the same physical computing resources.

Structurally, virtual private cloud is part of another larger cloud infrastructure. Physical infrastructure could be shared in previous NIST deployment models. Privacy could be a potential issue in the virtual private cloud.

Learning through example, is a preferred way to understand a new concept. Amazon VPC starts with the networking layer. An Amazon VPC instantiation is tied to a registered Amazon Web Services user account, which is managed by an organization administration. Through specific coding at network and hardware layers, this VPN is labeled as an isolated landscape from other virtual private clouds in the same cloud infrastructure. Through automatic or manual configuration, Internet Protocol addresses, subnets, routing tables, gateways, user security, authentication, authorization, and access controls are defined in the context of

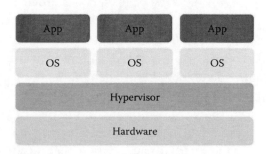

FIGURE 9.4   Virtual partitioning.

a particular virtual private cloud system. A subnet is a specific range of Internet Protocol addresses restricted to a particular virtual private cloud. Therefore, a company's internal and external networks can make use of different Internet Protocol subnets to connect various virtual private clouds to other systems on the Internet and internal infrastructures. All data traffic is encapsulated in nonrepudiated virtual private cloud labels. Multiple layers of security, security groups, and network access control lists are defined to enhance the resilience and security in the virtual private cloud. All users of Amazon VPC can create respective virtual private clouds tagged against a universally unique Amazon Web Services ID. All are configurable items at user choices, and this instantiates the uniqueness of each Amazon VPC created.

A dedicated and well-regulated Internet gateway is used to provide well-controlled network segments and dynamic subnets. This provides a direct and well-monitored communication channel between user-configured Amazon VPC and the Internet.

9.4 VIRTUAL PRIVATE CLOUD MITIGATION ON KEY ISSUES

Cloud computing is a new IT (from academics to commercial enterprises) since the coming of the millennia. Early adopters of this new technology and business paradigm face with insufficient security controls leading to commercial loss in data breaching and information leakage. Key security issues are grouped into several big categories (Beach, 2014; Porwal et al., 2012; Sotomayor et al., 2009): trust, architecture, identity management, software isolation, data protection, and availability. Cloud computing is an amalgamation of technologies from service-oriented architecture, virtualization, web technology, and utility computing. Substantially numbers of the security issues surface when blending different technologies together. Unlike conventional internal enterprise information system of which the native company boundary protects all processes and data, cloud computing stresses on sharing and multitenancy. A thought-provoking paradigm shift is deemed to deperimeterize the previous organizational infrastructure, and displace system and business applications. Here is the detailed elaboration of security issues that can be mitigated through the virtual private cloud.

9.4.1 Trust

When a company subscribes to cloud computing services, the organization releases all direct controls over certain security aspects. This demands an unprecedented level of trust from the cloud computing users onto the cloud services providers. After migrating from the internal IT landscape to the cloud ecosystem, business applications and data are processed and stored outside the walls of a company. Cloud landscape's firewall and other security controls take the company to a next level of inherited risk.

Insider threat is a renowned vulnerability in many companies. Cloud service is a share-oriented approach. Multitenancy dictates cloud subscribers to share computing resources and store them in a single instance of computing infrastructure. This act of outsourcing internal business processes and data operation to external cloud services violates the trust level normally bestowed in the internal platform. Further, insider threats can extend to current or former employees, company affiliates, contractors, and those having access to a company's enterprise networks. Numerous cases happen around involving fraud, sabotage, espionage, and information theft. One famous case is customer data theft in Tesco leading to senior management's stepdown.

Virtual private cloud locates within the company's premises such that conventional security measures and controls can be reused. All virtual private cloud accesses happen within the office boundary such that inherited trust on the traditional information system applies to the virtual private cloud.

9.4.2 Composite Services

Cloud computing environment does not follow the conventional information system design to have everything constructed for the stakeholder in concern. It is mashed in nature. Cloud computing operators compose their services and product offerings through nesting and layering with peer cloud operators. One good example is a SaaS company constructing the products and services offering through bundling the services and products from PaaS and IaaS providers. Dynamic subcontracting through third-party service providers is common in cloud computing. Moreover, security controls over third parties and accountabilities raise concerns.

Trust is not transitive from primary cloud operators to third-party subcontractors. Service-level agreements could be a remedy for this situation. Virtual private cloud is the ultimate trust generator because all cloud services and products are confined in subscribers' premises. Liability and performance assurance can be closely monitored with guarantee.

9.4.3 Visibility

A loss of internal control happens when a company moves all internal process and data to subscribed cloud services. This raises security alerts in securing companies' systems, business applications, customer data, and confidential organization data. Those shortfalls in security, management, procedural controls, and technical controls should be fixed with new external systems.

Virtual private cloud is housed in a company's premise. Management can solicit high visibility in the security of indoor virtual private clouds. Network and system-level monitoring happens in office premises. Policy and procedures can be enforced instantly due to high proximity in the virtual private cloud. This applies to software system life cycle, security controls, and third-party subcontractors' processes.

9.4.4 Risk Management

Public and community clouds sit outside the boundary of subscribers. Direct controls are loosened to cause a big issue in risk management. Business management would feel comfortable with anticipated risks, if they can exert higher and more controls over systems and business processes, confidential data, and equipment. Virtual private cloud maintains tight controls in the hands of company management. This high degree of control offers options to weigh alternatives, set priorities, and act decisively.

Virtual private cloud provides a conventional mentality for internal control persons to assess and manage various risks. The system landscape in the virtual private cloud and

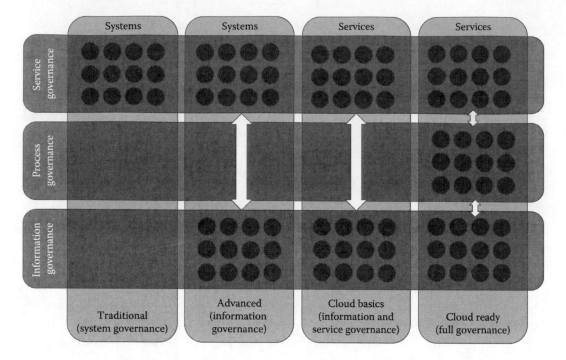

FIGURE 9.5   Cloud internal controls.

conventional technology systems are similar. Internal control officers (Figure 9.5) can verify the functioning of cloud-based subsystems simply. This enhances the effectiveness of security controls extensively because virtual private cloud is similar to internal enterprise business systems.

9.5 NEXT STEPS IN VIRTUAL PRIVATE CLOUD

Virtual private cloud is a new evolution in cloud computing. Some critical developments are noted (Beach, 2014; Moghaddam et al., 2011; Wood et al., 2009), and the details are as follows:

- *Architecture*: In a common cloud computing architecture, all systems components reside on the Internet to provide services to cloud computing subscribers. Only the cloud services provide know the actual physical locations of the associated cloud infrastructure. Virtual private cloud moves back to subscribers' premises and utilizes external resources for scale-up requirements. This enhances the reliability and scalability logic of the underlying framework. Secure virtual machines are the construction units in the virtual private cloud for quick deployment across the company's borders. Systems and business applications in the virtual pirate cloud employ Internet-accessible interfaces to ensure quick adaption.

- *Attack surface*: Hypervisor or virtual machine monitor (Figure 9.6) is an additional software piece to run multitenancy such that all virtual machines and subscribers

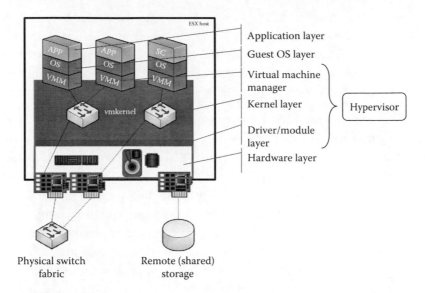

FIGURE 9.6 Hypervisor attack surface.

can run in isolated environments without the chance of compromise. In the virtual private cloud, hypervisors offer administrative operations, such as launching, migrating, and terminating VM instances, in addition to housing the clients' environments. Secure virtual machines are encrypted through the subscribers' identity. Hypervisor's bare metal nature imposes a new attack surface. Hackers can take over the hypervisor instantly. In the virtual private cloud, multitenancy is used to run multiple clients' processes and data in a single instance. Hypervisor security exposure is minimized.

- *Software virtualization of network and storage*: Software virtualization is a new trend in conventional hardware-dominated areas, including networking equipment and storage. This new technological trend offers the ability to generate instant configurable network switches and routers, which facilitate a quick provision of cloud-based resources. Virtual private cloud is a blend of Internet-based cloud resources and internal technology resources. Inflexibility is noted in manually reconfiguring all physical networking devices and storage when activating the virtual private cloud environment. Software virtualization facilitates a quick adjustment to computing resources, network connections, and cloud storage when relocating components in the virtual private cloud.

- *Client-side defense*: Substantial works move back to the company's premises through the virtual private cloud. Conventional cloud front ends use web browsers only, but virtual private cloud allows more business applications to run on the native mode to access virtual private cloud resources. Full-scale end-point client security must be upheld, and this can be achieved through well-proven personal computer security tools. Nonetheless, continuous updates of security patches are recommended to avoid exposure to unknown vulnerabilities. New client architecture in the virtual private cloud should be empowered to cater for increasing the availability and use of social media, personal e-mail and web mail, and publicly available sites. Numerous risks might impair the security of the virtual private cloud's front-end architecture. The conventional procedure of security hardening can be adopted in this perspective to prevent unsolicited keystroke logging.

- *Identity management*: Cloud computing generates substantial concerns in data sensitivity and privacy of information. Unauthorized access and wrong authentication are two primary concerns. In the virtual private cloud, a strong identification and authentication framework must exist to provide a secure and robust operational landscape. There are key components in the virtual private cloud: the indoor internal cloud infrastructure of a subscriber and the compliment Internet-based cloud resources. Identity federation is a new approach to handle this special identity management requirement. Security Assertion Markup Language (SAML) is adopted in many cloud operators to perform authentication. This tool simplifies the administrative works in user administration and authentication. SAML serves as a medium of exchange security information, such as assertions related to a subject or authentication information, between cooperating domains. Related request and response messages are mirrored over the Simple Object Access Protocol.

- *Access control*: Authentication is a way to verify the truth identity of cloud computing subscribers and users. There is a need to adapt user privileges and controls over access to cloud resources. Access control is a core complement to identity management discussed previously. One particular standard surfaced is eXtensible Access Control Markup Language (XACML) for steering access to cloud resources. XACML (Figure 9.7) offers a mechanism of making authorization decisions and transferring decisions of both authentication and authorization across entities. High security measures are installed to ensure XACML to safeguard from unauthorized disclosure, replay, deletion, and modification.

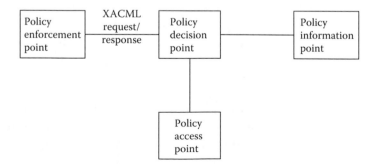

FIGURE 9.7 XACML.

9.6 SUMMARY

Virtual private cloud evolves naturally in cloud computing landscape to address risks, vulnerabilities, and business concerns in public and community clouds. Private cloud attempts to address the security gaps in the emerging cloud computing architecture. This innovative approach takes the best of internal enterprise systems and cost advantages of the cloud computing framework, which can advocate a high adoption of cloud computing. More development in the virtual private cloud can be noted in the following areas: virtual partitioning, fine-grained privacy level, configurable security, and access controls.

REFERENCES

Ahmed, M., Chowdhury, A., Ahmed, M., & Rafee, M. M. H. (2012). An advanced survey on cloud computing and state-of-the-art research issues. *IJCSI International Journal of Computer Science Issues, 9*(1), 1694–0814.

Beach, B. (2014). Virtual Private Cloud. In *Pro Powershell for Amazon Web Services* (pp. 67–88). Springer.

Chaves, D., Aparecida, S., Uriarte, R. B., & Westphall, C. B. (2011). Toward an architecture for monitoring private clouds. *IEEE Communications Magazine, 49*(12), 130–137.

Doelitzscher, F., Sulistio, A., Reich, C., Kuijs, H., & Wolf, D. (2011). Private cloud for collaboration and e-Learning services: From IaaS to SaaS. *Computing, 91*(1), 23–42.

Durkee, D. (2010). Why cloud computing will never be free. *Queue, 8*(4), 20.

Jadeja, Y., & Modi, K. (2012). Cloud computing-concepts, architecture and challenges. Paper presented at the 2012 International Conference on Computing, Electronics and Electrical Technologies (ICCEET).

Jansen, W., & Grance, T. (2011). Guidelines on security and privacy in public cloud computing. *NIST Special Publication, 800*, 144.

Keahey, K., Figueiredo, R., Fortes, J., Freeman, T., & Tsugawa, M. (2008). Science clouds: Early experiences in cloud computing for scientific applications. *Cloud Computing and Applications, 2008*, 825–830.

Krautheim, F. J. (2009). Private virtual infrastructure for cloud computing. *Proceedings of HotCloud*.

Lee, K. (2012). Security threats in cloud computing environments. *International Journal of Security and Its Applications, 6*(4), 25–32.

Marston, S., Li, Z., Bandyopadhyay, S., Zhang, J., & Ghalsasi, A. (2011). Cloud computing—The business perspective. *Decision Support Systems, 51*(1), 176–189.

Mell, P., & Grance, T. (2011). The NIST definition of cloud computing.

Moghaddam, F. F., Cheriet, M., & Nguyen, K. K. (2011). Low carbon virtual private clouds. Paper presented at the 2011 IEEE International Conference on Cloud Computing (CLOUD).

Porwal, A., Maheshwari, R., Pal, B., & Kakhani, G. (2012). An approach for secure data transmission in private cloud. *International Journal of Soft Computing and Engineering (IJSCE) ISSN*, 2231–2307.

Sabahi, F. (2011). Cloud computing security threats and responses. Paper presented at the 2011 IEEE 3rd International Conference on Communication Software and Networks (ICCSN).

Sotomayor, B., Montero, R. S., Llorente, I. M., & Foster, I. (2009). Virtual infrastructure management in private and hybrid clouds. *IEEE Internet Computing, 13*(5), 14–22.

Wood, T., Gerber, A., Ramakrishnan, K., Shenoy, P., & Van der Merwe, J. (2009). The case for enterprise-ready virtual private clouds. *Usenix HotCloud*.

III

Implementing Security in a Private Cloud

CHAPTER 10

The Hybrid Cloud Alternative

Daniel Ching Wa

CONTENTS

10.1 INTRODUCTION

Authoritative definition of cloud computing comes from the US National Institute of Standards and Technology (NIST) shown in Figure 10.1. It defines four models (Mell and Grance, 2011) of cloud deployment models: public cloud, private cloud, and hybrid cloud and community cloud.

Public cloud deployment framework facilitates all subscribers' access to cloud computing systems through a simple and intuitive user interface. It could be a web browser on a desktop personal computer or a smartphone. Meter-based payment is configured to allow users to pay as the business go. No deposit or fixed fee is included. Access and usage are controlled on time slots allocated. The paradigm of utility billing, as in water and electricity, can be found in the cloud computing ecosystem. In the end, the high information technology expense can be minimized. Moreover, public cloud deployment is vulnerable to the issue of security at large. Both applications and data situated in the public cloud infrastructure is prone to malicious software attacks aiming to steal information for profit. Security checking and validation must be upheld to mitigate this big risk. Further, strong identity management must be in place in subscribers' internal systems and shared external cloud servers to ensure no leakage of confidential data. Tight security measurements should not, however, impair the operation efficiency.

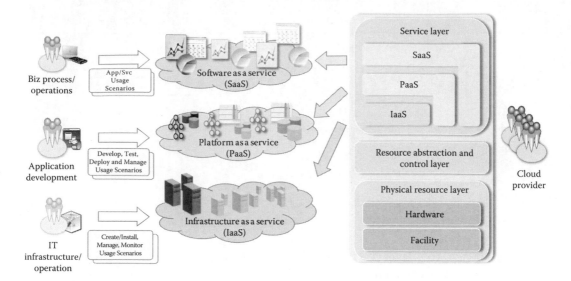

FIGURE 10.1   NIST cloud architecture (www.nist.org).

Private cloud, on the contrary, is a cloud computing system running in the subscriber organization's office or isolated data center. Apparently, this private cloud model is good for management in security, maintenance, upgrades, deployment, and other uses. This model is similar to intranet. Public cloud owns all computing resources, systems, and business applications, which are shared among all subscribers on the Internet; private cloud operators pool all cloud computing resources to be available for all users of subscribers. The cloud computing resources are presumed to be controlled by a subscriber organization. Definitely, security is at high position, because only subscribers' users can access the respective hired private cloud.

Community cloud is a social project in which companies jointly construct and use a common cloud computing infrastructure. Common requirements and policies form the backbone in the community cloud model. This community cloud infrastructure might be in a member's premise or shared on a third-party premise.

Hybrid cloud gets the name through a combination of public cloud and private cloud (Géczy et al., 2013). Inside this cloud, a private cloud system is connected to one or more external public cloud services through secure channels. This can maintain the high confidentiality in the private cloud; it is a secure way to control company data, systems, and business applications; and the subscriber can enjoy the flexibility in allowing the third-party access to own data and systems hosted in the respective private cloud.

10.2 WHY HYBRID CLOUD

Many enterprises are moving their internal enterprise systems to the cloud computing infrastructure these days. Private cloud gives good security feature (Ramgovind et al., 2010); whereas public cloud delivers low costs. The adopters of the private cloud go for enhanced security in order to meet compliance requirements. Users of the public cloud enjoy a high degree of flexibility, scalability, and low cost. Sooner or later, many business owners, especially

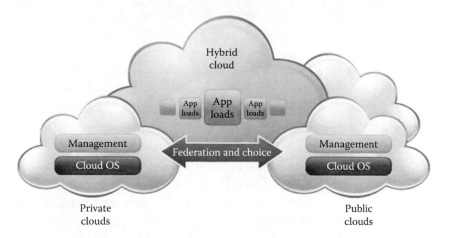

FIGURE 10.2   Hybrid cloud.

small and medium-sized companies, realize that not all of their information assets are mission critical. Hybrid cloud (Figure 10.2) is an emerging substream in this cloud computing movement so as to capture the best features in the private and public clouds.

In general commercial operation, many basic processes and applications show a peak workload when running in internal information systems. The scalability and quick provision of the public cloud saves a substantial cost of expanding the internal information systems. Nonetheless, there are sensitive and critical assets demanding top security offered in a private cloud. Hybrid cloud computing architecture is a natural option to address this pressing business needs. This can strike a balance from high security and compliance to flexibility and low costs.

Many cloud implementations are expanding their operation such that there is a growing demand to mesh up different cloud systems. This can improve the bandwidth, scalability, flexibility, and resource utilization. Hybrid cloud architecture (Figure 10.3) bears the aim

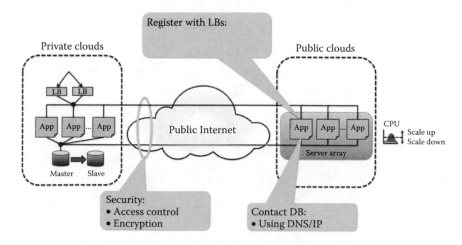

FIGURE 10.3   Hybrid cloud integrating with public and private clouds.

to integrate internal data centers to the external cloud environment. This builds a new horizon in cloud dynamics and scalability (Flores et al., 2011).

When a company, in particular small and medium-sized ones, expects a better higher scalability in operating respective internal data center solutions without compromising security, the dynamicity of the hybrid cloud computing system is the natural solution. It is a smooth transition from public and private clouds to a hybrid cloud system. Further, the metering in the hybrid cloud framework is commonly executed in a consumption-based manner. This pay-on-the-go approach is complemented with automated provisions and procedures.

Architecturally, hybrid cloud operation facilitates subscribing companies to control a continuous exchange of critical and sensitive information between internal information systems and external cloud computing resources (Suresh and Prasad, 2012). There are smart and secure controls exerted at all levels of this exchange. This includes cloud servers and storage, company storage and servers, internal and external networks, and online business's payment gateway.

The emergence of Internet of Things (IoT) is another application of the hybrid cloud framework (Gubbi et al., 2013). IoT can be managed in the public side of the hybrid cloud, and extracted information can be cascaded back to the private side of the hybrid cloud. All communication is handled through the single channel of hybrid cloud operator. Applications can be located in warehousing, transportation, factory equipment, and office building. The hybrid cloud addresses the exponential growth in IoT. High demands in bandwidth, storage, and computing capabilities are catered through the public cloud component of the hybrid cloud operator.

Disaster recovery and business continuity (Mell and Grance, 2009) are inherited in the hybrid cloud architecture (Figure 10.4). It offers a good isolation of handling sensitive and critical workloads. At the same time, a degree of flexibility of functions and performance is built in the hybrid cloud. This facilitates a subscriber to carry out disaster recovery when needed. This enables hybrid cloud users to perform disaster recovery through resources

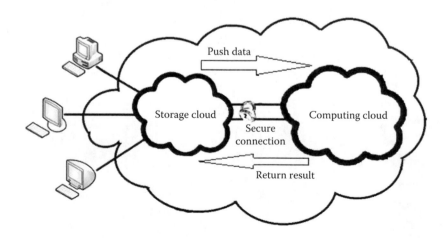

FIGURE 10.4 Hybrid cloud for business continuity.

redeployment in the hybrid cloud framework on one hand and to run the normal business operation on the other hand. This is a true realization of business continuity. Loss is minimized in case of system outage.

Many industry veterans feel comfortable on the concept of the hybrid cloud, and one of them is Oracle's CEO Larry Ellison. He honors the hybrid cloud system facilitating information, which is accessible and independent of devices and locations (Witt III, 2010). This indicates a critical paradigm shift in computing, and a list of some advantages noted is as follows:

- The cost of entry into the cloud computing landscape is low, and this attracts many small and medium-sized companies. Public cloud offers share-based, expensive, and powerful computing resources for intensive business analytics in exchange for low-security confinement. Still, the internal information system gives a high confidence to the corporate management. The debut of the hybrid cloud system offers dynamic provisioning (see Figure 10.5) of computing resources across the internal environment and cloud landscape highly possible.

- Unlike conventional internal information systems, cloud providers give clients an almost immediate access to software and hardware resources. No upfront capital investments and other expenses are demanded. This generates a faster time to market for business and sounds important to small and medium-sized companies. Hybrid cloud is good at extending legacy internal information systems to vast supplies of cloud resources purely at an operational expense. Through strong identity management and multitenancy in cloud technology, all user data and processes are confined in a totally isolated environment. This creates a very adaptive process to all enterprises. If the number of internal users grows substantially, all new demands are

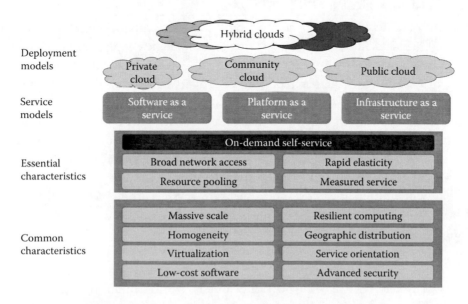

FIGURE 10.5 Hybrid cloud on-demand structure for fast provisioning.

shared through the hybrid cloud's internal resources to deliver a stochastic balance and achieve an economy of scale.

- Hybrid cloud computing allows subscribing enterprises to scale quickly between internal and external systems. All computing resources in the hybrid cloud are configured through software. Quick provision and deployment are fast enough to meet *ad hoc* requirements. There are software programming interfaces in the hybrid computing system to allow more systematic and well-controlled scaling up or down in computing resources.

- In this converging architecture, mobile interactive applications, which are sensitive to the location, environment, and context, could respond quicker in real time to information from sensors monitoring humidity, stress, and independent information services. Hybrid cloud dynamicity allows massive parallel batch processing to dissect terabytes of data in a short period of time. Critical and sensitive data are housed in internal servers, and the complex process data analytics can be performed through parallel execution in external cloud servers through the hybrid cloud framework. The workflow can be controlled through software development as well. This dynamic business analytics expands swiftly through the hybrid cloud landscape to employ a huge amount of computer resources so as to understand customers, buying habits, and supply chains. Hybrid cloud maintains high security through internal controls and offers unlimited computing resources through external computing resources. At large, all clumsy and time-consuming computing are offloaded to cloud servers to fine-tune the availability of network bandwidth and reduce the associated latency for performance.

10.3 DIFFERENCE FROM HYPERVISOR

Virtualization is a key technology supporting the cloud computing platform (Sotomayor et al., 2009). This facilitates low-cost systems and business applications developed to achieve multitenancy. Both on-premise single tenant or cloud-based multitenant can enjoy the quick provisioning through virtualization. This is being considered as a viable and alternative route to conventional multitenancy.

In the hybrid cloud environment, virtualization can separate computing resources and services from the underlying physical hardware of delivery. Virtual systems can be created and run under a single physical system housed in the hybrid cloud infrastructure. The core objective of virtualization is the consolidation of physical hardware for the sake of technology operation efficiency and higher cost savings. There are few characteristics in virtualization complementing the operation of hybrid cloud computing (Sotomayor et al., 2009):

- *Partitioning*: Data, applications, and operating systems are confined in a single physical system but are being portioned out as hybrid cloud resources, according to subscribed terms and conditions.

- *Isolation*: In virtualization, there are many virtual machines in isolation from hosting physical hardware. A physical mechanism of isolation applies to provide virtual machines from a crash in a particular virtual machine. Data are not shared in this isolation model, and thus, it is a guarantee of integrity and consistency (see Figure 10.6).

- *Encapsulation*: In virtualization, all virtual machines are stored and represented as a single file. Therefore, hybrid cloud administration can identify the operations easily. This encapsulation framework (Figure 10.7) could protect subscriber's data, systems, and business applications seamlessly.

- *Server virtualization*: One physical server in the hybrid cloud infrastructure is partitioned into several multiple virtual servers. Random access memory, central processing unit, hard disk, and network controller are virtualized at the same time for all virtual machines to run each subscriber's data, systems, and business applications.

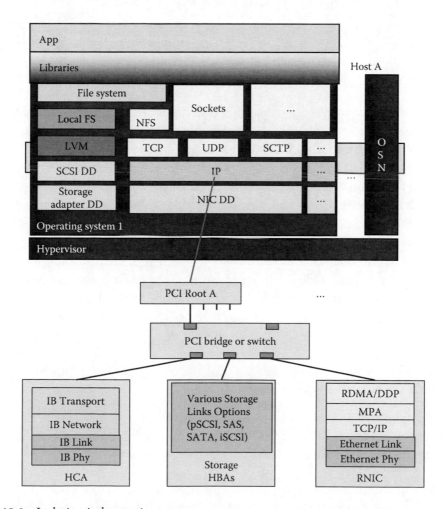

FIGURE 10.6   Isolation in hypervisor.

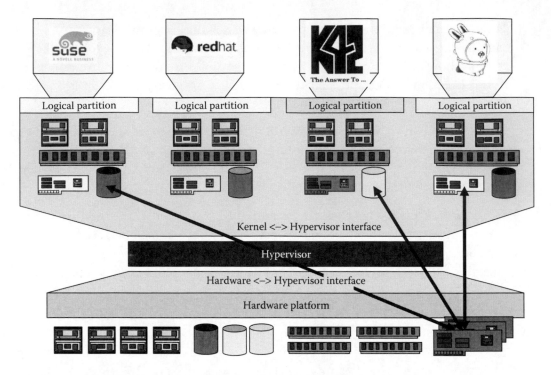

FIGURE 10.7   Encapsulation through hypervisor partitioning.

In course of virtualization development for hybrid cloud infrastructure, hypervisor evolves from server virtualization worthy of discussion. Hypervisor is a piece of software directly communicating with all hardware, including computing, network, and storage devices. It acts as a representative of multiple operating systems from hybrid cloud subscribers to share a single cloud hardware host. Function wise, it acts as a traffic cop to ensure a smooth concurrent access of all virtualized instances to access the physical host in an orderly manner. Physically, hypervisor is located at the lowest levels of the hosted hardware and employs a thin layer of software code to enable dynamic resource sharing. Owing to the fact that there are so many different operating environments in the hybrid cloud computing landscape, hypervisor is bestowed as an ideal delivery channel. The scope of a hypervisor is to emulate the functions of underlying hardware platforms without the hassle of physically copying data, systems, and business applications onto the hosting hardware. There are basically two kinds of hypervisors currently running in the hybrid cloud ecosystem (Seshadri et al., 2007):

- Type 1 hypervisor executes directly on the hosting hardware in order to achieve higher efficiency. This is a bare metal approach.

- Type 2 hypervisor relies on the hosting operating system. This is an emulation approach. The key benefit is the ability to cope with different kinds of input–output devices demanded from clients.

The beauty of a hypervisor is to carry all weight-lifting works. All hybrid cloud applications and data are running in virtual and isolated partitions. High protection and resiliency are observed. Hypervisor serves similar function as in virtualization, but acts faster, quicker, directly communicating with bare metal, and resources efficient. Hybrid cloud infrastructure uses more hypervisors on the server side.

10.4 TREND IN HYBRID CLOUD

A cloud computing paradigm has less than two decades of history. Public and community clouds are pioneers owing to the instant adoption of open-source development sectors. Gradually, it moves into the corporate arena leading to the debut of the private cloud. Unfortunately, the cost tag is huge to hinder the adoption of small and medium-sized companies. Hybrid cloud evolves to blend the best from both public and private clouds. This new development (Li et al., 2013) happens less than 3 years, and the trends observed in a hybrid computing landscape are discussed in Sections 10.4.1 through 10.4.3.

10.4.1 Administration Agent

Big hybrid cloud infrastructure vendors, such as Amazon® EC2, Microsoft® Azure, and Rackspace®, offer a simple and flexible system management interface to swiftly reallocate workloads and processing capacity from the existing on-premise applications to the hybrid cloud's resources out on the Internet. Boutique cloud technology firms, such as SolarWinds®, giving agentless systems and application monitoring for both on-premise information system and servers and applications situated in the public area of the hybrid cloud environment. This hybrid cloud administration agent integrates well with firewall, network bandwidth, and other security measures. Hybrid cloud disregards the location of the internal and external infrastructures. This integrated and simple administration agent is able to monitor servers, data, systems, and applications across the hybrid cloud ecosystem. SolarWinds is a good example of this emergent hybrid cloud development. It can handle thousands of hardware, networks, operating systems, data, and application monitoring. Its application monitoring system has the ability to discover available measurements and metrics in custom-made applications through the use of various protocols. No scripting is needed. Military standard Federal Information Processing Standards (FIPS)-compatible 2048 bit transport layer security (TLS) encryption is employed to protect all communications across the hybrid cloud environment.

10.4.2 Up-to-Date Inventory

Hybrid cloud landscape is composed of internal systems and internet equipment. Some are virtual devices created only in a time period. A new approach of technology inventory is adopted such that all records of resource sharing are kept for auditing. This includes the actual sharing and partition information. Those recordings can be used for capacity management.

10.4.3 Big Data, IoT, and Mobility

They create exponential data through mobile devices. Bring your own device (BYOD) blurs the division between the company and personal data. This fits into a blended mode of the hybrid cloud in which a company's internal information systems merge with the public cloud and personal facilities. Mobile devices inject increasing numbers of new data acquisition points causing a fragmentation in public and enterprise clouds and enterprise cloud segments. Ramping demands happen in areas, such as database as a service. Soon or later, a ubiquitous approach appears to result in a generalized "as-a-service" model. This is the ultimate goal of a hybrid cloud framework. Increasing the adoption of big data, IoT, and mobile devices is positioned as major drivers for increasing the adoption of hybrid cloud services in the medium term. They are ubiquitous in nature. Many modern businesses lay out policies for BYOD and social media, and install sensors around the companies. In sum, an explosion of mobile, structured, and unstructured data happens, and the hybrid cloud system is the ideal platform for the planning and swift execution.

More and more companies realize shortcoming in virtualization and the importance of private cloud computing to enterprise customers. In the short run, enterprises are paving the way toward a full-scale private cloud capability. When business processes, systems, and business applications, have to go hand in hand with (and adjusting for) ever-changing commercials (so as to reap instant and quantifiable monetary benefits), cloud services operators should be able to take a quantum leap (change) in service offerings. Hybrid cloud ecosystem starts with a combination of public and private clouds. There is a self-evolving mechanism in the hybrid cloud infrastructure to constantly develop to maintain a good integrating ability for business processes and legacy applications. In turn, the hybrid cloud model gives a unique competitive advantage to subscribing organizations through dynamic workload rebalancing between in-house facility and public cloud resources. No capital investment is required.

Taking a short and a medium term, the hybrid cloud will mingle more intensively with big data, IoT, and mobility. An explosive requirement is happening to connect internal systems to the public cloud environment through a hybrid cloud infrastructure. Later, in-house systems and business applications should be designed and validated as "hybrid cloud ready." In the long run, a possible way of environment consolidation could happen to make all internal systems to be pluggable with the public cloud infrastructure. Hybrid cloud interface is a default feature in all new internal information systems.

10.5 OPENSTACK: HYBRID CLOUD PIONEER

OpenStack is originated from a pilot development in the US National Aeronautics and Space Administration aiming to provide a dynamic, flexible, and scalable platform for massive information processing (Sefraoui et al., 2012). Hybrid cloud is designed to span across different cloud deployment models. OpenStack has options for private and public clouds. OpenStack private cloud runs natively with OpenStack public cloud to form the hybrid cloud option. Further, OpenStack cloud operator has a native interface with non-OpenStack cloud operator, such as Amazon Web Services. Technically speaking, OpenStack is inherited as a universal connector for any kind of public cloud operators to construct the dynamic hybrid cloud architecture.

OpenStack launches various hybrid cloud constructions for disaster recovery, business continuity, development and testing, and federation with the community cloud. Thus, allowing cloud users to exchange information, systems and business applications across different cloud computing providers.

In OpenStack design, the hybrid cloud bears an aim to support legacy systems in short term and mobilizes a transition to the general cloud landscape. Hybrid cloud design caters for internal systems that are not fully controlled by an internal information system architect. Hardware, software, and application programming interfaces of the third-party cloud systems have to align with the existing OpenStack cloud landscape. The architecture in OpenStack-based systems has an effect on the cloud operator and consumer's ability to work natively. OpenStack tools exist to provide all necessary functionalities to connect internal information systems to the OpenStack cloud environment.

There is an OpenStack cloud management platform (CMP) to manage both internal and external cloud systems, users, operators, and consumers. The CMP can log in to Internet resources to instantly form a public cloud instance. This dynamicity is a critical feature of the OpenStack hybrid cloud architecture.

OpenStack is extensible through the third party's commercially available products. The paradigm of OpenStack dictates that there is no single CMP able to meet the needs of all hybrid cloud uses under all scenarios. Innately, hybrid cloud deployment generates complex scenarios for both business and technology personnel. Special care should be taken to mitigate the incompatibility between workloads and cloud architecture. Smooth integration across different cloud providers is the highest priority. Continuous cloud monitoring is a critical aspect to implement in hybrid cloud installation. Exploring insight into a different cloud technology is needed to create a holistic view of all components for hybrid cloud models. Application programming interfaces provide a dynamic management layer for the hybrid cloud administrator to automate the mobilization of hybrid cloud components within OpenStack landscape.

Application and system agility should be assured when implementing the OpenStack hybrid cloud. This allows a higher availability in resources for deploying all cloud instances such that each component in the OpenStack hybrid cloud quickly spins up cloud instances to solve capacity issues, such as complete unavailability of a single cloud instantiation.

Application readiness is an automated item in the OpenStack hybrid cloud. Enterprise workloads have a dependency on the underlying cloud infrastructure for availability. Hybrid cloud workloads are designed to handle fault tolerance. Generically, hybrid cloud applications are coded to recover if entire racks, and/or data centers, and/or full infrastructure show outage.

Seamless component upgrade is built inside the OpenStack hybrid cloud. Close-to-zero disruption is anticipated through incremental changes. Auto-rollback is available for failure recovery.

Good maintainability is a mandate requirement for the OpenStack hybrid cloud. There are substantial participations of the third-party systems, processes, and applications. Hybrid controls involve heterogeneous controls that could cause the maintainability issue. OpenStack develops some automation components to enhance system maintainability.

In the OpenStack hybrid cloud, most workloads are stored through the instances in hypervisor technology. There is a challenge in hypervisors not able to open and read all images in the hybrid cloud. The underlying reason is that the OpenStack hybrid cloud is composed of a heterogeneous cloud architecture. Therefore, standardization of a hypervisor-compatible image format must be done to ensure a smooth integration in the hybrid cloud.

Network service is a key constructor when building a hybrid cloud architecture. Scalability is another critical factor in forming the underlying hybrid cloud framework. High availability of the hybrid cloud should be considered at the same time. The common approaches adopted in OpenStack implementations are active–hot standby, active–passive, and active–active.

Security is a prerequisite in the course of constructing an OpenStack hybrid cloud. Data traffic must be secured across the cloud front end, cloud computing resources, and other end points. All business and regulatory requirements must be considered and fulfilled in the hybrid cloud.

Hybrid cloud demands mature backup and restore mechanism. Data replication is the best way of protecting object stores in the hybrid cloud infrastructure. There are synchronous and asynchronous mirroring commonly employed to keep object stores in back-end storage systems.

Data integrity and data availability are the second tier of consideration in hybrid cloud data protection. Here, it has to admit that replication strategy influences the disaster recovery method. Natively, replication should be viable across different cloud racks, data centers, and geographical regions. This enhances the value of data locality, which improves data accessibility from the nearest or fastest storage next to hybrid cloud systems and business applications. Nonetheless, extra data replication should be avoided for unnecessary performance issues.

10.6 SUMMARY

Hybrid cloud is a promising option to address practical business concerns. Current public and private cloud solutions can only handle isolated business situations. Continuous merger and acquisition complicate business landscape to demand a quick provision and deployment approach. Hybrid cloud is a blend of all known cloud technologies. OpenStack is an open source to realize this paradigm of hybrid cloud.

REFERENCES

Flores, H., Srirama, S. N., and Paniagua, C. (2011). A generic middleware framework for handling process intensive hybrid cloud services from mobiles. Paper presented at the Proceedings of the 9th International Conference on Advances in Mobile Computing and Multimedia.

Géczy, P., Izumi, N., and Hasida, K. (2013). Hybrid cloud management: Foundations and strategies. *Review of Business and Finance Studies*, 4(1), 37–50.

Gubbi, J., Buyya, R., Marusic, S., and Palaniswami, M. (2013). Internet of Things (IoT): A vision, architectural elements, and future directions. *Future Generation Computer Systems*, 29(7), 1645–1660.

Li, Q., Wang, Z.-y., Li, W.-h., Li, J., Wang, C., and Du, R.-y. (2013). Applications integration in a hybrid cloud computing environment: Modelling and platform. *Enterprise Information Systems*, 7(3), 237–271.

Mell, P., and Grance, T. (2009). Effectively and securely using the cloud computing paradigm. *NIST, Information Technology Laboratory*, 304–311.

Mell, P., and Grance, T. (2011). The NIST definition of cloud computing.

Ramgovind, S., Eloff, M. M., and Smith, E. (2010). The management of security in cloud computing. Paper presented at the Information Security for South Africa (ISSA).

Sefraoui, O., Aissaoui, M., and Eleuldj, M. (2012). OpenStack: Toward an open-source solution for cloud computing. *International Journal of Computer Applications, 55*(3), 38–42.

Seshadri, A., Luk, M., Qu, N., and Perrig, A. (2007). SecVisor: A tiny hypervisor to provide lifetime kernel code integrity for commodity OSes. *ACM SIGOPS Operating Systems Review, 41*(6), 335–350.

Sotomayor, B., Montero, R. S., Llorente, I. M., and Foster, I. (2009). Virtual infrastructure management in private and hybrid clouds. *IEEE Internet Computing, 13*(5), 14–22.

Suresh, K., and Prasad, K. (2012). Security issues and security algorithms in cloud computing. *International Journal of Advanced Research in Computer Science and Software Engineering, 2*(10).

Witt III, W. F. (2010). Keep your feet on the ground when moving software into the cloud. *JDCTA, 4*(2), 10–17.

CHAPTER 11

Identification and Privacy in the Secure Cloud

Sarbari Gupta

CONTENTS

11.1 INTRODUCTION

When a system is hosted in the cloud, every user is by definition a "remote" user. Normal as well as privileged users have to authenticate their digital/online identity to the system over a shared public medium such as the Internet (when the system resides in the public cloud) or a medium that is shared within a community (when the system resides within a community cloud). Once the user's authenticated identity is established with a certain level of confidence or assurance, the system provides the user access to the functions and features of the system based on the roles and privileges authorized for that identity. Thus, establishing the identity of the user is the foundation for determining the user's access to the data and services provided by the system.

In the modern-day world, we are often required to share our personally identifiable information (PII) with other parties in order to establish our identity or to obtain certain types of services. For example, to obtain services from a health-care service provider, we will typically need to share a great deal of PII to allow the health-care provider to arrive at an appropriate diagnosis; the provider may also generate an additional PII through his or her diagnoses and diagnostic test results. When such services are provided through a cloud-based system, there are many benefits as well as drawbacks. For example, the personal data are more easily shared with other service providers (such as health-care providers) who need access to the data quickly. However, the user loses control over his or her personal data—the accuracy of the data, the aggregation of the data, what the data are used for, and whom the data are being shared with. The fact that most cloud systems have multiple parties who contribute to the administration and provisioning of the services makes privacy controls quite a bit more challenging in such systems.

11.2 IDENTITY IN THE CLOUD

This section discusses the concept of identity authentication and its implication for cloud systems. It also discusses the fundamentals of identity in the cloud, the concept of identity assurance, and the considerations for selection of identity authentication technologies and models for the cloud.

11.2.1 Fundamentals

There exist a wide variety of identity authentication mechanisms that can be used with cloud systems. There are three widely accepted factors of authentication:

- Something you know—such as a secret or a passphrase

- Something you have—such as a key or a badge

- Something you are—such as your fingerprint or your facial image

Single-factor authentication involves the use of one of the three factors, whereas multifactor authentication involves the use of two or even three factors of authentication. Recent advances and availability of other technologies enable the use of other nonstandard factors to augment the level of assurance of authentication—for example, reliable global positioning system data or computer network address may serve to further strengthen an authentication performed using one or more of the classic factors. The most prevalent identity authentication mechanism involves the use of a username and password combination—the user establishes a username for his or her identity and a shared secret (password) that is known only to the user and the system. Every time that user returns to that target system, he or she proves his or her identity by being able to provide his or her username and the matching password. At some point, the user may need to change his or her password or retire his or her use of that username/password pair.

An entity that issues and maintains digital identities and credentials for users is called an identity provider. The set of processes involved in supporting the life cycle phases of digital identity is called digital identity management. The life cycle phases of a digital identity include the following:

- *Identity proofing and registration*—The user provides proof of his or her identity through available documentation.

- *Token and credential issuance*—Following identity proofing and registration, the identity provider and user establish a token that allows the user to authenticate his or her identity. In this context, a token is something that is controlled by the user and contains a secret that allows the user to prove his or her identity to an identity provider. The identity provider may also establish a credential that binds the user's identity to the token.

- *Identity authentication and usage*—The token and credential are used multiple times by the user to authenticate his or her digital identity and obtain services from one or more online service providers.

- *Token and credential management*—The token and credential may need updates to account for usage periods, loss, corruption, or replacement. These management activities are performed by the identity provider as needed.

- *Identity decommissioning*—The user's digital identity and the related token and credential are terminated when no longer needed or when the life term of the identity has been reached. As a part of the retirement phase, the token and credential need to be destroyed effectively so that they cannot be reused.

11.2.2 Identity Authentication Assurance

The National Institute of Standards and Technology (NIST) Special Publication (SP) 800-63-2 provides guidelines for electronic authentication for US federal government information systems and contains widely recognized principles for online authentication. This publication asserts that the assurance level of an online remote authentication process is the low watermark of the assurance level of five component processes:

1. *Identity proofing*: The techniques and methods by which the user establishes his or her identity to the identity provider. Possible options with decreasing levels of assurance include in-person identity proofing with government-issued identity documentation, remote identity proofing using notary services, online identity proofing using knowledge-based questions and answers, and self-proclaimed identity.

2. *Token*: The types of technology used for the token has a great impact on the overall assurance of the identity authentication activity. Possible token types defined by

SP 800-63-2 with increasing levels of assurance include Memorized Secret Token; Pre-registered Knowledge; Look-up Secret Token; Out of Band Token; Single-factor One-Time Password Device; Single-factor Cryptographic Device; Multi-factor Software Cryptographic Token; Multi-factor One-Time Password Device, and Multi-factor Cryptographic Device. It may be noted that NIST SP 800-63-2 does not recognize a biometric (metrics related to human characteristics) as a secret suitable for remote authentication over a shared network but allows the use of biometrics to unlock another local token (such as a cryptographic device), which can then be used for remote authentication to an online system. However, many other communities have effectively used biometric factors for remote authentication after conducting a risk assessment and applying appropriate risk mitigation techniques.

3. *Token and credential management*: The processes by which tokens and related credentials are managed through the identity management life cycle have an impact on the assurance of the identity. These processes include initial issuance and reissuance of tokens and credentials, renewal of credentials, revocation prior to the end of term, and final decommissioning. The rigor of these processes and the extent to which they are resistant to typical threats determine the assurance of the token and credential management processes.

4. *Communication protocols*: Remote authentication (such as to cloud systems) requires the use of communication protocols between the user, the service provider, and potentially other parties such as identity providers and attribute providers. The strength of the protocols being used between the various parties and their resistance to online attacks determine the assurance level of the authentication process. Strong protocols include properly implemented Secure Sockets Layer and Transport Layer Security, whereas weak protocols include unencrypted channels over which sensitive data such as passwords are exchanged.

5. *Assertions*: Identity authentication serves a very useful purpose for establishing the identity of the user. However, in many cases, the service provider needs additional information associated with the identity (such as the role and membership status) in order to make decisions regarding the access privileges that the user should be granted. Assertions are statements about an identity that provide additional information to facilitate authorization and access control decisions. Assertions are sent from a source to the service provider that can review the assertions to make authorization decisions. The techniques for assembling, transmitting, and protecting the assertion (such as with encryption and/or digital signature) determine the assurance level of the assertion and contribute toward the assurance of the overall identity authentication process.

11.2.3 Identity Authentication Considerations for Cloud Systems

Cloud providers need to consider a number of dimensions when building and/or selecting their identity authentication implementations. Sections 11.2.3.1 through 11.2.3.5 discuss some of the key considerations, including identity assurance, types of tokens, whether the identities are internal or external to an organization, methods of identity proofing, and techniques for validation of identity credentials.

11.2.3.1 Required Assurance Level

A cloud service provider needs to determine the assurance level of the identity authentication mechanisms it wants to employ. The services provided by the cloud system may vary widely from providing publicly available information based on search criteria to collecting or disseminating the critical information related to national security, banking, or human safety. In order to determine what types of identity authentication technologies and processes are suitable to support the cloud services provided, best practices dictate that cloud service providers should perform an electronic authentication risk assessment (see Office of Management and Budget Memorandum M-04-04 for example) to determine the potential impacts of improper or compromised authentication. Based on the potential impacts, cloud service providers and cloud customers need to adopt identity authentication token types, credentials, and life cycle processes that effectively mitigate the risks arising from erroneous or compromised identity authentication [1].

11.2.3.2 Token Types

Current best practices for cloud systems dictate that administrative and privileged users should use at least two-factor authentication techniques in order to mitigate the risk of a compromised authentication. Regular or unprivileged users of a cloud system may use a variety of authentication tokens and credential types based on the criticality and sensitivity of the data and services provided through the cloud system and the impact of a compromised authentication balanced against cost and usability.

11.2.3.3 Internal or External Identities

Cloud service providers can choose to act as identity providers for their users or to accept digital identity credentials issued by external identity providers. The decision to serve as an identity provider implies that the cloud provider has to support all of the life cycle phases for the identities it manages. Some of these areas are described in Sections 11.2.3.4 and 11.2.3.5. If the cloud service provider elects to accept identities issued by one or more external identity provider(s), then it must implement an effective means for validating these external identity credentials and establishing trust in these credentials as described in Section 11.2.3.5.

11.2.3.4 Identity Proofing

If a cloud service provider selects to serve as an identity provider to its user base, then it must be able to provide a practical mechanism for identity proofing and registration of its users. Medium to high assurance identity credentials require that the user undergo a face-to-face identity proofing step. As cloud service providers are typically not geographically local to their user bases, in-person identity proofing may not be a feasible option. In such circumstances, cloud service providers may need to use digital identity credentials issued by one or more third-party identity provider(s). For each such third-party identity provider, the cloud service provider needs to establish a trust validation mechanism in order to validate the identity credentials issued by the identity provider. This may be challenging in an environment where multiple identity providers using a variety of authentication technologies need to be accepted by the cloud service provider.

11.2.3.5 Credential Validation

When external identity credentials are used to authenticate to a cloud service, the cloud provider must decide which and how many such external identity providers with which to integrate. The cloud provider must also decide whether to accept more than one token and credential technology type—for example, the cloud provider may decide to only accept public key infrastructure credentials as a method of authentication, or it may decide that for some subset of its user bases, it will also accept password-based authentication. For each such type of token and credential technology accepted from an external identity provider, the cloud provider must implement appropriate credential validation systems (such as certificate validation and certificate revocation checking).

11.3 PRIVACY IN THE CLOUD

Despite the new possibilities created through the storage, processing, and sharing of sensitive personal data in the cloud, a host of new concerns and issues arise related to the security and privacy of such data [2]. This section discusses the basic concepts in the realm of privacy and the implications for cloud systems.

11.3.1 Fundamentals

A typical cloud system is managed by multiple providers and administrators at different levels of the application stack. Thus, every piece of information collected, handled, distributed, and stored in a cloud system is potentially accessible to many layers of administrative users from several organizations. Additionally, multitenancy cloud systems host applications and data belonging to multiple customer organizations—the boundaries of protection between the various tenants of the cloud infrastructure are enforced through technical and/or administrative mechanisms which are outside the control of the tenants. Privacy concerns therefore arise with respect to PII collected, handled, and transmitted by the cloud systems as well as new PII generated by the system through interactions with its users. For example, a cloud system that allows the user to purchase medical supplies online will generate PII for the user based on the history of actual purchases made through the system—the data related to purchases made may indicate the types of physical conditions and diseases for that user.

Users are therefore justifiably concerned about the protection of their PII residing or being generated in the cloud. Organizations that are subject to privacy compliance requirements—such as those imposed by the Health Insurance Portability and Accountability Act (HIPAA) over Protected Health Information (PHI)—are also concerned about the protection of the PII handled by the cloud systems used by the organization. Significant penalties may be levied against such organizations for noncompliance with privacy statutes, and legal action may be brought on by end users who have suffered loss of privacy due to a data breach.

11.3.2 Understanding Privacy

Privacy is more than protecting the confidentiality of personal information. The Fair Information Practice Principles (FIPPs) are widely accepted in the United States and internationally as an overall framework for privacy and serve as the basis for analyzing privacy risks and determining appropriate mitigation strategies. The FIPPs also serve as a foundation for establishing trust in the privacy practices of organizations and to help organizations avoid tangible and intangible costs resulting from privacy compromise incidents. The FIPPs embody the following eight core principles:

1. *Transparency*—The reasons for the collection and use of PII must be clearly revealed.

2. *Individual participation*—The individual whose PII is being gathered and used must be able to review the PII and given a chance to correct any inaccuracies.

3. *Purpose specification*—The reasons for the collection and/or use of PII must be clearly articulated.

4. *Data minimization*—The least amount of PII needed to achieve the end purpose must be collected and handled.

5. *Use limitation*—The PII must not be used for purposes other than that for which it was originally gathered.

6. *Data quality and integrity*—The accuracy and currency of the PII must be maintained during the period of use.

7. *Security*—The PII must be provided technical protection during its storage, transmission and use.

8. *Accountability and auditing*—The provider must be held responsible for the proper handling and protection of the PII, and periodic auditing must be performed to determine the level of compliance with the provider's written privacy policies.

The HIPAA Privacy Rule establishes national standards to protect individuals' personal health information and applies to a broad range of organizations that deliver or facilitate the delivery of health-care and conduct transactions electronically. It requires appropriate safeguards to protect the privacy of PHI, sets limits and conditions on the uses and disclosures that may be made of such information without patient authorization, and gives patients the rights to examine and obtain a copy of their health records, and to request corrections.

11.3.3 Privacy Considerations for Cloud Systems

When designing and implementing cloud systems that generate, store, or process sensitive personal data, cloud providers need to consider a number of dimensions in order to best serve their customers while complying with regulatory requirements. Sections 11.3.3.1 through 11.3.3.5 describe several key considerations for such cloud systems.

11.3.3.1 Scope of PII

Cloud providers must determine the scope and extent of PII (if any) that is essential for providing their services. For example, a student financial support cloud service needs to collect a large amount of sensitive personal information for its students and their parents. Even if PII is not necessary for the core services, the cloud provider must closely examine its services to see if PII is collected or generated for one or more of the following reasons:

- *Account management*—The cloud provider may need to collect the basic information about its users in order to establish a local account for the user and deliver services.

- *Personalization*—The cloud provider may collect user information and user preferences in order to provide a more personalized user experience within the cloud system.

- *Transactional data aggregation*—As transactional information builds up through the repeated use of the cloud service by the user, the aggregated information may reveal a personal profile for the user (such as gender, ethnicity, and age group).

11.3.3.2 Privacy Impact Assessment

Once the types of PII handled or generated by the cloud system are identified, a privacy risk assessment should be performed to determine the potential impacts of compromise to the confidentiality, integrity, and availability of such PII handled by the system. Based on the severity of the impact, appropriate technical and process measures must be taken by the cloud provider to mitigate the risks down to an acceptable level. For example, PII may be encrypted while in transit and at rest to protect against confidentiality loss.

11.3.3.3 Compliance Requirements

The cloud provider must identify if there are regulatory and statutory requirements for privacy protection that apply to the types of services it provides. For example, cloud services that support health-care-related functions are subject to the HIPAA Privacy Rule. If regulatory requirements apply, the cloud provider must identify, document, and implement compliance mechanisms.

11.3.3.4 Privacy Policy

As described earlier in the FIPPs, privacy protections are multidimensional in nature. The foundation for sound privacy protection implementation by a cloud service provider is its documented privacy policy. A written description of the privacy policy forces the articulation of privacy practices by the cloud provider and allows the cloud customer to determine whether the privacy policy is adequate for his or her needs. A comprehensive privacy policy must address each principle of the FIPPs. The privacy policy must be published in a manner that is easily available to its user population. Ideally, it must be written in plain and easy-to-understand terms.

11.3.3.5 Records Maintenance

The cloud provider must maintain records to prove that it is complying with its published privacy policy. If regular privacy audits are conducted, the resulting audit reports must be maintained. These records may be provided at the request of users or upon legal action.

11.4 SUMMARY

Establishing the identity of the user with a given level of confidence is the foundation for determining the user's access to the data and services provided by the system. A number of considerations are provided for cloud service providers to select the attributes of an identity management approach that serves the needs of the cloud provider as well as its customer base.

Similarly, when cloud service providers handle PII, the user may potentially lose control over his or her personal data—the accuracy of the data, the aggregation of the data, what the data is used for, and whom they are being shared with. The fact that most cloud systems have multiple parties who contribute to the administration and provisioning of the services makes privacy controls quite a bit more challenging in such systems. A number of considerations are provided for cloud providers to develop an effective approach to protecting the privacy of the PII entrusted to them.

REFERENCES

1. Burr, William et al., *NIST Special Publication 800-63-2 Electronic Authentication Guideline*, NIST, 2013.
2. Jansen, Wayne and Grance, Timothy, *NIST Special Publication 800-144 Guidelines on Security and Privacy in Public Cloud Computing*, NIST, 2011.

CHAPTER 12

Private Cloud Security and Identification

Daniel Ching Wa

CONTENTS

12.1 INTRODUCTION

Public and private clouds are dominating the current subscription of cloud computing resources. Users can either enjoy the low cost of shared, fast computing resources in public and community clouds or take advantage of conventional enterprise information system security and controls in the private cloud. Nonetheless, subscriber identity (Bertino et al., 2009) is the key attribute when defining instances in multitenancy. System images (Chun et al., 2011) from virtualizations depend on the subscriber's identity. In the bare metal cloud framework, hypervisor is bounded toward the subscriber's identity as well. The emerging hybrid cloud creates virtual, software-configurable, and dynamically re-deployable cloud computing resources objects through a binding to the subscriber's corporate identity and delegated user identity.

Identification (Olden, 2011) is apparently the cornerstone in the general cloud architecture (Figure 12.1). Owing to all shared nature in the cloud paradigm, information isolation

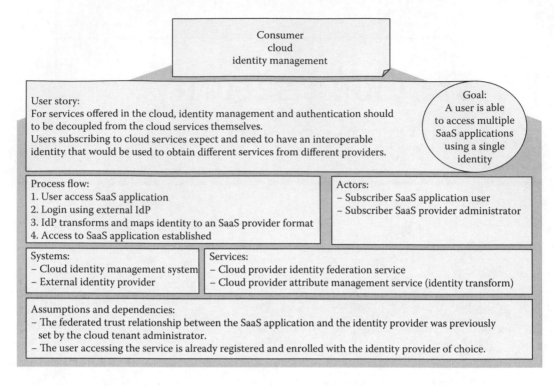

FIGURE 12.1   Cloud identity management. IdP, identity provider.

and privacy are key concerns to cloud operators and users. In this chapter, various identity management and encryption approaches are examined to elaborate the value contribution to the general cloud ecosystem.

12.2 *K*-ANONYMITY FOR IDENTITY AND PRIVACY

Standing from a privacy management point of view, all user identity and associated behavior records should not be uncovered, identified, and singled out in a straightforward manner. The life cycle of data (Gedik and Liu, 2005) is a hierarchy-based generalization algorithm able to classify the captured data in a cloud landscape (Figure 12.2). It can maximize the categorization accuracy and minimize the information loss such that privacy is assured. Common data anonymity algorithm is based on generalization through creating subsets of indistinguishable information segments from the general dataset. There are two main camps of generalization (He and Naughton, 2009): single-dimensional generalization and multidimensional generalization. Alternate ways of anonymizing data are as follows: (1) marginal publication releasing different segments in the concerned dataset onto different subsets of attributes, (2) perturbation swapping values to augment indistinguishability of records, (3) anatomy publishing quasi-identifier values and sensitive attributes in separate tables to minimize the probability of linking attacks, and (4) condensation of which the objective in concern is to release only selected statistics about each quasi-identifier group.

K-anonymity (Sweeney, 2002) first scrutinizes all data that might have inadvertently been revealed leading to anonymity compromise (Figure 12.3). Then categorization

Data life cycle	Privacy principles	Privacy protection measures
Collection/ generation	Proportionality and purpose specification	Data minimization
Storage	Accountability, security measures, sensitive data	Confidentiality
Sharing and processing	Lawfulness and fairness, consent, right of access	Data access control
Deletion	Openness, right to delete	Confidentiality

FIGURE 12.2   Privacy evolution in cloud computing.

Released table

	Race	Birth	Gender	ZIP	Problem
t1	Black	1965	m	0214*	Short breath
t2	Black	1965	m	0214*	chest pain
t3	Black	1965	f	0213*	hypertension
t4	Black	1965	f	0213*	hypertension
t5	Black	1964	f	0213*	obesity
t6	Black	1964	f	0213*	chest pain
t7	White	1964	m	0213*	chest pain
t8	White	1964	m	0213*	obesity
t9	White	1964	m	0213*	Short breath
t10	White	1967	m	0213*	chest pain
t11	White	1967	m	0213*	chest pain

External data source

Name	Birth	Gender	ZIP	Race
Andre	1964	m	02135	White
Beth	1964	f	55410	Black
Carol	1964	f	90210	White
Dan	1967	m	02174	White
Ellen	1968	f	02237	White

Example of *k*-anonymity, where *k*=2 and
Ql = {*Race, Birth, Gender, ZIP*}

FIGURE 12.3   *K*-anonymity tables.

taxonomy is applied on the data to generalize into less informative values. The underlying reason is to mitigate inference attacks. Information loss is minimized through limiting the nodal degree of the tree hierarchy in which the generalization hierarchy is mapped. Trees located at a high nodal degree show both high classification accuracy and high data anonymity, but indicate a higher information loss. High nodal degree having several subvalues tends to have difficulty in showing distinction between values competently. A heuristic approach is suggested to minimize the information loss on one hand and maximize classification accuracy and anonymity on the other hand. This approach (Nergiz et al., 2009) works through bounding each tree's nodal degree with a threshold value. Then an evaluation is done through computing the cost–benefit trade-off between information loss and classification accuracy. In case of information loss higher than a preset threshold, the depth of tree is changed to include a new node. The approach works well on categorical data. Conventionally, categorical data are more apparent in information loss than numerical data.

Data sanitization can then be achieved through *K*-anonymity schemes. It offers an elegant and cost-effective way of not disclosing private information (Figure 12.3) and making the information publishable to the public concurrently. The idea of generalizing data is to develop anonymity in the course of disclosing the same piece of information. The suppression of explicit attributes in the information concerned is not sufficient enough to guarantee anonymity.

K-anonymity is a heuristic implementation (Nergiz et al., 2009; Sweeney, 2002) considering cases of numerical and categorical data and yielding good performance in privacy preservation. *K*-anonymity algorithm is keen on preventing accurate inferences of sensitive attributes. There are variants of *k*-anonymity algorithms developed for computing generalization with minimum information loss. By far, *K*-anonymity is simple to configure and install in all cloud deployment models.

12.3 ELLIPTIC CURVE FOR EFFICIENT KEY

Encryption is a common practice in data protection. It could be in the form of symmetric or asymmetric structure. Speed of coding and decoding is key concern. Elliptic curve (Gampala et al., 2012) is an emerging development in encryption claiming fast execution through small key size (Figure 12.4). It is a class of cubic curves having group laws. It is possible to add points on an elliptic curve such that it is easier to solve discrete logarithm problem over a finite field.

Elliptic curve cryptography (ECC) is a kind of public key cryptography (Hankerson et al., 2006) based on the algebraic structure of elliptic curves over finite fields. One key benefit of non-ECC cryptography, that is, those taking plain (Bailey and Paar, 2001) as a basis, is the achievement of the same level of security through smaller size keys. ECC is good for its smaller key size, which reduces storage and transmission requirements. Compared to other encryption algorithms, a 256-bit ECC public key provides comparable security (Gura et al., 2004; Lauter, 2004; Liu and Ning, 2008) to a 3072-bit Rivest–Shamir–Adleman (RSA) public key. It is applicable for encryption, digital signatures, pseudo-random generators,

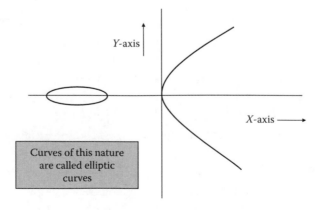

FIGURE 12.4 Elliptic curve.

and confidential tasks. Several integer factorization algorithms, such as (Dixon and Lenstra, 1993), employ elliptic curve.

Public key cryptography (Figure 12.5) uses intractability (Paillier, 1999) of certain mathematical problems. One key-associated problem is difficult to factor a large integer composed of two or more large prime numbers. In elliptic curve-based protocols, there is a major issue (Hankerson and Menezes, 2011) of "elliptic curve discrete logarithm problem" in which there is a limited chance of finding discrete logarithm of a random elliptic curve element with respect to a publicly known base point (Figure 12.6). ECC security capability depends on the functionality to compute a point multiplication and the inability to compute the multiplicand given the original and product points. Therefore, the size of ECC is a control factor of elliptic curve success.

There are several discrete logarithm-based protocols for elliptic curves. One of them is Diffie–Hellman key agreement scheme (Herzog, 2003). Another one is Elliptic Curve Integrated Encryption Scheme or Elliptic Curve Augmented Encryption Scheme, or simply the Elliptic Curve Encryption Scheme (Fujisaki and Okamoto, 1999). Digital Signature Algorithm uses Elliptic Curve Digital Signature Algorithm, whereas Edwards-curve Digital Signature Algorithm uses Schnorr signature (Lee et al., 2001). The US National Security Agency develops Suite B (Law and Solinas, 2007), which is intended to protect both classified and unclassified national security systems and information, exclusively on ECC for digital signature generation and key exchange. Owing to the economy of key size, low computing power, and faster key manipulation, elliptic curve is taking a root in all cloud systems' identity management.

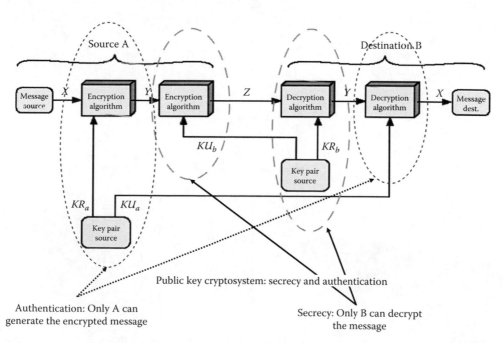

FIGURE 12.5 Public key encryption.

$$y^2 = x^3 - 4/3x + 16/27$$

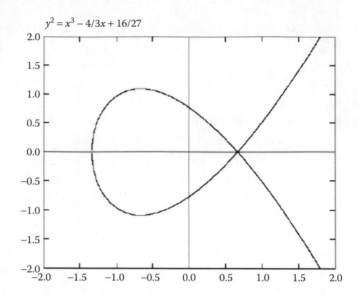

FIGURE 12.6   Elliptic curve solving point.

12.4 HOMOMORPHIC FOR ENCRYPTION ARITHMETIC

One common issue noted in data encryption is the preworks of decrypting before running information processing. When decrypting data for information processing, three issues are exposed: (1) Time of decoding could be very long, if the length of encryption key is more than 1024 bits; (2) huge amount of computing resources in chip and storage are demanded; and (3) the chance of data stealth when processing data after encryption. Homomorphic encryption (Atayero and Feyisetan, 2011) gives a promise to the information process on encrypted information without the need of decrypting it first (Figure 12.7). It is a form

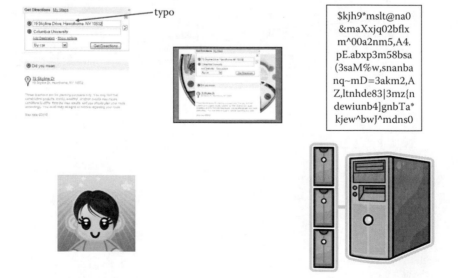

FIGURE 12.7   Homomorphic computing in encryption.

of encryption allowing computations and other information processes on encrypted data objects through cipher text, and then producing an encrypted result. There is no data distortion on the encrypted result and can be verified through decoding. In the public cloud, it is safe to store cryptographically scrambled data objects using a secret key. Moreover, there is no protection during the decoding of an encrypted cloud store object, when executing information processing. Hackers can listen to cloud processing and attack when detecting the process of decryption. Homomorphic encryption is a theoretical advancement to maintain secrets when doing information processing.

Public cloud focuses on low-cost computing resources through equipment sharing such that data protection and encryption are not of priority. Private cloud can deploy common encryption because all processing happens within company premises. The biggest issue is the hybrid cloud. Quick provision and redeployment are expected to integrate the internal information infrastructure and the external cloud structure. If a company's confidential data are decoded out on the Internet landscape, there is a chance of data leakage, hacking, and compromising. Homomorphic encryption is a desired feature in the communication system architecture for hybrid cloud. This encryption technology, allows the chaining of different services, from the internal infrastructure and external cloud system, without exposing the handling of data.

Homomorphic encryption scheme allows computations to be run on the data in the hybrid cloud without the preworks of decryption. A homomorphic encrypted search engine (Brenner et al., 2011; Brinkman, 2007; Gentry, 2010; Micciancio, 2010) can take in encrypted search strings and look up an encrypted index when surfing the Internet. A homomorphic encrypted financial database can run safely in the cloud environment to allow users to check financial information confidently. This avoids exposing confidential data in the public and hybrid clouds so as to enhance data confidentiality and privacy. Technically speaking, homomorphic encryption schemes are hardened by design to facilitate a wider use in hybrid cloud computing. High confidentiality of processed data is ensured. Further, the homomorphic property of cryptosystems is used to form secure systems. There are variants of homomorphic cryptosystems performing either partial or full encryption. This cryptosystem is intentionally malleable to perform computations securely.

Partial homomorphic encryption (Cramer et al., 2001) allows users perform special calculations on the encrypted data, but not others. One good example is an IBM researcher Craig Gentry in 2009. Gentry's method inserts immense computational requirements to computational tasks, which could run a little bit simpler if working on unencrypted data. Then, a tweak is to multiply an encrypted function roughly by a million and half many zeroes. This instantly speeds up the encrypted calculation. Gentry employs lattice-based cryptography by using the first plausible construction for a fully homomorphic encryption scheme. It allows addition and multiplication operations on ciphertexts so as to perform an arbitrary computation. In the end, this discovery leads to MacArthur "genius" grant for crypto research.

Armed with a quick success in partial homomorphic encryption, development moves onto homomorphic encryption (Gentry, 2009). This allows homomorphic computational operations on ciphertexts to run additions, multiplications, quadratic functions, and so on. If a cryptosystem can support an arbitrary computation on encrypted data, it can be classified as fully homomorphic encryption. This critical feature enables the construction of automation programs for desirable functionality. Encrypted inputs can produce an encryption result. There is no decryption happening. In an untrusted environment, such as public cloud, fully homomorphic cryptosystem preserves data confidentiality, integrity, and privacy.

Homomorphic encryption scheme is limited to low-degree polynomials (Stehlé and Steinfeld, 2010) over encrypted data. The underlying reason is due to the fact that ciphertext is noisy and growing in the course of adding and multiplying ciphertexts. This noise will only stop when the resulting ciphertext is indecipherable. A big issue in doing information processing in encrypted data is speed and performance. Ciphertexts in homomorphic encryption scheme are compact because the encrypted key lengths are not influenced by the complexity of the operation function on encrypted data. New development in homomorphic cryptosystems includes the following:

- The Brakerski–Gentry–Vaikuntanathan cryptosystem (Gentry et al., 2012)

- The Brakerski's scale-invariant cryptosystem (Coron et al., 2014)

- The NTRU-based cryptosystem (Coglianese and Goi, 2005) from Lopez-Alt, Tromer, and Vaikuntanathan

- The Gentry–Sahai–Waters cryptosystem (Alperin-Sheriff and Peikert, 2014)

12.5 CHECKLISTS FOR ENCRYPTION, SECURITY, AND PRIVACY

The debut of the hybrid cloud surfaces a new technology horizon where sensitive, classified, and strictly confidential materials, including text, voice, general form of data, pictures, and other machine-readable information commuting between highly secure private cloud and open public cloud. Privacy protection is noted in K-anonymity; fast, small, and powerful encryption evolves out of elliptic curves; and finally full information processing is possible in homomorphic encryption.

In the arena of general cloud computing, there are nonetheless certain areas of attentions worthy of special focus to raise the competence level in identity and privacy.

12.5.1 Software Isolation

Multitenancy (Figure 12.8) takes a dominating role in contemporary cloud computing and achieves a great flexibility of on-demand provisioning of trusted and accountable services, low cost, quick benefits, and high efficiencies through economies of scale (Wahbe et al., 1994). This consumption-based technology landscape drives cloud computing providers to ensure a high degree of dynamic and flexible delivery of service to subscribers on one hand and upholds a high degree of user resources isolation. Multitenancy is achieved through multiplexing and clustering of virtual machines from mutually exclusive cloud users onto the piece of physical cloud server. This solicits a state of total isolation in software pieces, including data of all kinds, systems and business applications, identity, security profiles, and privacy setting.

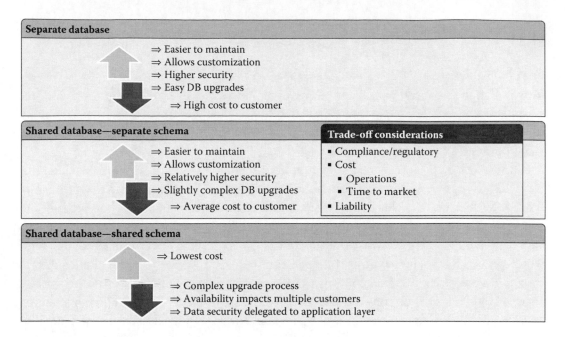

FIGURE 12.8   Multitenancy schema.

12.5.2 Hypervisor Complexity

Hypervisor is the director and communicator between host (including bare metal and hosted operating systems) and guest environments (Vasudevan et al., 2013). Security of cloud computing environment relies on the maturity of supporting software kernel to control the confinement and execution of processes. Hypervisor is configured to run concurrent multiple guest systems. In practice, many hypervisors are bulky and comparable to an operating system. This creates a negation in hypervisor's advantage. Two examples are Xen (Chisnall, 2008), which is a hypervisor using modified Linux kernel to execute a privileged partition for input/output operations, and KVM (Beloglazov et al., 2012), which modifies a Linux kernel. Therefore, the choice of hypervisor impairs the performance and efficiency in the cloud computing environment.

12.5.3 Data Protection

Most cloud providers offer data storage in a shared environment. It is collocated with information from other customers. A cloud subscriber must control which information is moved to the cloud environment to ensure security, integrity, and privacy. Access controls and encryption must be in place to prevent unauthorized access and information compromise. Strong identity controls give strong authentication of the user's identity in cloud computing.

12.5.4 Data Sanitization

This is a good practice in using all cloud computing deployment models. High security and privacy is preserved. Data sanitization involves the removal of sensitive data from cloud storage points. It applies to backup as well. This can avoid sensitive and confidential data kept in obsolete cloud providers' equipment.

12.5.5 Availability

This is a mandate in all cloud computing deployments to allow all computing resources accessible and usable at any time. If availability is affected temporarily or permanently, financial loss follows. Common threats to availability are denial-of-service attacks, equipment outages, and natural disasters.

Temporary outages (Figure 12.9) are noted in some big cloud services providers disregarded of high service reliability and availability. A good example is Amazon's Simple Storage Service (S3) in February 2008 (Palankar et al., 2008) to cause a 3-hour outage. One subscriber Twitter was seriously affected. In June 2009, S3 was hit by a lightning storm and caused a 4-hour outage. Most cloud operators give a service level at 99.999% reliability, which means 8.76 hours of downtime per annum. This indicates that all cloud subscribers should prepare individual contingency plans to handle the restoration and recovery in case of cloud services disruption. This can avoid a single point of failure in cloud storage services. Maybe, a backup cloud service provider can be employed to ensure nonstop business services for critical operations.

A denial-of-service attack (Lawson et al., 2010) causes cloud outage as well (Figure 12.10). It saturates cloud computing resources with bogus requests. An attacker only uses few computers or a botnet to make this attack and quickly uses up a large amount of cloud resources. The dynamic provisioning in cloud services can mitigate the impact of this denial-of-service attack. Careful planning in the network infrastructure is deemed.

12.5.6 Value Concentration

Before the debut of cloud technology, company information assets are bounded with the company walls. This situation changes substantially in the cloud computing era. (Shiller, 2009) such that cloud-based information store is the same as a bank vault. Thus, cloud-based information stores, become targets of cyber criminals who are aiming for financial gains.

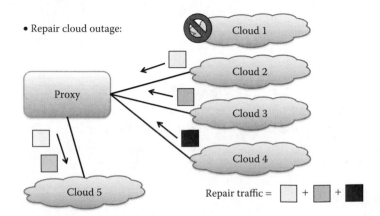

FIGURE 12.9   How to repair a cloud outage.

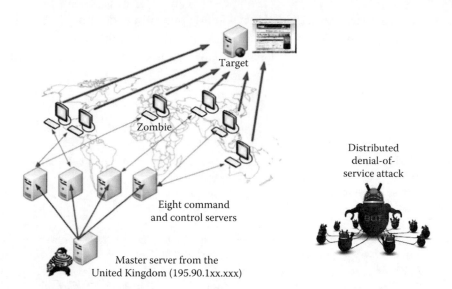

Target

Zombie

Distributed
denial-of-
service attack

Eight command
and control servers

Master server from the
United Kingdom (195.90.1xx.xxx)

FIGURE 12.10   Denial-of-service attack in clouds.

There are cases of attacks at cloud computing operators. A Twitter employee's e-mail account was exploited (Jansen, 2011) through answering a set of security questions. Captured information, was then used to access business files, that were stored on the company's enterprise Google Apps account. This is a typical cross-cloud attack. A similar case was noted in Amazon Web Services (AWS) where a registered e-mail address is the key for authentication credentials for accessing all AWS resources (Bausch, 2003). A hacker pretends to reclaiming passwords through reset by e-mail. Through controlling the mail system or network eavesdropping, the reset e-mail is hijacked in the middle for the hacker to successfully break in the compromised AWS account.

Therefore, it is critical for cloud computing subscribers to shield their use of cloud from the general awareness so as not to catch the attention of organized cyber criminals. Continuous identity and privacy changes are encouraged on cloud users. This includes a constant change in the cloud subscribers' identity to reduce the chance of guessing. Encrypted identity and login token could be an optimal option.

12.6 SUMMARY

In the evaluation of public, private, community, and hybrid clouds, cost and performance are the benchmarks for reference. Security and privacy bear another cornerstone in all cloud computing ecosystems as well. Emerging technology, such as federated trust, is still being considered in cloud implementation. In cloud computing, a high assurance in security and privacy becomes an elusive goal of security researchers and practitioners for cloud computing.

Contemporarily, cloud computing infrastructure focuses on trusted computing and cryptography. Cloud users' data should be protected according to the existing information policies. A good starting point to preserve a high standard in identity, security and privacy can be found in privacy and security standards, regulatory and compliance issues, service-level requirements and penalties, change management processes, continuity of service provisions, and termination rights. Cloud computing adoption, in certain ways, is a campaign in risk management. There are needs to consider both qualitative and quantitative factors in this risk impact analysis. The normal practice is to strike a balance across available safeguards, expected benefits, and accountability for security. Overcontrols lead to an inefficient and ineffective cloud operation.

REFERENCES

Alperin-Sheriff, J., and Peikert, C. (2014). Faster bootstrapping with polynomial error. In *Advances in Cryptology—CRYPTO 2014* (pp. 297–314). Springer.

Atayero, A. A., and Feyisetan, O. (2011). Security issues in cloud computing: The potentials of homomorphic encryption. *Journal of Emerging Trends in Computing and Information Sciences*, *2*(10), 546–552.

Bailey, D. V., and Paar, C. (2001). Efficient arithmetic in finite field extensions with application in elliptic curve cryptography. *Journal of Cryptology*, *14*(3), 153–176.

Bausch, P. (2003). *Amazon Hacks*. O'Reilly Media, Inc.

Beloglazov, A., Piraghaj, S. F., Alrokayan, M., and Buyya, R. (2012). *Deploying OpenStack on CentOS Using the KVM Hypervisor and GlusterFS distributed file system*. Cloud Computing and Distributed Systems (CLOUDS) Laboratory Department of Computing and Information Systems, The University of Melbourne, Australia.

Bertino, E., Paci, F., Ferrini, R., and Shang, N. (2009). Privacy-preserving digital identity management for cloud computing. *IEEE Data Engineering Bulletin*, *32*(1), 21–27.

Brenner, M., Wiebelitz, J., Von Voigt, G., and Smith, M. (2011). *Secret program execution in the cloud applying homomorphic encryption*. Paper presented at the 2011 Proceedings of the 5th IEEE International Conference on Digital Ecosystems and Technologies Conference.

Brinkman, R. (2007). *Searching in Encrypted Data*. University of Twente.

Chisnall, D. (2008). *The Definitive Guide to the Xen Hypervisor*. Pearson Education.

Chun, B.-G., Ihm, S., Maniatis, P., Naik, M., and Patti, A. (2011). *Clonecloud: Elastic execution between mobile device and cloud*. Paper presented at the Proceedings of the Sixth Conference on Computer Systems.

Coglianese, M., and Goi, B.-M. (2005). MaTRU: A new NTRU-based cryptosystem. In *Progress in Cryptology-INDOCRYPT 2005* (pp. 232–243). Springer.

Coron, J.-S., Lepoint, T., and Tibouchi, M. (2014). Scale-invariant fully homomorphic encryption over the integers. In *Public-Key Cryptography–PKC 2014* (pp. 311–328). Springer.

Cramer, R., Damgård, I., and Nielsen, J. B. (2001). *Multiparty Computation from Threshold Homomorphic Encryption*. Springer.

Dixon, B., and Lenstra, A. K. (1993). *Massively parallel elliptic curve factoring*. Paper presented at the Advances in Cryptology—EUROCRYPT'92.

Fujisaki, E., and Okamoto, T. (1999). *Secure integration of asymmetric and symmetric encryption schemes*. Paper presented at the Crypto.

Gampala, V., Inuganti, S., and Muppidi, S. (2012). Data security in cloud computing with elliptic curve cryptography. *International Journal of Soft Computing and Engineering*, *2*(3), 138–141.

Gedik, B., and Liu, L. (2005). *Location privacy in mobile systems: A personalized anonymization model*. Paper presented at the Proceedings of the 25th IEEE International Conference on Distributed Computing Systems.

Gentry, C. (2009). *Fully homomorphic encryption using ideal lattices*. Paper presented at the STOC.

Gentry, C. (2010). Computing arbitrary functions of encrypted data. *Communications of the ACM*, *53*(3), 97–105.

Gentry, C., Halevi, S., and Smart, N. P. (2012). Homomorphic evaluation of the AES circuit. In *Advances in Cryptology—CRYPTO 2012* (pp. 850–867). Springer.

Gura, N., Patel, A., Wander, A., Eberle, H., and Shantz, S. C. (2004). Comparing elliptic curve cryptography and RSA on 8-bit CPUs. In *Cryptographic Hardware and Embedded Systems-CHES 2004* (pp. 119–132). Springer.

Hankerson, D., and Menezes, A. (2011). Elliptic curve discrete logarithm problem. In *Encyclopedia of Cryptography and Security* (pp. 397–400). Springer.

Hankerson, D., Menezes, A. J., and Vanstone, S. (2006). *Guide to Elliptic Curve Cryptography*. Springer Science+Business Media.

He, Y., and Naughton, J. F. (2009). Anonymization of set-valued data via top-down, local generalization. *Proceedings of the VLDB Endowment, 2*(1), 934–945.

Herzog, J. C. (2003). *The Diffie-Hellman key-agreement scheme in the strand-space model.* Paper presented at the Proceedings of the 16th IEEE on Computer Security Foundations Workshop.

Jansen, W. (2011). *Cloud hooks: Security and privacy issues in cloud computing.* Paper presented at the 2011 44th Hawaii International Conference on System Sciences.

Lauter, K. (2004). The advantages of elliptic curve cryptography for wireless security. *IEEE Wireless Communications, 11*(1), 62–67.

Law, L., and Solinas, J. (2007). Suite B cryptographic suites for IPsec.

Lawson, J., Wolthuis, J., and Cooke, E. (2010). System and method for mitigating a denial of service attack using cloud computing. Google Patents.

Lee, B., Kim, H., and Kim, K. (2001). *Strong proxy signature and its applications.* Paper presented at the Proceedings of SCIS.

Liu, A., and Ning, P. (2008). *TinyECC: A configurable library for elliptic curve cryptography in wireless sensor networks.* Paper presented at the International Conference on Information Processing in Sensor Networks.

Micciancio, D. (2010). A first glimpse of cryptography's Holy Grail. *Communications of the ACM, 53*(3), 96–96.

Nergiz, M. E., Clifton, C., and Nergiz, A. E. (2009). Multirelational k-anonymity. *IEEE Transactions on Knowledge and Data Engineering, 21*(8), 1104–1117.

Olden, E. (2011). Architecting a cloud-scale identity fabric. *Computer, 44*(3), 52–59.

Oliveira, S. R. (2003). *Protecting sensitive knowledge by data sanitization.* Paper presented at the null.

Paillier, P. (1999). *Public-key cryptosystems based on composite degree residuosity classes.* Paper presented at the Advances in Cryptology—EUROCRYPT'99.

Palankar, M. R., Iamnitchi, A., Ripeanu, M., and Garfinkel, S. (2008). *Amazon S3 for science grids: A viable solution?* Paper presented at the Proceedings of the 2008 International Workshop on Data-Aware Distributed Computing.

Shiller, R. J. (2009). *The New Financial Order: Risk in the 21st Century.* Princeton University Press.

Stehlé, D., and Steinfeld, R. (2010). Faster fully homomorphic encryption. In *Advances in Cryptology—ASIACRYPT 2010* (pp. 377–394). Springer.

Sweeney, L. (2002). k-Anonymity: A model for protecting privacy. *International Journal of Uncertainty, Fuzziness and Knowledge-Based Systems, 10*(5), 557–570.

Vasudevan, A., Chaki, S., Jia, L., McCune, J., Newsome, J., and Datta, A. (2013). *Design, implementation and verification of an extensible and modular hypervisor framework.* Paper presented at the 2013 IEEE Symposium on Security and Privacy.

Wahbe, R., Lucco, S., Anderson, T. E., and Graham, S. L. (1994). *Efficient software-based fault isolation.* Paper presented at the ACM SIGOPS Operating Systems Review.

CHAPTER 13

Secure Management of Virtualized Resources

Roberto Di Pietro, Flavio Lombardi, and Matteo Signorini

CONTENTS

13.1 INTRODUCTION

The last few years have witnessed an increasing success of cloud computing services. In particular, infrastructure as a service (IaaS) has brought unprecedented flexibility and scalability to the services offered over the Internet. However, enterprises are still reluctant to embrace IaaS backed by the fear of loosing control over their data and computation. Physical resources in the IaaS cloud are managed by the cloud service provider (CSP), offering virtual hosts exposed to customer access (see also Figure 13.1) [1].

Such a large collection of resources within virtual hosts is maximized among customers (also known as tenants) with the objective to achieve the best result (i.e., to provide the best service) at the least cost (i.e., by sharing the very same physical hardware over multiple

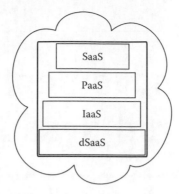

FIGURE 13.1 Cloud computing layers. SaaS, software as a service; PaaS, platform as a service; dSaaS, data storage as a service. (Wylve and Bikeborg, Cloud computing layers, Wikimedia Foundation, Inc., San Francisco, CA. https://commons.wikimedia.org/wiki/File:Cloud_computing_layers.svg.)

virtual hosts). Heterogeneous physical and virtual resources can be used to split and process the same problem (see Figure 13.2 and also MapReduce [2]). Once virtual resources (such as virtual networks, virtual data, and virtual processors) have been assigned to tenants, these latter ones have complete access to them and can rearrange them in order to better fit their needs. As an example, virtual memory and virtual networks given to the tenant by the CSP can be further redistributed by the tenant over different virtual machines (VMs) in order to build a specific topology aimed at providing some services. This process is called virtual resource to virtual resource (VR2VR) [3] management and many solutions have been already proposed to manage it [4,5].

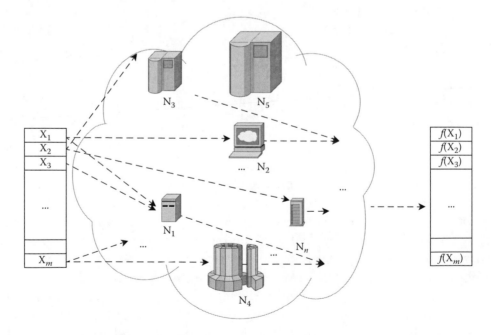

FIGURE 13.2 Cloud services can help splitting and offloading complex tasks over possibly heterogeneous virtual nodes.

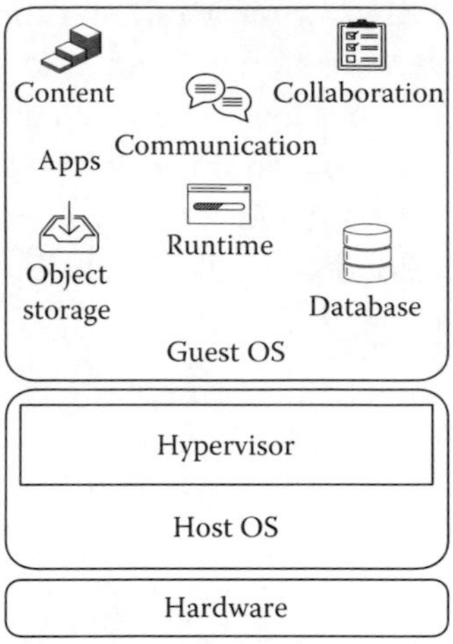

FIGURE 13.3   Cloud applications and (virtual) resources.

Unlike VR2VR that is managed and controlled by the tenant owning them, virtual to physical resource mapping (VR2PR) is managed by the CSP and is transparent to the tenant (see also Figure 13.3). The problem arises when CSPs leverage multitenancy to maximize their revenues. In this case, the same physical resource is assigned to multiple virtual resources that are provided to different tenants. This implies colocation of VMs from different tenants on a single physical host. As such, physical disk storage, networks, graphic cards, and so on are shared by different tenants at the same time. In such a way, VMs assigned to a tenant might get hacked by other VMs assigned to different tenants that leverage physical resources that are colocated within the same physical machine. This colocation can lead to different issues as follow:

- *Information leakage*: By reusing the same physical hardware to allocate virtual resources, tenants might be able to exploit forensic tools to recover sensitive data from previous tenants.

- *Performance degradation*: Malicious tenants colocated in the same physical host might be able to overuse computational power with high central processing unit (CPU)-intensive colocated VMs with the final goal of degrading victim's performances.

- *Service disruption*: Malicious tenants sharing physical resources with their victim might be able to lead the hardware to unexpected behaviors, thus causing a service disruption against the victim.

So far, many different studies showed the existence in the real world of colocation vulnerabilities of such physical resources [6–9]. Obtained results show that completely preventing multitenants from sharing the same physical resources is practically unfeasible and propose as an alternative to simply expose risks and placement decisions directly to tenants [6]. Another solution [3] proposes an attribute-based solution in which tenants can express constraints over both virtual and physical resource allocation. As a toy example, tenants can classify data sensitivity as "high," thus avoiding other VMs using the same physical host to be colocated. In this way, colocation will not be allowed for virtual resources working on high-sensitive information, thus lowering the chance of data leakage. All these solutions try to solve the multitenancy colocation security issues all at once. However, many different layers can be defined within cloud resource virtualization, and each of them can benefit from *ad hoc* solutions. Cloud computing services are usually classified into four types (see also Figure 13.1):

- Software as a service
- Platform as a service
- Infrastructure as a service
- Data storage as a service

However, this classification is more related to business issues than to security issues. As such, a new classification based on layers has been proposed to better describe and analyze security and privacy issues from a technical standpoint. The new classification is composed by the following layers (see also Figure 13.4) [10]:

- Application
- Operating system
- Hypervisor
- Hardware and software primitives

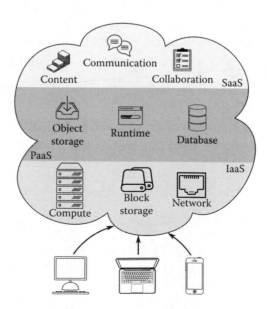

FIGURE 13.4   An alternative view of cloud layers more tied to actual security issues. SaaS, software as a service; PaaS, platform as a service.

In the classification proposed in [10], an additional layer "web" has been defined and described; however, as web services run on top of hardware and software resources as already introduced with the first four layers and as web services do not have their own resources to be managed but rather rely on the underlying VM resource set, this fifth layer will not be discussed here.

In the following, all the aforementioned layers will be introduced, and for each one, a state of the art will be given. The solutions proposed so far in literature aimed at addressing security will be described. Further, privacy issues derived from colocation and reallocation issues will be surveyed.

13.2 VIRTUALIZATION SECURITY

In the past few years, the virtualization technology showed its potential within a cloud eco-system by bringing different benefits such as cost-efficiency, increased uptime, improved disaster recovery, and application isolation [11–13]. However, on the other face of the coin, virtualization also threatened the cloud computing by opening new attack vectors as the following ones:

- *Hypervisor*: In a virtualized system, hypervisor is a software element that sits in between the host and each guest in order to allow the access to physical resources while protecting them from attackers. Usually, this layer is transparent to a non-privileged user running into the guest, but, as the user gets more power and privileges, the existence of the hypervisor comes to light. Attackers can then exploit hypervisor vulnerabilities to gain access to both the host system and other guests. Hypervisors are designed to provide interfaces for a wide multitude of hardware elements and devices. In fact, they can also provide emulation capabilities, whereas a specific hardware element is not present within the host system. However, this rises the points of failure as old drivers might not get patched on time. As a toy example in 2006, two rootkits were developed to demonstrate how a malicious user might get complete control over the host system and all its VMs [14,15]. More recently, a vulnerability in floppy disk interface [16] proved that this attack vector is still exploited by attackers and that more attention should be taken in hardening the hypervisor.

- *Resource allocation*: The main goal of virtualized environments is the physical resource sharing. VMs are usually executed on demand at runtime in order to provide services, infrastructures, platforms, and so on, thus making the resource allocation and management process as much dynamic as possible. The result is the capability of providing access to resources beyond physical constraints, thus increasing revenues. However, resource sharing can thwart the security of the host system as well as of its VMs. In fact, negligence in cleaning resources before giving them to others can lead to severe data leakage. As a toy example, data written into volatile or persistent storage elements can be stolen by others who have access to the same elements.

- *Pivoting*: VMs usually provide services open to the outside world. As such, users can reach and login into the VM as needed. Once inside, malicious users might exploit application vulnerabilities to compromise the VM and to use that VM as a starting point to reach other VMs hosted within the same host or within other hosts. Usually, such kinds of attacks are monitored by looking for malicious network traffic, but if the VM under attack belong to the same host, exchanged messages might be handled locally, thus avoiding network activities and making the pivoting attack harder to mitigate.

- *Migration attacks*: VMs are frequently moved between different hosts for load balancing or disaster recovery, and this process, named "migration," is usually accomplished by copying the image of the VM over the network. However, such a network can have an attacker (see the pivoting attack above) listening on the channel and eavesdropping everything that is exchanged between different hosts. In this case, the attacker might be able to accomplish a man in the middle attack if the channel is not encrypted or it could simply dump the network traffic for later offline attacks.

All these attacks showed how VMs and physical machines hosting them can be thwarted by attackers able to move from one VM to another, from one VM to the host machine, or simply willing to jeopardize the security of the VM by itself. The following is an example of possible solutions that are aimed at mitigating those attacks:

- *Hypervisor*: Attacks based on vulnerabilities in the implementation of the hypervisor can be easily mitigated by constantly updating the hypervisor. This means that patches to 0-day vulnerabilities should be provided as fast as possible and not-supported or outdated elements, such as old device drivers, should be purged from the mainstream source code and provided only when expressly required.

- *Resource allocation*: This attack is aimed at stealing information when it is not wiped out correctly. The only way to avoid such an attack is to carefully delete and overwrite all the resources either persistent or volatile that have been previously assigned to other VMs.

- *Pivoting*: The first approach in addressing the pivoting attack is based on the analysis of internal communications between guests hosted by the same host machine rather than only the inbound and outbound traffic. Furthermore, malicious network behaviors within the network should be analyzed looking for a well-known pattern by intrusion detection systems and intrusion prevention systems, thus avoiding an attacker from jumping from one VM to another.

- *Migration attacks*: To avoid migration attacks and the stealing of VMs while in transit, it is suggested that any information exchanged between guests gets first encrypted before it left the virtual machine. Using strong encryption keys will not avoid an attacker from stealing the data being exchanged but will make that data useless for the attacker and harmless for the owner.

After introducing the aforementioned security issues and solutions, in the remaining of this chapter, we will further delve into virtual resource management. In particular, we will deal with real hardware offering virtual resource sharing to cloud hosts, tasks, and services. In order to do that, we describe the characteristics of the current technology.

13.3 HARDWARE RESOURCES

Multitenancy service developers usually assume the underlying hardware and software elements to be reliable and secure, even though this is not really always the case. As an example, the isolation is assumed to be effective and to work as expected. However, as a toy example, side channels were found in Pentium processors due to the shared memory hierarchy being used [17]. The study showed how such a Pentium 4 hyper-threading technology should be avoided in VM monitors to enforce critical security policies and avoid severe information leakage as for OpenSSL keys.

This is just an example of how hardware vulnerabilities might leak sensitive information as their colocation and reallocation might lead to severe breaches. Four main hardware resource management vulnerabilities will be analyzed more in detail in Sections 13.3.1 through 13.3.3.

13.3.1 CPU Virtualization

Studies showed in the past that resource utilization does not exceed 40% of hardware capabilities mainly due to the following: (1) Most virtualized resource pools are usually static and do not provide live migration of VMs, and (2) data center workloads have eruptive demands, thus leading to conservative consolidation decisions, and user interactive performances tend to drop when they must contend for busy resources. All these cause critical application performances to be poor, thus pushing CSP in finding new ways to increase the utilization of server computational resources while providing a high level of security.

The most used approach in workload management is based on capping techniques aimed at distributing resources among collocated workloads in a nonwork conserving mode [18–26]. Examples of this approach consist in limiting CPU resources by establishing caps for non-critical workloads that are allowed to access only a limited percentage of allocated physical resources. However, if dynamic reallocation solutions are not in place, those caps can limit the usage of CSP physical machines, even though any critical workload is running leading to resource waste and a lower overall server utilization. Other solutions as the one proposed by Diao and coworkers [27] prioritize and dispatch incoming requests to service agents based on the service-level agreement (SLA) attainment target in a simulation testbed [27]. Others exploited the existing approaches such as CPU shares, XEN CPU weights, or Linux real-time priorities to interactively collocate jobs [28,29] and mix them with batch jobs [30,31]. Others cap-based approaches have been proposed in the past few years focused on the management of mixed batch and transactional workload profiling [18]. A workload profiler monitors resource consumption and utilization, and estimates CPU average needs to be assigned to single applications or whole VMs, and then the system predicts the performance of the transactional application for a given CPU resource allocation. As an example, Bubble-Up [19] exploits CPU consumption predictions to collocate workloads within the same server. This solution is based on "bubbles," as the name suggests, where applications are individually enclosed to be profiled. By profiling each application, a consumption prediction is made and based on that workloads are selected to be placed within the same server or within different servers. This approach proved to work well for specific scenarios such as the one described within the paper, but application profiling might be challenging and predictions not really accurate, thus leading to workload misplacement. Unlike Bubble-Up, in Q-Clouds [20], the resource consumption is not predicted or estimated, but it is rather computed while running the VM in an initial execution when it is profiled to collect quality of service (QoS) requirement information. After this first run, the Q-Clouds scheduler then leaves a prescribed amount of unused resources on each server and dynamically adjusts virtual central processing unit (VCPU) caps of the VMs through the Hyper-V hypervisor. Another solution based on the prediction and expectation of resource consumption is the one based on the active coordination [32] approach in which a multidimensional vector is used to collect VM resource expectations. Other solutions are classified as hybrid as they exploit both prediction and profiling capabilities [22,33]. To be more specific, they use historical profiled data to predict future resource consumption and workload demands; as well as, a reactive controller that handles unforeseen events.

Sandpiper [28] is a different solution that rather than being based on profiles or estimations for workload predictions, it is based on the monitoring of resource consumption and VM relocation whenever a VM runs out of resources. The relocation is accomplished from overloaded to underutilized physical hosts by using a black box (operating system (OS) and application agnostic) and a gray box (OS and application dependent). Sandpiper has been implemented and tested in Xen, and results showed its ability to resolve a single-server hot spot within 20 s and to scaling well to larger data center environments. Another solution is the one proposed by Blagodurov and coworkers [34] in which instead of using caps on the resource allocation, the server utilization is improved while meeting the SLAs of critical workloads by prioritizing resource access using Linux cgroups weights.

13.3.2 GPU Virtualization

The widespread adoption of virtualized environments have led some users in leveraging on VMs whenever they need to optimize resources. Although the same virtualization paradigm also applies to graphics processing units (GPUs), VMs have to fulfill special requirements in order to be able to give access to host-based GPU resources. Furthermore, as for standard virtualization, GPU virtualization also has different models [35], which are as follows (see the CUDA support comparative table [Table 13.1]):

- *Device Passthrough*: In this model, the GPU is connected directly to the VM as if the guest would have direct access to it. As such, only one guest at time can access the GPU. As an example, VMware calls this model virtual Direct Graphics Accelerator.

- *Time sharing*: This approach is similar to the device passthrough as direct access to the GPU is given to a single VM. However, that single VM does not have the monopoly on the usage of the GPU. Hence, time slots are signed to different VMs, which in turn will all be able to use the GPU.

TABLE 13.1   GPU Virtualization CUDA Support

	vSphere	Hyper-V	Virtual Box	XenServer	Linux
Passthrough	✓	✗	✓	✓	✓
Time sharing	✗	✗	✗	✗	✗
Partitioning	✗	✗	✗	✓	✗
Live migration	✗	✗	✗	✗	✗

- *Partitioning*: The host GPU is split into virtual GPUs, each of which is given to a single VM.

- *Live migration*: It is the ability to move a running VM from one VM host to another without downtime.

These models define how the GPU gets distributed among the VMs (see also Figure 13.5). However, once VMs have access to the GPU, the interaction between the guest and the real resource can be achieved in two different ways thus defining a back-end virtualization or a front-end virtualization [36]. The back-end virtualization approach gives a direct connection between the VM and the hardware, whereas the front-end virtualization poses an intermediate layer between the guest and the hardware that leverages on APIs. Examples for front-end virtualization of GPUs are vCUDA [37], gVirtuS [38], rCUDA [39], GViM [40], and VOCL [41].

As GPUs are mainly used for computation tasks, security concerns about GPU virtualization are mainly focused on data leakage. This can occur either by directly accessing data owned by the victim and stored within the GPU memory or by exploiting side channels. In [42], Christin and coworkers have depicted two adversary models.

- *Serial adversary*: This attacker has access to the same GPU or the same GPU memory of the victim before or after the victim. Hence, it can seek for traces previously left by the victim in different GPU memories.

- *Parallel adversary*: This attacker has access to the same GPU or the same GPU memory of the victim but in the same moment.

13.3.3 Network Virtualization

With the advent of cloud computing, network devices became more and more powerful over the past few years. All these devices started to join what goes under the name of cloud network, that is, a huge ecosystem built on top of physical network cards virtualized and provided as a service to multiple tenants. This cloud network is another good use case to show how resource management and reallocation of physical resources within a virtualized environment has to be protected to prevent information leakage and service disruption (see Figure 13.6). Resource management in the cloud network can even become worse, if "middle-boxes" such as proxy servers are used. In fact, albeit

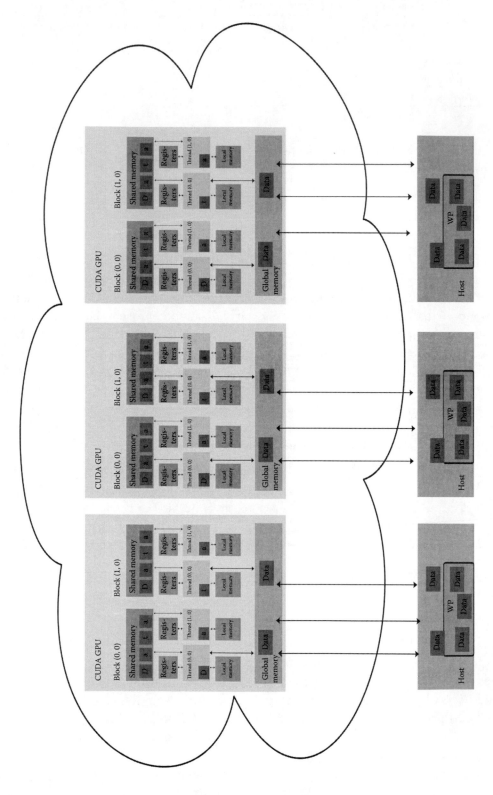

FIGURE 13.5 GPU cloud and GPU internals. Computing resources are transparently shared over clients.

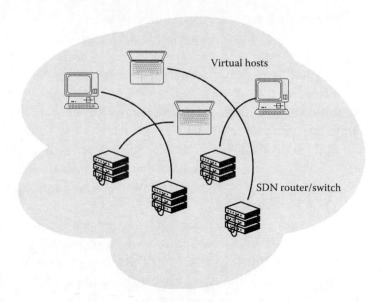

FIGURE 13.6   SDN allows dynamic reconfiguration of virtual networks for cloud computing.

such middle-boxes can provide many different benefits for network performances, they also make the network more complex, thus leading to a more complex resource management [43–45].

The involvement of such middle-boxes within cloud networks also brings security challenges in the resource management process. Network resource placement and configuration play a key role in the design of security policies. As a toy example, middle-box security elements such as firewalls and intrusion detection systems can be installed and placed at different positions to satisfy different security needs, and each position can have benefits and issues, thus requiring a complex configuration. Furthermore, different security network devices can have different purposes and security functions, thus being required to be placed at different locations and respecting different topologies to achieve the maximum results. This is usually an administrator's responsibility, but most of the time it is quite hard to predict all the possible network threats in order to design and to place into the right places all the network security devices. As such, it is of paramount importance to maximize the resource utilization of preinstalled and already existing middle-boxes as well as abstract them to provide virtual network resources with a simple interface that tenants can use to create more secure services.

Trying to solve the complexity of network security resource management, many different studies have been proposed over the past few years. OpenSafe [46] and Jingling [47] provide a script language to monitor networks. Sekar and coworkers proposed new approaches for network intrusion detection systems and network intrusion prevention system deployment [48] through packet inspection and load balancing [49]. Raza and coworkers introduced an approach to route packets to network monitoring points [50] while [10] focusing more on security monitoring in clouds by considering characteristics of different security devices and by designing different routing algorithms and response strategies for security needs. Other studies such as Nettle [51] and Frenetic [52] proposed a language-centric approach to program OpenFlow (OF) networks based on the principle of functional reactive programming. OF networks distinguish themselves from legacy network infrastructure by rethinking the relationship between the data and control planes of the network device. They adopt the paradigm of highly programmable switch infrastructures [53] enabling software to compute an optimal flow routing decision on demand. Solutions proposed with FortNOX [54] and its follow-up work, FRESCO [55], proposed another kind of approach to OF security challenges by designing a framework that facilitates the rapid modular composition of OF-enabled detection and mitigation modules. Seungwon and coworkers proposed with Avant-Guard [56] another solution for software-defined network (SDN) and its OF framework. More in detail, in Avant-Guard, Seungwon and coworkers focused on two specific security issues that belong to OF: (1) the inherent communication bottleneck that arises between the data plane and the control plane and (2) the boost of flow dynamic changing detection and reaction within the data plane. Their implementation proved to be practically feasible with an overhead of just 1% but also effective, thus providing resilience to an important adversary model that may hinder the SDN adoption.

All the aforementioned approaches showed the security issues raised by middle-boxes within cloud networks. This problem became even worse when such middleboxes started to be virtualized and provided within VMs. This new approach called network function virtualization [57] shares the same common vulnerabilities with the other virtualized resources. Studies in the past few years have already started to propose viable solutions to harden virtualized network devices. As an example, Shin and coworkers [58] proposed a slightly different approach to NSV as their solution does not need to convert network middle-box functions into VMs, and relocate and centralize them into a single place but rather relies on flow redirection toward existing preinstalled security devices on demand. Furthermore, their work is aimed at providing security virtualization by enabling security response functions and user-friendly security policy scripts to be used by administrators and tenants. As for [58] based on the flow redirection, other studies focused on similar approaches with the design of middle-box policy enforcement with SDN. Standard interface for multiple platform link evaluation [44] is one of those, aimed at controlling middle-box-specific traffic steering without mandating any placement or implementation constraints on middle-boxes and without changing current SDN standards. Another solution has been proposed with FlowTags [59], an extended SDN architecture in which middle-boxes add tags to outgoing packets in order to be later used on switches and middle-boxes for systematic policy enforcement.

13.4 HYPERVISOR-LAYER RESOURCES

Hypervisor-layer techniques isolate tenants by providing separate VMs. This section describes security issues for virtual machine managers (VMMs) and VMs, respectively. In particular, relevant security details, as well as possible remedies and approaches, will be given in Sections 13.4.1 and 13.4.2.

13.4.1 VMM Security

VMMs have a critical role for hypervisor and thus should be trustworthiness; however, in recent years, we have witnessed with attacks to VMMs based on vulnerabilities, rootkits, and so on, of which the most important ones are listed as follows:

- *VMM vulnerabilities*: As a complex piece of software, VMMs can suffer from vulnerabilities as any other software (see Figure 13.7). One of the most important researches showed that this is the one that exploited fuzzy techniques to audit the source code of the major VMMs and emulators [60]. In this work, three threat levels have been defined ranging from "total compromise" to "normal compromise" and finally to "abnormal termination." The result of the study was that none of the analyzed VMs tested was robust enough to withstand the testing procedure. Multiple exploitable flaws have been found that allowed an attacker restricted to a virtualized environment to reliably escape onto the host system.

- *VM-based rootkits*: As a standard rootkit can subvert the operating system it belongs to, VM-based rootkit can subvert the host machine as well as all the virtual guests running on top of it. Furthermore, although traditional kernel rootkits insulate themselves in the OS kernel, VM-based rootkits live in the VMM layer, thus being resilient from a kernel rootkit detector. During the last year, different VM-based rootkits have been proposed showing their weaknesses. As a toy example, VMware has been analyzed looking for the stealthiness of VM-based rootkits by measuring installation and boot times as well as memory footprints [15]. Another VM-based rootkit named BluePill [61] (see also Figure 13.8) also proved to be capable of installing itself on the fly. BluePill proved to be particularly dangerous as it can leverage on advanced micro devices storage virtualization manager-nested virtualization features, thus making it able to insulate itself within the VMM layer.

- *VMM transparency*: Another security concern tied to VMMs is detectability. The recognition of the underlying environment may help an attacker to thwart the VMMs, the host machine, and all the guest VMs. Furthermore, virtual honeypot hosting malicious code in the cloud needs to thwart the VM detection, thus rising the need of transparent VMMs. In [62], Garfinkel and coworkers showed that a complete transparency is not practically feasible. In fact, their results proved that by challenging the VMs, they were always able to find some discrepancies between the physical host and the virtual guest. Another study based on fuzzy benchmarks [63] showed a similar result. In that work, the authors were able to identify four identification weakness quadrants, each of which described some vulnerabilities that made an attacker able to distinguish between a VM and a physical machine. Also Di Pietro and coworkers [64] (see Figure 13.9) underline the importance of having a transparent VM and a set of tools for actively monitoring VMs.

- *Platform integrity*: In virtualized environments, it should be assumed that the underlying VMM and OS are trusted. In fact, starting from those trusted components, additional layers can be controlled in order to build a chain of trust where every layer of the software stack is responsible for the security of the next one in the chain. Terra [65] has been proposed as a trusted VMM that assigns different VMs to different applications to isolate them and control them one by one. Furthermore, as each application may deploy optimized OSs, the chain of trust can be preserved even within the VM. Unlike Terra, other works based their solution on trusted

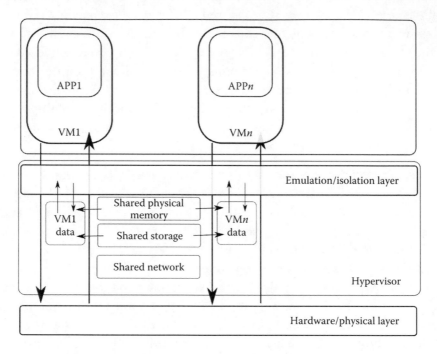

FIGURE 13.7   VMMs are complex pieces of software often vulnerable to attacks.

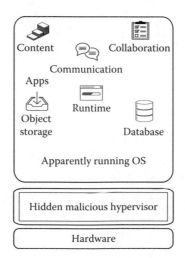

FIGURE 13.8   Bluepill-like attack.

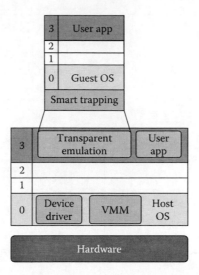

FIGURE 13.9   A transparent VMM allows better monitoring of VMs.

platform modules (TPMs). Virtual TPM [66] is one of those designed as a software embodiment of the TPM accessible within VMs.

13.4.2 VM Security

On top of VMM are VMs, where tenants reside. VMs are usually assumed to be isolated between each other. However, this is not always the case. As already described in Sections 13.4 and 13.4.1, vulnerabilities can be exploited to bypass VMM security control and attack VMs running on the same physical host. Furthermore, this scenario gets even worse in a multitenancy environment where VMs share physical and virtual resources colocated on the same host. The major VM security issues in a multitenancy environment are as follows:

- *Introspection*: VM debugging and introspection techniques (see Figure 13.10) available to hypervisors can be an advantage for integrity and a thread to VM confidentiality. In fact, malicious users may break out from their VMs (as discussed in Sections 13.4 and 13.4.1) and exploit the VMM to debug and profile other VMs. A solution capable of this is the VIX tool suite [67]. This suite relies on the mapping of DomU virtual memory address into Dom0 and is able to track VM behaviors.

- *Redundancy cancellation*: VMs are usually guaranteed to execute within an isolated environment. This protects their information from being accessed by other tenants but also slow down performances. In a multitenancy environment where there is not such a physical complete isolation and resources are shared and allocated within the same physical machine, solutions such as sHype [68] enable resource sharing among VMs without compromising security. sHype enforces strong isolation at the granularity of a VM, thus providing a robust foundation on which higher software layers can enact finer-grained controls.

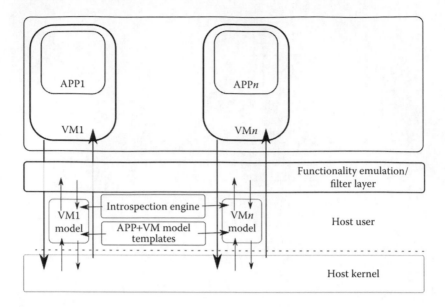

FIGURE 13.10   Semantic introspection allows better monitoring of VMs.

13.5 OS RESOURCES

OS security has been the target of large research efforts over the past 40 or more years, and it is now considered a well-established area. The main themes and achievements of past research are Kernel Integrity efforts and privilege separation attempts. They are summarized in Sections 13.5.1 and 13.5.2.

13.5.1 Kernel Integrity

OS kernel vulnerabilities may lead to an introduction of covert malware inside the kernel (kernel rootkit). This could be prevented by employing VM introspection techniques. Among them is NICKLE [69], a VMM extension performing memory shadowing and runtime kernel code integrity checks. NICKLE is claimed to be a widely applicable technique for multiple VMMs, such as QEMU, VirtualBox, and VMware. VM introspection is also successfully adopted in CloRexPa [70], an approach modeling and monitoring guest OS and guest application behavior in a scalable way.

13.5.2 Privilege Separation

Privilege separation approaches manage accesses and separate user privileges. OS security mechanisms are the basis for these approaches. In particular, discretionary access control (DAC) allows users to configure the more suitable access policy. Nevertheless, DACs are vulnerable to malware and easily subject to buggy system configurations that can easily cause failures in system security. mandatory access control (MAC) approaches enforce sysadmin-specified polcies, which are monitored using runtime hooks. This approach is more secure because individual users cannot tamper with their file access policies.

Examples of MAC implementations are Security Enhanced Linux and AppArmor [71], widely deployed on Linux production machines all over the world. Various MAC auditing tools exist such as VulSan [72], encoding security policies, system states, and system rules using logic programs. VulSan creates the attack graph and the vulnerability surface once given attack scenarios.

Nevertheless, they cannot handle ambient authority, which results in enabling an application to fully access user data. To cope with the issue, Capsicum capabilities [73], that is, an extension of UNIX file descriptors, were introduced. Capsicom reflects rights on specific objects such as files or sockets and may be delegated from process to process in a granular way in the same manner as other file descriptor types via inheritance or message passing. Such extension supports application compartmentalization, the decomposition of monolithic application codes into components that will run in independent sandboxes to form logical applications.

13.6 APPLICATION RESOURCES

Application-level resource isolation techniques provide logical resource isolation for user data. Relevant techniques are discussed in subsections 13.6.1 and 13.6.2. In particular, secure data storage issues will be dealt with first.

13.6.1 Secure Data Storage

Recent research on secure user data storage aimed at maintaining its usability are introduced below. In particular, we have to deal with encrypted data manipulation, data integrity, and data redundancy cancellation:

- *Encrypted data manipulation*: User data are confidential and have to be protected from unauthorized access. Among the many proposed approaches, progressive elliptic curve encryption [74] is a promising type of proxy reencryption [75], allowing the very same piece of data to be encrypted multiple times using different keys such that the final ciphertext can be decrypted in a single run with a single key. By adopting this mechanism, a data owner may encrypt data before uploading it to a service provider's server, which, upon request, reencrypts it by using the public key of the authorized party who wishes to access it, and the party receives and decrypts it with a single key. It is worth stressing that the service provider does not possess any key to decrypt the data here; thus, only the data owner can access the data. This enables secure usage of an untrustworthy service provider. However, users may wish to manipulate their encrypted data stored in the provider's server (e.g., retrieve data) without decrypting that at the server in order to preserve confidentiality. Homomorphic encryption [76,77] could achieve that. It is a form of encryption in which a specific algebraic operation performed on the plain text is equivalent to another (possibly different) algebraic operation performed on the ciphertext. With this scheme, CSPs can perform complicated processing of data without being able to see it. This helps make cloud computing compatible with privacy.

- *Data integrity*: Techniques to ensure storage correctness (i.e., data integrity) across multiple servers or peers have been proposed in the past [78,79,80]. A different approach was taken by Wang and coworkers [81], designing a scheme that supports secure and efficient dynamic operations on data blocks, including data update, delete, and append. Such scheme allows the user to generate a homomorphic precomputed token that is erasure coded and stored locally. This is used to detect a misbehaving server.

- *Data redundancy cancellation*: Deduplication, a technique that stores only a single copy of redundant data and provides links to that copy instead of storing other actual copies of the data, is now widely used by cloud storage providers to efficiently store data. Yet, such deduplication may cause security risks, as discussed by Harnik [82]. In fact, such deduplication can be used as a side channel to reveal information about the contents of other users' files and as a covert channel by which malicious software can communicate with the outside world, regardless of the firewall settings of the attack machine. In order to address such issues, Harnik discussed three different schemes: using encryption to prevent deduplication, performing deduplication at the server, and setting a randomized threshold for running deduplication. Even though these are not perfect solutions, they provide some privacy guarantees while slightly reducing the benefit of deduplication.

13.6.2 User Data Isolation

Individual user data need to be isolated to preserve privacy. Two major approaches for that are introduced below. They are mainly process isolation and selective decryption techniques.

- *Process isolation*: Data in a multitenant system needs to be carefully treated so that it cannot be mixed with another user's. Information flow control (IFC) [83] tags data entering the system and isolates the data belonging to different users. Papagiannis and coworkers [84] implemented IFC constraints in the Erlang programming language by leveraging its shared-nothing computation, message passing, and lightweight processes to provide uniform privacy preservation in a highly concurrent application;

- *Selective decryption techniques*: User data needs to be read by the intended users, but must not be read by the others. To enable that, cryptographic techniques enabling selective decryption have been researched. One fundamental technique enabling that is the identity-based encryption scheme [85], which enables a user specified by an identity to decrypt data. Kang and Zhang [86] designed a mutual authentication system that allows users in the same domain to securely share data for cloud storage by using the technique. There could be benefit in endowing decryption rights to a group of users instead of a single user designated by an identity, and Liu and coworkers [87] implemented a hierarchical identity-based architecture based on the hierarchical identity-based encryption system proposed by Gentry and Silverberg [88]. It predefines user structure, and decryption keys are created following the structures. Attribute-based encryption (ABE) provides more flexible decryption key assignment, and Li and coworkers [89] defined access structures of files so that a user can access a file only if the user's attributes satisfy the file's access structure. Note that the original ABE is proposed by Sahai and Waters [90], extensions of which are available in [91–93]. By combining assorted techniques including the aforementioned ones, Kamara and Lauter [94] introduced an architecture for a cryptographic storage service that assumes untrusted service providers.

13.7 SUMMARY

This chapter has discussed a large set of virtual resource management security issues. Security challenges and approaches have been introduced. The resulting survey has given a broad view of security issues of multitenant cloud computing, mainly focused on the issues related to resource isolation techniques. Based on the survey, this chapter has discussed different technical approaches to solve the main security issues. Some layers, such as the hypervisor and adaptive antenna system, are still evolving, and their security techniques have yet to be improved further. Others services and layers are approaching a certain technical maturity. As such, in order to more securely use cloud computing services, users might consider operational security. However, security operations and their automation need to be further investigated to improve their efficiency and effectiveness in alleviating security risks. Tackling security issues from both technical and operational aspects will eventually foster larger success of multitenant cloud computing.

REFERENCES

1. Wylve and Bikeborg. Cloud computing layers. Wikimedia Foundation, Inc.: San Francisco, CA. https://commons.wikimedia.org/wiki/File:Cloud_computing_layers.svg.
2. Jongse Park, Daewoo Lee, Bokyeong Kim, Jaehyuk Huh, and Seungryoul Maeng. Locality-aware dynamic VM reconfiguration on map reduce clouds. In *Proceedings of the 21st International Symposium on High-Performance Parallel and Distributed Computing*, pp. 27–36, ACM: New York, 2012.
3. Khalid Bijon, Ram Krishnan, and Ravi Sandhu. Mitigating multi-tenancy risks in IaaS cloud through constraints-driven virtual resource scheduling. In *Proceedings of the 20th ACM Symposium on Access Control Models and Technologies*, pp. 63–74, ACM: New York, 2015.
4. KhalidZaman Bijon, Ram Krishnan, and Ravi Sandhu. A formal model for isolation management in cloud infrastructure-as-a-service. In ManHo Au, Barbara Carminati, and C.-C. Jay Kuo, editors, *Network and System Security*, volume 8792 of *Lecture Notes in Computer Science*, pp. 41–53, Springer International Publishing, 2014.
5. Khalid Bijon, Ram Krishnan, and Ravi Sandhu. Virtual resource orchestration constraints in cloud infrastructure as a service. In *Proceedings of the 5th ACM Conference on Data and Application Security and Privacy*, pp. 183–194, ACM: New York, 2015.
6. Thomas Ristenpart, Eran Tromer, Hovav Shacham, and Stefan Savage. Hey, you, get off of my cloud: Exploring information leakage in third-party compute clouds. In *Proceedings of the 16th ACM Conference on Computer and Communications Security*, pp. 199–212, ACM: New York, 2009.
7. Venkatanathan Varadarajan, Thawan Kooburat, Benjamin Farley, Thomas Ristenpart, and Michael M. Swift. Resource-freeing attacks: Improve your cloud performance (at your neighbor's expense). In *Proceedings of the 2012 ACM Conference on Computer and Communications Security*, pp. 281–292, ACM: New York, 2012.

8. Yinqian Zhang, Ari Juels, Michael K. Reiter, and Thomas Ristenpart. Cross-VM side channels and their use to extract private keys. In *Proceedings of the 2012 ACM Conference on Computer and Communications Security*, pp. 305–316, ACM: New York, 2012.

9. Yinqian Zhang, Ari Juels, Michael K. Reiter, and Thomas Ristenpart. Cross-tenant side-channel attacks in PaaS clouds. In *Proceedings of the 2014 ACM SIGSAC Conference on Computer and Communications Security*, pp. 990–1003, ACM: New York, 2014.

10. T. Takahashi, G. Blanc, Y. Kadobayashi, D. Fall, H. Hazeyama, and S. Matsuo. Enabling secure multitenancy in cloud computing: Challenges and approaches. In *2012 2nd Baltic Congress on Future Internet Communications (BCFIC)*, pp. 72–79, 2012.

11. G. C. Deka. Cost-benefit analysis of datacenter consolidation using virtualization. *IT Professional*, 16(6):54–62, 2014.

12. M. Caliskan, M. Ozsiginan, and E. Kugu. Benefits of the virtualization technologies with intrusion detection and prevention systems. In *2013 7th International Conference on Application of Information and Communication Technologies (AICT)*, pp. 1–5, 2013.

13. G. Minutoli and A. Puliafito. GliteVM: How science and business may benefit from virtualization. In *Eighth IEEE International Symposium on Network Computing and Applications, 2009*, pp. 126–129, 2009.

14. Edward Ray and Eugene Schultz. Virtualization security. In *Proceedings of the 5th Annual Workshop on Cyber Security and Information Intelligence Research: Cyber Security and Information Intelligence Challenges and Strategies*, pp. 42:1–42:5, ACM: New York, 2009.

15. S.T. King and P.M. Chen. Subvirt: Implementing malware with virtual machines. In *2006 IEEE Symposium on Security and Privacy*, pp. 14–327, 2006.

16. Geffner Jason. VENOM: Virtualized Environment Neglected Operations Manipulation. http://venom.crowdstrike.com/, May 2015. [Online].

17. John Scott Robin and Cynthia E. Irvine. Analysis of the Intel Pentium's ability to support a secure virtual machine monitor. In *Proceedings of the 9th Conference on USENIX Security Symposium—Volume 9*, pp. 10–10, USENIX Association: Berkeley, CA, 2000.

18. David Carrera, Malgorzata Steinder, Ian Whalley, Jordi Torres, and Eduard Ayguadé. Enabling resource sharing between transactional and batch workloads using dynamic application placement. In *Proceedings of the 9th ACM/IFIP/USENIX International Conference on Middleware*, pp. 203–222, 2008.

19. Jason Mars, Lingjia Tang, Robert Hundt, Kevin Skadron, and Mary Lou Soffa. Bubble-up: Increasing utilization in modern warehouse scale computers via sensible co-locations. In *Proceedings of the 44th Annual IEEE/ACM International Symposium on Microarchitecture*, pp. 248–259, 2011.

20. Ripal Nathuji, Aman Kansal, and Alireza Ghaffarkhah. Q-clouds: Managing performance interference effects for QoS-aware clouds. In *Proceedings of the 5th European Conference on Computer Systems*, pp. 237–250. ACM: New York, 2010.

21. Xiaoyun Zhu, Don Young, B.J. Watson, Zhikui Wang, J. Rolia, S. Singhal, B. McKee, C. Hyser, D. Gmach, R. Gardner, T. Christian, and L. Cherkasova. 1000 islands: Integrated capacity and workload management for the next generation data center. In *International Conference on Autonomic Computing, 2008*, pp. 172–181, 2008.

22. Zhikui Wang, Yuan Chen, D. Gmach, S. Singhal, B.J. Watson, W. Rivera, Xiaoyun Zhu, and C.D. Hyser. Appraise: Application-level performance management in virtualized server environments. *IEEE Transactions on Network and Service Management*, 6(4):240–254, 2009.

23. Rui Wang and Nagarajan Kandasamy. A distributed control framework for performance management of virtualized computing environments: Some preliminary results. In *Proceedings of the 1st Workshop on Automated Control for Datacenters and Clouds*, pp. 7–12, 2009.

24. D. Minarolli and B. Freisleben. Utility-based resource allocation for virtual machines in cloud computing. In *2011 IEEE Symposium on Computers and Communications (ISCC)*, pp. 410–417, 2011.

25. Emerson Loureiro, Paddy Nixon, and Simon Dobson. A fine-grained model for adaptive on-demand provisioning of CPU shares in data centers. In *Proceedings of the 3rd International Workshop on Self-Organizing Systems*, pp. 97–108, 2008.

26. I. Goiri, Kien Le, M.E. Haque, R. Beauchea, T.D. Nguyen, J. Guitart, J. Torres, and R. Bianchini. Greenslot: Scheduling energy consumption in green datacenters. In *2011 International Conference for High Performance Computing, Networking, Storage and Analysis (SC)*, pp. 1–11, 2011.

27. Yixin Diao and Aliza Heching. Closed loop performance management for service delivery systems. In *2012 IEEE Network Operations and Management Symposium*, pp. 61–69, 2012.

28. Timothy Wood, Prashant Shenoy, Arun Venkataramani, and Mazin Yousif. Black-box and gray-box strategies for virtual machine migration. In *Proceedings of the 4th USENIX Conference on Networked Systems Design and Implementation*, pp. 17–17, 2007.

29. Akkarit Sangpetch, Andrew Turner, and Hyong Kim. How to tame your VMS: An automated control system for virtualized services. In *Proceedings of the 24th International Conference on Large Installation System Administration*, pp. 1–16, USENIX Association: Berkeley, CA, 2010.

30. O. Sukwong, A. Sangpetch, and H.S. Kim. Sageshift: Managing SLAs for highly consolidated cloud. In *2012 Proceedings of the IEEE INFOCOM*, pp. 208–216, 2012.

31. Bin Lin and Peter A. Dinda. Vsched: Mixing batch and interactive virtual machines using periodic real-time scheduling. In *Proceedings of the ACM/IEEE SC 2005*, p. 8, 2005.

32. M. Kesavan, A. Ranadive, A. Gavrilovska, and K. Schwan. Active coordination (act)—Toward effectively managing virtualized multicore clouds. In *2008 IEEE International Conference on Cluster Computing*, pp. 23–32, 2008.

33. A. Gandhi, Yuan Chen, D. Gmach, M. Arlitt, and M. Marwah. Minimizing data center SLA violations and power consumption via hybrid resource provisioning. In *Proceedings of the 2011 International Green Computing Conference and Workshops*, pp. 1–8, IEEE Computer Society: Washington, DC, 2011.

34. Sergey Blagodurov, Daniel Gmach, Martin Arlitt, Yuan Chen, Chris Hyser, and Alexandra Fedorova. Maximizing server utilization while meeting critical SLAs via weight-based collocation management. In *2013 IFIP/IEEE International Symposium on Integrated Network Management*, pp. 277–285, 2013.

35. Saad Rahim. State of GPU virtualization for cuda applications. Acceleware Ltd.: Calgary, Alberta, Canada. http://acceleware.com/blog/ state-gpu-virtualization-cuda-applications-2014, 2014.

36. Micah Dowty and Jeremy Sugerman. GPU virtualization on vmware's hosted I/O architecture. *SIGOPS Operating System Review*, 43(3):73–82, 2009.

37. Lin Shi, Hao Chen, and Jianhua Sun. vCUDA: GPU accelerated high performance computing in virtual machines. In *IEEE International Symposium on Parallel Distributed Processing*, pp. 1–11, 2009.

38. Giulio Giunta, Raffaele Montella, Giuseppe Agrillo, and Giuseppe Coviello. A GPGPU transparent virtualization component for high performance computing clouds. In Pasqua D'Ambra, Mario Guarracino, and Domenico Talia, editors, *Euro-Par 2010—Parallel Processing*, volume 6271 of *Lecture Notes in Computer Science*, pp. 379–391. Springer: Berlin, Germany, 2010.

39. J. Duato, A.J. Pena, F. Silla, R. Mayo, and Quintana-Orti E.S. rCUDA: Reducing the number of GPU-based accelerators in high performance clusters. In *International Conference on High Performance Computing and Simulation*, pp. 224–231, 2010.

40. Vishakha Gupta, Ada Gavrilovska, Karsten Schwan, Harshvardhan Kharche, Niraj Tolia, Vanish Talwar, and Parthasarathy Ranganathan. GViM: GPU-accelerated virtual machines. In *Proceedings of the 3rd ACM Workshop on System-Level Virtualization for High Performance Computing*, pp. 17–24, ACM: New York, 2009.

41. Shucai Xiao, P. Balaji, Qian Zhu, R. Thakur, S. Coghlan, Heshan Lin, Gaojin Wen, Jue Hong, and Wu-chun Feng. VOCL: An optimized environment for transparent virtualization of graphics processing units. In *Innovative Parallel Computing*, pp. 1–12, 2012.

42. Clementine Maurice, Christoph Neumann, Olivier Heen, and Aurelien Francillon. Confidentiality issues on a GPU in a virtualized environment. In Nicolas Christin and Reihaneh Safavi-Naini, editors, *Financial Cryptography and Data Security*, volume 8437 of *Lecture Notes in Computer Science*, pp. 119–135. Springer: Berlin, Germany, 2014.

43. Justine Sherry, Shaddi Hasan, Colin Scott, Arvind Krishnamurthy, Sylvia Ratnasamy, and Vyas Sekar. Making middleboxes someone else's problem: Network processing as a cloud service. In *Proceedings of the ACM SIGCOMM 2012 Conference on Applications, Technologies, Architectures, and Protocols for Computer Communication*, pp. 13–24, 2012.

44. Zafar Ayyub Qazi, Cheng-Chun Tu, Luis Chiang, Rui Miao, Vyas Sekar, and Minlan Yu. Simplifying middlebox policy enforcement using SDN. In *Proceedings of the ACM SIGCOMM 2013 Conference on SIGCOMM*, pp. 27–38, ACM: New York, 2013.

45. Aaron Gember, Robert Grandl, Junaid Khalid, and Aditya Akella. Design and implementation of a framework for software-defined middlebox networking. In *Proceedings of the ACM SIGCOMM 2013 Conference on SIGCOMM*, pp. 467–468, ACM: New York, 2013.

46. Jeffrey R. Ballard, Ian Rae, and Aditya Akella. Extensible and scalable network monitoring using OpenSafe. In *Proceedings of the 2010 Internet Network Management Conference on Research on Enterprise Networking*, pp. 8–8, 2010.

47. Glen Gibb, Hongyi Zeng, and Nick McKeown. Outsourcing network functionality. In *Proceedings of the First Workshop on Hot Topics in Software Defined Networks*, pp. 73–78, ACM: New York, 2012.

48. Vyas Sekar, Ravishankar Krishnaswamy, Anupam Gupta, and Michael K. Reiter. Network-wide deployment of intrusion detection and prevention systems. In *Proceedings of the 6th International Conference*, Co-NEXT'10, pp. 18:1–18:12, ACM: New York, 2010.

49. Victor Heorhiadi, Michael K. Reiter, and Vyas Sekar. New opportunities for load balancing in network-wide intrusion detection systems. In *Proceedings of the 8th International Conference on Emerging Networking Experiments and Technologies*, CoNEXT'12, pp. 361–372, ACM: New York, 2012.

50. Saqib Raza, Guanyao Huang, Chen-Nee Chuah, Srini Seetharaman, and Jatinder Pal Singh. Measurouting: A framework for routing assisted traffic monitoring. *IEEE/ACM Transactions on Networking*, 20(1):45–56, 2012.

51. Andreas Voellmy and Paul Hudak. Nettle: Taking the sting out of programming network routers. In *Proceedings of the 13th International Conference on Practical Aspects of Declarative Languages*, pp. 235–249, Springer-Verlag: Berlin, Germany, 2011.

52. Nate Foster, Michael J. Freedman, Rob Harrison, Jennifer Rexford, Matthew L. Meola, and David Walker. Frenetic: A high-level language for OpenFlow networks. In *Proceedings of the Workshop on Programmable Routers for Extensible Services of Tomorrow*, pp. 6:1–6:6, ACM: New York, 2010.

53. Nick McKeown, Tom Anderson, Hari Balakrishnan, Guru Parulkar, Larry Peterson, Jennifer Rexford, Scott Shenker, and Jonathan Turner. OpenFlow: Enabling innovation in campus networks. *SIGCOMM Computer Communication Review*, 38(2):69–74, 2008.

54. Philip Porras, Seungwon Shin, Vinod Yegneswaran, Martin Fong, Mabry Tyson, and Guofei Gu. A security enforcement kernel for OpenFlow networks. In *Proceedings of the First Workshop on Hot Topics in Software Defined Networks*, pp. 121–126, ACM: New York, 2012.

55. Seugwon Shin, Phillip Porras, Vinod Yegneswaran, Martin Fong, Guofei Gu, and Mabry Tyson. Fresco: Modular composable security services for software-defined networks, 2013.

56. Seungwon Shin, Vinod Yegneswaran, Phillip Porras, and Guofei Gu. AVANT-GUARD: Scalable and vigilant switch flow management in software-defined networks. In *Proceedings of the 2013 ACM SIGSAC Conference on Computer & Communications Security*, pp. 413–424, ACM: New York, 2013.

57. L.R. Battula. Network Security Function Virtualization (NSFV) towards cloud computing with NFV over Openflow infrastructure: Challenges and novel approaches. In *ICACCI, 2014 International Conference on Advances in Computing, Communications and Informatics,* pp. 1622–1628, 2014.

58. S. Shin, H. Wang, and G. Gu. A first step towards network security virtualization: From concept to prototype. *IEEE Transactions on Information Forensics and Security,* PP(99):1–1, 2015.

59. Seyed Kaveh Fayazbakhsh, Vyas Sekar, Minlan Yu, and Jeffrey C. Mogul. FlowTags: Enforcing network-wide policies in the presence of dynamic middlebox actions. In *Proceedings of the Second ACM SIGCOMM Workshop on Hot Topics in Software Defined Networking,* pp. 19–24, ACM: New York, 2013.

60. T. Ormandy. An empirical study into the security exposure to host of hostile virtualized environments. *taviso.decsystem.org,* 2007.

61. Joanna Rutkowska. Subverting vista kernel for fun and profit. *Black Hat Talk,* 2006.

62. Tal Garfinkel, Keith Adams, Andrew Warfield, and Jason Franklin. Compatibility is not transparency: VMM detection myths and realities. In *Proceedings of the 11th USENIX Workshop on Hot Topics in Operating Systems,* pp. 6:1–6:6, USENIX Association: Berkeley, CA, 2007.

63. Jason Franklin, Mark Luk, Jonathan M. McCune, Arvind Seshadri, Adrian Perrig, and Leendert van Doorn. Remote detection of virtual machine monitors with fuzzy benchmarking. *SIGOPS Operating System Review,* 42(3):83–92, 2008.

64. Flavio Lombardi and Roberto Di Pietro. Secure virtualization for cloud computing. *Journal of Network and Computer Applications,* 34(4):1113–1122, 2011.

65. Tal Garfinkel, Ben Pfaff, Jim Chow, Mendel Rosenblum, and Dan Boneh. Terra: A virtual machine-based platform for trusted computing. In *Proceedings of the Nineteenth ACM Symposium on Operating Systems Principles,* pp. 193–206, ACM: New York, 2003.

66. Stefan Berger, Ramón Cáceres, Kenneth A. Goldman, Ronald Perez, Reiner Sailer, and Leendert van Doorn. vTPM: Virtualizing the trusted platform module. In *Proceedings of the 15th Conference on USENIX Security Symposium—Volume 15,* USENIX Association, Berkeley, CA, 2006.

67. Brian Hay and Kara Nance. Forensics examination of volatile system data using virtual introspection. *SIGOPS Operating System Review,* 42(3):74–82, 2008.

68. Reiner Sailer, Trent Jaeger, Enriquillo Valdez, Ramon Caceres, Ronald Perez, Stefan Berger, John Linwood Griffin, and Leendert van Doorn. Building a MAC-based security architecture for the Xen open-source hypervisor. In *Proceedings of the 21st Annual Computer Security Applications Conference,* pp. 276–285, IEEE Computer Society: Washington, DC, 2005.

69. Ryan Riley, Xuxian Jiang, and Dongyan Xu. Guest-transparent prevention of kernel rootkits with VMM-based memory shadowing. In *Proceedings of the 11th International Symposium on Recent Advances in Intrusion Detection,* pp. 1–20, Springer-Verlag: Berlin, Germany, 2008.

70. Roberto Di Pietro, Flavio Lombardi, and Matteo Signorini. CloRExPa: Cloud resilience via execution path analysis. *Future Generation Computer Systems,* 32:168–179, 2014.

71. Z. Cliffe Schreuders, Tanya McGill, and Christian Payne. Empowering end users to confine their own applications: The results of a usability study comparing SElinux, AppArmor, and FBAC-LSM. *ACM Transactions on Information and System Security,* 14(2):19:1–19:28, 2011.

72. Hong Chen, Ninghui Li, and Ziqing Mao. Analyzing and comparing the protection quality of security enhanced operating systems. In *NDSS.* The Internet Society, 2009.

73. Robert N. M. Watson, Jonathan Anderson, Ben Laurie, and Kris Kennaway. Capsicum: Practical capabilities for UNIX. In *Proceedings of the 19th USENIX Conference on Security,* pp. 3–3, USENIX Association: Berkeley, CA, 2010.

74. Gansen Zhao, Chunming Rong, Jin Li, Feng Zhang, and Yong Tang. Trusted data sharing over untrusted cloud storage providers. In *2010 IEEE Second International Conference on Cloud Computing Technology and Science (CloudCom),* pp. 97–103, 2010.

75. Masahiro Mambo and Eiji Okamoto. Proxy Cryptosystems: Delegation of the power to decrypt ciphertexts. *IEICE Transactions on Fundamentals of Electronics, Communications and Computer Sciences*, 80A(1):54–63, 1997.

76. Craig Gentry. Fully homomorphic encryption using ideal lattices. In *Proceedings of the Forty-First Annual ACM Symposium on Theory of Computing*, pp. 169–178, ACM: New York, NY, 2009.

77. Craig Gentry. Computing arbitrary functions of encrypted data. *Communications of the ACM*, 53(3):97–105, 2010.

78. Thomas S. J. Schwarz and Ethan L. Miller. Store, forget, and check: Using algebraic signatures to check remotely administered storage. In *Proceedings of the 26th IEEE International Conference on Distributed Computing Systems*, pp. 12–, IEEE Computer Society: Washington, DC, 2006.

79. Mark Lillibridge, Sameh Elnikety, Andrew Birrell, Mike Burrows, and Michael Isard. A cooperative internet backup scheme. In *Proceedings of the Annual Conference on USENIX Annual Technical Conference*, pp. 3–3, USENIX Association: Berkeley, CA, 2003.

80. Kevin D. Bowers, Ari Juels, and Alina Oprea. Hail: A high-availability and integrity layer for cloud storage. In *Proceedings of the 16th ACM Conference on Computer and Communications Security*, pp. 187–198, ACM: New York, 2009.

81. Cong Wang, Qian Wang, Kui Ren, and Wenjing Lou. Ensuring data storage security in cloud computing. In *17th International Workshop on Quality of Service, 2009*, pp. 1–9, 2009.

82. Danny Harnik, Benny Pinkas, and Alexandra Shulman-Peleg. Side channels in cloud services: Deduplication in cloud storage. *IEEE Security and Privacy*, 8(6):40–47, 2010.

83. Andrew C. Myers and Barbara Liskov. Protecting privacy using the decentralized label model. *ACM Transactions on Software Engineering and Methodology*, 9(4):410–442, 2000.

84. Ioannis Papagiannis, Matteo Migliavacca, David M. Eyers, Brian Shand, Jean Bacon, and Peter Pietzuch. Enforcing user privacy in web applications using erlang. *Web 2.0 Security and Privacy*, 2010.

85. Dan Boneh and Matt Franklin. Identity-based encryption from the Weil pairing. In Joe Kilian, editor, *Advances in Cryptology—CRYPTO 2001*, volume 2139 of *Lecture Notes in Computer Science*, pp. 213–229. Springer: Berlin, Germany, 2001.

86. Lishan Kang and Xuejie Zhang. Identity-based authentication in cloud storage sharing. In *2010 International Conference on Multimedia Information Networking and Security*, pp. 851–855, 2010.

87. Qin Liu, Guojun Wang, and Jie Wu. Efficient sharing of secure cloud storage services. In *2010 IEEE 10th International Conference on Computer and Information Technology*, pp. 922–929, 2010.

88. Craig Gentry and Alice Silverberg. Hierarchical id-based cryptography. In Yuliang Zheng, editor, *Advances in Cryptology—ASIACRYPT 2002*, volume 2501 of *Lecture Notes in Computer Science*, pp. 548–566, Springer: Berlin, Germany, 2002.

89. Jin Li, Gansen Zhao, Xiaofeng Chen, Dongqing Xie, Chunming Rong, Wenjun Li, Lianzhang Tang, and Yong Tang. Fine-grained data access control systems with user accountability in cloud computing. In *2010 IEEE Second International Conference on Cloud Computing Technology and Science (CloudCom)*, pp. 89–96, 2010.

90. Amit Sahai and Brent Waters. Fuzzy identity-based encryption. In *Proceedings of the 24th Annual International Conference on Theory and Applications of Cryptographic Techniques*, pp. 457–473, Springer-Verlag: Berlin, Germany, 2005.

91. Vipul Goyal, Omkant Pandey, Amit Sahai, and Brent Waters. Attribute-based encryption for fine-grained access control of encrypted data. In *Proceedings of the 13th ACM Conference on Computer and Communications Security*, pp. 89–98, ACM: New York, 2006.

92. Melissa Chase and Sherman S.M. Chow. Improving privacy and security in multi-authority attribute-based encryption. In *Proceedings of the 16th ACM Conference on Computer and Communications Security*, pp. 121–130, ACM: New York, 2009.

93. Shucheng Yu, Cong Wang, Kui Ren, and Wenjing Lou. Achieving secure, scalable, and fine-grained data access control in cloud computing. In *Proceedings of the 29th Conference on Information Communications*, pp. 534–542, IEEE Press: Piscataway, NJ, 2010.
94. Seny Kamara and Kristin Lauter. Cryptographic cloud storage. In *Proceedings of the 14th International Conference on Financial Cryptography and Data Security*, pp. 136–149, Springer-Verlag, Berlin, Germany, 2010.

Designing Cloud Security and Operations Models in the Changed Geopolitical Environment

Thorsten Herre

CONTENTS

14.1 INTRODUCTION

Cloud computing and cloud services became the new driving buzzwords over the past couple of years and will redefine many enterprise information technology (IT) organizations and the way how IT systems and critical business solutions are operated in the future. Every industry and even governments are affected, and no one can ignore the upcoming changes any more. A long time the epicenter of this cloud movement and cloud solution development was very US centric and driven with the open and unrestrictive Internet in mind. This chapter outlines some of the challenges and developments in the world, which could make the usage of cloud more complicated due to newly emerging country-specific laws, regulations, and industry standards.

14.2 TRADITIONAL HOSTING VERSUS CLOUD SERVICES

In its core, the "cloud" is not totally new. Outsourcing and external hosting models were used by companies for many years. Also in those cases, the enterprises had to decide if they can trust the hosting partner and want to store or even process their business critical data in a foreign country, data center, or if they can accept the risk of potential data access by partner employees. There are legal frameworks, contracts, and even certifications and attestation standards available for such hosting partners to prove to their customers that a secure and reliable operation is maintained. So what's new in the cloud?

Figure 14.1 shows how the cloud services and operation models changed the setup and responsibilities between the cloud service provider and the customer. The introduction of virtualization and new ways to share all kinds of IT-related services brought a big push to the hosting or cloud market. It was cheaper and more effective for many customers to only rent the IT resources (e.g., storage, CPU workloads, or complete applications) on demand to be able to scale flexible based on their own business. Also the cloud offered a new model of IT Infrastructure system design and consumption. Everything is a cloud-based (meaning virtualized, potentially shared, and Internet facing) service, which can be used together with

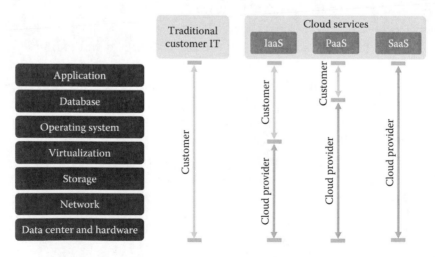

FIGURE 14.1   Traditional IT versus cloud services. IaaS, infrastructure as a service; PaaS, platform as a service; SaaS, software as a service.

other cloud services. In other words, it is more like a modular set of granular IT services, that is ready any time, and indefinitely scalable.

Companies such as Amazon [1], Microsoft [2], Apple, Google, VMware, or open-source projects such as OpenStack [3], Docker, and Chef are at the forefront of this movement. Another disruptive idea was the way how complete servers, systems, or landscapes are set up, cloned, reused, or automated. One approach was the "DevOps" method [4] that tried to deeply integrate the software development cycle with the IT operation models.

14.3 SILICON VALLEY AND THE WORLD

Like many development in the IT space, the influence of US inventions, US standards, and US-based companies is significant. Silicon Valley plays of course a key role. The developers located in this area mostly have the free Internet and US cultural or regulatory ideas in their mind when they built new cloud solution or cloud services. The idea that there is one gigantic global cloud that could serve all countries equally and with the same configuration and processes was not uncommon in the past. This is the reason why many existing cloud solutions were optimized for US needs and US markets. Unfortunately, in some cases, especially if we talk about processing business critical or regulated data in the cloud, this US-centric approach will not work for the rest of the world. The cloud service providers finally recognized this issue and changed their solution, for example, for the EU or Asia market accordingly. However, there are still frictions in some areas (e.g., EU privacy laws) that need to be watched closely before a cloud solution is bought.

14.4 DIFFERENCES BETWEEN THE CLOUD CONSUMER AND THE ENTERPRISE WORLD

There is a major difference between the cloud consumer business and the enterprise business. In the consumer world, the end user basically has to accept the terms and conditions as long as he or she complies with the basic requirements of the local laws. Nevertheless, if you look at the terms in many well-known cloud-based services, it is clear that especially for free solutions, the customer has to pay with his or her data. When have you last read the whole updated iCloud terms or the customer data usage rights of Facebook, Spotify, Google Mail, Twitter, or WhatsApp? The customer should be aware of the prize he or she pays for the usage, and in the end, he or she could decide not to use these cloud-based services any more. There are in most cases only two options: accept the existing terms or reject them which will basically terminate the service usage. However, of course, it is very unlikely that these companies change their business model or terms only due to some disgruntled end users that disagree with the way their data are reused for advertising, marketing analytics, or other purposes.

In the enterprise market, however, the cloud customer companies will not accept terms that endanger or expose their business data. Especially in Europe, these companies are very hesitant to move their core business data into the cloud and would like to negotiate special terms or contract depending on their industry standards and internal company policies. The cloud service provider is a subcontractor like anyone else for them and needs to follow their purchasing process. For example, will most European

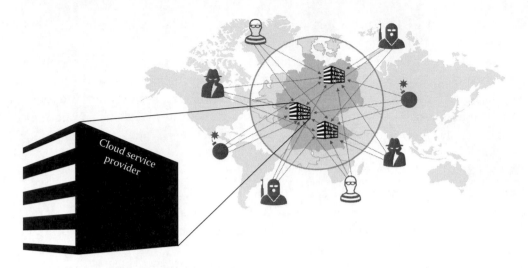

FIGURE 14.2   Cloud provider under attack.

customers insist in local storage of their data (e.g., within the country of the corporate headquarter or at least within the boundaries of the European Union). Figure 14.2 shows how the cloud service provider becomes the central point of attraction for many attackers, spies, or criminals due to his or her concentration of customer data in one location or within one cloud service. Therefore, a very high and vigilant security is a key feature for every enterprise cloud provider.

Similar notions arise from Asian, Russian, or Australian companies. One global cloud with maybe only US-based data centers would be a problem for such companies. The cloud provider reacted and ensures now a local data center usage, which in some cases can even be selected by the customer. Some cloud solutions call this feature "availability zone" or "region" [5]. Other examples could be added, but it is fair to say that the enterprise market was one of the key drivers and those new features.

14.5 COUNTRY- AND INDUSTRY-SPECIFIC DEVELOPMENTS

Many country- and industry-specific requirements exist at the moment and must be considered by cloud service providers with ambitions to sell into the global enterprise cloud market. Unfortunately, there is not one central cloud standard or cross-country cloud regulation, besides the well-known service organization controls (SOC)1/2 attestations as defined in the ISAE3402 [6] or International Standards for Assurance Engagements (SSAE)16 [7]. These SOC audits ensure that a cloud provider or a hosting service provider has some level of controls in place and can offer a reliable operation. It is not per se a cloud-specific attestation and was formerly also known as SAS70 Reports for the old application or server hosting business. In the same way, the internationally known ISO27001 certificate [8] confirms a high level of security controls and a security management framework, but this is also not cloud specific. Most cloud service providers perform all these certifications and attestations to have a good foundation and baseline for their business. Many are also a member of the Cloud Security Alliance (CSA) and work with other companies in the definition of, for example, a cloud security standard and certification model (STAR certification) [9]. The challenge remains that additional local regulations of certain industries (e.g., health care, finance, credit card industry, pharmaceutical industry) or countries must also be followed in the cloud setup and operation. Sometimes, this is quite difficult because these regulations did not consider the special nature of the cloud services or operational models. The examples discussed in Sections 14.5.1 through 14.5.5 should outline some of those cases.

14.5.1 Example: Russia

Russia, for example, doesn't care so much about international certifications such as ISO27001 or European- or US-defined attestations such as SOC1/2. They have their own standards and certifications. The Russian companies are not willing to use cloud solutions if the data are stored outside of Russia. The newly introduced Russian regulation even restricts the storage of Russian citizen data even more [10]. Therefore, Russian companies could not so easily use a human resource cloud solution that manages their employees and operates, for example, out of a data center in the United States. If the cloud provider decides to serve these customers out of Russia, he or she must go through a detailed vetting and approval process involving several Russian telecommunications authorities [11] and maybe even the federal security service (FSB). Encryption should use a Russian-developed encryption algorithm called GOsudarstvennyi STandard (GOST) and all encryption hardware or software must be approved by the authorities upfront. This could be a problem, if the cloud software, for example, can't use a different encryption algorithm and is hard-coded to the international encryption standards such as ASE and RSA. The cloud solution itself must be checked in security functionality, and special operational and security concepts must be created. In most cases, a "Federal Service for Technical and Export Control" (FSTEC) certification and approval is needed. Figure 14.3 explains the three basic steps for using FSTEC-certified hardware and software for the cloud solution; as well as, explaining how to perform a security and data protection attestation for the solution and all its components itself. And in the end, Figure 14.3 also explains how to get registered for the Russian market, including all of the necessary approvals and licenses.

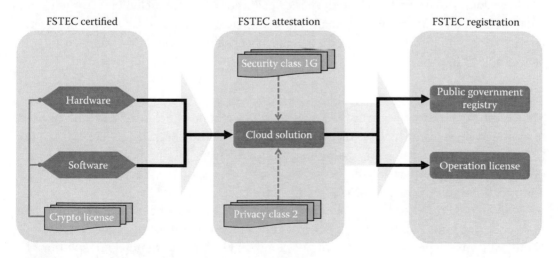

FIGURE 14.3   FSTEC attestation and registration.

Needless to say, all documentation and governmental forms must be filled out in Russian. The financial and operational impact for the cloud service provider is significant.

14.5.2 Example: China

A foreign (e.g., US or EU) company is not allowed to sell or offer cloud services on its own. The cloud provider always needs a local Internet service partner (e.g., China Telecom) to sell and operate the cloud with their help [12]. This creates a certain dependency to the local partner and limits the business options of the cloud provider. Also China is known for its restrictive Internet usage policies that will also apply to Internet facing cloud services. Therefore, potential censorship and reporting channels to the government could be needed, which may violate the cloud provider principles. In the end, he or she would not like to connect this China cloud solution directly to his or her global cloud network and may consider a stand-alone variant for China.

14.5.3 Example: European Union

Europe and Australia are very strict in terms of customer data usage, especially if the data contain personal data of end users. Even if the cloud solution is a global setup, it may be necessary to add certain functionality for European or Australian users with regard to data retention policies, customer-controlled data processing settings, data encryption options, or opt-in principles. Europe also has a high level of country-specific regulations on top of the European ones that make the market even more complex. Many companies such as Microsoft, Google, Facebook, or Amazon have long-standing discussions with the Europeans about the necessary protection of its citizens and industries. The Safe Harbor Program [13] between the United States and Europe was questioned and seen as insufficient by some EU members to protect EU data. New international agreements between the United States and Europe try to harmonize the regulations and standards to enable additional business. The cloud solutions could also be benefitted from that, but these discussions take many years and the cloud business can't wait so long. For the cloud service provider, it means that he or she can't extend his or her business into new countries or markets without checking if his or her current cloud infrastructure and data processing environment are actually allowed to be used. Figure 14.4 shows the different restrictive data protection and privacy legislation in various countries. Even though this is only an example, it shows how fragmented the legislation is around the world.

14.5.4 Example: Credit Card Industry

The credit card industry demands that all used IT solutions, including subcontractors or outsourced services, comply with their Payment Card Industry/Data Security Standard (PCI/DSS) [14] for secure processing of credit card data. Figure 14.5 lists the 12 main domains and topics that need to be covered with corresponding security measures and controls to be able to get a PCI/DSS certification.

This must be certified by independent auditors on a regular basis. The PCI/DSS standard contains hundreds of single measures and controls that must be implemented in the cloud solution. Depending on the kind of cloud service provider and cloud solution that is in scope, such a PCI audit is a high-effort endeavor. The PCI/DSS requirements define

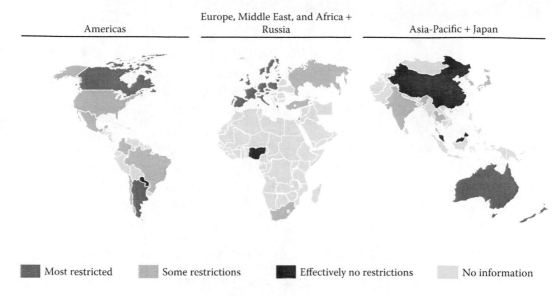

FIGURE 14.4 World map of data protection laws.

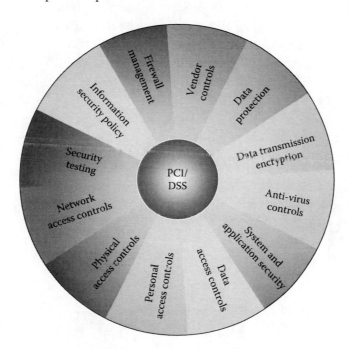

FIGURE 14.5 PCI/DSS domains.

rules not only for the operation but also for the design of the cloud software itself. Similar to other industry standards, the cloud service provider must plan a new functionality with these requirements in mind and also adopt this in his or her cloud development life cycle. It is a very specific view on the cloud data processing and cloud service delivery compared to other standards. The main focus lies in the credit card fraud prevention, after the credit card industry suffered some painful incidents in the past.

14.5.5 Example: Pharmaceutical Industry

The pharmaceutical industry focuses more on the change management processes and the traceability of all actions performed in a system either by end users or especially by administrators. Therefore, they want assurance from the cloud service provider and special tools that allow deep reporting, logging, and monitoring of their cloud solution and cloud data. The provider needs to offer such extensive and flexible monitoring and logging functions to be able to sell into such markets successfully. Of course, there are also other aspects of data security besides the pure change management and logging that are relevant for those systems as well [15]. These customers may, for example, insist in cryptographic electronic signatures similar and document rights management functionality. This would demand the capability for cryptographic key handling and an integration of such signature aspects into the cloud software design.

14.6 PUBLIC SECTOR AND GOVERNMENT CLOUD CHALLENGES

A special challenging area is the public sector that consists of the governmental and military customers. To a certain degree, commercial companies fall under these regulations if they deeply interact, produce, sell, or process military or government data or products. Not surprisingly, the requirements and regulations by these governmental customers are not harmonized between the countries. Basically, every country defined its own rules. Figure 14.6 shows an example of various government and industry-specific certification and attestation standards grouped by region and industry types.

Of course, there are some similarities with regard to encryption usage, but this only helps a little because the encryption software or hardware must be certified by each individual government. Also they of course demand that their data are stored locally and only administrated by local citizens. This is a challenge for the cloud service provider if he or

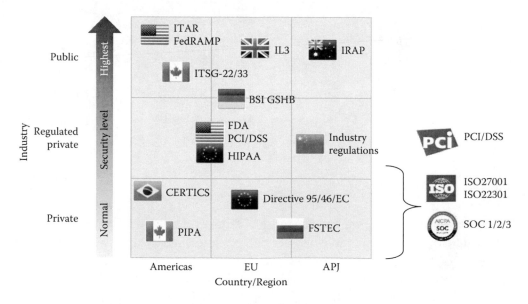

FIGURE 14.6 Country- and industry-specific certifications.

she operates with a global shift based following the sun support model and has no local country-specific resources for the cloud operation around the clock (7 × 24).

Additional to these technical cloud infrastructure and cloud operational aspects, the solution and services must be certified by local standards. Therefore, in the end, you may have dozens of isolated and country-specific cloud implementations of your cloud service to serve these customers. It is questionable if such an effort and fragmentation of the global cloud service makes sense from a business and a financial point of view.

14.6.1 The US Federal Risk and Authorization Management Program

Many US government agencies have the need to work with contractors or to operate, for example, their own IT systems. It was decided that a unified and government-wide risk management program would be needed to manage such outsourcing or multiagency information systems. The Federal Risk and Authorization Management Program (FedRAMP) addressed such needs by defining security monitoring and cloud computing requirements. The FedRAMP process defines five major roles and participants:

- The cloud service provider
- The US agency that wants to use the cloud services
- A joint authorization board that reviews and approves the cloud provider or the cloud solution for governmental usage
- Potentially a third-party assessor that assists in the review and vetting process
- The FedRAMP Program Management Office that provides support and coordination services to the aforementioned parties

The main purpose of this review and approval process is to ensure that the cloud solution and cloud operator comply with the needed information security measures and also to analyze the remaining risk for the government. Figure 14.7 shows this assessment process by listing the needed review and approval steps and by showing the corresponding workflow. After the initial steps, the process goes into a continuous

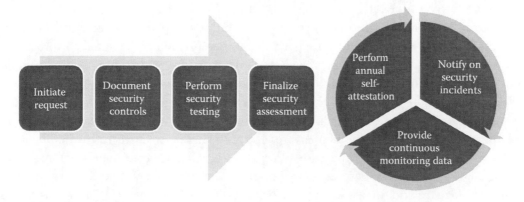

FIGURE 14.7 FedRAMP assessment process.

monitoring and annual review cycle to ensure that the originally achieved compliance is not lost over time.

A third task is to reduce the overall costs and to monitor potential duplication of effort (cost-effectiveness analysis). As a result, the United States has interagency-approved and defined security baselines that can be implemented by the cloud service provider. If such a cloud provider is FedRAMP compliant and approved, it will automatically enable him or her to serve all kinds of agencies without the need to build agency-specific government cloud implementations.

The National Institute of Standards and Technology (NIST) was defined as a technical advisor for the FedRAMP. It helped to define the FedRAMP process and the underlying security requirements. It is important to note that the NIST is not the implementing organization. The governance and implementation of the FedRAMP lies with the Federal CIO Council.

In that context, the NIST has created a special publication 800-53 for cloud computing [16]. It also develops the Federal Information Processing Standards (FIPS) that, for example, regulate the use of encryption [17]. It is responsible for the US configuration baseline, which gives clear guidance for various software products with regard to secure configuration and operation.

It is therefore clear that a cloud provider needs to implement these FIPS and NIST requirements to be able to be approved by the FedRAMP. The US government cloud customers will in most cases only buy a cloud solution that is FedRAMP compliant and approved.

14.6.2 German BSI and "IT-Grundschutz" Certification

The German Federal Office for Information Security (in German abbreviated as BSI) defines the information security standards for governmental agencies and contractors. It has a similar role like the US NIST or the Communications Electronics Security Group (CESG) in the United Kingdom. Their area of expertise focuses on all layers of the security configuration and operation. It also helps citizens to propose Internet security measures. Therefore, it educates the public and the government with regard to security threats and countermeasures. Their main focus of course is the security support of the government IT systems.

One additional function is the definition of the "IT Grundschutzhandbuch" [18]. It is a catalog of baseline security measures (Grundschutz) grouped by security domains and protection needs. It contains hundreds of single measures that are linked to threats and risks. The catalog defines modules such as "Infrastructure," "Networks," "Applications," and "IT-Systems" that contain subtopics such as "Server-room," "Workplace," "VPN," and "Web-Server". These submodules than contain a list of all the relevant risks and measures or safeguards. Therefore, you can, for example, look only at the security measures to protect your office space. Additionally, all measures and risks/threats are also grouped in their own catalogs (e.g., organizational measures vs. technical infrastructure measures) and interlinked. Figure 14.8 shows these security modules or building blocks and how they interact with the safeguard and threat catalog to provide a full 360° view on certain aspects such as the Network.

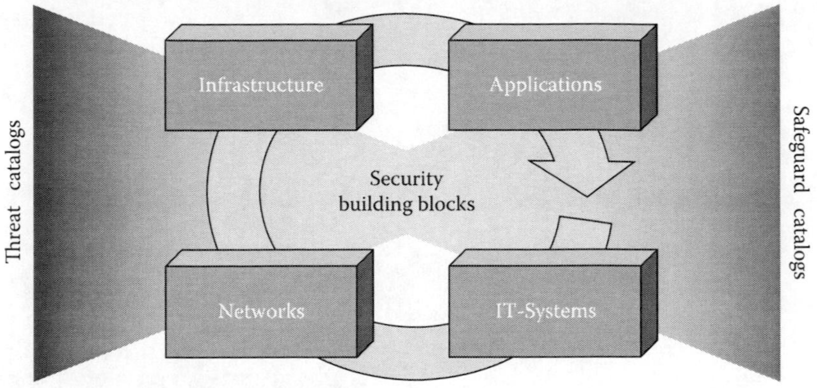

FIGURE 14.8   IT-Grundschutz catalogs.

The amount of measures that have to be applied is defined by the protection goals for the governmental data. A cloud provider could choose, for example, a medium protection level and certify against it by implementing all the related security measures in the relevant modules. The IT-Grundschutz as defined by the BSI also insists in implementing an information security management system and risk management processes. In that regard, it is similar to the ISO27001. The IT-Grundschutz certification and audit is performed by external assessors that are trained and approved by the BSI.

All government IT systems must comply with the IT-Grundschutz, but the BSI also recommends that other German commercial companies implement it to increase their security levels. Currently, an IT-Grundschutz certification is not necessarily mandatory for cloud providers that want sell to German agencies, as long as these providers have similar certifications such as ISO27001 and provide the necessary assurance that their cloud is secure and reliable operated.

14.6.3 Australian Signals Directorate and Information Security Registered Assessors Program Compliance

The Australian Signals Directorate (ASD) created an Information Security Registered Assessors Program (IRAP) to provide the framework for assessing IT systems or cloud services that want to process, store, or transmit governmental data up to the top secret level. The ASD has a similar role like the US NIST and provides also an Information Security Manual (ISM) that outlines for various secrecy levels the necessary technical and organizational measures [19]. For example, it defines encryption algorithms down to the key length or technical implementation, or it defines color codes or labels for network cables. It also requests that for certain governmental data only, ASD certified equipment can be used. This puts a lot of pressure on the cloud services architecture because the used hardware or software may not be allowed and need to be replaced by certified ones. It shows that the ISM contains hundreds of very specific requirements that need to be matched against the cloud solution and cloud provider operational processes. In the end, this could lead to the risk that a completely separated cloud solution has to be operated

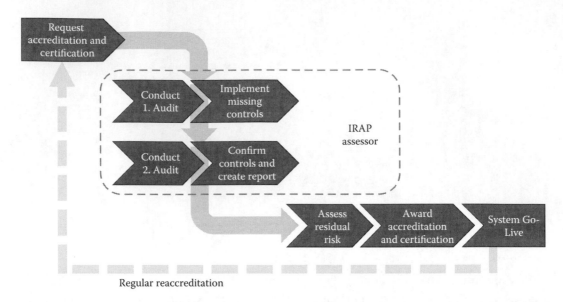

FIGURE 14.9   IRAP accreditation process.

and maintained. The IRAP assessor is an ASD-approved third party that has the skills to perform this assessment and to define the gaps toward the ISM. The cloud provider should then fix all identified gaps before the IRAP assessor comes back and looks deeper into the solution to find out if all findings are solved. He or she will then issue a report to the certification authority (also ASD) that makes the final decision on whether an IRAP certification can be granted. Figure 14.9 shows the basic steps that are needed to get the necessary IRAP certification and accreditation in a process diagram. These audit and assessment steps are repeated in certain intervals depending on the targeted cloud solution and processed data types. Most importantly, there are two audit steps: the first stage only to identify the gaps and missing controls and the second audit to confirm the implemented controls and draft the actual report. The assessor himself or herself will not award the certification. This is done by the authorities based on the provided audit report and remaining risk.

14.7 CONSEQUENCE OF THE CURRENT GEOPOLITICAL ENVIRONMENT

As a consequence of the fact that the different countries and local needs of the cloud customers will not be harmonized short term, it is crucial for a cloud service provider to offer various cloud deployment options and security configuration capabilities to meet these goals and sign these customers. There are three aspects of the various cloud deployment options and security configuration capabilities: First, the cloud service itself must be capable to fragment and process customer data and cloud solutions in an industry or country specific way. This includes the way the cloud service provider uses his or her own administrators for daily cloud operation. This is more a question of the overall design and used shared back-end infrastructure. Second, the cloud services and functionality must provide the needed configuration options and security measures. Last but not least, the whole design and cloud service operation must be certified by the local applicable regulation to get the necessary permits by, for example, the government, and to ensure the trust into the solution by the local cloud customers.

14.7.1 Decentralized Cloud Designs and Services

If the cloud service provider wants to sell his or her services into a global enterprise market and in various countries, it will be necessary to think about the general cloud service and back-end design. "One size fits all" will most likely not be sufficient for those customers. The notion to have one design and one global cloud based on, for example, US design principles and standards will be challenged or blandly rejected right away. However, it is not commercially reasonable for the cloud provider to install local clouds in every country. As a compromise, at least a regional installation (e.g., the United States, the European Union, and Asia-Pacific) should be considered. If we want to put this into a metaphor, we could define the following: Instead of one big cloud service bubble, the actual cloud is more like a "foam" of many smaller and regional cloud bubbles that are glued together and share certain services, design principles, or can interact in a controlled way with each other. For example, the various countries have their own local data storage in local data centers, but the design of these data centers, the physical security policies, or the hardware setup is always the same. The local implementation is a fork or clone of another, for example, central cloud implementation and shares the back-end infrastructure or the graphical user interface or the network services. The same applies for the cloud software and applications.

In any case, the amount of variants and modifications should be limited to a minimum and always be linked to, for example, a master or default cloud service design.

14.7.2 Country- and Industry-Specific Security Models

To be able to fulfill the discussed requirements, the cloud service provider must implement a set of security controls that are flexible and granular enough. A complete logging of all administrative activities is an absolute must. To be on the safe side, the cloud solution and services should be built in a way that most or even all administrative activities by the provider will not allow access to customer data. Also the best operation model for the cloud provider would ensure that in daily operation, all administrative tasks are done by, for example, automation frameworks and not manually by people. For example, the login of a cloud provider administrator into a hypervisor server or the firewall should only happen in emergency or rare incident cases. All default incidents should be solved automatically by, for example, some expert system that tries to fix or rebuild failed cloud service back-end components before the auto-repair system triggers an actual cloud provider administrator. These measures and design concepts reduce the need for direct access by administrators in general by 80%.

The customer data should also be stored in the cloud always in encrypted form. It would be even better, if the encryption keys are not known to the cloud provider and stored, for example, in a system on the customer site. The integrity and confidentiality of these data would be ensured if a cloud administrator is able to directly or indirectly access customer data.

The cloud provider must operate (e.g., with partners) multiple data center sites in the world. At least two data centers per region or even two per country are needed to be able to store the primary systems and backup data in a certain legal area. Governmental or military customers should be treated completely separated from the other commercial private industry sector. A dedicated and isolated installation is often needed.

The cloud provider support model and operation teams mostly cover the whole world in a 7 × 24 setup. It would be recommended to have some key support or operation staff in each region or in special key countries.

14.7.3 Security Considerations for Cloud Customers

The cloud customer must first of all know his or her own industry-specific requirements and country or legal regulations. These requirements must be mapped to the cloud engagement and the planned business case. It makes a difference in the security design and responsibilities if the cloud solution is completely operated by the cloud provider (e.g., software as a service) or if there are shared responsibilities and a more open design/toolbox environment like in a pure infrastructure-as-a-service cloud. The CSA checklists could be a starting point to analyze the planned cloud usage and to come up with clear questions and a requirement catalog for the cloud provider. The customer must also understand the cloud services and check the available isolation and security configuration options. Is a public cloud sufficient? Should a customer-specific private cloud [20] setup be used? Is encryption mandatory for the data storage and processing? Should the data be stored outside of the country? Are foreigners allowed to manage the cloud services that host customer data? These are some of the questions that need to be discussed.

The cloud customer has also to decide if he or she wants to set up and use one global cloud application or system instead of having multiple instances that run independently. Maybe it makes sense for the customer that the local subsidiary of a country runs his or her own cloud-based, for example, vendor management, human resources, or customer relationship solution, which is later on consolidated into one big central database and analytics system. This increases, of course, the complexity and administrative effort tremendously and should be avoided whenever possible.

The basic security measures such asa clearly defined user access and permission management, a security patch management, some security configuration policies, the network communication setup, the security monitoring or the intrusion detection, and anti-malware management solution should be applied in the same way across all the cloud solutions. They can be seen as a baseline that every cloud system or application must comply to. The country- and industry-specific security requirements are than added on top as an extension. Figure 14.10 shows such an example network topology for a private cloud setup with dedicated security gateways and network access controls.

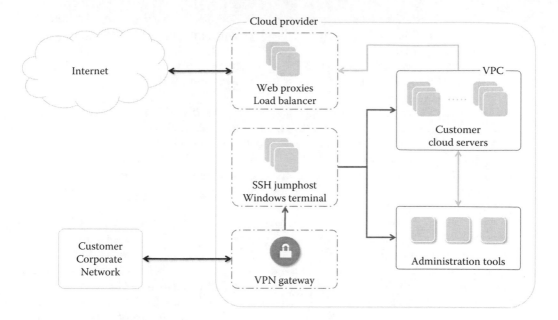

FIGURE 14.10   Example private cloud architecture.

14.8 SUMMARY

In sum, there is not one global cloud solution that fits all the needs of its customers. Instead the cloud business is still evolving and adopting to the feedback and needs of the customers and carefully tries to balance the cloud principles and cost-reducing measures with special requirements and modifications that are needed for certain customers. The important part is a cloud service design that can be extended and adopted to the needs of the customer and a baseline or back-end cloud infrastructure that already fulfills most of the various requirements by extensive certification and audit activities. In the end, it is a business case decision by the cloud providers how far they want to go.

The past few years of cloud business and cloud solution offerings showed a clear move by the providers toward a more flexible and open environment. They integrated new requirements from a legal contractual or technical feature perspective and used open standards or open-source solutions. The hope remains that the governments can agree to some international standards and will not go to the path of further isolation or Internet segmentation that will harm the global cloud business.

REFERENCES

1. Sajee Mathew. *Overview of Amazon Web Services*. Whitepaper. Amazon Web Services: Seattle, WA. November 2014. https://d0.awsstatic.com/whitepapers/aws-overview.pdf.
2. Gethyn Ellis. *Microsoft Azure IaaS Essentials*. Packt Publishing. May 2015.
3. Tom Fifield, Diane Felming, Anne Gentle, Lorin Hochstein, Jonathan Proulx, Everett Toews, Joe Topjian. *OpenStack Operations Guide—Setup and Manage Your Openstack Cloud*. O'Reilly Media. September 2015. http://docs.openstack.org/ops/.

4. *The ABCs of Continuous Release and Deploy in a DevOps Approach.* Technical White Paper. IBM: Somers, NY. May 2013. http://public.dhe.ibm.com/common/ssi/ecm/ra/en/raw14324usen/RAW14324USEN.PDF.

5. *Amazon Elastic Compute Cloud: User Guide, Regions and Availability Zones.* Amazon Web Services: Seattle, WA. April 2015. http://docs.aws.amazon.com/AWSEC2/latest/UserGuide/using-regions-availability-zones.html.

6. *Assurance Reports on Controls at a Service Organization (ISAE 3402).* International Auditing and Assurance Standards Board. June 2011. http://isae3402.com.

7. *Statement on Standards for Attestation Engagements No. 16 (SSAE 16).* Auditing Standards Board of the American Institute of Certified Public Accountants (AICPA). April 2010. http://ssae16.com.

8. *ISO/IEC 27001—Information Security Management Standard.* International Organization for Standardization (ISO): Vernier, Switzerland. 2013. http://www.iso.org/iso/home/standards/management-standards/iso27001.htm.

9. *SA Security, Trust & Assurance Registry (STAR).* Cloud Security Alliance Group: Seattle, WA. 2015. https://cloudsecurityalliance.org/star/#_overview.

10. *On Amendments to Certain Legislative Acts of the Russian Federation for Clarification of Personal Data Processing in Information and Telecommunications Networks.* Russian Federal Law No. 242-FZ. July 2014. http://www.rg.ru/2014/07/23/persdannye-dok.html.

11. *Register of Operators Engaged in the Processing of Personal Data.* Government of the Russian Federation. Federal Service for Supervision of Communications, Information Technology and Mass Media (Roskomnadzor). September 2015. http://rkn.gov.ru/personal-data/register/.

12. Steve Dickinson. *Foreign SaaS in China: Get off of my Cloud.* China Law Blog. Harris & Moure: Seattle, WA. April 2015. http://www.chinalawblog.com/2015/04/foreign-saas-in-china-get-off-of-my-cloud.html.

13. European Parliament and Commission. 2000/520/EC: Commission Decision of 26 July 2000 pursuant to Directive 95/46/EC of the European Parliament and of the Council on the adequacy of the protection provided by the safe harbour privacy principles and related frequently asked questions issued by the US Department of Commerce. July 2000. http://eur-lex.europa.eu/LexUriServ/LexUriServ.do?uri=CELEX:32000D0520:EN:HTML.

14. *Payment Card Industry (PCI) Data Security Standard—Requirements and Security Assessment Procedures.* Version 3.1. PCI Security Standards Council: Wakefield, MA. April 2015. https://www.pcisecuritystandards.org/documents/PCI_DSS_v3-1.pdf.

15. Martijn Jansen. *Troopers Security Conference: How to Work Towards Pharma Compliance for Cloud Computing.* ERNW Enno Rey Netzwerke GmbH: Heidelberg, Germany. 2014. https://www.troopers.de/media/filer_public/1c/77/1c7755d9-6d3e-46ea-a099-3fe303cab1c2/troopers14-how_to_work_towards_pharma_compliance_for_cloud_computing-martijn_jansen.pdf.

16. *Security and Privacy Controls for Federal Information Systems and Organizations.* Revision 4. National Institute of Standards and Technology. January 2015. http://nvlpubs.nist.gov/nistpubs/SpecialPublications/NIST.SP.800-53r4.pdf.

17. *Security Requirements for Cryptographic Modules.* Federal Information Processing Standard. FIPS PUB 140-2. May 2001. http://csrc.nist.gov/publications/fips/fips140-2/fips1402.pdf.

18. Isabel Münch, Michael Hange. *IT-Grundschutz-Catalogues.* 13th version. German Federal Office for Information Security (BSI). 2013. https://gsb.download.bva.bund.de/BSI/ITGSKEN/IT-GSK-13-EL-en-all_v940.pdf.

19. Dr Paul Taloni. *Information Security Manual—Controls 2015.* Version 2015. Australian Signals Directorate: Kingston ACT, Australia. 2015. http://www.asd.gov.au/publications/Information_Security_Manual_2015_Controls.pdf.

20. *Amazon Virtual Private Cloud: Getting Started Guide.* Amazon Web Services: Seattle, WA. April 2015. http://docs.aws.amazon.com/AmazonVPC/latest/GettingStartedGuide/vpc-gsg.pdf.

CHAPTER 15

Continuous Private Cloud Security Monitoring

Thorsten Herre

CONTENTS

15.1 INTRODUCTION

Monitoring is an essential part in any information technology (IT) system operation and plays a key role in the cloud security area as well. Without a proper continuous monitoring, we are blinded against all kinds of data manipulation, theft, or data destruction, and we can't predict nor control the behavior of our cloud system or applications. It is clear that this would be an unacceptable situation for any business critical data processing or development activity in the cloud. Private clouds allow a more isolated and dedicated setup of system landscapes or cloud data processing compared to a pure public cloud service and therefore enable also more complex security monitoring architectures that are under the control of the cloud customer. This would not be possible in public cloud solutions due to the shared aspects of underlying resources or infrastructure and due to the limitations of modifications or control by a single customer over the whole cloud operation itself. This is the reason why most enterprise businesses prefer a private cloud for critical business systems to ensure that they stay in control over various aspects of the cloud architecture, service delivery, and data processing. The monitoring and especially the security monitoring can be customized to meet the company's security policies, protection goals, or regulatory industry requirements. It enables the necessary transparency and creates trust between the cloud service provider, the cloud customer, cloud application users, and involved partners.

This chapter outlines some core principles and best practices for security monitoring of IT systems especially within the context of cloud, and it will point out the cloud-specific activities that must be considered by a cloud system administrator.

15.2 CLOUD SECURITY MONITORING GOALS

The security aspects of cloud servers are very similar to the security measures that are applied in a traditional on-premise or hosting server environment, and the same ideas must be considered for the monitoring as well. In our new highly connected digital world, many businesses require a shift from complex practices of the past to simple practices of the future. This paradigm shift must be considered also in the monitoring setup and can be achieved by focusing on three basic security questions or threats that the cloud server or monitoring environment need to solve:

- Is my customer or corporate data secure and protected in the cloud system?

- Is the cloud operations secure, reliable, and compliant to my industry standards?

- How can I trust the cloud data processing, transfer, or storage?

Figure 15.1 shows how operational monitoring and security monitoring have often conflicting goals or different main focus points. Therefore, the goal must be to target the

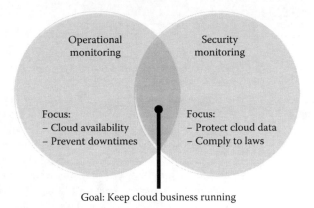

FIGURE 15.1 Operational versus security monitoring.

intersection of both worlds that will provide a secure and also high-available operation. Only if both aspects are monitored, the cloud business can succeed.

The Security Monitoring and Cyber Security (Security Incident) Management setup of the cloud system can address these points by implementing preventive, detective, or corrective measures. Table 15.1 outlines these measures in more detail and give some example implementations. As a prerequisite to implement those measures, it is necessary to be aware of the used cloud resources, data center locations, involved users, logging activities, or cloud service provider events, and to be able to correlate this information with history data that were collected, for example, over the last couple of months. The monitoring system can only be effective if these data sets are known, collected, and understood by the cloud system architect or administrator.

15.3 FUNDAMENTAL PRINCIPLES IN CLOUD MONITORING

To be able to design an effective and security aware cloud monitoring, it is crucial to understand the IT layers where monitoring can happen, the type of monitoring that is applicable to these layers, the responsibilities for such monitoring, and the technologies or tools that are provided either by the cloud service provider or by installing self-developed or third-party monitoring applications in the cloud system environment. The implementation of security monitoring capabilities must be considered and planned from the get-go. New cloud landscapes, systems, or servers shall only go live if the security monitoring is in place and shows no pending noncompliance or issue. This ensures that new installations are forced to be in a "secure-by-default" state and provide better transparency over the whole life cycle of a cloud system. Depending on the cloud solution itself, the level of access to monitoring data may also vary; for example, in an infrastructure-as-a-service (IaaS) environment, certain aspects of network and all aspects of data center facility and hardware monitoring are done by the cloud service provider. The cloud customer may get only some generic monitoring status report or no data at all. In a platform-as-a-service (PaaS) environment, the customer or cloud administrator may be limited to monitor only the behavior of his application. All other aspects of the cloud infrastructure and security environment are monitored and maintained by the cloud service provider.

TABLE 15.1 Examples of Security Measures

Type	Security Measure	Description
Prevent	Security requirements framework	Clear definition of the security requirements that are applicable to the cloud system; the monitoring concept is part of this overall security framework and collects the required security KPIs/events
	State-of-the-art security measures	Monitoring data provided and countermeasures implemented by intrusion detection and prevention systems; setup of network access list and firewall rules; anti-malware protection; file and configuration integrity checks; administrative activity monitor; data leakage prevention
	People enablement	Continuous security awareness trainings for cloud administrators; security forensic training and dry-run exercises for cyber security monitoring teams; secure design workshops for cloud developers and architects that are documented and monitored
Detect	Security deviation management	Implement data integrity and change management monitoring within the application, database, or OS to detect suspicious modifications in cloud configurations, the user database, key database tables, or the operating file system/storage objects. If possible, enable auto-remediation to fix detected deviations immediately
	Threat and vulnerability detection	Perform regular vulnerability scans from within the cloud landscape and from the Internet with a feedback loop to the monitoring and security incident process for continuous improvement and maybe auto-remediation
	Security monitoring center	Install a 7 × 24 security monitoring environment and reaction team that supervises the data processing and integrity of the whole cloud landscape on every level (network, OS, storage, database, application)
React	Security response management	Ensure that a security incident, crisis, or emergency management process is in place and known to all involved parties; attach this process to the given security monitoring systems and the security incident communication interfaces of the used cloud provider; perform regular trainings
	Threat and vulnerability management	Implement auto-remediation or automatic countermeasure systems based on vulnerability scan results; e.g., implement a security patch; fix the unsecure configuration; block certain network traffic that could exploit the vulnerability

15.3.1 Cloud Monitoring Layers

The cloud solution must be monitored end to end, which means that it must cover all aspects of the cloud landscape from the hardware and network up to the application itself. A holistic monitoring concept is recommended for all kinds of critical and highly productive cloud systems. In a private cloud environment, we differentiate the layers discussed in Sections 15.3.1.1 through 15.3.1.7, which may be monitored individually by either the cloud service provider or the cloud customer and administrator.

15.3.1.1 Facility Layer

The cloud facility layer consists of the physical infrastructure of the data center(s) where the cloud is hosted. This includes all physical locations that are used to process, transmit, or store cloud systems and their respective customer cloud data. Monitoring at this layer considers data center operations, energy consumption, environmental impact, and physical security, such as surveillance, physical access controls, and architectural resilience.

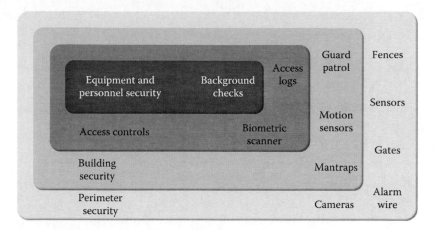

FIGURE 15.2   Data center security monitoring.

Figure 15.2 shows these aspects and data center security domains with some practical examples. It also visualizes how these domains built on each other from the external perimeter security up to the inner server room and people security measures.

All these aspects are monitored by the cloud data center provider and confirmed or tested by independent auditors at regular intervals (e.g., yearly) based on the certification and attestation needs of the cloud provider. The cloud customer has in general no access to this monitoring data and can only read the reports provided by the independent third-party auditors. In some private cloud environments, a customer may be allowed to receive a regular report that includes some security access log information to his or her dedicated equipment or cloud system environments. However, in a true cloud-based setup, there is no identifiable customer server anymore, and physical access and maintenance is handled the same across all customers. Also all other aspects of the facility operation and monitoring are solely controlled by the cloud provider. The purpose and scalability of cloud implies that the customer does not need to deal with physical hardware, sizing, energy consumption, or capacity management any more. Therefore, the monitoring is also not of any concern by the customer as long as the cloud provider is able to deliver the agreed service levels and availabilities. In the end, the cloud customer focuses on the facility layer on the availability and regular confirmation of the applicable cloud data center certifications and industry standards maybe combined with a yearly on-site audit and/or data center visit.

15.3.1.2 Hardware Layer

This monitoring layer focuses on the physical components of the computing, storage, and networking equipment. The hardware monitor will inform the cloud service provider about failures of storage disks, unstable RAM memory modules, failing power units or cooling fans, CPU errors, network card issues, or similar hardware-related defects. In most cases, a hardware defect will not immediately cause a downtime of the cloud service or data loss, because every hardware component within a server, storage unit, or network component is implemented redundantly. Only the failure of multiple components at the same time may cause a certain disruption. In a public or private cloud environment, the hardware is owned and maintained by the cloud service provider, and therefore, the customer has no visibility or responsibility for hardware layer monitoring.

15.3.1.3 Network Layer

The cloud network layer consists of the communication links and paths within a cloud, between clouds, and between the cloud and the user. The communication within the cloud back end (e.g., the hypervisor server or the storage clusters) and the management or automation framework used by the cloud service provider to operate and to provide his or her cloud services is monitored by the provider himself or herself. The customer has no insight into the monitoring of these back-end components. Nevertheless, the cloud provider may offer some services that inform the customer about irregular behavior that has its origin on virtual cloud servers owned by the customer or if the customer is targeted by other virtual cloud servers or the Internet itself. In such cases, the internal cloud intrusion detection and security monitoring can have a side effect of monitoring also the behavior of customer systems. Besides the security monitoring, the provider will also focus on network bandwidth consumption, network access control list violations, firewall behavior, and overall network performance in his or her cloud backbone environment.

The network communication within a virtual private cloud customer landscape and the customer connection between the cloud and the customer on-premise network is in the responsibility of the customer. The provider may offer certain configuration and monitoring options but will in most cases not actively reconfigure and monitor it. The customer has to analyze the network access list violations, the security group configuration, and logs, and act accordingly. It is recommended to define a monitoring and security concept for the network topology used by the cloud systems (e.g., filtering the Internet or subnet traffic between the cloud servers) and to integrate the resulting log entries into the customer network security monitoring solution like a customer Security Incident and Event Management (SIEM) system [1]. If such a system is not in place or available, the customer could use the cloud provider automation frameworks to define some event triggers and messaging queues (e.g., cloud automation sends an e-mail to the administrator on certain network events or even changes some access list to block traffic temporary). The diagram in Figure 15.3 outlines a possible network security architecture of such a private cloud environment. All these components such as routers, firewalls, intrusion prevention (IPS) or detection systems (IDS), virtual private network (VPN) gateways, web proxies, and other security appliances create security logs that need to be analyzed.

15.3.1.4 Operating System Layer

On the operating system (OS) layer, we have to differentiate the host and guest OSs, and the hypervisors running the virtual machines (VMs). The host servers and hypervisor software are owned by the cloud service provider and therefore also monitored by the provider. The cloud customer has only limited ability to monitor or configure these components via the Administrative user interfaces (e.g., Web-Consoles) or via direct application program interface (API) calls. In general, the cloud administrator can monitor the status of his or her VMs and manage the deployment (e.g., ensuring that the VMs run in a certain availability zone, network configuration, or have a specific setup for storage, memory, or CPU usage). Certain

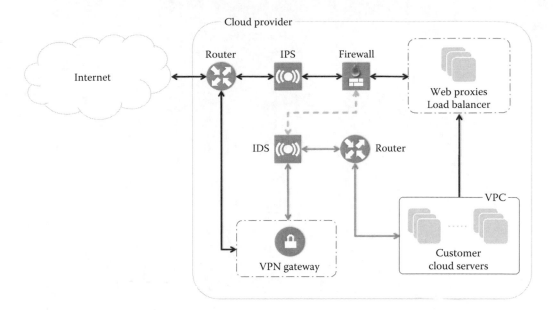

FIGURE 15.3   Network security architecture.

general performance indicators are provided to the cloud customer, but the detailed host OS and hypervisor monitoring and log management are not accessible for the customer. The cloud provider will ensure that his or her host server farm is secured and reliable. The security monitoring by the provider on this level in general includes integrity checks of the host OS configuration, the network ports opened or active connections from the host servers, some malware protection and intrusion prevention monitoring, and of course the monitoring of the OS users and all administrative activities. Due to the fact that the host and hypervisors are set up in a very standardized way, the cloud service provider knows all possible processes activities, network data transfers, or administrative commands that are allowed and possible over the lifetime of the whole server farm. This enables the security monitoring to watch for any deviations that can be considered as security event and potential attack. Figure 15.4 shows the responsibilities for hypervisor and virtual server monitoring.

The VM OS, however, could contain any kind of software applications and network communication to the outside world and is therefore much more difficult from a monitoring perspective. The VM must be monitored by the cloud customer because only he or she knows which application needs which kind of special monitoring. From a security perspective, the standard monitoring for viruses, malware, or illegal network connection attempts to apply to the virtual server as well combined with some application-specific monitoring. A good best practice is to ensure proper timestamps (e.g., by using a time service like network time protocol [NTP]) and to collect all OS log events centrally. If the VM is highly sensitive, it is recommended to monitor also the changes of key OS files to ensure that these files are not tampered with or changed to an insecure configuration. The OS user setup and user permissions must be monitored for changes to detect the creation of new local administrative accounts. Additionally, all administrative activities must be logged and analyzed.

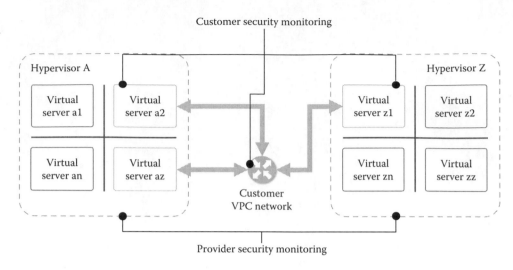

FIGURE 15.4   Hypervisor and virtual server monitoring.

15.3.1.5 Middleware Layer

In a cloud environment, the middleware layer normally represents the PaaS and software-as-a-service (SaaS) models. It consists of the software layer between the user application and the underlying OS.

In a SaaS cloud solution, the customer only inserts his or her configuration and data into an already existing cloud-based shared application. The customer has no direct control over all aspects of the application and instead has a specially designed customization and configuration environment to model his or her application instance to his or her specific industry or company needs. The cloud service provider is mainly responsible to monitor the SaaS solution, including security aspects. The customer has no direct way to deploy own applications or to change the operational or monitoring design aspects of the solution. Some selected performance indicators such as general availability or security incident reports are provided by the cloud solution to the customer.

A PaaS environment also allows the customer to deploy his or her own applications within the platform or framework provided by the cloud solution. In many cases, the PaaS cloud allows development by the customer and therefore a much higher grade of customization and data processing options. As a result of this approach, the customer has some responsibilities to monitor his or her application and data processing, especially if it is not covered by the basic platform (security) monitoring offered and operated by the cloud service provider. The security monitoring on that level includes, for example, the monitoring of application data transmissions, user permissions/roles, and web-based attack scenarios.

15.3.1.6 Application Server Layer

This monitoring layer consists of the user applications running in the cloud. In a private cloud environment, the cloud customer can install any kind of application on his or her VMs and must consider the necessary security monitoring. The cloud provider will not take any responsibility of application misconfiguration, compromises, or data loss. The monitoring is in the sole responsibility of the cloud customer and his or her cloud server administrator. If the application provides a web-based interface and interacts directly with the Internet, it is recommended to install a web application firewall as additional protection and monitoring element. Most cloud providers offer also some additional monitoring services that could be integrated if the application setup allows it. The different areas of application security monitoring are shown in Figure 15.5. Business critical applications in the cloud should ensure that all these listed aspects are implemented and executed either continuously or on a regular basis.

Also the cloud provider will still monitor the network traffic and inform the cloud customer, in case a massive attack is targeted from or to the cloud servers. Application monitoring on that level should also include the security settings of the application (e.g., setup of encrypted connections such as hypertext transfer protocol [HTTPS]), critical user permissions, critical data changes (e.g., data deletion), and suspicious log entries (such as logon failed events).

15.3.1.7 User Layer

In our definition, the user layer consists of the end users of the cloud applications and the applications running outside the cloud, for example, a web browser of the end user or a graphical user interface (GUI) application used by the end user to access the cloud systems remotely. The end user could have many different roles such as cloud administrator, application power user, review or read-only user or even down to anonymous user access for everyone. For administrators, due to their privileged access into the cloud environment, it is crucial to ensure that they use a secure client environment. Therefore, their laptops, portable computers, tablets, or mobile phones must be integrated into the corporate security monitoring system by having, for example, a malware protection solution, a host IDS, a software inventory, or a network access control system in place. Additionally, these clients need to be integrated into a central domain (e.g., active directory) to ensure central user and permission

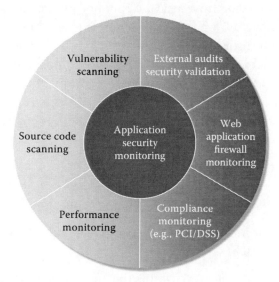

FIGURE 15.5   Aspects of application security monitoring.

handling or enforced group policies on the client machine. The clients also need to be up to date with security patches. All of that must be centrally monitored to detect clients that are potentially insecure or even compromised. Of course, all of these activities run outside of the cloud environment and are therefore in the responsibility of the cloud customer.

15.3.2 Types of Cloud Monitoring

The monitoring activities could be grouped based on their purpose and type. These types of monitoring will give the cloud administrator insight into the cloud system health, proper function of the cloud applications, and data processing [2]. It will allow tracking of the availability or usage of the system, create some performance statistic data, or provide auditability of all critical (e.g., administrative) activities. These monitoring data will allow to guarantee the agreed or expected service levels for the cloud services or the overall cloud application. In a well-designed cloud system, a combination of these monitoring types is needed to cover all aspects of daily operation. Section 15.3.2.1 discusses briefly all types of monitoring to provide a basic overview after we dive into more details of the security monitoring part itself.

15.3.2.1 Health Monitoring

The "health" of a cloud system is defined as the capability of such system to process requests or data within the boundaries of the defined performance parameters. Therefore, the purpose of monitoring such "health" is to constantly verify that all components of the cloud system function as expected. The overall health status of a system could be represented by traffic light icons, for example, the color "red" indicating a failed or stopped component versus the color "green" confirming the proper working of other parts of the cloud system. Another way to display the health could be a numeral statistic that shows the overall load or deviation from a norm value. In this case, for example, a 100% load of the CPU or network component would indicate that no further requests can be processed and the system is overloaded. Also a measure could be an indication how far the system parameters currently deviate from the usual values (e.g., arithmetic average). This could be a warning sign of unhealthy behavior or even suspicious activities by the cloud system users or potential internet attacks against the system. In most monitoring visualizations provided by the cloud service provider, the system administrators can drill down from a high-level report to each subcomponent to pin point the actual reason for an unhealthy cloud system. To determine the security health of a cloud system, the following raw data can be used:

- User login and activity events
- System logs and security/trace log events of the application
- CPU, memory, network, and storage performance indicators of the virtual servers and cloud storage system
- Cloud provider monitoring logs covering the underlying virtualization, hardware, or overall security environment

Besides the actual continuous monitoring, an alerting system should also be in place to react, in case the cloud system goes into an "unhealthy" state. Most cloud providers offer an integration of the monitoring in their automation or alerting queue functionality [3]. For example, you can configure an automated reaction based on certain monitoring alerts. The easiest reaction could be an automated alert mail to the administrator. In more sophisticated scenarios, the monitoring could detect a failure of the application servers and automatically trigger the start of a replacement VM application server instance and stop the faulty one. The automation scripts could also try to repair the affected cloud application server by resetting some configurations or restating the affected services or blocking malicious network traffic or user activity.

15.3.2.2 Availability Monitoring

The availability monitoring is strongly linked to the aforementioned health monitoring. In its core, the health monitoring also provides key performance indicators (KPIs) that can be used for the availability monitoring and analysis. The health monitoring focuses on the real-time view of the cloud system, whereas the availability monitoring has also the historical view to be able to identify trends and availability statistics, for example, over a whole month or year. This can be used to identify peak loads, resource, or performance bottlenecks within a certain time frame to optimize the cloud system (e.g., if it fails periodically due to an unknown root cause) or to detect suspicious activities [e.g., denial-of-service (DOS) attacks]. Availability data are stored in database systems to provide such an historical and analytical view. A cloud service provider monitors the availability of his or her services to prove his or her compliance to the agreed service levels or uses it for billing purposes as well. In most cases, the cloud system administrators add their own availability and health monitoring on top of the already provided cloud service monitoring to cover all the components that are in the sole responsibility of the cloud customer.

The source of logging data used for the availability monitoring is similar to the health monitoring with an additional focus on the endpoint monitoring. This means that the monitoring system performs certain checks on key components in a regular fashion that mimic the behavior of a cloud system end user or web service system user. For example, it could check the login capability, execute certain transactions or API calls, and confirm that these activities are successfully completed within the cloud system.

The availability of a system or subcomponent is often calculated as the percentage value using the total availability time and considering the overall downtime. A basic formula that reflects these values could look like this:

$$\text{Availability } (\%) = \left[\frac{(\text{Total time} - \text{Total downtime})}{\text{Total time}} \right] \times 100$$

In a cloud environment, the definition of "availability" and "downtime" is important because it could be referenced in the contractual agreement and service-level agreements (SLAs). The cloud customer should know which kind of system or cloud service availability the provider guarantees and how this availability is actually calculated.

15.3.2.3 Performance Monitoring

The overall performance of a cloud system besides the pure general availability is also a very important monitoring aspect. The system may be available and therefore "green" in the availability monitoring, but the performance of certain actions or the responsiveness of the system toward the end user may be too bad for a productive and satisfying usage. This is the reason why the cloud administrator should also define some KPIs, which are still acceptable for productive usage of the system. These KPIs could contain the following metrics:

- The reaction time to user inputs on the graphical user interface or web service

- The business transaction completion times that include data processing, transmitting, or storing time frames

- The number of concurrent user requests

- The volume of network traffic and amount of open sessions

- The number of processing errors

- The time it takes to start processing a request after it is initiated

- The overall performance of the underlying cloud infrastructure such as the following:

  - The number of running processes or threads

  - CPU load

  - Memory utilization

  - Storage and network I/O rates (e.g., the amount of written bytes to the cloud storage, network packet errors)

Like the availability monitoring, the collected KPI data are stored for historical and analytical analyses. Similar to the discussed health alerts, the cloud administrator could leverage the automation frameworks to implement an alerting and counter measure system, which could detect a pending overload of the application servers and automatically trigger the start of another VM server instance to be able to process this peak load and ensure the availability of the scenario. This is summarized as an autoscaling feature and sometimes a functionality that is directly supported by the cloud service provider. The cloud setup enables such easy scalability options due to the fact that the whole cloud system is already set up as a virtual instance and uses the cloud provider configuration utilities. In the past, an administrator had to set up and start another instance manually and integrate this new server into the existing landscape. Now in the cloud, scaling up or down the whole landscape becomes less of a manual activity and more of an automated "self-healing" function of the cloud system itself.

KPIs are in general reported via percentages or total values for a given topic. The trigger value upon which an alert or counter measure is executed is either defined manually by the administrator or system owner or calculated based on historical data (e.g., averages) and experiences.

15.3.2.4 Security Monitoring

The security monitoring itself can be seen as a subset of the already discussed monitoring activities and event or log collection that focuses on security relevant activities in a cloud system, which could indicate endangering the cloud data integrity and confidentiality, or even indicate an overall attack on the availability of the cloud system or cloud web services. However, focusing on the monitoring data collected by the performance, availability or health monitoring is not sufficient for the security monitoring, because certain security threats such as massive data downloads, data manipulation, user account misuse, or data deletion may not be covered by those monitoring activities. The system may be up and running within the given parameters but still suffer an undetected attack on its cloud data or user base. This is the reason why the security monitoring adds additional security events and key performance parameters that need to be considered in every productive cloud system. Figure 15.6 shows the basic cycle of this security monitoring that consists of the planning, monitoring, and action parts. The planning defines a log concept based on the discovered assets or cloud systems, the monitoring executes the log concept, and the action is necessary if a security threat or incident is detected. This could lead to an escalation and taskforce creation. After the incident or threat is averted, the process goes back to the planning and monitoring.

FIGURE 15.6   Security monitoring cycle.

We need to address two aspects of this security monitoring. One is the direct monitoring of suspicious behavior by users or suspicious access or changes to cloud system data. This is a real-time monitoring of actual security attacks executed against the cloud system. Security logs, data flow monitors, IDS, and anti-malware protection solutions are part of this. However, the security monitoring tries to identify and watch over all existing security flaws, vulnerabilities, or attack vectors that could be used by a hacker or attack as entry point into the cloud system. Typical examples of those monitors are the security patch and vulnerability scanner, the network access lists and firewall rules, the user and access management controller, or the system configuration scanning solution. This part of the security monitor alerts or even reacts on missing security patches, open firewall ports, or unsecure configuration settings in the OS, cloud database services, or the application. Additionally, together with the identity management system, it observes and prevents weak user passwords, failed login attempts, or critical or unusual permissions granted for users. In sum, the security monitoring must at least detect threats such as the following:

- DOS attacks by overloading the cloud system with requests

- Identification of security vulnerabilities and attempts to execute them against the cloud system (security exploit) even without a valid user

- Attempts to take over existing (privileged) user accounts by guessing (brute force), resetting passwords, or hijacking the user session of someone else

- Attempts to create a new user account with privileged permissions using flaws in the user management system setup or the application session handling

To differentiate real attacks and threats from usual activities of cloud users and cloud administrators, it is necessary to define a clear baseline or behavior pattern that outlines normal operation. For example, the amount of acceptable log-on failed attempts/events per time could be a trigger to identify an active attack. Modern intrusion detection or web application firewall systems perform such a baseline definition as one of their core functions to assist the cloud administrator and security team to get rid of too many false-positive security alerts.

The cloud system administrator should consider the use of a central security event correlation and alerting engine. This can be implemented by using a SIEM solution. Many vendors of such solutions provide a cloud ready deployment option as a VM image (cloud appliance) or they allow at least an integration of the cloud systems and cloud provider security logs into their SIEM solution, which may be installed on-premise at the customer site [4].

15.3.2.5 SLA and Usage Monitoring

Commercial cloud providers offer a service-level agreement (SLA) that contains guarantees of certain service availabilities, operational response times, or throughputs. The customer relies on such availabilities for his or her cloud system and should also watch over the compliance to these targets. Downtimes or performance issues caused by the cloud provider have a direct financial or billing impact to the cloud customer, and the provider may be liable for damages. KPIs for such an SLA monitoring consist of the following:

- The overall cloud service uptime or downtime percentages
- The number of application or VM faults, exceptions, and so on
- The number of successful/failing cloud service requests
- The overall network performance or network packet loss
- Cloud storage write/read performance or cloud storage data loss
- Concurrent user performance and user request response times

The cloud provider should enable the customer to collect or review such KPIs on a regular basis, aligned with the billing cycle (e.g., monthly).

The usage monitoring is even more relevant for the cloud billing, because it documents and outlines the cloud service usage and consumption over a period of time. This monitoring or report contains information about the used CPU times, memory or storage spaces, and the network activities. In some cloud solutions, even the user activities are logged and used for the billing. Additionally, all administrative commands are monitored because some of them might be billed as well. In general, the cloud service provider offers such a report to the customer automatically as part of his or her internal monitoring and billing process [5]. He or she may use this information also to enforce existing quotas (e.g., allowing only a finite amount of users or limiting the storage or VM usage).

The cloud system administrator may add a usage monitoring for his or her own applications and VM processes that are not covered in the provider's usage report. The setup depends on the used cloud environment. In a SaaS cloud, the usage monitoring and reporting is done solely by the provider, whereas in an IaaS solution, the provider covers only his or her services, excluding all customer-specific applications and VM usage activities. The usage monitoring can also be used like the performance monitoring to identify hot spots or peak activities within the cloud system to optimize and scale the system for better response times. Usage data may also be collected for statistical or marketing reasons to analyze the behavior patterns or to sell the collected data to analytics third parties.

15.3.3 Cloud Security Monitoring Responsibilities

After discussing the layers and types of monitoring especially in a cloud environment, we can summarize and list the responsibilities and security monitoring targets for each layer in a matrix view. This can be used as a checklist in a cloud system setup to ensure that all relevant security monitoring aspects have an owner and are appropriately covered by monitoring solutions operated either by the cloud customer or by the cloud service provider himself or herself. The responsibility is different for some layers in an IaaS versus a PaaS or a SaaS cloud solution, as shown in Table 15.2.

TABLE 15.2   Example: Security Monitoring Responsibilities and Scoping

Monitoring Layer	What Is Monitored	How Is It Done	Cloud Type	Who Does the Monitoring (Responsible)
Facility/data center	Building access, perimeter/fences, environmental risks, equipment exchange	Security guards, biometric access control, closed circuit television, background checks, regular audits, certifications	IaaS, PaaS, SaaS	Cloud service provider
Hardware	Hardware replacement and maintenance, secure destruction/wiping of media, hardware BIOS or CPU security functions	Secure disk disposal process (e.g., shredder, degaussing), security checks on hardware delivery, metal detectors, loading bay area closed circuit television, CPU/basic input/output system security settings active in OS	IaaS, PaaS, SaaS	Cloud service provider
Network	Network traffic, Internet requests, hypervisor setup, VLAN or VPN configuration	Firewall and ACL monitoring, IDS/IPS, web application firewall, security groups, regular audits, certifications	IaaS PaaS, SaaS	Cloud service provider and cloud customer Cloud service provider
OS (hypervisor)	Security groups (ACLs), network traffic, security settings, patch level, VLAN setup, running VMs	Security groups and configuration monitor, IDS, SIEM, patch, and vulnerability scans, certifications	IaaS, PaaS, SaaS	Cloud service provider
OS (VMs)	Security configuration, running services, open shares, local/remote users, security patch level, security logs, VM image checksums, cloud APIs	SIEM, antivirus and host intrusion detection system solution, cloud VM console, file integrity checker, identity management (user access management system)	IaaS PaaS, SaaS	Cloud customer Cloud service provider
Middleware/database	Security and encryption settings, security and activity logs, user and access permission, data change logs	SIEM and log analytics, central database management console, identity management (user access management system)	IaaS PaaS, SaaS	Cloud customer Cloud service provider
Cloud application	Encryption setup, user and access permission, cloud data read/write logs (transaction logs), open network ports, Internet activities	IPS, web application firewall, vulnerability scanner, regular application security audits, certifications	IaaS, PaaS SaaS	Cloud customer Cloud service provider

15.4 ELASTIC MONITORING IN THE CLOUD

It is important to keep the special properties of a cloud environment in mind and to use them for the cloud monitoring setup as well. The cloud providers offer various additional automation and monitoring services out of the box that can be combined and integrated into a flexible and, to some degree, intelligent monitoring system that is even capable of triggering automatic responses or repair activities. Elastic monitoring configurations achieve these goals.

Another aspect is the fact that the monitored environment could change constantly due to its virtualization features. VMs may be added or replaced; functionality or applications may shift between cloud servers, IP addresses may be volatile or dynamically assigned, and storage or CPU resources are resized on the fly. Cloud monitoring needs to be elastic to accommodate also for these aspects of the cloud environment, and it needs to support runtime configuration changes.

For autonomous and proactive cloud management, monitoring data is required to provide an accurate representation of the cloud state and needs to be delivered in a timely fashion in order to enable quick decisions in the face of changes.

Overall this means that the cloud monitoring solution must constantly scan and observe changes in the cloud infrastructure or cloud application landscape to be able to provide a complete monitoring status. Therefore, it must discover new cloud resources and configurations automatically and update the corresponding monitoring dashboards, groups to include, for example, the new discovered VMs. The cloud provider tools are hereby a primary source of information. The monitoring services offered by the provider consider of course also these updates in the cloud environment.

The elastic monitoring feature is very important for the overall security monitoring as well. It ensures, for example, that all security events and logs are properly collected from all source systems, that the security patch status covers all cloud instances and components, or that a newly added cloud server is automatically reported in case of security configuration noncompliance.

In combination with auto-remediation features of the cloud automation frameworks, it even allows automatic responses to detected threats such as initiating the installation of missing patches, disabling unsecure network ports that are vulnerable to an attack, and deletion of noncompliant and potential dangerous user permissions or passwords. It can also be used as part of the default system installation or set up a procedure to allow network communication to the outside world only if the system is set up in a secure way and complies with the defined minimum security policies and standards. Therefore, this security monitoring would be a quality gate and workflow item in all changes to the cloud landscape.

15.5 CLOUD MONITORING TOOLS AND SERVICES

The cloud service providers understood that transparency and control in cloud operations is highly valued by enterprise cloud customers. These customers insisted in proper tools and reporting functionality before they are willing to migrate their productive business data into a cloud environment. For example, an IaaS/PaaS provider must be able to immediately expose fine-grained security specifications and details for the entire stack, including software versions, patch levels, firewall rules, tracking server snapshots, and user access rights.

The cloud service provider tools and APIs must provide this kind of information and also allow the configuration of customer-specific metrics and checks that should be executed/monitored in the customer cloud environment. The data must be provided in an easy consumable way (e.g., via a web-based graphical user interface) and also as protocol raw data in an international format (e.g., extensible markup language [XML], javascript object notation [JSON], comma-separated values [CSV]) that can be integrated into a commercial SIEM monitoring solution.

The tools must cover all cloud provider services such as network, virtualization layer, database tables, application user management, and configuration.

The data and tools must also cover all API commands and administrative functions executed by a cloud user. It must be possible without a doubt to identify every change in the cloud service configuration and the responsible entity or user. This includes, for example, all VM instance creation, deletion or change activities, modifications of network security groups, access control lists (ACLs), firewall rules, VPN settings, virtual local area network (VLAN) creation, assignments or changes, and all user permission changes.

The monitoring should also cover all additional cloud add-on services used by the customer such as the settings of an elastic load balancer, workflow and automation job schedules and assignments, autoscaling cluster events, and domain name system events.

The cloud provider should execute these monitor checks at least in a 1 minute cycle and should keep the monitoring logs for at least 6 months. Some providers offer additional metrics and cycles as a purchasable add-on service. The cloud customer must check which monitoring package is part of his or her cloud service and validate that the scope, monitoring cycles, and history features fulfill his or her needs and industry requirements.

Most cloud providers also allow the setup of customer-specific alerts for certain thresholds. These alarms are then created by the monitoring system of the cloud provider and could trigger a customer-specific incident or reaction process. E-mail alerting would be the minimum requirement for that. Better would be a full-fletched integration into the cloud workflow and automation engines or a customer-specific automated reaction based on his or her installed tools.

Last but not least, many cloud providers offer a comprehensive set of certifications and attestations by independent auditors. The most current reports and certificates are also made available to the cloud customer via the provider website and monitoring console.

15.6 BEST PRACTICES IN CLOUD SECURITY MONITORING

The cloud customer and cloud system administrator need to set up continuous real-time security audits for his or her cloud environment. Many corporations invest in very thorough, one-time "snapshot" security audits. This is the completely wrong approach. A security audit should be considered as a long-term, ongoing, real-time, continuous process. Instead of performing a security audit every 6 months, it should be performed every minute. This requires continuous monitoring and continuous assurance. And the audit procedure itself needs to adapt with the evolution of the overall system (elastic monitoring).

Based on the discussed monitoring principles and cloud-specific aspects, we are now able to define a minimum set of best practices for the private cloud security monitoring setup. These best practice examples can be used as a starting point but must be adjusted to the actual cloud landscape and used cloud services. As discussed previously, it makes a great difference if the cloud customer uses an IaaS cloud provider or a PaaS setup. Nevertheless, the basic requirements for cloud security monitoring will not change, only the responsibilities and used tools or monitoring solutions. It is key to make yourself familiar with the cloud monitoring features of your cloud service provider and the security needs of your cloud application and the hosted business data. These answers are then mapped to the best practices discussed in this section and will provide a clear guidance and monitoring concept, which will ensure a secure and reliable operation of the cloud solution itself.

15.6.1 Security Monitoring Logs

Traceability of activities must be ensured by appropriate logging in all relevant cloud services and components. Log entries must contain all critical events relevant to the cloud infrastructure. The security log process consists of log collection from various sources and the data normalization to ensure that these sources can be correlated and aggregated as next step. The resulting dataset is analyzed against existing patterns or for unusual behavior as shown in Figure 15.7. Some log analysis solutions even offer the recognition of an emerging DOS attack. A minimum set of critical events are considered to include the following:

- Successful user login

- Failed user logins

- User logoff

- User account change or deletion

- Service failures

- System starts and shutdowns

- Critical errors

FIGURE 15.7 Security logs workflow.

Additionally, a log entry should contain at least the following information (if relevant):

- A time stamp with date and current time
- Type of event
- Category of event
- Application/service
- Logon ID/account
- Source ID/IP/computer

Log files must be protected from unauthorized modification by the cloud service provider or the cloud customer (administrators). This could be achieved by using cryptographic controls (preventive controls) or by independent auditors that regularly check the integrity of these given logs and search for manipulation (detective control).

The log event should be collected every minute (if possible) and stored in the log file or log event database for at least 6 months. All log events must follow a clear time stamp to be able to compare different logs and to recombine and reconstruct a historical sequence of events based on the time stamps. This makes it absolutely mandatory that all cloud systems have a configured NTP to ensure this proper time stamp.

Log events must be centrally collected in a SIEM solution or at least in a "syslog" and "splunk" server monitoring environment. These central logging, monitoring, and analytics servers should have different administrators and a high secure configuration setup (system hardening) to reserve the log data and prevent manipulation or data deletion.

15.6.2 Consider Cloud Certifications

Check and ensure that the cloud provider has performed a SOC2 Type II Attestation [6,7] and an ISO27001 Certification [8] as a minimum base for secure and reliable cloud backend (infrastructure) operations. Check that the certifications and audit reports are still valid and ask for the next audit cycle. Review the findings or noncompliances outlined in these reports. Ask the cloud service provider also for the Statement of Applicability that defines the scope of the attestations and certifications to ensure that you understand which services or layers are monitored by these auditors and controls.

Also check for industry-specific certifications. For example, a payment card industry/data security standard (PCI/DSS) certification is absolutely mandatory if you want to process credit card data in the cloud environment. In the same way, the provider should have necessary certifications and compliance guarantees for other industries (e.g., Health Insurance Portability and Accountability Act [HIPAA] for health care, Federal Information Security Management Act/National Institute of Standards and Technology [FISMA/NIST], Food and Drug Administration/Good X Practice [FDA/GxP]).

In the past few years also, cloud-specific certifications emerged like the Security Trust Assurance Registry (STAR) certification by the Cloud Security Alliance (CSA) [9].

This certification will also show that the chosen cloud provider is serious in his or her attempt to provide a state-of-the-art cloud service for all kinds of critical businesses. Nearly all major cloud providers are members of the CSA and have a STAR certification/compliance available.

The CSA is also constantly updating and researching the cloud security aspects, including security monitoring. Their website can serve as another source of information and best practices in the area of cloud security monitoring.

The European Network and Information Security Agency (ENISA) is a similar European-based cloud alliance and was formed especially with the strong European laws (e.g., privacy laws) in mind. If a European cloud setup or usage is considered, it would be helpful to check the lasted best practices on their website as well.

15.6.3 Cloud Internal Vulnerability Monitoring

In case of an IaaS or PaaS cloud solution, vulnerability scans should be performed at a minimum of 4 time s a year, to ensure that the controls are met based on compliance and certification requirements. It should focus on the areas that are in the main responsibility of the cloud customer such as the application, database, or OS level. Such a vulnerability scan of the cloud servers and landscape is often mandatory for many audit frameworks or industry standards. Figure 15.8 shows such a vulnerability management and scanning process.

The cloud administrator must prioritize vulnerability remediation to reduce risk and impact to his or her cloud data and business processes. The assessed and prioritized vulnerabilities are followed up within the bug-fixing activities using the security patch and change management processes. The cloud service provider also performs such regular scans to his or her cloud service infrastructure to ensure that he or she can comply with his or her audit and

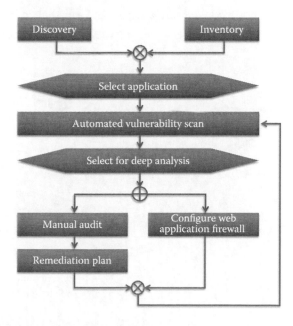

FIGURE 15.8 Vulnerability management process.

certification requirements and to monitor, for example, vulnerabilities that can endanger his or her customers. The cloud customer, however, should either use the available scanning services of the cloud service provider or install and run a vulnerability scan appliance from within his or her cloud network segment to be able to fully scan all cloud applications and servers. It is clear that such activities must be aligned with the terms and conditions of the cloud service, and the customer must clarify in which form such scans are allowed.

15.6.4 Internet Penetration Testing

All Internet-facing cloud systems or services (e.g., firewalls, load balancers, gateways, web application servers, etc.) must be validated by independent penetration tests. An external company should perform these tests up to 4-times per year, but at least once per year.

Findings from the penetration tests are followed up according to their criticality. The idea behind this activity is to execute a simulated attack and vulnerability scan the same way a cloud user or an Internet hacker would try to test the cloud application. This means that it tests the whole security infrastructure from a network, firewall up to the application session handling, and user management level. It also shows flaws in the cloud provider services (e.g., in case the firewalls or web servers are managed by the provider). Overall, it is very important to check with the provider upfront which kind of testing and scanning activity is allowed to prevent of being blocked or in violation with the cloud contract. The provider can't differentiate good customer-triggered scans from the ones that mean harm to the cloud service. Therefore, most providers are very restrictive when it comes to the ability to perform own scans and testing. Figure 15.9 shows the different aspects of such penetration testing and auditing, some of which are automated by tools or managed third-party services, and some audits are pure manual security analysis by impendent security experts or white hat hackers.

Of course, the cloud service providers in general perform their own external penetration tests and monitor their services with IDS. Due to security reasons, such penetration test results

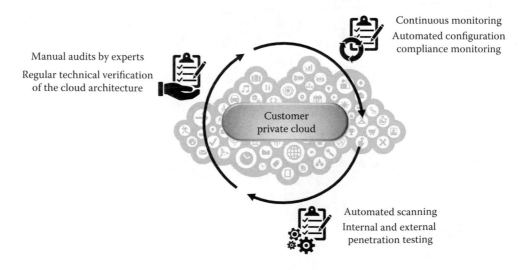

FIGURE 15.9   Penetration tests and audits.

may not be shared with the cloud customer. Ensure you get either the testing results or a certification report that outlines the execution of such penetration tests with no major findings.

15.6.5 Monitor Security Configurations and System Changes

All critical configurations, activities, and log events must be monitored. All configuration changes and administrative activities performed by the cloud provider APIs or web-based tools are logged by the provider and can be retrieved using the cloud provider monitoring, logging, and reporting services. The analytics (e.g., define good vs. suspicious events) is still something the cloud customer must perform on his or her own using some additional tools or services or by integrating the data in his or her SIEM solution and security incident process. Unfortunately, the usage of the cloud provider logs is not enough to cover the whole system activity and the changes on all components. Especially, in IaaS and PaaS setup some components (e.g., applications, OS) are in the responsibility of the cloud customer. The provider may only have some technical metadata but no real insight into these systems. Therefore, the following additional components must be monitored for suspicious behavior or unplanned changes:

- Network ACL settings and cloud server security group configurations

- All VM activity and API/admin commands

- Changes in user permissions and user account creation

- General deviating VM activity (CPU, state, memory, network activity)

- All storage read/write activity affecting critical business data

- Logs of established virtual path connection (VPC)/VPN connections

- The security patch status of the cloud server, the database, and the application

- Antivirus and anti-malware update status and virus event logs

- The IDS status and detection logs

- Changes to the OS, database, or application security configuration such as the following:

  - Changes in running (network facing) services

  - Changes in encryption settings

  - Changes in installed software packages

  - Changes in open shares, network folders, or Internet-facing web services

  - Changes in default system users or password policies

  - Changes in the logging configuration

  - Unusual direct changes in database (system) tables

To be able to detect unusual and suspicious activity or changes, it is of course necessary to define a baseline of allowed changes in daily operation. Therefore, the operation team must follow clear boundaries (e.g., not working with the root user; not changing the password policy setup), and the change/event logs must be analyzed over a certain time period to detect the level of normal change. The following points cloud help to come up with such a baseline and better understand your cloud system:

- Monitor the performance issues and peak activity

- Correlate changes that occur in your environment with changes in key metrics

- View the most recent changes for a given server or cluster

- Review all of the changes that a given employee made during a period of time

- Review all firewall changes during a period of time

- Review all of the changes that occurred before, during, and after an incident or outage

This will set the threshold for an automated monitor to alert in case of unusual network activity or unusual changes in the cloud system.

History data must also be preserved for later forensic analysis in case of a security breach or incident. It is recommended to store such data for at least 6 months. The logs must be stored in a redundant and high available environment. If you want to be on the safe side, you could even think about storing the logs in your local data center facility (if applicable), in another country, or by another cloud provider.

15.6.6 Security Incident Process and Abuse Handling

Apart from the actual continuous monitoring of the private cloud environment, it is also very important to integrate the events captured by the monitoring system or cloud provider solution into a security incident management system or a full-blown security incident and event management solution that is controlled and operated by the cloud customer or one of his or her partners/subcontractors. The security incident could be handled in general with the normal incident management, besides the fact that certain escalation steps or key stakeholders may be different (e.g., initial reaction times need to be faster, countermeasures must be in place swiftly, security teams and escalation managers should be involved from the start).

The cloud customer must also check the security incident process that is in place within the cloud service provider to define the necessary interfaces and notification channels. Some cloud providers offer hereby very proactive services such as an instant notification of possible hacking attempt or abuse behavior of customer cloud server instances as shown in Figure 15.10. Of course, it is also in the interest of the cloud provider to ensure that his or her customers and his or her backend services don't suffer from an immanent security vulnerability or system exploit. Therefore, as a side product of monitoring his or her own back-end (e.g., network) infrastructure, he or she also contributes to the security monitoring of the cloud customer and his or her systems as well.

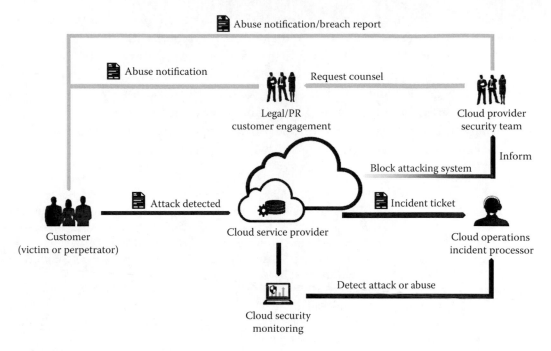

FIGURE 15.10   Security incident notification process.

Additionally, the monitoring done by the cloud provider for his or her back-end infra-structure and cloud service delivery is also part of most certification and attestation activi-ties. The cloud customer must review the provided certification reports to figure out which level of security monitoring and proactive vulnerability management is done by the provider.

The cloud providers have clear rules and engagement models in case of a detected abuse case and could terminate the affected cloud instance, application, or even the customer contract. The customer should be able to react on such provider security notifications in a timely manner to fulfill the terms and conditions as outlined in the contract between the cloud customer and the provider.

15.7 SUMMARY

Overall, the private cloud environment must be monitored similar to an on-premise solu-tion in terms of the security aspects. Topics such as secure system configuration, access lists and port opening, user access, and role permissions are important monitoring areas also in the cloud environment. The biggest differentiation lies in shared or distributed responsibilities for the monitoring. The fact that every aspect of operation must be seen as a cloud service and therefore different tools and general system setups applies. The cloud solutions in the world today can even offer better control and monitoring capabilities due to their strict service approach and force the customer to think about his or her operation model and system setup in a new way. In the end, every customer cloud installation and solution should use the monitoring framework and logging capabilities of the cloud ser-vice provider. It is up to the customer to use this toolbox in a smart way and to define the needed monitoring KPIs and security event management processes. The big advantage of using a cloud provider (regardless if this is an IaaS, PaaS, or SaaS solution), is the high level of already available security measures and cloud service security monitoring. Here, the provider must ensure that he or she can provide a reliable and resilient operation which can stand up against basic attacks or vulnerabilities. As a cloud customer, you can profit from these measures and don't need to take care of, for example, data center physical security or hypervisor virtualization security. The starting point is a customer landscape-specific monitoring concept that is aware of the cloud provider capabilities and services and defines its needs based on the processed customer data and business overall.

REFERENCES

1. Joshua Brower. SANS Institute Whitepaper. *The Security Onion Cloud Client—Network Security Monitoring for the Cloud*. 2013. http://www.sans.org/reading-room/whitepapers/detection/security-onion-cloud-client-network-security-monitoring-cloud-34335.
2. Gethyn Ellis. Managing and Monitoring Virtual Machines. Chapter 5 in *Microsoft Azure IaaS Essentials*. Packt Publishing Ltd. 2015.
3. *Amazon CloudWatch: Developer Guide*. Amazon Web Services: Seattle, WA. 2015. http://docs.aws.amazon.com/AmazonCloudWatch/latest/DeveloperGuide/acw-dg.pdf.
4. *Intelligent Monitoring for your AWS Infrastructure, Systems and App*. Stackdriver: Boston, MA. 2015. http://www.stackdriver.com/event-logging/.
5. *AWS CloudTrail: User Guide*. Version 1.0. Amazon Web Services: Seattle, WA. 2015. http://docs.aws.amazon.com/awscloudtrail/latest/userguide/awscloudtrail-ug.pdf.
6. *Assurance Reports on Controls at a Service Organization* (ISAE 3402). International Auditing and Assurance Standards Board. 2011. http://isae3402.com.
7. *Statement on Standards for Attestation Engagements No. 16* (SSAE 16). Auditing Standards Board of the American Institute of Certified Public Accountants (AICPA). April 2010. http://ssae16.com.
8. ISO/IEC 27001—Information Security Management Standard. International Organization for Standardization (ISO): Geneva, Switzerland. 2013. http://www.iso.org/iso/home/standards/management-standards/iso27001.htm.
9. SA Security, Trust & Assurance Registry (STAR). Cloud Security Alliance Group. Seattle, WA. 2015. https://cloudsecurityalliance.org/star/#_overview.

CHAPTER 16

Cloud Security Assessment and Authorization

Sarbari Gupta

CONTENTS

16.1 INTRODUCTION

Within the information security domain, the words "assessment" and "authorization" take on a special connotation. Assessment is the process of evaluating the effectiveness of information security techniques and processes implemented within an information system (with a defined boundary) against an established set of security requirements to determine the security risks that remain within the information system. Authorization is the organizational-level decision to accept the risks posed by an information system used or operated by the organization and the formal approval to allow the information system to become operational in production mode.

In this chapter, assessment and authorization methods and activities for cloud-based information systems are reviewed.

16.2 RISK-BASED MODEL FOR SECURITY ASSESSMENT AND AUTHORIZATION

The Federal Information Security Management Act (FISMA) is a part of the Electronic Government Act of 2002. It is a comprehensive framework that established the responsibilities and objectives for strengthening the security posture of information resources that support US Federal Operations and Assets.

Assessment and authorization are two of the six steps within the National Institute of Standards and Technology (NIST) Risk Management Framework (RMF), which was developed in response to the FISMA [1]. The NIST RMF defines a structured methodology for choosing, implementing, evaluating, and maintaining the effectiveness of security controls throughout the life cycle of an information system in a manner that is commensurate with the criticality of the system and the risks posed by the system to the broader organization. Figure 16.1 illustrates the six steps of the RMF along with the core NIST standards and

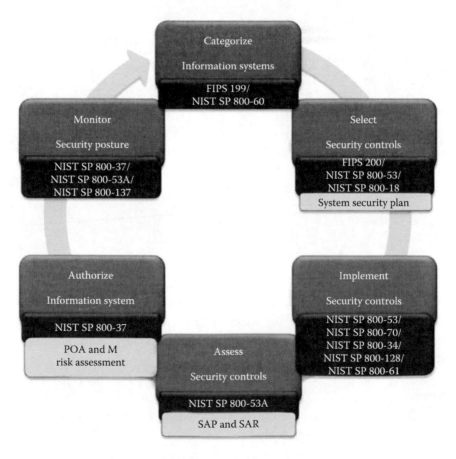

FIGURE 16.1 The NIST risk management framework.

guidelines that apply to each step as well as key documents that are produced in implementing the RMF. The six steps of the NIST RMF are as follows:

1. *Categorize.* Determine the criticality of the information system in terms of the potential impact of compromise to the information and the information system.

2. *Select.* Identify a minimal set of security controls (baseline) that are needed to mitigate risk to the information system based on its security categorization; tailor and supplement the security control baseline as needed based on an organizational assessment of risk.

3. *Implement.* Instrument the selected set of security controls and document the implementation status and how the controls are implemented.

4. *Assess.* Evaluate the security controls using appropriate evaluation methods to determine the extent to which the controls are implemented correctly, operating as intended, and producing the desired outcome with respect to security.

5. *Authorize.* Review the weaknesses identified through assessment and the risks posed to the organization to determine whether the risk is acceptable and the information system can be approved for operation.

6. *Monitor.* Evaluate the implementation status and effectiveness of the security controls on an ongoing basis as the information system undergoes change and the environment of operation evolves.

The security controls implemented as a part of the RMF are defined in the latest revision of NIST Special Publication 800-53 (currently at revision 4) [?] The focus of the RMF model is on risk identification, mitigation, and acceptance by the organization that owns or operates the target system.

16.3 CLOUD ASSESSMENT AND AUTHORIZATION

Cloud computing environments have some unique characteristics. For example, responsibility for system administration and security are often shared between multiple players. Many cloud environments are built to support multitenancy for computing platforms as well as storage media. By definition, cloud systems are "remote" to the user—thus, authentication to a cloud system is always conducted over a shared channel. Cloud systems are built using virtualized IT components (processors, storage, networking, etc.), thus bringing in additional avenues for attack and compromise.

In general, cloud environments engender a more diverse set of threat agents and threat events due to the inherently shared nature of these environments, the use of different technologies, and the presence of a larger set of actors. Thus, for systems that are implemented wholly or partially within a cloud environment, the uncertainties and shared environment necessitate additional security protections to achieve the same level of risk mitigation compared to traditional systems. Additionally, a fundamental promise of cloud services is the ability to build once and make available to multiple consumers/users of the service.

To provide a consistent set of security requirements for cloud-based information systems used by the US federal government, and to leverage assessments and authorizations of the same cloud service across multiple government customers, the Federal Risk and Authorization Management Program (FedRAMP) was developed as a joint effort between the General Services Administration, the Department of Defense, the Department of Homeland Security, and the NIST.

16.4 FedRAMP OVERVIEW

FedRAMP enables a federal organization to rapidly adopt cloud services that have been previously authorized for operation. A cloud service may receive provisional authorization from the FedRAMP Joint Authorization Board (JAB) or full authorization from a federal agency. A previously achieved FedRAMP authorization can be leveraged by one or more additional agencies that wish to engage the same cloud services, thus resulting in significant savings in cost and effort [3]. The FedRAMP framework includes the following major components:

- Standardized security control baselines for cloud systems at low and moderate impact levels addressing the specific threats and vulnerabilities that apply to cloud environments

- Set of templates for developing documents that comprise the security authorization package for a cloud system and guidelines for navigating the FedRAMP process

- Online training on the FedRAMP process

- Model for formal accreditation of FedRAMP Third Party Assessor Organizations (3PAOs) that are approved to conduct independent security control assessments of cloud services

- Rigorous review of FedRAMP authorization packages submitted for Provisional Authorization to Operate (p-ATO) by the FedRAMP JAB

- Guidance and standardized contract language for inclusion of FedRAMP requirements into acquisition documents

- Repository of authorization packages for cloud services that can be leveraged government-wide

In a memorandum to Federal Chief Information Officers dated October 2011 (and entitled "Security Authorization of Information Systems in Cloud Computing Environments"), the Office of Management and Budget (OMB) established that executive departments and agencies shall use FedRAMP when conducting risk assessments and security authorizations. This also includes the granting of ATOs for all executive departments or agencies that use cloud services; as well as, ensuring that applicable contracts appropriately require that credentials service providers (CSPs) comply with FedRAMP security authorization requirements [4]. A CSP is compliant with FedRAMP requirements and processes if all of the following conditions are met:

- Security package uses the required FedRAMP templates.

- All FedRAMP security controls have been met either directly or through compensating controls (where allowed).

- The CSP has been assessed by an independent assessor who has no conflict of interest or bias with respect to the system.

- An authorization letter for the p-ATO or full ATO is on file with the FedRAMP Program Management Office (PMO).

16.5 FedRAMP STAKEHOLDERS

The OMB memorandum [4] also defines executive department and agency responsibilities in developing, implementing, operating, and maintaining FedRAMP. The four main stakeholders in the FedRAMP program and process [3,4] are as follows:

- *Cloud service provider* (*CSP*): Entity that provides cloud services that are of potential interest to federal agencies. The CSP is responsible for implementing the security controls needed to comply with the appropriate FedRAMP security control baseline and documenting the security implementation. The CSP retains a 3PAO to conduct an independent security control assessment.

- *Federal agency customer*: Federal organization that wishes to contract with a CSP to obtain specific services. The agency is responsible for following FedRAMP processes for authorizing the cloud system/service prior to operation.

- *FedRAMP PMO and JAB*: Centralized entities that are responsible for establishing and maintaining the FedRAMP processes and templates, facilitating JAB provisional authorizations, and publishing the authorization packages for CSPs.

- *3PAO*: Independent parties that are accredited to perform security assessments of CSPs. 3PAOs are responsible for following FedRAMP processes for assessment, developing the needed assessment documentation using FedRAMP templates, and providing and defending an authorization recommendation for the CSP.

16.6 FedRAMP DOCUMENTATION

A FedRAMP Authorization Package consists of a number of documents in addition to the three core documents—system security plan, security assessment report, and plan of actions and milestones (POA&M) [5]. FedRAMP provides templates for many of these documents. Some templates are mandatory, whereas others are optional as long as an equivalent content is included in the documents. Table 16.1 lists all of the documents required for a FedRAMP authorization package and the availability and use of the FedRAMP-provided templates.

TABLE 16.1   Availability and Use of FedRAMP Templates

Document Name	FedRAMP Template Use—Mandatory/ Optional/Unavailable
Control Tailoring Workbook	Mandatory
Control Information Summary	Mandatory
FIPS 199 Categorization	Mandatory
e-Authentication Risk Assessment	Optional
Rules of Behavior	Optional
Privacy Threshold Assessment	Optional
Privacy Impact Assessment	Optional
Information System Security Policies	Unavailable
System Security Plan	Mandatory
Configuration Management Plan	Unavailable
IT Contingency Plan	Optional
Incident Response Plan	Optional
SAP	Mandatory
SAR	Mandatory
POA&M	Optional

16.7 FedRAMP AUTHORIZATION PACKAGE REPOSITORY

CSP authorization packages that are posted to the FedRAMP repository can be leveraged by other agencies that wish to contract with the same CSPs to obtain services. Authorization packages can be submitted for inclusion into the FedRAMP repository through one of the following three possible paths:

- *JAB*: Packages that are submitted for review and provisional authorization by the JAB receive a very rigorous review by the FedRAMP PMO-appointed Information System Security Officer as well as the members of the JAB. For these packages, it is mandatory that a 3PAO be engaged for the independent security assessment. Once p-ATO has been granted by the JAB, the package and p-ATO memorandum are published to the FedRAMP repository and can be easily leveraged by any agency that wishes to contract with the associated CSP.

- *Agency*: In this path, the authorization package is submitted by the CSP to the agency that wishes to contract with them. The CSP engages a suitable assessor to conduct the security control assessment and assembles the authorization package. The agency is responsible for reviewing the package to ensure that it meets all FedRAMP requirements as well as additional agency-specific requirements. Once the agency decides to grant an ATO to the CSP, the authorization package can be sent to the FedRAMP PMO for publishing in the FedRAMP repository. Any other agency that wishes to contract with the same CSP can then choose to leverage the existing authorization package to determine the extent of additional documentation or testing that may be needed in order to grant ATO from a second agency.

- *CSP supplied*: For this path, the CSP does not need either p-ATO or agency ATO in order to publish their security authorization package. The CSP engages a suitable security assessor, prepares the authorization package, and submits to the FedRAMP PMO for publication in the FedRAMP repository. Although published, the package does not go through any accuracy or quality reviews. Agencies can choose to leverage the published package to conduct a thorough review of compliance with FedRAMP as well as agency-specific requirements prior to issuing an ATO. If an ATO is granted, the package moves from the "CSP Supplied" path to the agency path.

It may be noted that the level of rigor of the reviews in the three paths is progressively less intense from the first to the third. Conversely, the time frame for achieving authorization is significantly less for agency versus JAB packages. By definition, a CSP Supplied package has not received authorization.

16.8 FedRAMP ASSESSMENT

The FedRAMP process has been developed to ensure that all CSPs that achieve FedRAMP compliance are assessed in a standardized manner [5]. The CSP selects an independent assessor consistent with the authorization path it selects—a FedRAMP-approved 3PAO is mandatory for the JAB p-ATO path but optional for the agency ATO path. The selected assessor is responsible for preparing a security assessment plan (SAP) using the FedRAMP-provided template, which must be approved by the CSP prior to the commencement of testing. The SAP must also be approved by the FedRAMP JAB (for JAB p-ATO path) prior to testing. In performing the assessment of the CSP, the assessor must use the FedRAMP-provided Security Assessment Test Cases (which are based on NIST SP 800-53A and augmented to account for the uniqueness of cloud systems) and document the findings in the test cases template.

Automated scans (authenticated and nonauthenticated) and penetration testing are mandatory under FedRAMP. The CSP is required to run source code scans if the CSP develops and uses custom code as a part of its offering. FedRAMP provides guidance on the methodology for conducting these technical test steps.

The Security Assessment Report (SAR) is developed by the assessor at the conclusion of the assessment activity using the FedRAMP-provided template and includes the assessor's recommendation on whether the CSP is ready for authorization. For the JAB p-ATO path, the assessor briefs the FedRAMP PMO and JAB on the results of the assessment and the basis for the authorization recommendation.

16.9 FedRAMP AUTHORIZATION

FedRAMP supports two basic authorization models for CSPs: JAB p-ATO and agency ATO. These two authorization models are described in Sections 16.9.1 and 16.9.2, respectively.

16.9.1 JAB Provisional ATO

In this model, the CSP applies to the FedRAMP PMO for JAB p-ATO and prepares the FedRAMP documentation in accordance with the available templates and guidance.

The FedRAMP PMO and JAB review and approve the documentation at each step before the CSP can move to the next step of the process. For example, the SSP has to be approved prior to development of the SAP; the SAP has to be approved prior to commencement of the actual testing and the development of the SAR. The CSP needs to engage a FedRAMP-approved 3PAO to perform the assessment. The results of the assessment are documented in the SAR and presented to the JAB by the assessor. The entire authorization package is reviewed rigorously by the JAB. The CSP makes adjustments as needed to bring it to the level of compliance and quality required by the JAB. When the JAB is satisfied that the authorization package meets all of the technical and quality requirements, the CSP is granted p-ATO. The authorization package is then uploaded to the FedRAMP repository by the FedRAMP PMO.

16.9.2 Agency ATO

In this model, the CSP works with a specific agency end customer to obtain ATO for the solution built around the cloud service/system provided by the CSP. The agency appoints a suitable senior person as the authorizing official for the cloud system. The CSP works with the agency to determine the boundaries of responsibility (between the CSP and the agency cloud customer) for the various security controls included in the relevant FedRAMP baseline. The CSP prepares the FedRAMP documentation in the same manner as in the JAB ATO using the FedRAMP templates and guidelines. The agency approves the FedRAMP documentation at each step. The CSP selects an independent assessor (who may or may not be a FedRAMP-approved 3PAO) that prepares the SAP. When the agency approves the SAP, the assessor performs the assessment using the FedRAMP-provided templates, test cases, and guidelines. The assessor prepares the SAR and the CSP prepares the corresponding POA&M. The agency authorizing official reviews the entire authorization package against the context of the agency's mission and risk tolerance and grants ATO to the cloud system if the risk is brought under an acceptable level. The agency can then choose to submit the CSP's authorization package to the FedRAMP PMO for uploading to the FedRAMP repository.

16.10 LEVERAGING FedRAMP AUTHORIZATION FOR CLOUD SERVICES

The FedRAMP repository includes the authorization packages for CSPs that have achieved p-ATO or agency ATO. An agency that wishes to utilize the services of a CSP that has already achieved authorization can request the FedRAMP PMO to provide access to the relevant authorization package. The agency authorizing official can then review the package against the backdrop of his or her mission and risk profile to determine whether to grant ATO to the CSP as is or to request changes to the security control implementation or documentation. The agency may also request a partial or full assessment if they are not satisfied with the existing SAP or SAR. However, in most cases, the agency will accept the existing authorization package with minimal changes and grant ATO to the CSP for use within that agency. Additional agencies that wish to use the same CSP will go through a similar process to grant ATO to the CSP for their agency. In effect, the authorization package that is produced once will be reused multiple times as many agencies decide to use the same CSP, thus saving the government as well as the CSP lots of time, effort, and money.

16.11 STRENGTHS AND WEAKNESSES OF FedRAMP

Sections 16.1 through 16.10, describe the most significant facets of FedRAMP. Although there are many obvious benefits of the FedRAMP approach to cloud authorizations, there are a few drawbacks as well. The major benefits of FedRAMP include the following:

- A standardized set of requirements, templates, and processes for cloud authorizations that can be leveraged across all agencies and departments

- Enabling a higher level of confidence in the security of cloud systems, thus promoting more rapid cloud adoption by agencies

- Ability to leverage existing authorizations for a CSP across multiple agencies, resulting in huge savings in cost, effort, and time

Despite the aforementioned benefits, there are some drawbacks to the current FedRAMP approach. The most significant weaknesses of FedRAMP are listed as follows:

- The FedRAMP downplays the fact that agencies still have to review the CSP authorization package to issue an agency-level ATO for the CSP. In most cases, the agency will have to implement a significant subset of the security controls that are part of the relevant baseline (such as AC-1 Access Control Policy and Procedures and AC-2 Account Management) for the simple reason that these controls can only be implemented at the agency level. For all of the controls that are (or should be) the agency's responsibilities, the agency must prepare an authorization package and grant ATO prior to using/operating a production instance of the cloud system. The FedRAMP *Agency Guide for FedRAMP Authorizations* conveys this message clearly—however, the message is frequently lost in the louder messages about the ease and cost-effectiveness of leveraging existing p-ATO or agency ATO for a CSP. The result is that agencies are assuming that CSP authorization is all they need to start using the cloud service. This is a security risk because the security controls that should have been the responsibility of the agency are not getting the security review and authorization that is needed.

- The FedRAMP JAB provisional authorization process presents a significant bottleneck for issuing authorizations to CSPs. The JAB review process is very intense and frequently involves multiple iterations with the CSP and the 3PAO, which can take many months and sometimes several years to complete. Only a handful of CSPs have been able to achieve p-ATO since the time the FedRAMP program became operational, and there is a huge backlog of CSPs that are going through the authorization process. This has translated to a slowing down of cloud adoption by agencies because they have very few JAB-authorized CSPs to choose from at this time. The demand for cloud authorization is much higher than that can be sustained by the FedRAMP JAB process.

- The FedRAMP JAB authorization is a very costly process for the CSP due to its lengthy duration and intensity. This has served as a great disincentive to small, innovative cloud providers who would otherwise like to sell their services to federal agencies.

Some of the foundational advantages of the cloud (such as rapid deployment and low cost) are negated by the costly and lengthy FedRAMP JAB authorization process. As a result, agencies are unable to realize some of the basic advantages of the cloud and are not able to access cloud service from small and innovative cloud providers.

- The FedRAMP JAB p-ATO process is inherently not a risk management process. The FedRAMP JAB does not have a mission beyond security of cloud systems and cannot make risk-based decisions on behalf of customer agencies that may use a particular CSP. Thus, the p-ATO process does not have the benefit of a context or backdrop against which to make a reasonable risk-based decision for authorization of a CSP. This is in direct conflict with the FISMA law and the NIST RMF, which is the basis for the FedRAMP approach.

16.12 RECOMMENDATIONS FOR A WAY FORWARD

The author of this chapter recommends that FedRAMP continue the outstanding work it is doing to standardize the security requirements and templates for cloud systems used by federal agencies. However, it would be recommended that the JAB p-ATO path be deprecated while promoting the agency ATO path as the way forward. This will result in the agency's making risk-based decisions to authorize cloud systems that lead to lower costs and shorter time frames for all parties and remove the bottleneck of the JAB p-ATO process. It would also be recommended that FedRAMP develop more detailed guidance on how to leverage agency ATOs for CSPs more effectively while maintaining or enhancing the security of federal cloud implementations. Finally, it would be recommended that FedRAMP continue its role in enforcing continuous monitoring of agency-authorized CSPs.

16.13 SUMMARY

Federal departments and agencies are required to follow the FedRAMP assessment and authorization model for all cloud services that they implement or utilize [4]. The FedRAMP program provides a standard set of processes and templates for cloud security assessment and authorization that ensures a certain degree of consistency and assurance in the security of these cloud services [3]. Despite the benefits of the FedRAMP model, the FedRAMP JAB represents a significant bottleneck in the path for rapid adoption of cloud services by federal government, and the JAB p-ATO process represents a very costly and lengthy process for managing risk in adopting cloud solutions.

REFERENCES

1. Joint Task Force Transformation Initiative. *NIST Special Publication 800-37 Revision 1 Guide for Applying the Risk Management Framework to Federal Information Systems*, February 2010.
2. Joint Task Force Transformation Initiative. *NIST Special Publication 800-53 Revision 4 Security and Privacy Controls for Federal Information Systems and Organizations*, April 2013.
3. FedRAMP. *Guide to Understanding FedRAMP*. Version 2.0, June 2014.
4. VanRoekel, Steven. *Security Authorization of Information Systems in Cloud Computing Environments*. Office of Management and Budget (OMB) Memorandum, December 8, 2011.
5. FedRAMP. *FedRAMP Security Assessment Framework*. Version 2.0, June 2014.

CHAPTER 17

Assessment and Authorization in Private Cloud Security

Roberto Di Pietro, Flavio Lombardi, and Matteo Signorini

CONTENTS

17.1 INTRODUCTION

Cloud computing is nowadays a well-established computing model that provides many advantages to organizations (service providers and users) in terms of massive scalability, lower cost, and flexibility. The cloud computing paradigm has become a mainstream solution for the deployment of business processes and applications. In the public cloud vision, infrastructure, platform, and software services are provisioned on a pay-as-you-go basis [1].

Nevertheless, the level of service and the nonfunctional properties of cloud applications are still an open problem. In the past few years, the research community has been focusing on the nonfunctional aspects of the cloud paradigm, especially with respect to security aspects. However, despite these technical and economical benefits, many potential cloud consumers are still hesitant to adopt cloud computing due to security and privacy concerns.

The cloud migration rate is not as fast as it could be, primarily due to the serious security and privacy issues that exist in the paradigm. This is especially relevant when considering the authorization and security assessment issues in the cloud environment.

Given the reduced cost and flexibility of cloud computing, a migration to such approach and related technologies is compelling for many subject matter experts (SMEs). However, major concerns for SMEs migrating to the cloud include the confidentiality of their information (here authorization issues come into play) and liability for incidents (here a security auditing process can help). Governments are also interested in using cloud computing to reduce information technology (IT) costs. However, personal information over citizens is a delicate subject, especially as regards legal and regulatory issues. The complexity of such issues calls for a novel set of approaches in terms of security assessment and authorization issues.

17.2 TECHNOLOGICAL BACKGROUND

Cloud computing offers pay-as-you go elastic services at different layers (see also Figure 17.1) [2]. The separation offered by such layers is useful security-wise. Nevertheless, the complexity of the present middleware implementation introduces a number of potential attack surfaces that only an in-depth security analysis can help protect.

Cloud security issues are very challenging, given the heterogeneity of cloud middleware, given the lack of adequate formal security requirements, and finally given the lack of a stable categorization of security techniques. In addition, there is the usual need of balancing between security, flexibility, and performance, and a lack of transparency on cloud activities and jobs. Many state-of-the-art research work presents partial, *ad hoc* solutions, which only consider and address part of the problem. This situation renders a general evaluation of the state of the art on cloud security difficult. Furthermore, complicating factors include potential interference between security mechanisms at different

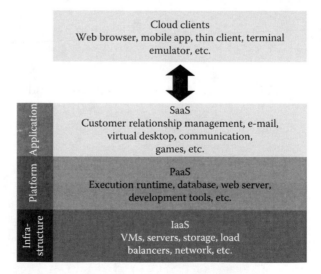

FIGURE 17.1 Cloud computing layers and most common applications. (Wylve and Bikeborg, *Cloud Computing Layers*, Wikimedia Foundation, San Francisco, CA, 2010.)

levels of the cloud stack [1]. In Section 17.3, we will start delving into risk assessment potential solutions that help in getting closer to the main cloud security issues.

17.3 RISK ASSESSMENT

One of the critical aspects to address the security of a cloud system is the possibility of producing a satisfactory risk assessment for the given platform. Cloud computing can refer to several different service types, including application/software as a service (SaaS), platform as a service (PaaS), and infrastructure as a service (IaaS). The risks and benefits associated with each model will differ and so will the key considerations in contracting for this type of service. In Section 17.3.1, we survey the most relevant discussions and proposals that are aimed at addressing the risk assessment need.

17.3.1 ENISA Cloud Computing Risk Assessment

As regards cloud computing risk assessment, the European Network and Information Security Agency (ENISA) has contributed an in-depth study [3] to produce an informed assessment of the security risks and benefits of using cloud computing, providing security guidance for potential and existing users of cloud computing (see also Figure 17.2) [3]. The ENISA security assessment is based on three use case scenarios:

- SME migration to cloud computing services

- The impact of cloud computing on service resilience

- Cloud computing in e-government (e.g., eHealth)

The ENISA's cloud computing risk assessment explains, based on concrete scenarios, cloud computing implications for network and information security, data protection, and privacy. It shows security benefits of cloud computing and its risks, covering technical, policy, and legal implications. Most importantly, it exposes concrete recommendations on how to address the risks and maximize the benefits.

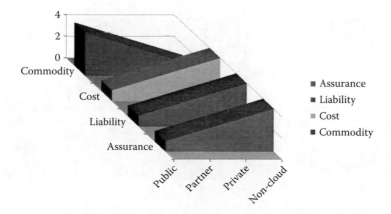

FIGURE 17.2   Evaluating the main risk parameters for different kinds of cloud approaches. (European Union Agency for Network and Information Security, *Cloud Computing Risk Assessment*, ENISA, Heraklion, Greece.)

17.3.2 CSA STAR Self-Assessment

Cloud Security Alliance and Security, Trust & Assurance Registry (CSA STAR) [4] is a free, publicly accessible registry that documents the security controls provided by various cloud computing offerings. CSA STAR Self-Assessment that is free and open is interesting and useful as it allows cloud providers to submit self-assessment reports that document their compliance to CSA best practices (see also Figure 17.3).

CSA STAR Self-Assessment has been particularly successful with major cloud players, including Amazon Web Services, Box.com, HP, Microsoft, and Red Hat submitting entries into the registry. These cloud providers recognized the need to provide transparency and assurance of their cloud services to corporations and end users, who are increasingly requesting visibility into the security controls provided by various cloud computing offerings [4]. Cloud providers can submit two different types of reports to indicate their compliance with CSA best practices:

The Consensus Assessments Initiative Questionnaire (CAIQ), which provides industry-accepted ways to document what security controls exist in IaaS, PaaS, and SaaS offerings. This questionnaire provides a set of over 140 questions a cloud consumer and cloud auditor may wish to ask of a cloud provider. Providers may opt to submit a completed CAIQ. The Cloud Controls Matrix (CCM), which provides a control framework that gives a detailed understanding of security concepts and principles that are aligned to the Cloud Security Alliance guidance in 13 domains. As a framework, the CSA CCM provides organizations with the needed structure, detail, and clarity relating to information security tailored to the cloud industry. Providers may choose to submit a report documenting compliance with CCM. All IaaS, SaaS, and PaaS providers can use CSA STAR to perform a self-assessment.

In addition to cloud provider self-assessments, CSA STAR also provides public visibility to solution providers who have integrated CAIQ, CCM, and other governance risk compliance (GRC) Stack components into their compliance management tools. This induces customers extend their GRC monitoring and reporting across their enterprise and in concert with multiple cloud provider relationships.

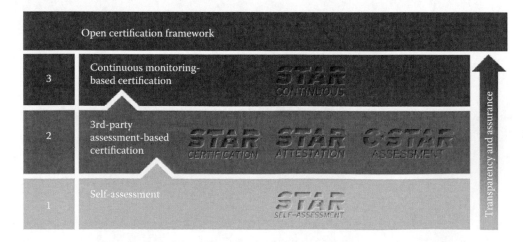

FIGURE 17.3 The CSA STAR certification framework.

17.3.3 Quantitative Assessment

The advantage of a quantitative assessment approach is that it allows the comparison of the robustness of cloud vendor offerings to cloud providers, consumers, and regulation agencies. To obtain such a quantitative approach, it is then needed a meticulous and structured data collection that measures threat events probability, thus being able to assess risks as a product of the probability of a security compromise and its potential impact or consequence. However, so far, few solutions have been proposed for fully quantitative risk assessment as the main limitation for this approach is the lack of structured analysis approaches that can be used for risk assessment in the cloud environment. Frameworks such as quantitative impact and risk assessment framework for cloud security (QUIRC) [5] tried to solve this limitation with the definition of new impact metrics such as the following:

- *Low impact*: Derived by the loss of confidentiality, integrity, availability, mutual trust, or mutual auditability with limited adverse effect on organizational operations, organizational assets, or individuals. For example, such an impact could (1) cause degradation in business capability to an extent and duration that the organization is still able to perform its primary functions, but the effectiveness of the functions is noticeably reduced; (2) result in minor damage to organizational assets; (3) result in minor financial loss; or (4) result in minor harm to individuals. In the context of cloud computing, an organization may be defined as any business unit participating directly as a tenant on a given cloud platform, including end customers who use the cloud services.

- *Moderate impact*: Derived by the loss of confidentiality, integrity, availability, mutual trust, or mutual auditability with serious adverse effect on organizational operations, organizational assets, or individuals A serious adverse effect means that, for example, the aforementioned loss might (1) cause a significant degradation in mission capability to an extent and duration that the organization is able to perform its primary functions, but the effectiveness of the functions is significantly reduced; (2) result in significant damage to organizational assets; (3) result in significant financial loss; or (4) result in significant harm to individuals that does not involve loss of life or serious life-threatening injuries.

- *High impact*: Derived by the loss of confidentiality, integrity, availability, mutual trust, or mutual auditability with severe or catastrophic adverse effect on organizational operations, organizational assets, or individuals. Adverse effects on individuals may include, but are not limited to, loss of the privacy to which individuals are entitled under law. A severe or catastrophic adverse effect means that, for example, the loss might (1) cause a severe degradation in or loss of business capability to an extent and duration that the organization is not able to perform one or more of its primary functions; (2) result in major damage to organizational assets; (3) result in major financial loss; or (4) result in severe or catastrophic harm to individuals involving loss of life or serious life-threatening injuries. These definitions are based heavily on the Federal Information Processing Standards (FIPS) descriptions, with appropriate modifications for the cloud applications.

Albeit, QUIRC proved to be feasible. The challenge and difficulty of applying such a quantitative approach, is the precise collection of historical data for threat events probability calculation; which requires data input from those to be assessed cloud computing platforms with their vendors.

17.3.4 Assessment as a Service

The dynamic nature of the cloud makes traditional, more static assessments of resources and their configuration ineffective [6]. Given that the cloud is increasingly "on demand," risk assessments applied to the cloud has to be on demand too. Although the underlying policy infrastructure by which a cloud service provider (CSP) (or consumer) applies resources to meet business objectives can and should be assessed. This foundation should be complemented with ongoing policy compliance to verify that the objectives are met in operation.

Cloud computing should be assessed "as a service." Indeed, the same characteristics of the cloud that make it hard to assess with existing tools also make it easy to assess with new ones, especially the metering that is already built in for billing and service-level assurance.

Risk assessment as a service, is a new paradigm for measuring risk as an autonomic method [7]; which follows the on-demand, automated, multitenant architecture of the cloud. This is a way to get a continuous "risk score" of the cloud environment, with respect to a given tenant, a specific application, or, more generally, for use by new tenants and applications.

We envision such assessments as being made available in real time by one or more of the entities in the cloud ecosystem. For instance, a cloud provider could perform continuous self-assessments as a best practice through evaluation of its own runtime environment; a trusted third party could assess the provider on an ongoing basis through privileged access to certain internal measurement interfaces or a consumer could assess the provider through nonprivileged access. The third avenue is exemplified in approaches such as proofs of retrievability [8,9].

In each case, the dynamic assessment service would rest on a foundation periodic, underlying static assessments. Static assessments should focus on the elements of the provider's underlying IT infrastructure and governance that (1) changes infrequently and (2) drives security and privacy in the dynamic environment. This again points to the importance of assessing security and privacy policies, policy enforcement mechanisms, and policy compliance mechanisms.

Because a provider may itself be a consumer of services from other providers, it is reasonable to expect that a provider would also be assessing the providers it relies on, thus addressing the point discussed previously about the recursive nature of cloud computing. Indeed, even if the ultimate business consumers and their customers are not directly assessing providers, the providers themselves will likely be assessing one another.

The addition of real-time assessment capabilities into the cloud environments parallels managed security services whereby an external provider monitors the internal security of a conventional data center. The results of such services are kept confidential to the relevant organization. In the cloud, the comparable results would, like the cloud itself, be open to all consumers.

An assessment service for the cloud involves more than just the automation of traditional surveys and scoring systems. The metrics must also be adapted to the nature of cloud computing, for instance, the dynamic allocation of resources and multitenancy. Updating a traditional assessment to address cloud characteristics, then applying it manually, although accurate in principle, still may not fit the dynamic nature of the new environment.

17.4 AUTHORIZATION AND THE CLOUD

Many different kinds of security and authorization policies have been introduced over the years. The peculiarities of the cloud call for a scalable and effective approach to security and isolation, with particular regard toward authorization issues. This is so because the resources (computing, storage, and network) that are available to cloud services and users are large and as such potentially security sensitive. In this section, we will more specifically delve into relevant results and validated approaches in this area.

As Zahoor [10] mentions, an authorization process can be more specifically regarded as to determine who can access what resources, under what conditions, and for what purpose. Authorization policies are high-level descriptions of these access rules. In the past few years, the widespread adoption of the cloud computing has introduced new opportunities and the associated challenges. Cloud computing has provided a model in which the resources are pooled, shared, and provided on demand over a network. From a client perspective, the exact location of the resources is unknown/not relevant as they are dynamically provisioned. However, with all the benefits associated with the cloud are some major challenges in terms of security and privacy. When the applications are moved to the cloud, we need new models for enforcing security [10].

The cloud-based federated authentication is a hot research area. Approaches such as Security Assertion Markup Language™ (SAML) [11] aim at providing single sign-on for federated environments. However, the authorization challenges in cloud-based applications are overly complicated. In fact, as an example, authorization has to take into consideration the context, apart from content. Furthermore, authorization assertions that refer to policies should be specified to be handled. This will allow considering and automating policy requirements such as role/group abstractions, fine-grained constraints, and temporal aspects.

A systematic analysis of the existing authorization solutions in the cloud and an evaluation of their effectiveness against well-established industrial standards are proposed in [12]. Their analysis can help organization to assess/choose the best authorization technique for deployment in the cloud. In fact, they also present a case study along with simulation results and illustrate the procedure of using our qualitative analysis for the selection of an appropriate technique, following cloud consumer requirements. The general shortcomings of the existent access control techniques prevent effective scalable authorization on the cloud. Masood and Shibli [12] also suggest a solution to this major security challenge—access control as a service (ACaaS) for the SaaS layer. Finally, they conclude that a meticulous research is needed to incorporate advanced authorization features into a generic ACaaS framework that should be adequate for providing high level of extensibility and security by integrating multiple access control models.

Cloud computing is defined as delivering of computing resources as a service. Data security and access control are key components for any cloud service. The service-level agreements are negotiated when a service provider registers with an enterprise. This chapter proposes an authentication and authorization interface to access a cloud service. Service selection is acquired via monitoring of security measures provided by a service provider through Security Service Level Agreements (Sec-SLAs). The enterprise and employee validation is performed through two-level authentication mechanisms. Single sign-on mechanisms for users and services make the proposal more efficient. Features such as denial of service, man in the middle attack, and access control rights of employees are also handled.

Cloud computing is defined as delivering of computing resources as a service. Discovery of reliable resource provider and access control are key components of cloud computing. Service-level agreements are negotiated between the service provider and the enterprise. Bajpai et al. [13] propose authentication interfaces to access a cloud service. User authentication token is required to validate whether the user is a registered employee of enterprise or not. Service authentication token is required to validate the access right of a user for service. Service selection is acquired via monitoring of security measures of services provided by a service provider through Sec-SLAs at the enterprise end, thereby completely relieving the end user from the nitty-gritty of service providers in comparison to approaches proposed in the past. Single sign-on mechanisms for users and services are used. Features such as denial of service, man in the middle attack, and access control rights of employees are also handled.

As depicted in the work of Zahoor et al. [10], access control and authorization has been an active research area since decades, and the focus of traditional research approaches has been the role-based access control (RBAC) model and its variations (see Figure 17.4) [14]. Task-based access control extends the traditional model by considering task-based contextual information. Unfortunately, RBAC suffers from role explosion. Some approaches have investigated the use and challenges for RBAC in a distributed environment [10]. In contrast to RBAC models, the attribute-based access control (ABAC) model subsumes RBAC and provides more flexibility and expressiveness than this latter. In a collaborative context, ABAC is thus the preferred model as it is more suitable for situations in which

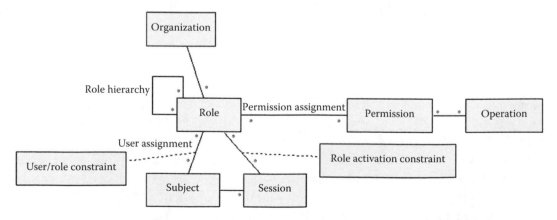

FIGURE 17.4 A sample RBAC diagram. (FuzzyBSc., *Role Based Access Control*, Wikimedia Foundation, San Francisco, CA, 2013.)

finer granularity and context-aware authorizations are required. Zahoor et al. [10] define their own policy model on top of a formal language event calculus.

As regards policy languages for network and security management, page description language (PDL), request for expressions of interest (REI), assembler source language (ASL), VALID, organization based access control (OrBAC), and component definition language (CDL) are formal policy languages. None of them actually provides a satisfying solution, In particular, ASL, OrBAC, and VALID, as well as eXtensible Access Control Markup Language XACML), are not usable in a dynamic environment as they are not event based [10]. Furthermore, policy languages such as REI, PDL, and Ponder need additional processing (meta-policies) for conflict handling. Many XACML extentions have been proposed in the literature. However, in distributed environments, it is not easy for a user to define his or her own policy using XACML.

17.4.1 CatBAC

The CatBAC meta-model is based on the concept of category and makes it possible to formalize hybrid policies, which can combine several elements of the classical access control models [15]. In CatBAC, the cloud provider initially recovers the high-level policy of this company, which must be abstract. The meta-model will be refined in an abstract model of access control representing this policy. This abstract model will be sent to the various sites of the company allowing the local security administrators to refine it in a concrete model by respecting the low-level security policy and the constraints locally required. The concrete model will be used to treat the coming access requests from its corresponding site. The CatBAC approach generalizes the use of the category concept and applies it to all basic elements of access control. As such, an abstract level that connects categories "assignment relation" (AR) is used to express authorizations (permission, prohibition) that are called "abstract authorizations" (AAs). "Concrete authorizations" (CAs) represent instead the access control decisions in relation to concrete entities such as subject, resource, action, and context. Such decisions are based on the assignment of these entities to categories and on the existence of an abstract authorization between these categories. On this basis, Khamadja et al. [15] define three types of relations for modeling access control. AA associates the four categories (subject, resource, action, and context) to express permission and prohibition. AR associates concrete elements of access control with their corresponding categories to express low-level policies. CA associates concrete elements to express concrete decisions of access control, and it is based on the two relations mentioned previously. CatBAC is interesting as it allows cloud providers to leverage an access control security solution that can be seen as a cloud service where users can define their own low-level policies in a way that these policies can be refined correctly from the abstract policy defined by their cloud provider.

17.4.2 Hierarchy Attribute-Based Access Control

Hierarchy attribute-based access control (HABAC) is a model that supports users and attribute hierarchies [16]. This model introduces attribute hierarchies as a natural means of structuring attributes to reflect an organization's line of authority and responsibility. The fundamental idea of the HABAC model is that security administrators assign individual user entities to attributes and assign permissions to attributes. In addition, a set of sessions is included in the HABAC model. Each session is a mapping between a user entity and an activated subset of attributes that are assigned to the user entity.

HABAC defines basic data elements called users entities (UENTITIES), attributes (ATTRS), objects (OBS), operations (OPS), and permissions (PRMS). Furthermore, it includes a set of sessions where each session is a mapping between a user entity and an activated subset of attributes that are assigned to the user entity. It gives the definitions of some relations such as UA relation, UH relation, active hub (AH) relation, assigned users, sessions attrs, and avail session perms. User hierarchies are also defined by HABAC as well as inheritance relationships between user entities. In fact, the core of the HABAC model is the concept of the user entity relations and the attribute relations [16]. General and limited user hierarchies are included in the user hierarchy. On the one hand, general user hierarchies support not only multiple inheritance of permissions among attributes but also multiple inheritance of user membership among user entities. On the other hand, limited user hierarchies only support simple hierarchy structure such as trees or inverted trees.

HABAC allows fine-grained data access control for cloud computing. It achieves such goal by exploiting ciphertext policy attribute-based encryption (CP-ABE) and uniquely combining it with techniques of user hierarchy and attribute hierarchy.

17.5 SECURITY ASSESSMENT AND THE CLOUD

Rizvi et al. [17] describe some critical cloud computing security factors. They developed a security metric tool to provide information to cloud users about the security status of a given cloud vendor. The primary objective of the proposed metric is to produce a security index that describes the security level accomplished by an evaluated cloud computing vendor. The resultant security index will give confidence to different cloud stakeholders and is likely to help them in decision making, increase the predictability of the quality of service, and allow appropriate proactive planning if needed before migrating to the cloud. To show the practicality of the proposed metric, we provide two case studies based on the available security information about the two well-known CSP. The results of these case studies demonstrated the effectiveness of the security index in determining the overall security level of a CSP with respect to the security preferences of cloud users.

Cloud security risk assessment is discussed in [18], where the possibility of calculation of information security risks in cloud computing system is discussed, and fuzzy cognitive maps and artificial neural networks are used to help provide a possible solution. Among actual cloud security assessments, Gusev et al. [19] analyzed the security vulnerabilities of Eucalyptus cloud from inside and outside and determine that Eucalyptus server nodes are more vulnerable from inside, rather than from outside of the cloud, whereas virtual machine (VM) instances have the same security vulnerability risks inside both from and outside.

As regards network segregation and security, Donevski et al. [20] have assessed the security of the OpenStack cloud. They prove that OpenStack cloud multitenant environment rises new security vulnerabilities risks from inside the cloud, for both the tenants and the OpenStack cloud provider. The results of such assessments proved that segregating the networks in OpenStack rises additional security vulnerability risks only for CSP from inside but remain the same for the tenants. Security vulnerability risks are also the same for the CSP outside from the OpenStack cloud. However, segregating the networks in OpenStack can increase the security vulnerability risks for the tenants using Windows VM instances. Although Windows-based VM instances are detected with security vulnerability risks, they can be secured by implementing existing patches or reconfiguration.

17.6 AUTHORIZATION AND THE CLOUD

As discussed by Chadwick and Fatema [21], there is a strong need for a policy-based authorization infrastructure that a cloud provider can run as an infrastructure service for its users. Such a system/policy will protect the privacy of user data by allowing the users to set their own privacy policies, and then enforcing them so that no unauthorized access is allowed to their data. The infrastructure has to ensure that the user privacy policies are stuck to their data, so that access will always be controlled by the policies even if the data are transferred between cloud providers or services. This infrastructure also has to ensure the enforcement of privacy policies, which may be written in different policy languages by multiple authorities such as legal, data subject, data issuer, and data controller. A resolution strategy is needed to resolve the conflicts among the decisions returned by the different policy decision points.

Abstract cloud computing is considered one of the most dominant paradigms as it offers cost-effective services on demand such as SaaS, IaaS, and PaaS. However, with all of these services promising facilities and benefits, there are still a number of challenges associated with utilizing cloud computing such as data security, abuse of cloud services, malicious insider, and cyberattacks. Among all security requirements of cloud computing, access control is one of the fundamental requirements in order to avoid unauthorized access to systems and protect organizations' assets. Although various access control models and policies have been developed such as mandatory access control and RBAC for different environments, these models may not fulfil the cloud's access control requirements. As discussed by Younis et al. [22], this is because cloud computing has a diverse set of users with different sets of security requirements. It also has unique security challenges such as multitenant hosting and heterogeneity of security policies, rules, and domains. This chapter presents a detailed access control requirement analysis for cloud computing and identifies important gaps, which are not fulfilled by conventional access control models. It also proposes an access control model to meet the identified cloud access control requirements. We believe that the proposed model not only can ensure the secure sharing of resources among potential untrusted tenants but also has the capacity to support different access permissions to the same cloud user and gives him or her the ability to use multiple services securely.

17.7 RELEVANT RELATED WORK

Several works have been devoted to the evaluation of risks in the cloud and to the identification of vulnerabilities, threats, and attacks that would target the cloud infrastructure. Fernandes et al. [23] provide one of the most complete details of vulnerabilities, threats, and attacks to the cloud infrastructure.

Gruschka and Jensen [24] present a taxonomy and a classification of cloud security attacks based on the notion of attack surface. After modeling the cloud as a set of three entities, including users, services, and cloud providers, they define each attack as a set of interactions within this model. First, they claim that attacks targeting the interactions between users and services are similar to the ones known for traditional distributed communications (e.g., denial of service, structured query language [SQL] injection, cross-site scripting). However, attacks proper of a cloud environment also involve interfaces managed by the cloud provider. Then, they identify six attack surfaces that are used, possibly in a combination, to perform an attack. Finally, they describe some successful attacks on sample cloud environments. Ardagna et al. [1] take a similar approach to threat modeling, categorizing chapters on vulnerabilities, threats, and attacks according to the application level, tenant on tenant, and provider on tenant/tenant on provider. This also includes: relevant vulnerabilities, threats, and attacks, and their mapping to attack surfaces and involved security properties.

Application-level vulnerabilities, threats, and attacks have threatened information and communication technology (ICT) infrastructure since the early days of the Internet, and they mainly target the interactions between users and services. In other words, they focus on services and data at the highest level of a cloud stack and consider the SaaS service model. In particular, Gruschka and Iacono [25] present a weakness in the simple object access protocol (SOAP)-based control service of Amazon EC2 against signature wrapping attacks, originally described in McIntosh and Austel [26]. The attacker was able to modify an eavesdropped message faking the digital signature checking algorithm and executed commands on behalf of legitimate users. Jensen et al. [27] present security issues in cloud computing, considering extensible markup language (XML) signature, browser security, cloud integrity, and flooding attacks. They also introduce the cloud malware injection attack, where a malicious user tries to add a malicious service implementation and confuse the cloud provider by letting it consider the malicious service as a normal one. Somorovsky et al. [28] test the security of the cloud control interfaces of Amazon public cloud and of a private cloud based on Eucalyptus. The results show that in both cases, the control interfaces can be compromised by means of signature wrapping attacks. The authors propose a novel methodology for the analysis of public cloud interfaces and discuss possible countermeasures to the identified attacks. Chonka et al. [29] focus on two attacks that can target the cloud, namely, hypertext transfer protocol (HTTP)-based denial of service and XML-based denial of service [30]. In particular, they recreate these attacks, present a solution to identify the source of an attack, and introduce an approach (Cloud Protector) to detect and filter these attacks. In principle, this kind of attacks could also apply to the tenant-on-tenant attack surface. Bugiel et al. [31] provide an analysis of threats to confidentiality and privacy in the cloud that successfully extract sensitive information from Amazon machine images and exploit secure shell (SSH) vulnerabilities.

Tenant-on-tenant vulnerabilities, threats, and attacks are typical of virtualized environments where different tenants share a common infrastructure and may reside on the same physical hardware. Researchers working in this area mainly consider scenarios where a malicious tenant tries to attack other tenants colocated on the same hardware, exploiting misconfiguration and vulnerabilities on the virtualization infrastructure (e.g., VM isolation). In other words, tenant-on-tenant vulnerabilities, threats, and attacks focus on resources, processes, and data at the lowest levels of a cloud stack and consider the Paas and IaaS service models. Ristenpart et al. [32] describe an attack to information confidentiality of running service instances. Their attack is based on the fact that an attacker VM and the target service are on the same hardware, and therefore, the former can launch an attack by generating traffic and monitoring its own (or the hypervisors) performance. Aviram et al. [33] discuss the problem of timing channels in the cloud and present an approach to prevent timing attacks based on provider-enforced deterministic execution, whereas Pearce et al. [34] discuss the concerns due to intermittent interference in a virtualized environment.

Provider-on-tenant and tenant-on-provider vulnerabilities, threats, and attacks are specific of the cloud where users, enterprises, and business owners move their assets to an untrusted infrastructure. Researchers working in this area mainly consider scenarios where the cloud provider is malicious (or at least honest but curious) and attacks its tenants (provider-on-tenant). Alternatively, they consider contexts in which one or more compromised tenants (e.g., botnets for denial-of-service attacks) are used to attack the cloud infrastructure (tenant-on-provider). In other words, provider-on-tenant and tenant-on-provider vulnerabilities, threats, and attacks focus on resources, processes, and data delivered using the IaaS service model. In the following summary, we provide an overview of chapters that focus on provider-on-tenant and tenant-on-provider attack surface.

17.8 SUMMARY

This chapter has discussed various cloud computing security issues, in particular regarding authorization and security assessment. Security challenges and approaches have been introduced. The result is a broad survey that tries to shed a light on security issues of cloud computing, mainly focusing on the issues related to security assessment and authorization. Based on the survey, this chapter discussed the differences between the various approaches; some are still evolving, and their security has yet to be improved further, whereas others are more technical mature. As such, in order to securely make use or offer cloud computing services, users and providers need to perform an accurate analysis of their needs and of the security requirements that have to be fulfilled. Nevertheless, critical security aspects still have to be further investigated to improve their effectiveness in alleviating security risks. Tackling security issues from both technical and operational aspects will eventually foster larger deployment of cloud computing.

REFERENCES

1. Claudio A. Ardagna, Rasool Asal, Ernesto Damiani, and Quang Hieu Vu. From security to assurance in the cloud: A survey. *ACM Computing Surveys*, 48(1):2:1–2:50, July 2015.
2. Wylve and Bikeborg. *Cloud Computing Layers*. Wikimedia Foundation: San Francisco, CA. 2010. https://commons.wikimedia.org/wiki/File:Cloud\computing\layers.svg.
3. European Union Agency for Network and Information Security (ENISA). *Cloud Computing Risk Assessment*. ENISA: Heraklion, Greece. http://www.enisa.europa.eu/activities/risk-management/current-risk/risk-management-inventory/rm-process/risk-assessment.
4. Cloud Security Alliance. Seattle, WA. https://cloudsecurityalliance.org/star.
5. P. Saripalli and B. Walters. QUIRC: A quantitative impact and risk assessment framework for cloud security. In *IEEE 3rd International Conference on Cloud Computing*, pp. 280–288, July 2010.

6. Burton S. Kaliski, Jr. and Wayne Pauley. Toward risk assessment as a service in cloud environments. In *Proceedings of the 2Nd USENIX Conference on Hot Topics in Cloud Computing*, pp. 13–13, USENIX Association: Berkeley, CA, 2010.

7. Jeffrey O. Kephart and David M. Chess. The vision of autonomic computing. *Computer*, 36(1):41–50, January 2003.

8. Ari Juels and Burton S. Kaliski, Jr. Pors: Proofs of retrievability for large files. In *Proceedings of the 14th ACM Conference on Computer and Communications Security*, pp. 584–597, ACM: New York, 2007.

9. Christian Cachin, Idit Keidar, and Alexander Shraer. Trusting the cloud. *SIGACT News*, 40(2):81–86, June 2009.

10. E. Zahoor, O. Perrin, and A. Bouchami. Catt: A cloud based authorization framework with trust and temporal aspects. In *2014 International Conference on Collaborative Computing: Networking, Applications and Worksharing (CollaborateCom)*, pp. 285–294, October 2014.

11. Christian Mainka, Vladislav Mladenov, Florian Feldmann, Julian Krautwald, and Jörg Schwenk. Your software at my service: Security analysis of saas single sign-on solutions in the cloud. In *Proceedings of the 6th Edition of the ACM Workshop on Cloud Computing Security*, pp. 93–104, ACM: New York, 2014.

12. Rahat Masood, MuhammadAwais Shibli, Yumna Ghazi, Ayesha Kanwal, and Arshad Ali. Cloud authorization: Exploring techniques and approach towards effective access control framework. *Frontiers of Computer Science*, 9(2):297–321, 2015.

13. Durgesh Bajpai, Manu Vardhan, Sachin Gupta, Ravinder Kumar, and DharmenderSingh Kushwaha. Security service level agreements based authentication and authorization model for accessing cloud services. In Natarajan Meghanathan, Dhinaharan Nagamalai, and Nabendu Chaki, editors, *Advances in Computing and Information Technology*, volume 176 of *Advances in Intelligent Systems and Computing*, pp. 719–728, Springer: Berlin, Germany, 2012.

14. FuzzyBSc. *Role Based Access Control*. Wikimedia Foundation: San Francisco, CA, 2013. https://upload.wikimedia.org/wikipedia/en/c/c3/RBAC.jpg.

15. Salim Khamadja, Kamel Adi, and Luigi Logrippo. Designing flexible access control models for the cloud. In *Proceedings of the 6th International Conference on Security of Information and Networks*, pp. 225–232, ACM: New York, 2013.

16. Shi-Xin Luo, Feng-Mei Liu, and Chuan-Lun Ren. A hierarchy attribute-based access control model for cloud storage. In *International Conference on Machine Learning and Cybernetics*, vol. 3, pp. 1146–1150, July 2011.

17. Syed Rizvi, Jungwoo Ryoo, John Kissell, and Bill Aiken. A stakeholder-oriented assessment index for cloud security auditing. In *Proceedings of the 9th International Conference on Ubiquitous Information Management and Communication*, pp. 55:1–55:7, ACM: New York, 2015.

18. Oleg Makarevich, Irina Mashkina, and Alina Sentsova. The method of the information security risk assessment in cloud computing systems. In *Proceedings of the 6th International Conference on Security of Information and Networks*, pp. 446–447, ACM: New York, 2013.

19. Marjan Gusev, Sasko Ristov, and Aleksandar Donevski. Security vulnerabilities from inside and outside the eucalyptus cloud. In *Proceedings of the 6th Balkan Conference in Informatics*, pp. 95–101, ACM: New York, 2013.

20. A. Donevski, S. Ristov, and M. Gusev. Security assessment of virtual machines in open source clouds. In *36th International Convention on Information Communication Technology Electronics Microelectronics (MIPRO)*, pp. 1094–1099, May 2013.

21. David W. Chadwick and Kaniz Fatema. A privacy preserving authorisation system for the cloud. *Journal of Computer and System Sciences*, 78(5):1359–1373, 2012.

22. Younis A. Younis, Kashif Kifayat, and Madjid Merabti. An access control model for cloud computing. *Journal of Information Security and Applications*, 19(1):45–60, 2014.

23. Fernandes et al. 2013.

24. Gruschka and Jensen. 2010.

25. Nils Gruschka and Luigi Lo Iacono. Vulnerable cloud: Soap message security validation revisited. In *IEEE International Conference on Web Services, 2009*, pp. 625–631, IEEE, 2009.

26. McIntosh and Austel. 2005.

27. Meiko Jensen, Jörg Schwenk, Nils Gruschka, and Luigi Lo Iacono. On technical security issues in cloud computing. In *IEEE International Conference onCloud Computing*, pp. 109–116, IEEE, 2009.

28. Juraj Somorovsky, Mario Heiderich, Meiko Jensen, Jörg Schwenk, Nils Gruschka, and Luigi Lo Iacono. All your clouds are belong to us: Security analysis of cloud management interfaces. In *Proceedings of the 3rd ACM Workshop on Cloud Computing Security Workshop*, pp. 3–14, ACM: New York, 2011.

29. Ashley Chonka, Yang Xiang, Wanlei Zhou, and Alessio Bonti. Cloud security defence to protect cloud computing against http-dos and xml-dos attacks. *Journal of Network and Computer Applications*, 34(4):1097–1107, 2011.

30. Mudhakar Srivatsa, Ling Liu, and Arun Iyengar. Eventguard: A system architecture for securing publish-subscribe networks. *ACM Transactions on Computer Systems (TOCS)*, 29(4):10, 2011.

31. Bugiel et al. 2011.

32. Thomas Ristenpart, Eran Tromer, Hovav Shacham, and Stefan Savage. Hey, you, get off of my cloud: Exploring information leakage in third-party compute clouds. In *Proceedings of the 16th ACM Conference on Computer and Communications Security*, pp. 199–212, ACM: New York, 2009.

33. Amittai Aviram, Sen Hu, Bryan Ford, and Ramakrishna Gummadi. Determinating timing channels in compute clouds. In *Proceedings of the 2010 ACM Workshop on Cloud Computing Security Workshop*, pp. 103–108, ACM: New York, 2010.

34. Michael Pearce, Sherali Zeadally, and Ray Hunt. Virtualization: Issues, security threats, and solutions. *ACM Computing Surveys*, 45(2):17:1–17:39, March 2013.

IV

Advanced Private Cloud Computing Security

CHAPTER 18

Advanced Security Architectures for Private Cloud Computing

Pramod Pandya and Riad Rahmo

CONTENTS

18.1 INTRODUCTION

In this chapter, the scope and the nature of privacy and security within the private cloud computing infrastructure are addresses. The private cloud resources are made accessible to cloud-based customers through the Internet Service Providers (ISPs). Private cloud is a type of cloud computing that delivers similar advantages to public cloud, including scalability and self-service, but through a proprietary architecture. Hence, private cloud architecture is best compatible for business with dynamic computing needs that require direct control over their infrastructure. A private cloud (also called an internal cloud) computing service offers its service to a single organization. The cloud private infrastructure can be located internal or external to an organization. Private cloud service is not a multitenant service in that sense; hence, one would be led to believe that security concerns would equally be minimal compared with public cloud computing service. The weakest link in any security configuration is the human element! In a private cloud, you have greater control over a data management system than public cloud platforms. This is because, they can either be local applications on the computing platforms or virtualizing them through cloud computing.

Just as data centers were both business and technical constructs to support data processing needs of businesses, cloud in some sense is more like a business construct, because the security and privacy in the cloud is handled more or less by the cloud service providers. A private cloud service could be utilized by a financial company that is required by regulation to store sensitive data internally and that will still want to benefit from some of the advantages of cloud computing within their business infrastructure, such as on-demand resource allocation. The private cloud computing service users no longer own the infrastructure; hence, the data security must be managed by the cloud service provider. This is a shift in paradigm and calls for redefining the governance of privacy and security. This in no way suggests that the consumer of cloud services need not be responsible for their data privacy and security, but should have service-level agreement with the cloud service provider, and identify appropriate levels of security and its compliance with the state in which they operate. Risk management must factor the threats specific to different deployment cloud models and devise solutions to mitigate these threats. Data confidentiality, integrity, and its availability in cloud deployment model are more susceptible to risk compared to noncloud deployment model. Secure cloud computing architecture must be a scalable one to respond to all insider and outsider threats as well as from natural disasters. Security can be breached at either or both at cloud infrastructure or along the Internet. Cloud computing services offer elasticity, rapid provisioning and releasing of resources, resource pooling, and high bandwidth access with security risks.

18.2 CLOUD SECURITY PROFILE

Next we itemize a number of security risks associated with the deployment of cloud computing. These risks must be addressed by the service provider and stated in the Service-level agreement. The client must understand the full implications of these risks, because they might be providing service to their clients. Of course, they are required to secure their clients' data [1]:

1. *Governance*: Because the computing infrastructure is not managed by the consumer, the governance of privacy and security is considerably lost, which must be compliance with the local state and federal regulations.

2. *Ambiguity in governance*: The cloud service provider has to address the privacy and security needs of all of its consumers, who could differ in their requirements as to what constitutes minimum governance.

3. *Regulatory compliance*: Consumers of cloud computing have to provide protection of their clients' data stored at the service provider facility, which in turn requires that the cloud service providers have appropriate certifications per state regulations.

4. *Security incidents*: Detection, reporting, and management of security breaches must be transparent and reported immediately to the consumers of cloud computing.

5. *Data protection*: Cloud computing service providers must ensure- and maintain mission critical data from corruption; and/or, unauthorized access, and provide comprehensive data backup procedures. Compromises to the confidentiality and integrity of data in transit to and from a cloud provider (man-in-the-middle).

6. *Data deletion*: Termination of service-level agreement with the consumer must explicitly require that the consumer data are completely and irrevocably deleted from the data storage medium. This scenario has legal ramifications in case the data are then sold in a secondary market.

7. *Business failure*: Cloud service provider may file bankruptcy, thus failing to continue to provide access to resources to their clients, which would adversely impact the business cycles of the consumers.

8. *Service interruptions*: Network service providers are the backbone of the cloud computing, who provide the connectivity between the cloud consumers and the cloud service providers.

18.3 CLOUD SECURITY MANAGEMENT—OVERVIEW

Security and privacy concerns faced by the cloud consumers require them to evaluate the risk and its management in the cloud environment, thus mitigating those risks. Of course, the most critical benefit offered by cloud computing is the lowering of the business cost.

18.3.1 Governance and Comprehensive Risk Analysis

Most businesses have well-established security objectives, strategies, and policies consistent with compliance requirements to protect their intellectual property and their clients' data. The framework for security policies are designed based on the risk analysis prediction and its impact on business revenues if the assets are compromised. Security and privacy needs in cloud computing differ from the traditional IT environment, but what is common to both of them is the impact of security breach on corporate assets. In the cloud computing, a breach of security would not only impact just one cloud computing client, but its ramification could far be reaching as other clients could also get breached. In this sense, the framework for security control policy has to factor in support for multiple clients. Cloud customers have to understand the risk they are exposed to, and hence, they need to impose their security controls in addition to the one provided by the cloud service provider, because not all the cloud customers desired the same level of service as regards infrastructure as a service, software as a service (SaaS), and platform as a service. As part of general governance, the cloud service provider would have to indemnify its customers if the breach in security occurred as a result of willful or negligence on the part of the service provider. Private cloud service providers do not have multiple locations of their data centers spread over geopolitical boundaries unlike the public cloud service provider, but the level of risk exposed to both types of service providers is not necessarily different. The International Organization for Standardization (ISO) is currently developing new standards, ISO/IEC 27017 [2] "Security in Cloud Computing" and ISO/IEC 27018 [2] "Privacy in Cloud Computing."

18.3.2 Audit and Reporting

The cloud service provider must generate audit reports of its services on a regular basis, which they must share with their clients as stated in the service-level agreement. The audit report should itemize the customer's logs of all data processing and data storage access activities, including any apparent anomalous activity.

More frequent security breaches have necessitated that the service provider must be mandated to enforce compliance regulations. Of course, not every state has uniform compliance regulations; and, this could be of major consequence to consumers. The audit report must additionally specify the following as implemented and managed by the service provider:

1. Overview of the risk assessment matrix should guarantee the integrity of consumers' data, even though they could be housed on the same physical media. The intent here is to make sure that one cloud customer does not unintentionally manage to access other cloud customers' data—privacy safeguard is of utmost value in private cloud computing.

2. Security controls as implemented are not to be viewed as a static configuration, but with a saleable design and controls; thus, if a breach is discovered, then appropriate actions can be taken to fix the design.

3. Security awareness program is normally not viewed as a critical component of information security. It is the human element that is the weakest link in the security design and control. Cloud computing service staff has to be trained in the security awareness program on a regular basis, which would highlight the damage that would have to be borne out if the protection of consumer data is not a priority.

18.3.3 Proper Protection of Data Information

Consumer data of any kind such as structured or unstructured, and stored in any format (encrypted or unencrypted) on media, is the life and blood of any corporation. Of course, when a corporation makes a determination to subscribe the services of a cloud computing entity, it has to be aware of the risk being exposed to their data. The corporation may decide to move only noncritical data to the cloud and maintain critical data locally within their IT infrastructure, thus reducing the risk factor. Over a time period, a corporation might find this division of data unpractical; hence, making a decision to move all of their corporate data in the cloud. The cloud computing service provider probably has a policy to distribute the customer data over its multiple data centers. In other words, the inherent nature of cloud computing, is one of data distribution, in order to overcome a single point of failure, so that the consumer has access to their data on a 24/7 basis. Cloud computing has increased the scope of security to both the data that is static and the data that is moving along the network; consequently, corporation has to take audit of its data assets.

Categorize data (structured as well as unstructured) into data sets; each of the data set would correspond to certain defined functions, which would represent business processes associated with different departments within a given corporation. Each of the department would have certain processing rights to those business processes, hence to the data sets. Here, we would have to define security privileges using some sort of "reflexive algorithm" assigned to each of the business processes, thus to the data sets. Of course, the chief information officer (CIO) would have the highest level of privilege to all the data sets. The reflexive algorithm would also identify the departments that have common access (inclusive) to data sets and those that have exclusive access—access management. Thus, the security policy now gets defined using the reflexive algorithm, and security controls get implemented. The next step would be to set up monitoring of business processes.

Security policy defined and controls implemented would ensure privacy of data sets consistent with local compliance regulations (Figure 18.1). Of course, the cloud computing service provider would also have to place security controls to protect its consumers' data sets.

Consumers must take a decision as regards the data sets that should be encrypted. This decision would depend on the nature of the data and how often is accessed. With the current encryption algorithm, the data would have to be decrypted on the fly for processing, thus adding cost, and latency to business cost factor.

18.3.4 Security Aspects of Private Cloud Networks

Any ISP that offers computing services to its customers is also susceptible to hacking and other forms of denial-of-service (DOS) attacks. Hence, the ISP must have the the intrusion detection system (IDS) and the intrusion prevention system (IPS) installed to monitor the network traffic and take appropriate action if an intrusion is detected. Similar to ISP's exposure to malicious network traffic, any cloud service provider would also be exposed to the same level of risk.

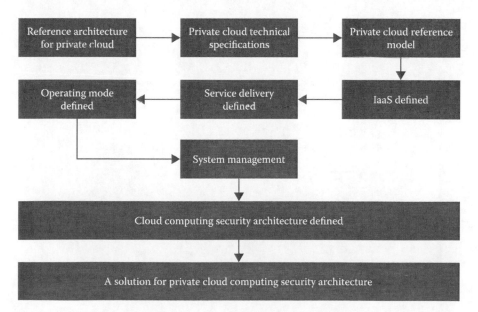

FIGURE 18.1   Reference architecture for private cloud. IaaS, infrastructure as a service.

Hence, the cloud service provider too would have installed IDS and IPS to provide network perimeter safety measures, thus being able to detect any malicious network traffic. The logical network design of the cloud computing resources must factor in a front-end router with a connection to Internet for providing services to the consumers. The back end of the router will connect to a perimeter firewall, which will support a demilitarized zone (DMZ). This DMZ will support possibly web-based services, e-mail, and domain name servers for external services. The perimeter firewall will provide a measure of access control and protection to the services in the DMZ. The back end of the perimeter firewall will be connected to an internal firewall, behind which all the cloud computing resources will be placed, as shown in Figure 18.2.

These resources, of course, will be configured in multiple segmented networks. Each of these segments may be configured as virtual local area networks (VLANs) to further provide a measure of protection to the resources from unauthorized access, as well as secure some degree of privacy among the consumers, as shown in Figure 18.3. With this mind, the following network controls must be strategically placed, in addition to traffic logs and reporting:

- Front-end router is possibly configured to block inbound and outbound traffic as per access control configuration parameters such as the network/internet protocol (IP) addresses, port numbers, and the protocols. This would filter the network traffic at the network layer model of the Internet.

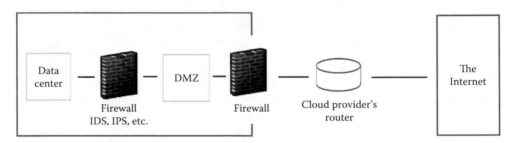

FIGURE 18.2   Private cloud service provider's logical network design.

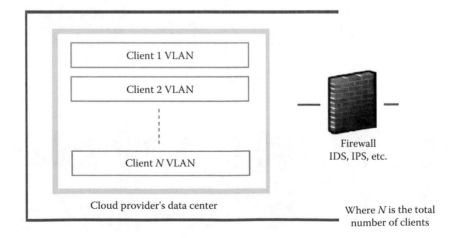

FIGURE 18.3   Segmentation of the data center network.

- Perimeter router would contribute additional stringently designed filtering (packet filtering) of the inbound/outbound network traffic, thus enabling the required access to the resources on the servers in the DMZ.

- Secure the network resources from DOS attacks. Preventing DDOS attacks would require further addition of a router with appropriate configuration.

- Configured as stateful inspection, it will make an entry for each established transmission control protocol (TCP) connection to guarantee that the three-way handshake was established for each of the connection, thus preventing from TCP session hijacking. It is configured as an application-level gateway to monitor allowable applications as defined.

- Combination of strategically placed IDS and IPS would permit deeper packet inspection to identify malicious packets such as worms, Trojan horses, and viruses. Host-based IDS/IPS would prevent modification of system resources. Network-based IDS/IPS would use signature and anomaly detection.

- Incident reporting to consumers must be a priority, because the consumers are liable for their customers' data—scope of the liabilities must be legally defined. Incident handling procedures must be clearly established, thus minimizing its impact on the downtime of service accessibility.

- Network logged information would be made available to the consumers, at the same time protecting the privacy of each of the consumers from one another—this would depend on how storage devices are configured and made available across segmented networks. Address the network logging and retention policy—logs made available on a periodic basis or on demand per consumer.

Service-level agreement should state the security policy adapted by the service provider in no uncertain terms. The damages incurred by the consumer in case of network breaches and the resulting scope of the liabilities should be stated explicitly. As the cloud service provider has many consumers, data breach in one consumer account should not impact on the privacy and security of the data of other consumers' accounts—of course, this would depend on the internal configurations of the data network such as VLANs, firewalls, and access to data storage.

18.3.5 Security Controls on the Physical Infrastructure

Local area networks (LANs) would be configured as VLANs; thus, consumers on one VLAN would never see or monitor traffic (VLAN hopping) on another VLAN. It is quite probable that a consumer may use software-driven application that could monitor and log traffic on VLANs, thus breaching network security for espionage purposes. This may appear to be not probable, but the number of cyber security breaches reported should not put us in a deniable sense!

Consumers could access the cloud services using VPN circuits from their home location, and then into VLANs. This would provide "site-to-site" to security and privacy. Of course, the use of VPN would require consumers to secure digital certificates (security socket layer/internet protocol security [SSL/IPsec]) from the service provider. We should remind the reader at this point that the consumer is now accessing services from the nonproprietary servers, and the digital certificates for secured connections have to be obtained from the service provider—infrastructure as a service is now called into play. Multiple consumers may have access to one server or distributed server design.

Does the cloud service provider support private VLAN (PVLAN)? PVLAN partitions layer 2 (data link layer from the open systems interconnection [OSI] model) broadcast domains in addition to VPN circuits that function at layer 3 (network layer). Thus, PVLAN just adds yet another layer of security (Figure 18.4).

The segmented internal network should be designed such that the cloud service provider network is as much as isolated from the consumers' network. The cloud service provider would need to keep the records of its customers, and this would need to be stored in a database or distributed databases somewhere on the network. The cloud service provider's network should be minimally integrated with the consumers' network and interconnected with a layer 3 switch. Traffic monitoring activities would take place on the consumers' network, but data generated has to be moved over to the service provider's network, and then to storage devices. This would require careful planning, and assessment in case breach, thus isolating the segments of networks without having to shut down the entire cloud services. The cloud services provider and its consumers would suffer both revenue loss and the integrity and the reliability of the service. Secured and scalable cloud architecture is extremely critical for a private cloud service provider, where revenues are generated in millions of dollars—economies of private cloud computing must address the cost/benefit from the consumers' perspective.

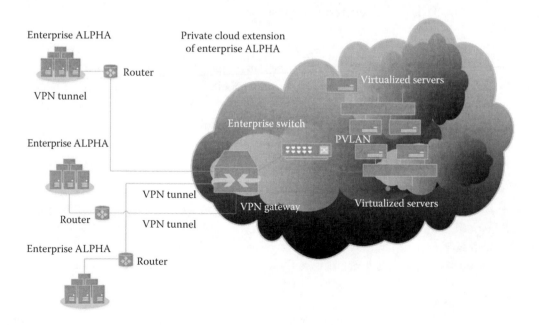

FIGURE 18.4 Data center extension to a private cloud.

Security in private cloud computing is venerable, because private cloud computing is a platform where consumers' sensitive data are stored either at one location or over distributed locations. The question we pose is as follows: Is the data encrypted on the storage device, or is it in a plaintext format! If the data is encrypted, then how secured it is and who is the guardian of encryption technologies. The cloud service provider would share the details of the encryption technology with its consumers—such as keys, digital certificates, and hash algorithms. We can conclude that privacy and security must be viewed as ever-evolving integration of art and information technologies.

Cloud computing platform must be physically located, even though it is in the cloud. Physical infrastructure and the facilities of the locations must be secured. The employees of the service provider must have a controlled access to the facility. The logs of the entry/exit must be kept and available to the consumers for audit purpose.

The physical infrastructure must be protected from natural disasters such as flooding, earthquakes, and fire. Proper maintenance/upgrade of the infrastructure should be performed to provide service level per contractual obligations. Cloud computing service should have uninterruptable access to electricity supply, and disruption of electric power should be factored in the design of the infrastructure. Every data center has backup, redundancy, and contingency plans, so should the cloud computing service provider—per its business plan.

18.3.6 Termination of Service-Level Agreement

The service-level agreement must stipulate the conditions that must be honored and implemented by the service provider upon termination of the service requested by the consumer. The service provider is responsible for storing the consumer's data on the storage media, as well as backing up the data periodically. Termination of service agreement would require that the consumer's data be deleted from the media, and be not traceable in future. This would require overwriting on the media where the consumer's data was stored as well as backed up. The entire history of the consumer would have to be deleted as required by the state laws—knowing perfectly well that there is a secondary market for data.

The consumer must be able to transfer all of its data from the service provider to its data center. If the service-level agreement requires that the service provider retain the consumer's data for a defined period, then it must be honored, in case the consumer decides to sign up for the cloud services in the near future!

18.4 SECURITY ARCHITECTURE MODEL

The private cloud model is closer to the more traditional model of data center used in the past by an enterprise but with the added advantages of virtualization. The features and benefits of private clouds therefore are discussed in Section 18.4.1.

18.4.1 Data Encryption Model

- *Security and privacy*: Access is restricted to connections made from behind the organization's firewall, dedicated leased lines such as T1/T3, and/or on-site internal hosting.

- *Configuration*: Private cloud is not a multitenant setup; hence, the ability to configure and manage it is more practical to achieve a tailored network solution. However, this level of control removes some of the economies of scale generated in public clouds by having a centralized management of the hardware.

- *Cost efficiency*: Private cloud model can improve the allocation of resources within an organization by ensuring the availability of resources to individual business functions on a real-time demand basis. Therefore, although they are not as cost-effective as a public cloud service due to smaller economies of scale and increased management costs, they do make more efficient use of the computing resource than traditional LANs.

- *Cloud bursting*: Providers may offer the opportunity to employ cloud bursting, within a private cloud offering, in the event of spikes on demand, much similar to in nature to frame relay bandwidth bursting. Private clouds can even be integrated with public cloud services to form hybrid clouds where nonsensitive functions are always allocated to the public cloud to maximize the efficiencies on offer.

Many models of cloud computing are based on different security features and algorithms, and especially e-commerce transactions need more security sensitive features because they operate in a cloud computing environment. Security models operating in cloud computing environments should provide security for a file and for the communication system. In this model, security algorithms are used for giving a secured communication process. Files are encrypted with advanced encryption standard (AES) algorithm in which keys are generated randomly by the system, and distributive servers may be used, thus ensuring higher security. The Rivest–Shamir–Adleman (RSA) algorithm is used for secured communication between the users and the servers.

The AES-based file encryption system is used in some of these models, and these models keep both the encryption key and the encrypted file in one database server. In such a setup, successful malicious attack in the server may open the whole information files to the hacker, which is not desirable. Some other models and secured architectures are proposed for ensuring security in the cloud computing environment. Although these models ensure secured communication between users and servers, but they do not encrypt the loaded information. Recently, some other secured models for cloud computing environment are also being researched [3,4]. However, these models also fail to ensure all criteria of cloud computing security issues.

In the proposed model, RSA encryption algorithm is used for secured communication. The cloud service provider would have to distribute its public key using public key infrastructure to its cloud clients. The cloud client would then encrypt (using RSA) its request using the public key. In the proposed security model, the cloud client would have to send a request for login. The cloud service provider would send to the client a password, encrypted using the client's public key. Next, the client will decrypt the password using the client's private key. Now the plaintext password will be used for login session. Thus, whenever a client wants to log in, the system will generate an encrypted password using the client's public key. The password in question may be assigned a cycle time, say, of 24 h before it expires. The cloud service provider would have to secure a set of public keys for the authorized clients in a file server, and the access to this file server would be limited to few IT personnel at the service provider.

After establishing a secured connection with the system, a client can upload or download the file(s). When a file is uploaded by a client, the system server encrypts the file using AES encryption algorithm. In the proposed security model, 128-bit key is used for AES encryption. Here, the 128-bit key is generated randomly by the system server. A single key is used only once for both encrypting and decrypting that file of the client for that instance only. This key is not further used in any instance later. The key is kept in the database table of the system server along with the client's account name. Before inserting the user account name, it is also hashed using md5 hashing.

18.4.2 Case Study Example: Internal LAN Security Architecture Components of Cloud Computing

In this section, we illustrate our discussion on private cloud computing with reference to a financial institution, MRT Credit Union, as a case study. MRT Credit Union uses the SaaS of Google Cloud Platform to provide a cost-efficient service.

MRT Credit Union located in Los Angeles (LA), California, is a growing small community bank. It offers banking services, mortgage, financial planning, loans, and retirement accounts. Some of the online services that MRT has to offer are obtaining e-statements, making electronic deposits, receiving electronic alerts, and paying bills online (bill pay). After several years of gaining new customers, the credit union is required to expand operations. A plan to open an additional branch in San Diego (SD), California, to serve its growing client base is currently in progress. Currently, MRT has an on-site data center in Los Angeles that supports its internal operations. Decisions must be made to obtain the important aspects of the network in regard to functionality, security, technical requirements, and system requirements of the four departments as laid out in the followings:

- *Business admin/executives*: The executives at MRT Credit Union consists of the chief executive officer, president, and executive management that provides leadership, operation techniques, research and development, and expertise of new development and efficiencies. The executives also serve to manage and make sound decisions concerning the operation of the credit union. In addition, the administrative staff at MRT offer human resource functions, which include recruitment, promotion, position classification, employee records, training, employee benefits, and compensation.

- *Marketing*: Marketing strategies are the delivery of advertising and exchanging what MRT Credit Union has to offer while promoting services. *Credit Union Times* reported that 40% of consumers switch to a credit union because they were satisfied with online services that their banks provided. Thus, is it extremely important to publicize the online services that we have to offer to the current and potential customers?

- *Finance/accounting*: The finance and accounting department at MRT provides financial statements and reports of the position and results MRT operations. This includes liabilities, income, expenses, and assets.

- *IT*: IT Services will assist MRT with the system design, implementation, and management of dependable IT infrastructures. MRT Credit Union's business operations are dependent on the reliability of the IT system. In addition, the most important concern for MRT is to secure the database of the client's information.

Instead of a traditional DMZ, our organization has opted to go with cloud-based SaaS provider for both our web and e-mail servers. This will be cheaper and easier for the bank to maintain. We choose to go with the Google Cloud Platform Live that has a number of services from hosting to application management and Big Data query capabilities [5]. In addition, all employees will be using Google apps to perform day-to-day word processing and other office duties. Google promises consistent CPU, memory, and disk performance as well as virtualized servers that never need to go down for maintenance (Google, 2014). This will free up our technical staff to focus exclusively on securing our in-house data center from break-ins. Figure 18.5 illustrates Google Cloud Platform that would provide SaaS.

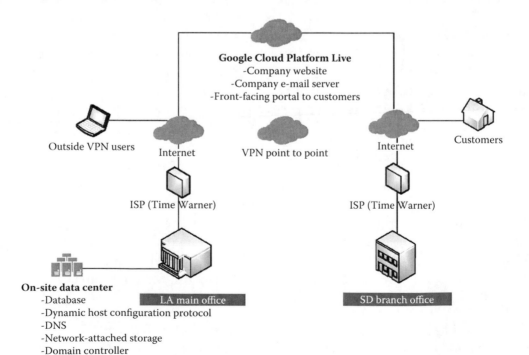

FIGURE 18.5   Google Cloud Platform.

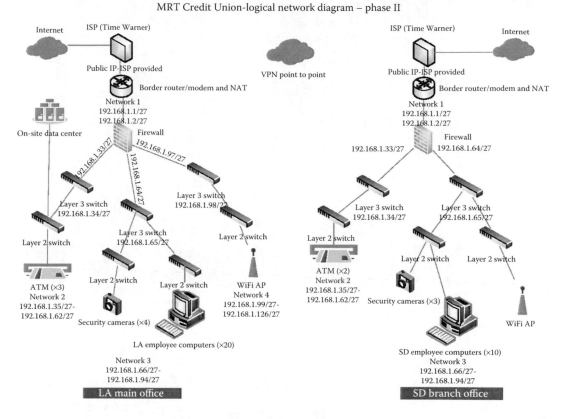

FIGURE 18.6   Internal LAN security configuration.

Figure 18.6 shows a schematic diagram of an internal LAN security component of a cloud computing service provider. Observe the placement of a perimeter router placed in front of an external firewall. The internal LAN architecture shows the placement of the internal firewall to further secure the network.

Figure 18.7 shows the LA IT data center of an internal security component of a cloud computing service provider. Observe the placement of a perimeter router placed in front of an external firewall. The internal LAN architecture shows the placement of the internal firewall to further secure the network.

18.5 SUMMARY

In this chapter, we reviewed the aspects of the private cloud computing security architecture. Our primary focus is on the private cloud, but some aspects of security are pertinent to the hybrid cloud. Cloud computing service provider has to offer service-level agreement to its potential customer, who may want to sign for cloud services. The service-level agreement is the most significant document that could provide a degree of satisfaction to the cloud client in case of breach of security. We should point out that management and assessment of security risks are both dynamic processes, as vulnerabilities get discovered, and security gets reassessed. Thus, the management of security is an ever-evolving process.

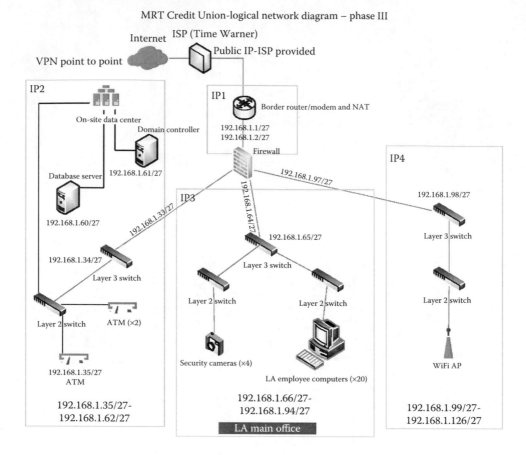

FIGURE 18.7 LA IT data center.

REFERENCES

1. Cloud Security Alliance. Security guidance for critical areas of focus in cloud computing V3.0, 2011.
2. Mike Edwards. Cloud computing ISO security and privacy standards: 27017, 27018, 27001, 2015.
3. Vaibhav Khadilkar, Anuj Gupta, Murat Kantarcioglu, Latifur Khan, Bhavani Thuraisingham. *Secure data storage and retrieval in the cloud*. University of Texas, 2011.
4. S. Srinivasan. Is security realistic in cloud computing?. *Journal of International Technology and Information Management*, 22(4), Article 3, 2014.
5. Google. Google Cloud Platform. Google.com. Retrieved November 25, 2014.

CHAPTER 19

Advanced Private Cloud Computing Security Architectures

Albert Caballero

CONTENTS

19.1 INTRODUCTION

Security can no longer be an afterthought; it must become a design consideration, which is at the core of every cloud deployment. For most public cloud subscribers, there is little ability to request modifications or additions to the architecture of their provider. Those customers able to build out a private cloud or able to subscribe to a certified shared cloud that is compliant with a particular set of standards, however, are able to drive security architecture and influence implementation. It is not sufficient to look at information security as maintaining the three basic pillars: confidentiality, integrity, and availability. Although these core concepts remain the holy grails of security, the protection mechanisms needed to ensure that these three pillars are sustained in a cloud environment can take many forms. Security controls need to have situational awareness and take into account customized tactics and methodologies in each of the following areas [1]:

- *Compute*: physical servers, operating system, CPU, memory, disk space, and so on

- *Network*: virtual local area networks, demilitarized zone, segmentation, redundancy, connectivity, and so on

- *Storage*: logical unit numbers (LUNs), ports, partitioning, redundancy, failover, and so on

- *Virtualization*: hypervisor, geolocation, management, authorization, and so on

- *Application*: multitenancy, isolation, load balancing, authentication, and so on

As illustrated in Figure 19.1, one philosophy security professionals can adopt is to consider security controls in three fundamental areas when designing an information security strategy: attack resiliency, incident readiness, and security maturity.

Attack resiliency helps protect core business assets from internal and external attacks by implementing strong technical controls and adhering to industry best practices. When considering how to protect assets and data in the cloud, it is important to make the distinction between public and private clouds. When protecting assets that are in a public cloud, the traditional protection mechanisms will not suffice, and in many cases, they will not apply because the subscriber will have little or no access to the underlying infrastructure or operating systems. When building a private cloud infrastructure, the data owners remain autonomous and are responsible for all of their own security operations, which can be a

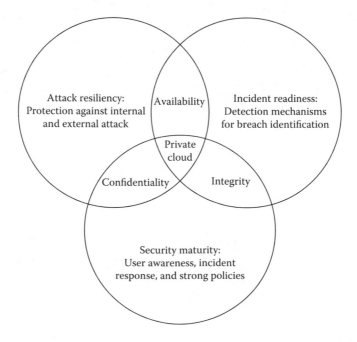

FIGURE 19.1   Information security strategy.

double-edged sword. If there isn't a highly skilled and experienced information technology (IT) team with a supporting security design architect or if the IT organization is not able to perform, automate, and deliver at the level of a service provider, then it is easy to let potentially dangerous considerations fall by the wayside.

Incident readiness is a key strategy component that can help in early detection of security breaches or incidents. When a security breach is detected, it is common for an organization to call in professional help from the outside to assist with incident response and recovery, especially if it runs its own private cloud. A major issue is that when the third party is engaged and appears on-site to help, the first thing it does is requesting relevant information such as log data, packet captures, and forensic images. If an organization has not put the necessary controls in place before the security incident occurs, then it often happens that all traces of the breach are overwritten or deleted by the time it's investigated. Tools that perform functions such as capturing event logs and vulnerability data, network packet inspection, end point recording, and live response will help build the visibility needed to effectively identify and respond to security incidents whenever they are discovered.

Even today, organizations have not reached a level of security maturity that will significantly deter attackers from attempting to compromise their data. Building a mature information security program with a comprehensive, risk-based strategy is necessary for other controls to be effective. Among the items that are part of mature information security programs are policies that make sense, a thorough incident response plan, and an all-inclusive user awareness program.

19.2 PRIVATE CLOUD ARCHITECTURE

There are many core concepts and characteristics behind the architecture of a private cloud, but the overarching goal remains to provide IT organizations with elastic and resilient compute environments that are highly automated and secured. This is accomplished by abstracting the physical infrastructure through virtualization of the operating system so that applications and services are not locked into any particular device, location, or hardware. That being said, it is critical that the infrastructure is designed in a way that delivers the services that the business needs and manages the workloads in a portable and dependable way. Organizations that want to build and maintain their own private cloud will need to take on a service provider mentality by taking a holistic approach to resource utilization, security operations, infrastructure resiliency, and availability design [2].

19.2.1 Design Characteristics

Server, network, storage, and application virtualization are the core components that make up most private clouds. The main difference is that in a cloud, provisioning these resources should be fully automated and scale up and down quickly. An important aspect of pulling off this type of elastic architecture is commodity hardware. A cloud needs to be able to provision more physical servers, hard drives, memory, network interfaces, and just about any operating system or server application transparently and efficiently. To be able to do this, servers and storage need to be provisioned dynamically and be constantly reallocated to and from different environments with minimum regard for the

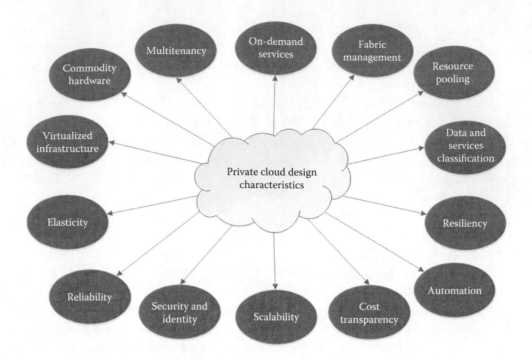

FIGURE 19.2   Characteristics of private cloud computing.

underlying hardware. Some key characteristics of a private cloud that help focus on the basic principles that differentiate a private cloud from a more traditional IT infrastructure [3,4] are as follows (please refer to Figure 19.2 for a more comprehensive list of cloud design characteristics):

- *On-demand services*: The always-on nature of the cloud allows for organizations to perform self-service administration and maintenance, over the Internet, of their entire infrastructure without the need to interact with a third party.

- *Resource pooling*: Cloud environments are usually configured as large pools of computing resources such as CPU, RAM, and storage from which you can choose to use or reallocate to a different business area.

- *Network connectivity*: The ease with which users can connect to the cloud is one of the reasons why cloud adoption is so high. Organizations today have a mobile workforce, which require connectivity to and from multiple platforms.

- *Elasticity*: A vital component of the cloud is that it must be able to scale up as the business demands it. A department or business unit may spin up new resources seasonally or during a campaign and bring them down when no longer needed.

- *Resiliency*: A cloud environment must always be available. The cloud is only as good as it is reliable, so it is essential that the infrastructure be resilient and delivered with availability at its core.

- *Multitenancy*: A multitenant environment refers to the idea that all tenants within a cloud should be properly segregated from each other. In many cases, a single instance of software may serve many departments, so for security and privacy reasons, it is critical that the organization takes the time to build in secure multitenancy from the bottom-up.

- *Security*: The primary areas of security remain infrastructure, network, system, and application—all of which require strong security controls and monitoring.

- *Identity*: Identity management and privileged access are top security concerns in the always-on private cloud; therefore, strong authentication, authorization, and user profiling mechanisms are required.

- *Data protection*: Data classification, separation, and security are extremely important in a private cloud due to the ubiquitous via shared resources.

- *Service classification*: Service classification as part of a service catalog allows for better standardization, increased predicatbility, and a higher level of service.

19.2.2 Converged Infrastructure

One of the most challenging aspects of building a private cloud infrastructure is determining what the bare metal components will be and the level of effort required to integrate them properly. Adding to the complexity of a multivendor environment is building a virtualization stack that is supported on all areas of the underlying hardware. To manage the acquisition and provisioning of all the components necessary to build a private cloud and configure technology that different vendors provide is not a menial task. Many times organizations realize that some major components such as network devices, physical servers, and storage solutions may not fully support one another or the hypervisor being used to virtualize the operating system, and cloud services may not be compatible. Due to the complexity associated with configuring all these physical and virtual technologies to work well together and all the considerations involved in building out the cloud environment, many vendors have introduced physical infrastructures and cloud stacks that are preconfigured to work together. Many organizations decide to leverage one of these standardized solutions with proven systems integrations that are provided as an all-in-one private cloud environment typically called a converged infrastructure. Figure 19.3 [1] shows an example of an all-in-one private cloud converged infrastructure delivered by VCE called a Vblock. Vblocks use Cisco UCS components for the compute and networking components with EMC storage and VMware as the hypervisor, and it is sold as a single solution for deploying a cloud environment.

The traditional process of scaling an infrastructure typically entails design, procurement, deployment, testing, and integration, all of which consume a tremendous amount of time. To avoid all of this time and effort, organizations are increasingly looking at some of the largest technology vendors to sell them preconfigured cloud solutions. Typically, the more common converged infrastructure vendors designed solutions specifically targeted to address one of the three major types of cloud services: infrastructure as a service (IaaS), platform as a service (PaaS), or software as a service (SaaS). The type of private cloud being

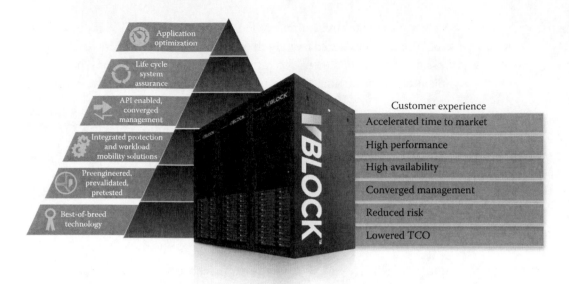

FIGURE 19.3   VCE-converged infrastructure for private cloud deployments. (VCE Company, LLC, *Enabling Trusted Multi-Tenancy with Vblock® Systems*, VCE Company, LLC, Richardson, TX, 2015.)

built and what services it is meant to deliver will determine which cloud technology stack or converged infrastructure is deployed:

- *VCE*: Vblock Systems are the most mature and tested converged infrastructures out there. VCE delivers a true converged infrastructure, leveraging Cisco compute and network technology, EMC storage and data protection, and VMware virtualization management. Vblocks are commonly deployed in IaaS and PaaS.

- *FlexPod*: The FlexPod solution leverages Cisco UCS computing and networking but is configured to use NetApp storage and can use a variety of hypervisors, so it is not tied into VMware as its primary virtualization technology. It is particularly useful to deploy a high-performance cloud service designed to run a nonstandard virtualization stack [5].

- *Oracle Private Cloud*: This solution can be described as a hyperconverged infrastructure that is purpose built to run a private cloud with a robust database back end. We have seen a trend toward delivering an entire private cloud in a single appliance that is designed specifically to run a resource-intensive cloud application in a more simplified and standardized way.

- *Nutanix*: Dell's flavor of a converged infrastructure focuses on commodity computing. It consists of enterprise class compute and storage systems using Intel-based servers and storage with a standard hypervisor. It allows an organization to build large, clustered environments with standard hardware easily adding nodes and capacity as needed.

- *VSPEX*: This is EMC's version of a converged infrastructure powered by EMC storage. Some times, an organization may have a need for a high-performance storage area network (SAN) or network attached storage (NAS) environment and needs to build a private cloud whose primary focus is delivering an elastic storage environment, this is what VSPEX excels at.

19.2.3 Virtualization Stacks and Automation

Similar to a converged infrastructure, the complexity required to deploy and maintain the virtualization layer of a cloud environment can be complex. There are a couple of efforts to build a common virtualization stack of software that will allow any organization to build the framework needed for a private cloud environment. This group of software components typically includes a management console, virtual machines, emulated devices, management services, and a user interface. Assessing which virtualization technologies will be used to manage each of these components has been simplified by the introduction of virtualization stacks and configuration management tools.

There are quite a few methodologies for the orchestration and deployment of cloud-based objects such as virtual systems, web applications, and management servers. One such methodology is a container-based technology that wraps software in a complete file system containing everything it needs to run on its own. This enables easy updating, deployment, and configuration of many services at once. This container technology is great for managing applications, but what of the infrastructure itself? For this, there are tools that allow users to script the provisioning of new platforms, users, and systems for full automation. Combining container-based technology that leverages configuration management software will give an organization the power to deploy a truly robust and reliable private cloud environment. The most common virtualization stacks and automation software for the cloud are listed as follows:

- *Docker*: Containers wrap up a piece of software in a complete filesystem that contains everything it needs to run: code, runtime, system tools, system libraries—anything you can install on a server. This guarantees that it will always run the same, regardless of the environment it is running in:
  - *Lightweight*—Containers running on a single machine all share the same operating system kernel, so they start instantly and make more efficient use of resources. Images are constructed from layered filesystems, so they can share common files, making disk usage and image downloads efficient.
  - *Open*—Containers are based on open standards allowing containers to run on all major Linux distributions and Microsoft operating systems with support for every infrastructure.
  - *Secure*—Containers isolate applications from each other and the underlying infrastructure while providing an added layer of protection for the application.
- *Chef*: It is a method to automate building, deploying, and managing the cloud. Infrastructure becomes as versionable, testable, and repeatable as the application

code. A Chef server stores your recipes as well as other configuration data. The Chef client is installed on each server, virtual machine, container, or networking device you manage called nodes. The client periodically polls Chef server for the latest policy and state of your network. If anything on the node is out of date, the client brings it up to date:

- *Development kit*—It contains everything you need to develop and test your infrastructure.

- *Analytics*—See and integrate the data with external systems such as log management and security information and event management (SIEM) tools ensuring that infrastructure is policy compliant.

- *Management*—It is a web-based console to control access via role-based access control (RBAC), edit and delete nodes, and reset private keys.

- *High availability*—It supports distributed replicated block devices and Amazon's elastic block storage volumes and the remapping of its elastic IP addresses.

- *Replication*—It is the central location for developing the policy.

- *Puppet*: This is an open source tool also designed to automate the configuration and provisioning of Windows and Unix-based systems with a ruby-based programming language and information files. It is an extremely powerful software that can be sufficient for the orchestation of most private clouds.

- *CloudStack*: It is an open source cloud management platform designed for creating, controlling, and deploying various cloud services and enables a private organization to implement many automations that would otherwise become extremely challenging to perform using different technologies.

- *OpenStack*: This platform actually brings together multiple interrelated stack-based projects in an effort to tie all cloud computing management into one interface that allows for the provisioning and rollout of any cloud service.

Figure 19.4 shows a sample of different hardware form factors and technology stacks that can be used to build a private cloud [5].

19.3 PRIVATE CLOUD SECURITY

Private cloud security requires all the components of a traditional defense in-depth strategy for protecting information systems. In addition to these best practices, there are implications and challenges unique to a private cloud that should be considered. If it is determined that the data being stored in the private cloud is mission critical, then more advanced security techniques may be required, including trusted multitenancy, data security, and identity management. It becomes an orchestration of operations, development, and security that needs to be delicately handled so that one of these critical aspects is not overlooked and easily exploited.

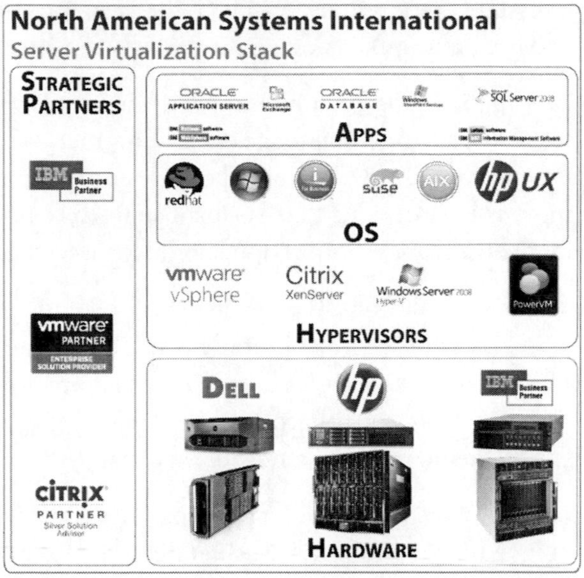

FIGURE 19.4   Private cloud hardware and virtualization stack.

19.3.1 Implications and Challenges

The type of business that will be conducted in your unique private cloud instance will determine the level of security required. Keeping the design considerations for each of the core components in mind is the first step in architecting a private cloud. Next, having a good working knowledge of the implementation options for converged infrastructures and cloud stacks can help drastically reduce the time and cost of deployment. To build a list of unique requirements for your cloud, there are some implications and challenges that should be analyzed before implementation begins. The goal is for an organization to develop an advanced security architecture design based on its usage model and a blueprint for its own private cloud security architecture. These implications and challenges are best described based on the following general criteria [3,6]:

- *Virtualization*: A core capability of virtualization is to abstract the hardware from the software allowing multiple instances of the software to emulate stand-alone hardware. This means that one physical system may house many servers, which all communicate and interact with each other on a virtual network over shared resources. Visibility into this virtualized computing infrastructure is important.

- *Infrastructure*: Life cycle management of hardware components, temperature controls, data center security, storage arrays, and network devices are all factors when building a resilient infrastructure. At each of these layers, there is a need to make decisions that will determine the availability and reliability of your cloud.

- *Platform*: Whether it is a resource-intensive back-end database or high-transaction web application, the platform that is being built on top of the infrastructure should be independently assessed. There will need to be basic security controls baked into the design before implementation to ensure a more robust platform.

- *Software*: Software applications require unique security testing to assure that the developer has not written vulnerable code. With commerical applications, vulnerability scans and penetration testing can be performed. When the software is developed in-house, more robust options that perform static and dynamic analyses of the code from development through production should be assessed.

- *Network*: In cloud implementations, the perimeter of the network is completely redefined. An organization's IT team must literally think outside of the box and assume that the entire Internet and every object connecting to it are now its own perimeters. Public network connectivity and interoperability with other clouds usually come hand in hand with the deployment of a new private cloud.

- *Data*: Data classification, security, and separation together help design a data protection strategy. Once data is properly classified, it can be separated into zones and properly protected at the level of security it deserves.

- *Client security*: Endpoint protection takes on a whole new meaning in the cloud. The end systems that are connecting to the cloud vary tremendously from tablets and phones to other cloud platforms, software applications, and business partners. There should be a clear strategy on how to implement client security for all types of connections the cloud environment is designed to handle.

- *Security monitoring and auditing*: Monitoring all events from every system in the private cloud, from hardware to hypervisor and up through applications, is a critical component of security. Most organizations do not take the time to properly plan and implement a robust, centralized logging solution.

- *Incident response*: Once an issue is identified, performing incident response, gathering forensic data, and analyzing security information may not be as straightforward as in a traditional IT infrastructure. There are areas in a cloud that may demand different capture techniques and analysis methods to arrive at root cause.

- *Legal issues*: In an organization that is geographically dispersed, running data centers in multiple countries need to be aware of the laws, regulations, and compliance standards that apply in each region. Most countries have different laws governing the seizure of corporate data and storing personal employee data outside of the country. Aside from international regulations, there may also be contractual obligations that dictate how data should be stored and transferred.

- *Attacker profiles*: Building a baseline for the activity of authenticated users helps define what the profile of an attacker may look like. An attacker must become an authenticated user to affect any damage on the infrastructure; therefore, security must be implemented, assuming that the attacker will already have privileged access.

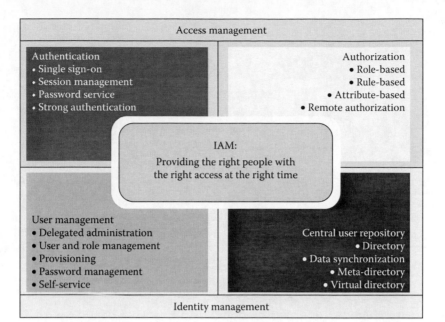

FIGURE 19.5   Identity and access management key components.

- *Identity and access management (IAM)*: Tracking the behavior and actions of each individual and asset in the cloud is specifically challenging due to its always-on nature and broad connectivity characteristics. IAM enables individuals to access the correct resources at the right time for the proper reasons, and if properly implemented drastically increases visibility and security. Figure 19.5 describes the key components of an IAM strategy, which are as follows:

  - *Authentication and authorization*: Strong authentication mechanisms with proper access rights in a cloud environment requires more scalable and avaialble solutions than those in a traditional IT infrastructure.

  - *Role-based access control*: Without role-based access controls, it will be impossible to maintain separation of duties, control privileged access, or maintain security against internal attacks.

  - *Single sign-on*: It is the ability to have a single location that will authenticate cloud users to any number of back-end applications and services.

  - *Federation of services*: Federated services are often used in cloud deployments, typically to extend the functionality of an internal network into the cloud. This common requirement is seen when deploying cloud-based technologies that need leverage Microsoft Active Directory or other internal services.

19.3.2 Security Operations Management

The main responsibility of any security operations center is incident management. Incidents can be considered anything from a combination of interesting events that are generated from one system to a widespread security breaches across the entire cloud. A strong security

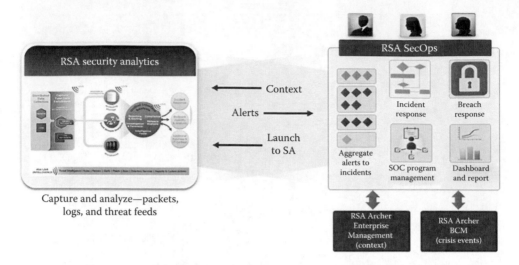

FIGURE 19.6   Security operations management by RSA.

operations team is needed to understand and distill security data from all the disparate systems used in a cloud environment and to properly identify and respond to incidents. It is essential to orchestrate people, process, and technology for proper incident analysis and breach response with focused workflows and intuitive dashboards. Figure 19.6 illustrates a sound security operations implementation. Some of the core elements to good security operations management are as follows [6]:

- Monitor and audit extensively.

- Automate security operations.

- Apply security best practices.

- Understand that isolation is key.

- Assume attackers are authenticated and authorized.

- Assume all data locations are accessible.

- Use strong cryptographic technologies.

- Limit routing and enforce segmentation.

19.4 ADVANCED SECURITY ARCHITECTURES

The cloud has so many usage models that every cloud experience is different and security cannot be assessed based on one set of standards or single reference architecture. There are many cloud security reference architectures published that are use case specific and take into account different business requirements. For example, it is possible that an organization is looking to build out an IaaS to run Windows-based servers in a traditional IT operation. This typically requires a well-known deployment architecture and can fit into traditional security management models. More complex use cases may involve deploying a PaaS or SaaS environment that is payment card industry (PCI) compliant or adheres to National Institute of Standards and Technology government standards. This type of environment may hold cardholder or employee data. If this is the case, then more customized security reference architectures with advanced security controls are required [1].

19.4.1 Security Reference Architectures

The major design consideration and criterion to keep in mind when considering security architectures for high security is multitenancy. At the core of a shared resource like a cloud environment, whether public or private, you can implement all the security you'd like, but if there is data leakage or security breaches between tenants in a cloud, it compromises the entire infrastructure. All of the security considerations recommended based on design should also be implemented in a multitenant fashion where it is clear which alerts, events, and activities correspond to which tenant or business unit. The most fundamental goals should be the following [7]:

- Maximum physical separation at each layer by tenant

- Maximum logical separation at each layer by tenant

- Implement security controls using partner tools on a per-tenant basis

Controls must take all reasonable measures to prevent unauthorized data leakage or resource reallocation between tenants. Figure 19.7 describes the basic separation of tenants within a private cloud. The three important concepts for your reference are as follows [1]:

- *Separation*: At the level of the open systems interconnection (OSI) model, primarily storage, network, and compute

- *Tenant*: A user, customer, organization, or department

- *Data*: Data in transit and at rest as well as network traffic

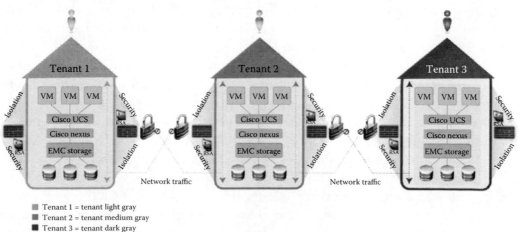

■ Tenant 1 = tenant light gray
■ Tenant 2 = tenant medium gray
■ Tenant 3 = tenant dark gray

FIGURE 19.7 Multitenancy and separation of tenants. (VCE Company, LLC, *Enabling Trusted Multi-Tenancy with Vblock® Systems*, VCE Company, LLC, Richardson, TX, 2015.)

19.4.2 Trusted Multitenant Infrastructure

There are different philosophies on how to decide which controls to put in place and how to implement them. It is common to hear that security in the cloud should be treated as a "wrapper" in which every transaction in the cloud goes through certain steps to determine the trust level and access permissions of each connection. That is an outside-in approach that considers many variables based on the best available information at the moment and will heavily depend on how solid your security infrastructure was built. An inside-out approach for example would be the Zero Trust model in which it assumes that every workload and transaction in the cloud will not trusted and design the architecture from the ground up with the highest level of segregation and security possible. For success in the security wrapper design, it is useful to set out with a Zero Trust model philosophy from the beginning, which advocates the tried and true motto: "Trust, but Verify." Specific Zero Trust model recommendations include the following:

- Include properly segmented networks, systems, and data with clear boundaries.

- Security built into the architecture design before final implementation is finalized.

- Inspect and log all traffic, security events, and host activity all the time.

- Strictly enforce access control policies based on a need-to-know basis.

- Ensure all resources are accessed in a secure and trusted manner.

When data separation, identity management, and trusted workloads are a requirement, a higher level of trust is needed. The underlying software that runs the infrastructure and all its moving pieces should be measured for continuous compliance of the cloud. This concept of continuous trust validation helps prove with real-time event logging that your data is where it says it is, and your systems are who they say they are. This low-level trust validation of the infrastructure is largely overlooked. It is extremely difficult to prove things such as data boundaries, geographic location, and virtual machine location without it. In addition, vulnerabilities have been exploited in firmware, basic input/output system (BIOS), routers, flash cards, and other hardware, which once compromised become invisible to the operating system. Whether embedded by a malicious insider at the factory or an overzealous third party in the supply chain, it remains a good idea to check all your systems before you rack them in the data center for the next few years.

To help measure and validate the identity of a system and measure any changes in its firmware, kernel modules, physical location, or system integrity, Intel has developed a Trusted Execution Technology (Intel TXT). Intel TXT is a hardware security technology that protects IT infrastructures against software-based attacks by validating the behavior of key components within a server or PC at start-up. This enables multitenancy with an assurance that your systems, data, and workloads can be trusted down to the hardware. A common use case is an organization deploying a shared private cloud for the HR and finance departments. Each of these workloads may reside on a dedicated server blade, but right next to those servers, there are R&D projects that share a separate server. In all cases,

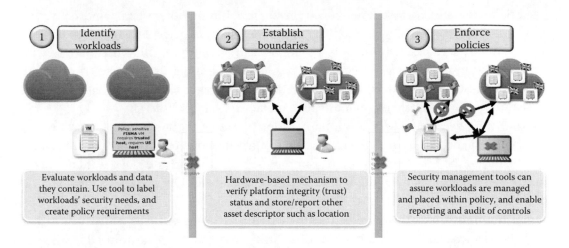

FIGURE 19.8 Trusted workloads. (VCE Company, LLC, *Enabling Trusted Multi-Tenancy with Vblock® Systems*, VCE Company, LLC, Richardson, TX, 2015.)

workloads must be separated and protected from each other. In this example, we'll take into account all the trusted multitenancy concepts. The idea would be to design a cloud environment where secure workloads can measure the trust of the underlying infrastructure and all client connections can be validated. Furthermore, we want to make sure that virtual systems residing on one physical server blade are never migrated to a different, untrusted server. A design as shown in Figure 19.8 would allow for full auditing of what is happening within both the physical and the virtual infrastructure [8,9].

19.5 SUMMARY

Security is a process, and it is also a mind-set. A mind-set that must be turned on prior to the decision of building a private cloud is made and continually reassessed throughout the entire process. A significant amount of emphasis has been placed on proper planning and security design by shedding some light on all the implications for deploying a private cloud. An understanding of all the layers of security that can be implemented in a cloud environment and recognizing where it is best implemented is critical to the success of any information security program. In a cloud environment, it is often not clear where best to place controls for proper policy enforcement and not to most effectively monitor the activity for full visibility into the environment. Many security breaches can be directly traced back to an area of the infrastructure in which activity is not properly monitored and logged or policy is not enforced due to some coverage gaps in security instrumentation.

Deploying a private cloud is clearly quite different than on-ramping services to a public cloud. A private cloud at first will initially require a significant investment of time and money but will definitely produce long-term savings by adding efficiencies resulting in a lower total cost of ownership. Reducing the time to deploy and the upfront costs of a private cloud is leveraging converged infrastructures for the underlying hardware and virtualization stacks for the cloud environment. Due to all the orchestration needed to effectively manage so many dynamic components in a cloud deployment, that automation becomes essential. To assist in the automation of tasks, provisioning of systems, and delivery of services, container-based technologies and configuration management tools can be leveraged in highly scalable environments. For high-security environments where data security, tenant separation, and trust integrity are paramount, consider deploying a trusted multitenant infrastructure leveraging hardware-based security technologies that continually measure the environment down to the bare metal for every transaction.

Analyzing every situation from many different angles is the nature of most security professionals, and when architecting security, a private cloud environment of this quality will be put to the test. Responsibly on-ramping services to a private cloud does not negate the need to protect your traditional IT infrastructure as well. Organizations must not only build incident readiness and attack resiliency into their initial private cloud design but also assure themselves that these protections are extended throughout the rest of the organization. Finally, maintaining a high level of security maturity by performing due diligence and producing strong policies around all your processes will help lead to a successful, robust, and secure private cloud implementation.

REFERENCES

1. VCE Company, LLC. *Enabling Trusted Multi-Tenancy with Vblock® Systems*. VCE Company, LLC: Richardson, TX, pp. 8–42, 2015. http://www.vce.com/asset/documents/trusted-multi-tenancy-with-vblock.pdf.
2. Peter Mell and Timothy Grance. *The NIST Definition of Cloud Computing*. The National Institute of Standards and Technology: Gaithersburg, MD, pp. 5–7, 2011. http://csrc.nist.gov/publications/nistpubs/800-145/SP800-145.pdf.
3. Bill Loeffler and Jim Dial. *Private Cloud Principles, Concepts, and Patterns*. Microsoft TechNet Article, Microsoft Corp., 2013. http://social.technet.microsoft.com/wiki/contents/articles/4346.private-cloud-principles-concepts-and-patterns.aspx.
4. Dob Todorov and Yinal Ozkan. *AWS Security Best Practices*. Amazon Web Services, pp. 1–52, 2013. http://media.amazonwebservices.com/AWS_Security_Best_Practices.pdf.
5. Cisco Corporation. *Architecture Overview for FlexPod with Microsoft Windows Server 2008 R2 and Microsoft System Center 2012*. pp. 45–83, 2012. http://www.cisco.com/c/dam/en/us/solutions/collateral/data-center-virtualization/microsoft-applications-on-ucs/ucs_flexpod_ms_netapp.pdf.
6. Bill Loeffler and Jim Dial. *Private Cloud Security Operations Principles*. Microsoft TechNet Article, Microsoft Corp., 2013. http://social.technet.microsoft.com/wiki/contents/articles/6658.private-cloud-security-operations-principles.aspx.
7. Brian Lowans, Neil MacDonald, and Carsten Casper. *Five Cloud Data Residency Issues That Must Not Be Ignored*. Gartner: Stamford, CT, pp. 13–25, 2012. https://www.gartner.com/doc/2288615.
8. Intel® Cloud Builders Guide. *Integrating Intel® TXT Enabled Clouds with McAfee Security Management Platform Leveraging Trapezoid Trust Control Suite*, pp. 6–12, 2013. http://trapezoid.com/images/pdf/Intel_Cloud_Builders_Trapezoid_McAfee.pdf.
9. Intel® Cloud Builders Guide. *Integrating Intel® IPT with OPT and Symantec* VIP for Dynamically Assigning Permissions to Cloud Resources*, pp. 4–21, 2013. http://trapezoid.com/images/pdf/Intel_Cloud_Builders_Intel_IPT_2013.pdf.

CHAPTER 20

Privacy Protection in Cloud Computing through Architectural Design

Wanyu Zang, Meng Yu, and Peng Liu

CONTENTS

20.1 INTRODUCTION

According to the recent estimate, security and privacy concerns in cloud computing may lead to loss up to $35 billion in cloud market by 2016 [1]. One fundamental root cause for the security and privacy concerns is the privilege design. Existing cloud computing platforms endow too much power to the cloud provider, much more than necessary, which at the same time creates great challenges to ensure the trustworthy of the computing platform to the cloud customers. We believe a legitimate cloud provider has no intent to do anything malicious against tenant data, but this does not mean his or her employees won't do any. A disgruntled or corrupted cloud administrator could do many of the following attacks. For example, because the administrator of cloud has full privileges over all cloud resources including memory and disk, the abuse of his privilege could disclose any client's secrets in the clouds. Also, a malicious insider may insert malicious code (e.g., a back door) into a hypervisor. Commodity virtual machine (VM) monitors (VMMs; hypervisor) are too large to be verified by the state-of-the-art verification techniques. Hence, it is not practical to remove all back doors or vulnerabilities through peer review during development (and testing) or review of hypervisor codes. In the worst case, the malicious administrator could exploit the existing bugs and back doors inside the hypervisor. The state-of-the-art provider-side security measures, including both physical and cyber, however cannot deal with the malicious insider threat.

An intuitive and simple solution is to encrypt sensitive data before a customer sends the data to an untrusted environment. However, simple encryption, such as advanced encryption standard (AES) and Rivest–Shamir–Adleman (RSA), does not allow arbitrary processing over encrypted data and getting the results by decryption. Theoretically, homomorphic encryption (HE) [2] can provide perfect security features to protect sensitive data in a remote untrusted environment, such as a cloud. Unfortunately, there is no practical implementation for homomorphic encryption, by hardware or software. Back in July 2009, a well-known cryptographic personality Bruce Schneier (https://www.schneier.com/) praised Craig Gentry's groundbreaking HE scheme, but pointed out that "Gentry's scheme is completely impractical ... Gentry estimates that performing a Google search with encrypted keywords—a perfectly reasonable simple application of this algorithm—would increase the amount of computing time by about a trillion." In May 2013, the International Business Machines (IBM) released an open source software package called HElib (https://github.com/shaih/HElib), a software library that implements HE. Although this is a big new step in cryptography, the HElib developers pointed out that "At its present state, this library is mostly meant for researchers working on HE and its uses. Also currently it is fairly low-level (set, add, multiply, shift, etc.), and is best thought of as 'assembly language for HE." Thus, protecting sensitive data on untrusted platforms remains extremely challenging.

A more practical solution uses special hardware architectures [3,4] to create compartments to isolate users or protect data. However, such hardware architectures are not readily available as commercial products and also need fundamental changes of the cloud infrastructures. Besides using special hardware architectures, researchers have also studied the possibilities to provide an answer using new computing architectures to protect user's privacy. For example, Overshadow [5] hides sensitive data from the supporting operating system (OS) through encryptions. However, it still needs to trust the whole hypervisor underneath the OS, and the size of hypervisor is too large to trust. Self-service cloud [6] is one important step toward privacy protection in clouds. Unfortunately, the trusted computing base (TCB) of self-service cloud includes too many components; thus, it is too large to verify. Current hypervisors typically have over a million lines of codes, which is not practical for security verification.

We have been successful in developing a user-configured privacy protecting a virtualization platform, MyCloud [7,8], with a small TCB in our preliminary work. However, MyCloud does not support many features found on popular cloud computing software such as VMWare, Xen, and keyboard, video, mouse (KVM). Providing privacy protection cloud-wide and providing agile construction and configuration of such platform remain a very challenging task. In this chapter, we introduce our experiences in architectural designs for privacy protections in clouds.

To achieve our goals of protection, we need to do the following: (1) Deprivilege the administrator, (2) authorize users to configure access to their contents, and (3) maintain a small TCB size. We will describe how to protect a user's privacy with negligible overhead while achieving similar security strength of HE in terms of our threat model described later in this chapter.

20.2 RELATED WORK

We have been successful in developing a user-configured privacy protecting a virtualization platform, MyCloud [7], with a small TCB in our preliminary work. We also developed a two-layer virtualization structure, SplitVisor [8]. In this section, we explain the differences between our work and related work.

When the cloud provider has full privileges over the VMM and users' VMs, there is no way that cloud users can protect their privacy. The first step to enable privacy protection in virtualization architecture design is to design the separation of privileges.

To address the threats from the administrative domain, previous work was tried to disaggregate privileges functionality of Dom0 into separated client VMs [6,9] or split VMM into two components [8]. In [9], the domain builder, which is part of the important privileged components, is moved out of the service domain into a small TCB. Conceptually, the most similar work to ours is self-service cloud (SSC) computing [6]. SSC allows client VMs to execute some management of privileges, which used to be provided in the administrative domain such as to access VM's memory and to execute CPUID instruction.

However, in these works, the TCBs are not minimized because all of them consider a full-functional hypervisor as part of the TCB. SplitVisor [8] splits VMM into two parts according to their functions: a smaller one regarded as minimized TCB in order to enforce isolation and a larger one to provide rich service functionality. Nevertheless, in SplitVisor design, clients have to upload a specialized guest VMM. Hence, the design is not compatible with current cloud computing schemes such as Amazon EC2.

Similar to SplitVisor, recent work also investigates the uses of nested virtualization to disaggregate some host VMM components to the guest VMM [10–12]. CloudVisor [10] uses nested virutalization to separate the hypervisor from the computing software stacks. It enforces strong isolation through a small host hypervisor below a guest hypervisor. However, it does not allow user-configured privacy protection. Also, performance loss may increase exponentially with nesting depth [13]. Xen-Blanket [11] allows users to build their own business by launching VMs on a guest VMM. However, the service provider still has full control over the host VMM. In such a case, a service provider has the ability to breach the client's privacy. Thus, clients cannot prevent the cloud administrators from accessing the client's privacy.

Besides the aforementioned architectural improvement attempts, there are many other researches [14] on encrypting client's sensitive data, and the encryption algorithms do not rely on the offer of service providers. Employees from the service provider cannot decrypt data without a user's private key. However, during computation, encrypted data should be decrypted into plaintext in memory. In other words, this work is not suitable for supporting arbitrary computing such as a full guest VM. Also, encryption and decryption will consume a lot computing resources.

Given the aforementioned efforts in separation of privileges design, there are also a lot of previous efforts to minimize the TCB of a cloud platform, which is also one of our design goals. In order to minimize the size of TCB (VMM and dom 0), NOVA [15,16] constructs a microkernel-based VMM including ~9K LOCs. Despite its thin TCB compared with commodity hypervisors, the complexity of the TCB is not markedly decreased because the microhypervisor still needs to manage complex duties, such as address space allocation, interrupt, and exception handling. Therefore, the thin TCB is still difficult to verify dynamically. Although seL4 [17] proposes a technique to verify a microkernel with ~8.7K LOCs, this method sacrifices functionality and usability.

At the same time, many researches have focused on removing the unnecessary virtualization component. MAVMM [18] and Trustvisor [19] are customized VMMs with minimized TCB. The size of the TCB is quite small (MVMM with ~3.2K LOCs and Trustvisor with ~2K LOCs for core functions), they can only handle a specific scheme and neither of them supports multiple VMs. In conclusion, these architectures are not suitable for serving commodity VMs.

Hardware vendors, such as Intel and advanced micro devices (AMD), are willing to provide hardware features to minimize TCB size. These features include system management mode (SMM) [20] and Trusted Execution Technology (TXT) [21]. SICE [22] utilize x86 SMM to isolate the TCB. The security of an isolated environment is guaranteed by the TCB, including hardware, basic input/output system (BIOS), and SMM program of ~300 LOCs. However, SICE supports only one VM, so it will not be compatible with any cloud platform. Flicker [23] is also considered a privacy protection solution based on CPU features [21]. Unfortunately, it only offers application-level protection and is not a general solution for VMs in the cloud.

NoHype [24,25] dynamically eliminates the VMM layer in order to narrow the hypervisor attack surface. Nonetheless, the disadvantage of NoHype is that it requires one VM per core on multicore processors and a preallocated nested page table. The two requirements restrict the number of VMs that can be simultaneously hosted on the physical platform and decrease the elasticity. Coreboot [26] is a promising way for the TCB minimization. It replaces the BIOS firmware with a lightweight system designed to perform a minimum number of initializing tasks and directly boot executable linkable format (ELF) images in ROM. However, coorboot has no virtualization component design in mind.

Compared with the previous work, MyCloud design reduces the TCB size by removing the control VM from the TCB. In MyCloud design, a cloud provider can only launch a deprivileged VM in order to do cloud management rather than having full privileges over the whole cloud platform. Thus, both separation of privileges and minimization of the TCB are achieved.

Unlike some researchers who reduce the privileges of cloud providers by extending the architecture of the cloud OS (e.g., OpenStack) [27], MyCloud minimizes the cloud provider's privileges on the cloud hypervisor, which is located lower than the cloud OS. Therefore, MyCloud is more secure because the TCB size is much smaller. Additionally, the cloud OSs work based on the support of cloud hypervisors (e.g., Xen and KVM), which may contain a lot of vulnerabilities.

Data protection-as-a-service (DPaaS) model [28] is a verifiable platform that can protect data integrity, control user access, allow users to audit the strength of data encryption, and secure execution isolation and trusted platform module (TPM). MyCloud can manage user access and protect users data by relying on hardware (CPU and mainboard) security features and TPM.

20.3 PROBLEM FORMULATION

In this section, we provide a formal description of our problems. Different from the previous work [29–31] that formulates virtualization requirements on the architecture, we describe the virtualization in a different way to derive security requirements.

20.3.1 Secure Resource Virtualization

A computer system state can be described by the combination of states of resources $\{M, D, l, psw\}$, where M is the memory state, D is the device state, L is the processor mode, and psw is the processor state. We consider virtualization as a function of resource mapping. Note that our notations will also handle nested virtualization [12,10]. A VMM (or hypervisor) maps a VM state into a lower level (hardware, if the lower level is not virtualized) machine state.

The mapping of VMM can be denoted by a virtualization function f that maps resources to resources at a lower level. We use V_m^n for the mth VM at the nth level of virtualization. Thus, $f(V^1) = \{M_1, D_1, l_1, psw_1\}$, $f(V^1) = \{M_2, D_2, l_2, psw_2\}$, ..., $f(V_k^1) = \{M_k, D_k, l_k, psw_k\}$. With these notations, the memory isolation requirements can be described as $(\forall i, j)$, $1 \leq i, j \leq k$, $i \neq j$, $M_i \cap M_j = \phi$.

The compromise of VMM, according to our definitions, will lead to the change of f. However, the change of f is not necessarily caused by compromising f. For example, f may

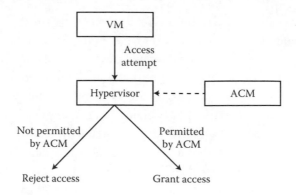

FIGURE 20.1   Access control using a hypervisor.

map the same VM to a different region of memory or dynamically allocate more memory to the VM. In such situations, f is not considered compromised.

The basic idea of integrating the access control into a hypervisor is shown in Figure 20.1. In the figure, a VM tries to access a specific memory location. The access can be intercepted by a hypervisor of the cloud platform. The access then is inspected against a preconifgured Access Control Matrix (ACM). If the VM does have permission over the memory location, for example, no privacy issues, the access will be granted. Otherwise, the access will be denial due to privacy protection.

Now we have sufficient entities to discuss access permissions allowed in the virtualization architecture. The ACM is shown in Table 20.1. In the table, ACM_i is the ACM of VM_i and CVM is for control VM. Note that the access permissions of our proposed architecture are completely different from any of the existing VMMs, as shown in the second row of the table. Actually, by filling different values into the second row of the table, we can get a full spectrum of possible hypervisor designs. Most existing designs assign full privileges to the CVM, which cause security problems once the CVM is compromised.

In sum, Table 20.1 describes a separation of privileges design that only CVM has permissions to do cloud management, and additional permissions are explicitly authorized by users through ACM_k. Note that a recent work [6] also proposed the separation of privileges design; however, it includes too many software components in the TCB. We will discuss our proposed solution in later sections.

TABLE 20.1   ACM of the Virtualization Architecture

Components	f	CVM	VM_i	VM_j	ACM_i	ACM_j
f	Full	Full	Full	Full	Full	Full
CVM	H	Full	A/M/D/ACM_i	A/M/D/ACM_j	R	R
VM_i	H		Full	ACM_j	R/W	
VM_j	H		ACM_i	Full		R/W

A, allocation; M, migration; D, deallocation; H, hypercall; R, read; W, write.

20.3.1.1 Secure Virtualization

It is important that virtualization is secure in terms of resource management and mapping from logic resources to physical resources. In the following, we specify what kind of virtualization or mapping of resources is considered *secure* virtualization. A hypervisor implements "secure virtualization" if the following conditions are met:

1. Nonoverlapping resource allocation. No allocable resource is allocated to multiple VMs simultaneously.

2. VM isolation. No VM can access any resource or state of resource allocated to others.

3. Integrity and correct implementation of hypervisor.

4. Deprivileged control VM. CVM cannot have more privileges than the following:

    a. Resource allocation and deallocation for VMs.

    b. VM management operations.

    c. User's explicitly authorized access to the user's VMs.

The isolation condition removes the possibility of side-channel attacks such as attacks through caches [32]. In our definition, resource allocation and isolation have been widely implemented in existing hypervisors. However, condition 4 is the most often overlooked condition, which causes many serious security flaws and problems. For example, once a fully privileged CVM is compromised, the full virtualization platform is exposed to the attacker and all users' VMs are taken over by the attacker. Moreover, a fully privileged CVM will make privacy protection "mission impossible," because a compromised CVM can mount VM introspection tools to peek into users' spaces and interpret all user VM states.

Therefore, in our definition of secure virtualization, we require that the CVM has minimum privileges necessary for cloud management. If allowed by users through ACM_k, the CVM can have more permissions.

20.3.2 Privacy Protection and Usability

At the hypervisor level, access control mechanism can only see memory contents, device status, and so on. These low-level binary data need to be translated into pieces of information that users care and can understand. For example, a general computer user may say "Please do not disclose my Social Security Number in the cloud." whereas a more advanced user may say "Please do not let anybody, including the cloud provider, to access my bank application in the cloud." However, nobody will request to "protect the contents at logical address 0xb9003ea8," as privacy protection.

The last request, although it can be understood by the lowest level of virtualization architecture, has no "usability" to users at all. The user's logical address is translated to the physical memory address by *f*, the hypervisor, through multiple levels of page translations on the x86 architecture and many other interconnection security agreements (ISAs).

The translation from high-level concepts to a low-level machine-understandable format needs the knowledge of software design and implementation. Virtual Machine Inspection Tools such as XenAccess* and LibVMI† can do translation and interpretation of low-level data of VMs. However, mapping from high-level concepts to low-level data is in another direction. Though it is challenging, it is a feasible work for implementation, with the help of software component in hypervisors.

A "monitoring mapping function," denoted by *g*, maps a data item at the OS or application level to physical addresses where the data item is actually stored. Using a data item as an example, function *g* can be implemented by the composition of two functions g_2 and g_1, where g_1 translates the data item into the OS's logical address space (implemented in the OS, through a system call), and $g2$ translates the logical address into the physical address space (implemented in the hypervisor, through a hypercall). As mentioned in our assumptions, we are not dealing with privacy protection on storage devices in the cloud. We assume that data are encrypted when they leave the VM, before stored on external devices.

The challenging part of privacy protection is not only on the construction of *g* that enables the mechanism of privacy protection. For example, if a user is very concerned about his or her social security number. The protection at the application level will be very challenging because the OS has no knowledge about the data flow or control flow of applications. A data item obtained from an application's input may be stored anywhere, even encrypted by a weak algorithm, in the application's memory space. Thus, taint analysis [33,34], dynamic instrumentation [35], or similar techniques need to be deployed if we want to track the exact location of a user-concerned data item, which currently introduces too much overhead.

A user may specify a higher abstract-level requirement like "I consider all my bank account information and processing results as privacy." To automatically and accurately identify exact data items or data structures in an application specified in the requirements requires more advanced analysis, for example, natural language processing, given the state-of-the-art technology.

The aforementioned analysis that maps the user's concepts into the OS's logical space is out of the scope of this proposal. We do consider mapping a particular process, or OS data structures, into memory addresses, such as the functions of XenAccess or LibVMI. Note that if we do not run dynamic analysis, we cannot stop an application leaking private information through network communications. Addressing these problems is out of the scope of this proposal.

Another usability-related problem is caused by interprocess communication (IPC) and resource sharing at the OS level. For example, if we choose an application *p* to protect privacy, it will be easy to identify *p*'s memory space and resource usage. However, *p* may

---

launch a tree of processes or threads and also have resource sharing with other processes, which requires privacy protection to cover more processes involved.

If the process pi has IPC or resource sharing with pj, we say that it has a privacy sharing relation, denoted by $pi \simeq pj$. Therefore, it is straightforward to conclude the theorem about privacy protection in Section 20.3.3.

20.3.3 Theorem of Boundaries of Privacy Protection

Given $\langle P, \simeq \rangle$, where P is a set of processes and relation $\simeq \subseteq P \times P$ is for resource sharing, to protect privacy of $p \in P$, the lower bound of privacy protection is p, and the upper bound of privacy protection is $\{q \in P \mid p \simeq_* q\}$. An intuitive example is to protect a process. In such a situation, the protected process, all child processes/threads, and all processes having IPC with the protected process, or any processes sharing resources with the protected process, should be protected as well.

20.3.4 Neutralized VM Monitoring

Virtual machine introspection (VMI) [36] implements function $g{-}1$. With the help of the knowledge of kernel data structures, a VM's internal state can be interpreted. Bringing in privacy protection we discussed in previous sections, user's requests for privacy protection will be mapped, by g, into a set of protected memory blocks. Assume that VMI can also access a set of memory blocks, with the support of hypervisor, then user privacy is compromised if and only if there are memory blocks storing privacy and being monitored through VMI:

Assume that users' privacy protection request to protect a set of memory blocks $P_s = \{B_1, B_2,..., B_m\}$, and cloud provider is able to monitor memory $VMI_m = \{b_1, b_2,..., b_n\}$. We define that the monitoring is "neutralized" if and only if $\forall i, j, 1 \leq i, j \leq m$, and $1 \leq i, j \leq n$, $B_i \cap b_j = \phi$. The monitoring mechanism has a similar problem to privacy protection—finding the correct boundary to fulfil the monitoring task. For example, current VMI tools reside in a fully privileged VM and can view all resources of the cloud platform. This capability is an overkill for monitoring and leaves no space for privacy protection. On the contrary, it will be an overkill for privacy protection if we design hypervisor to disable any access from the control VM, which completely disables the monitoring capability in the cloud. Definition of neutralized monitoring specifies meaningful monitoring capability without compromising users' privacy. It is also straightforward to conclude the theorem about boundary of neutralized VM monitoring in Section 20.3.4.1.

20.3.4.1 Theorem about the Boundary of Neutralized VM Monitoring

Assume that the cloud monitoring task needs to look at $L_m = \{l_1, l_2,..., l_k\}$, a set of data structures of the OS kernel, user space, TCP/IP stack, and so on, the lower bound of neutralized monitoring is $\bigcup_{i=1}^{k} g(l_i) - P_s$, and the upper bound of neutralized monitoring is P_s. This theorem explains how much memory protection is necessary based on our definition of neutralized monitoring.

20.4 OVERVIEW

Our virtualization architecture, MyCloud, aims at defending against all malicious activities trying to (locally or remotely) compromise the VMM of existing commodity cloud platforms, the guest VMM in our architecture, and break into users' privacy. In this section, we describe our basic assumptions about the cloud computing environment and discuss the kinds of threats that are considered in our architectural designs.

20.4.1 Threat Model and Assumptions

We assume that once compromised, the root software stack (of the existing commodity cloud platform) could be fully controlled by the adversaries. Thus, the adversaries are able to do the following types of attacks: (1) taking over the control of management/control VM of the cloud provider and then looking into VMs' memory and disk; (2) breaking into the management/control VM of the cloud provider and injecting the malicious code into the VMs; (3) directly exploiting the vulnerabilities of the VMM (the legacy root software stack with bulk size) and dumping secrets from VMs; (4) as an internal employee, launching insider attacks (not physically) to leverage the powerful management interfaces to steal tenants' private data.

First, we take the attacks from insiders into consideration, but we assume that overall the cloud provider entity, for example, the company, is benign and credible. We distinguish "service providers" from "system administrators." Normally, well-known enterprises such as Amazon and Microsoft are interested in protecting the client's privacy rather than revealing or snooping on users' privacy, which protects their reputation of running the cloud business. Thus, we assume that a service provider has no motivation or intention to breach users' privacy in the cloud or launch any physical attacks such as memory bus tapping. Therefore, physical attacks such as attacks to temper-resistant systems [37,38] or protection against other hardware attacks are out of the scope of this chapter. The physical attack requires special tools and definitely leaves some evidence physically. On the contrary, system administrators who are employed by services providers may have opportunities and motivation to filch the user's data for pursuing monetary benefits. Even if a system administrator is benign, he or she may make mistakes by accident and cause privacy breach. Therefore, system administrators are considered adversarial.

Second, the platform is physically secure (e.g., monitored by cameras, locked in a safe room, etc.) so that attacks via physical accesses are not possible. Third, the platform is equipped with trusted computing hardware, including the Core Root of Trust for Measurement (CRTM) and TPM, which allows the attestation to the integrity of the crucial components in TCB.

Third, system management random access memory (SMRAM) cache should not be poisoned. On AMD platforms, it has already been protected so that cache-poisoning attacks [39] are immunized. On Intel platforms, however, a proper configuration of the System Management Range Register (SMRR) [20] is required to ensure this assumption.

Finally, we assume that we can utilize the TPM equipped in hardware to measure the integrity of crucial components in TCB. Also, because the SMM of processors has already been protected from cache-poisoning attacks [39], we do not consider this type of attacks either. Similarly, on Intel platforms, a proper configuration of the SMRR is required to ensure this assumption.

Note that we do not try to derive which part of memory should be protected in order to protect a data item at high abstraction level, such as a social security number. This is out of the scope of this chapter. We provide protection mechanisms at the VMM level, but it is up to the guest VM, which regions of memory should be protected.

In this chapter, we assume that the swapped pages are encrypted in order to protect the guest VM space. Thus, the guest VM's privacy will not be compromised when part of the memory is swapped out to the disks.

20.4.2 TCB Integrity Measurement

The Root of Trust for Measurement (RTM) mechanism is commonly used to ensure the integrity of TCB, which mainly relies on the TPM chip. Specified by the Trusted Computing Group, the TPM chip can be used to authenticate hardware devices [40]. It can be found on almost all the motherboards of servers and high-end PCs. A unique and secret RSA Endorsement Key (EK) is generated for each TPM at the time of manufacture and will be permanently sealed inside the chip, and other sensitive data will be stored into shielded memory. A privacy certificate agency can authenticate a TPM according to its public EK. The main role of TPM chips in trusted computing is to act as the CRTM, which measures the integrity metrics of modules, holds them in Platform Configuration Registers (PCRs), and reports them in an authenticated way in remote attestation. For privacy concerns, EK is not allowed to be used as a platform identity directly. Instead, Application Identity Keys are created to sign these PCR values. A detailed example to establish TCB with TPM can be found in Terramodel [41]. Note that RTM can be either static or dynamic (SRTM and DRTM, respectively) [21].

20.4.3 Design Goals

One principle of MyCloud design is to provide privacy protection "mechanism" but "not the policy" themselves. More specifically, the primary goal of MyCloud is to enable configurable privacy protection by (1) allowing users to build their own ACM in the TCB and (2) reducing the TCB size to be more secure. The detailed design considerations are provided in Sections 20.4.3.1 through 20.4.3.4.

20.4.3.1 Configured Privacy Protection

By default, the control VM has no access permission to any of the guest VM unless the guest VM grants the permission. In other words, once the cloud provider allocates the memory resource to run a user's VM, the cloud provide will lose access permissions to the user's VM space, unless the user explicitly authorizes accesses. By default, no access permission is granted to the cloud provider.

An interesting argument will be whether the cloud provider should have right to get the resource back from a particular VM in order to protect the platform against denial-of-service (DoS) attacks. Either solution (allow or not) can be supported by our design through the configuration of the ACM in the VMM, depending on the cloud provider's service-level agreement (SLA).

20.4.3.2 TCB Minimization

The large size and high complexity of security-sensitive applications and systems software are primary causes of poor testability and high vulnerability [42]. Hence, the TCB size of the cloud architecture with MyCloud should be as small as possible. However, a small/simple TCB is not sufficient. There should be a strong protection mechanism to enforce the security of the TCB. Formal analysis [43] is usually used to verify the TCB correctness and security properties, and software model checking [44] can be utilized to verify the implementation. There are also approaches utilizing hardware-based dynamic measurement to secure TCB, such as Trustvisor [19] and Flicker [23]. All the aforementioned protection mechanisms, however, have restrictions on the TCB size. For example, the recent successful report of formal verification shows the capability of a general-purpose kernel with ~8.7K LOCs [43]. Therefore, we need to control the TCB size by including only security-related or crucial functionalities.

20.4.3.3 Weakening the Cloud Provider's Power

In order to alleviate the concerns of privacy leakage to the cloud provider's internal employees, the overpowerfulness of cloud providers should be dealt with. In the current cloud architecture, Xen,* for example, the cloud provider occupies the most privileged domain and handles all the operations with the authority to look into users' data and computation. In MyCloud-based architecture, the power of a cloud provider should be limited, as long as it can normally perform cloud resources management (allocation, revoking, and migration).

20.4.3.4 VM-Level Isolation

We choose the isolation granularity at the VM level. First, most of the current commercial public clouds provide the service in the infrastructure-as-a-service fashion (e.g., Amazon EC2†). Second, VM is a native and simple abstraction/encapsulation of privacy for each cloud user. Unlike protecting processes, protecting VMs does not require handling the complex and subtle semantic gaps. Third, protection at the VM level is more likely to preserve backward compatibility, without the need of modifying OS kernels and applications.

20.4.4 Architecture

Intel processors support virtualization extension through virtual machine extensions (VMX) [20], and AMD processors use SVM [45]. Once the virtualization extension is enabled by the processor, CPU will have two modes: root and nonroot. In each mode, there are four privileged levels from ring 0 to ring 3, where ring 0 has the highest privilege level. A stand-alone OS usually runs the kernel in ring 0 and applications in ring 3.

The VMM, running in the root mode, can specify what should be trapped and handled by VMM, such as extended page table (EPT) exceptions, page faults, and timers. When those privileged operations are run by a guest OS in the nonroot mode, it will trigger the mode transition to the root mode with a VMEXIT. After those privileged operations are

---

* An open source project at http://www.xen.org/.
† Amazon Elastic Cloud Compute service at http://aws.amazon.com/ec2/.

handled, VMM will enter the guest OS again through a VMENTRY. Note that the handling of those operations in VMM is transparent to guest VMs. There is a virtual machine control structure (VMCS), including both the host status and the guest status, for each VM when VMEXIT (VMENTRY) happens to record (recover) the running context of the VM.

Figures 20.2 and 20.3 show the architectures of both KVM and Xen, respectively. In both architectural designs, the host OS (control VM) does not have a separate VMCS for VM context switching, so it runs in the root mode.

As the results, the host OS has all privileges that the processor's root mode has. Therefore, the TCB of both designs includes the whole control VM (the host OS).

Moreover, because the control VM is in the root mode, it is able to manipulate the VMCS structures of all guest VMs, as well a the page tables of all other VMs. Under such designs, it is impossible to protect any guest VM from the control VM. VMI, for example, using XenAccess, can be done in the control VM. Thus, no privacy protection can be achieved.

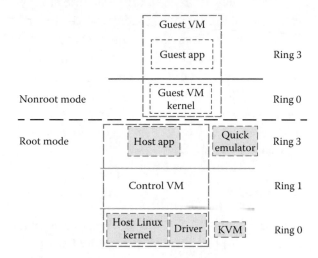

FIGURE 20.2   KVM architectures. Components of the TCB are shown in shadow.

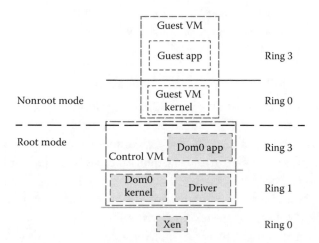

FIGURE 20.3   Xen architectures. Components of the TCB are shown in shadow.

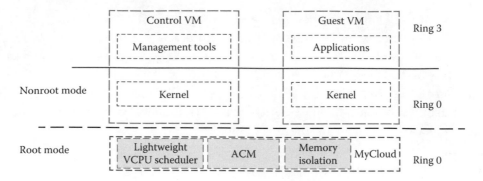

FIGURE 20.4   MyCloud architecture. Components of the TCB are shown in shadow.

Figure 20.4 shows the architecture of MyCloud. In MyCloud, only the VMM runs in the "root" mode, and VMM keeps security-related functionalities in the TCB. In our design, the scheduler is a timer-triggered preemptive scheduler against DoS attacks from any VM running on the platform. Memory isolation is also enforced by the VMM. In Section 20.5.2, we describe how memory isolation and devices are handled in MyCloud architecture.

In MyCloud design, there is no OS running in the processor's root mode. Therefore, no VM, including the control VM, is more privileged than others or can manipulate any others. The access permission is specified by an ACM in the VMM, following a separation of privilege design as described in Section 20.5.1. According to the ACM, the control VM can access a guest VM's space if and only if the guest VM explicitly grants the permission.

20.5 IMPLEMENTATION

MyCould uses EPT tables to isolate VMs, including the control VM. If a VM tries to access any memory location out of its space, it will trigger an EPT violation that causes a VMEXIT. Because the control VM has its own EPT and VMCS, it cannot access any other guest VMs either. The control VM has access to a resource table in the VMM about the current memory allocations. When creating a new VM, the control VM initiates a hypercall to allocate memory for the guest VM. The VMM handles the boot process of the new guest VM. By default, no access permissions are granted to the control VM to access the new guest VM space once the memory is allocated.

20.5.1 VM Isolation and User-Configured Access Control

In MyCloud architecture as shown in Figure 20.4, the cloud provider uses the control VM for cloud management. Our design completely removes the control VM from the root mode, and the cloud provider's privileges are specified in the ACM in the bottom layer in the root mode. Therefore, the platform has a depriviledged domain for the cloud provider.

The ACM, shown in Table 20.1, enables a user to choose what information in the user's VM space can be accessed by the cloud provider or other VM domains. In the table, ACM_i is the ACM of VM_i. Note that the access permissions of our proposed architecture are completely different from any of the existing cloud platforms, as shown in the second row of the table. Actually by filling different values into the second row of the table, we can get

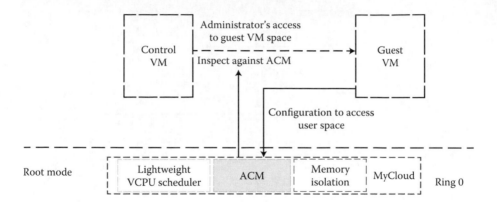

FIGURE 20.5   ACM in the hypervisor.

a full spectrum of possible hypervisor designs. Most existing designs assign full privileges to the control VM, which causes security problems once the control VM is compromised. Even worse, users have no privacy if the control VM has full privileges. Figure 20.5 shows how the ACM is included in the TCB of hypervisor design.

According to the ACM, each user can modify the access permissions to the user's space. By default, all accesses by other users, including the service provider, are prohibited. However, if a user likes, the user can grant access permissions to other users, or the cloud provider to enable information sharing or virus scan. Our access control mechanism protects a user's sensitive information in the user's space.

Furthermore, all existing technologies support page-level access control because violations are captured through page access-related exceptions. In such design, a sensitive data item will be overprotected because accesses to all other data on the same page will be trapped and prohibited. To protect sensitive data items more accurately, we create additional data structures to draw the boundary between sensitive data and nonsensitive data.

In MyCloud, ACM_i of a guest VM_i is implemented by an access control list (ACL) that specifies memory regions, VM identifiers, and access permissions. If a VM wants to access a memory region of other VMs, for example, doing VMI for virus scan, the VM initiates a hypercall to request the operation. VMM will check the request against the ACL of the VM being visited (see Table 20.2). If the access is permitted, the VMM will conduct the operation on behalf of the requesting VM. Otherwise, the access will be denied.

Because the memory region can be specified at the byte level, our protection provides byte-level access control. Also, because the protection is enforced in the procedure of a hypercall, it does not rely on paging mechanisms or exception handling either. Thus, it does not add overhead to EPT-based protections.

TABLE 20.2   An Example of the ACL of a VM VMk, $k = i$, and $k = j$

Resources	CVM	VM_i	VM_j
Memory [0 × b0, 0 × c900]		R	R/W
BIOS	R	R	

R, read; W, write.

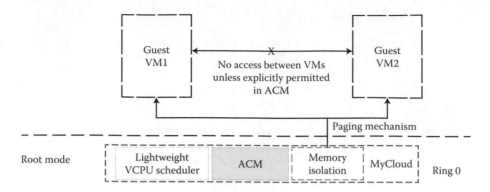

FIGURE 20.6   Memory isolation in the hypervisor.

Note that we do not need security keys for VMs to do the hypercall. The VMM manages VM identifiers and VMCSs for all VMs. It is impossible for one VM_i to set up ACM_j if $i = j$.

20.5.2 Memory and Device Virtualization

Figure 20.6 shows the memory isolation as part of the TCB of hypervisor design. Both Intel and AMD have extended two-layer address translation to three-layer address translation (nested paging). The guest page table specified by CR3 register in the guest VM is responsible for translating guest virtual addresses to guest physical addresses (GPAs). A new table called extended page table (EPT) controlled by the VMM is responsible for translating GPA to machine frame number. The address of EPT is specified by a VMCS field.

MyCloud maintains the EPT and memory management unit (MMU) will automatically translate GPA to machine address. Once set up, the memory translation process will be automatically done by MMU, and no interaction with the virtualization software is necessary. The VMM will only be called for EPT updating when an EPT violation exception happens.

Besides memory translation, I/O management is another important issue to consider. MyCloud utilizes the hardware extensions for virtualization, including input/output MMU (IOMMU) (VTd [46] for Intel and AMD-Vi [47] for AMD) and single root I/O virtualization (SR-IOV) [48], to minimize the TCB size. The IOMMU connects a direct memory access (DMA)-capable I/O bus to the main memory. Like a traditional MMU, which translates CPU-visible virtual addresses to physical addresses, the IOMMU takes care of mapping device-visible virtual addresses (also called device addresses or I/O addresses in this context) to physical addresses. With the help of IOMMU, devices can be directly assigned to VMs. This kind of direct assignment of devices provides very fast I/O and eliminates drivers from VMM. However, it prevents the sharing of I/O devices. To solve this problem, peripheral devices start to support SR-IOV to enable a single root function to be appeared as multiple separate physical devices, called virtual functions.

For a device that does not support virtualization, such as hard drives, there are two solutions. First, cloud users can mount internet small computer system interface (iSCSI) disks [49]. Second, MyCloud can redirect the disk I/O requests to the control VM, who controls the local disk. However, this solution exposes users' data to the cloud provider, so I/O encryption is required for it.

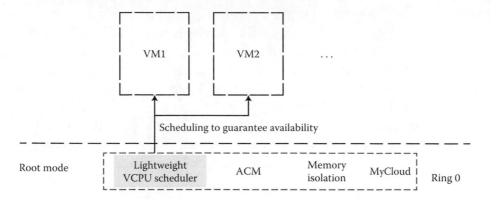

FIGURE 20.7 Scheduler in the hypervisor.

20.5.3 Scheduling

Figure 20.7 shows the scheduler as part of the TCB of hypervisor design. To simplify the system design, MyCloud currently supports two scheduling algorithms: round-robin and simple fair-sharing. In the case of round-robin scheduling, every VMCS is set to have a fixed amount of timer expiration time before the VMENTRY. Timer expiration will trigger a VMEXIT. In the current round-robin method, we only consider scheduling another VM when the timer expires. The drawback of this method is that it lowers the overall CPU utilization if the VM does not have a lot of things to do. We also implement an algorithm close to fire-sharing that evaluates more often on whether to schedule another VM to use the CPU upon the number of VMEXITs, which will improve the CPU utilization.

20.5.4 Cloud Management

Unlike the traditional architectures, the cloud provider only controls an unprivileged control VM in MyCloud design. The control VM is responsible for resource management. The management work is indirect and should be done through the interface provided by the VMM. Any resource allocation change requested by the control VM will be handled by the VMM.

Cloud users' key management is out of the scope of this chapter, whereas a key system is necessary to ensure authentication and cloud platform verification. We provide the following examples to explain that the cloud management is possible with a preconfigured public key system.

To create a VM, MyCloud will allocate the resources under the request from the control VM. The cloud user can remotely attest the platform and negotiate a session key with MyCloud. Afterward, the cloud user can upload an image along with the hash value encrypted by the session key. If MyCloud can successfully verify the image, it will launch the VM until a destroy request is received.

If the resources allocated to a cloud user are expired or no longer needed, MyCloud will destroy the data first, and then mark the resources as free space to the control VM. There can be an argument upon whether the control VM should be able to forcibly recollect guest VM's memory pages. If this is allowed, a compromised control VM may be a huge threat to the whole platform. Although MyCloud can clean all the content in the recollected memory pages, the effects due to missing pages would still leak side-channel information to the control VM. However, if the forcible recollection is not allowed, cloud providers may have a lot of troubles if they are not willing to continue providing service to some VMs. In such a situation, if we want to satisfy the users' desire of privacy, we must sacrifice the power of the cloud providers. For example, we can disable forcible recollection of memory but keep charging the users who do not give up the resources.

We are not trying to find out an ultimate solution to this argument. How to make such decision is business policy related and it is simply out of the scope of this chapter. Our design simply supports either way of decisions. Simply put, we provide security mechanisms but not policies.

Because the control VM's memory access is also restricted by the ACM, and any privileged CPU or I/O instructions will be captured and checked by the VMM, it is impossible for a cloud provider's internal employees to launch insider attacks.

20.6 EVALUATION

In our prototype implementation, the TCB size of MyCloud is ~5.8K LOCs. The comparison of the TCB size with other virtualization techniques is shown in Figure 20.8. MyCloud has the smallest TCB.

Our prototype is built on a hardware platform that has an Intel i7-2600 processor (with both VT-x and VT-d) running at 3.3GHz, an Intel DQ67SW Motherboard (Chip: Q67), 4 GB RAM, a 1 TB SATA hard disk drive, and an Intel e1000 Ethernet controller. We use Ubuntu 10.04 long-term support (LTS) with Linux kernel 2.6.32 for the VM. In order to evaluate the overheads of our platform, we compared the following five configurations:

1. Run an OS on a bare metal machine, labeled as "No_virt" in the figures.

2. Run MyCloud with only one VM, labeled as "One VM" in the figures.

3. Run MyCloud with two VMs. The lightweight round-robin scheduler will be triggered by VMX CPU timer, and the scheduling interval is 10 ms, labeled as "10ms" in the figures.

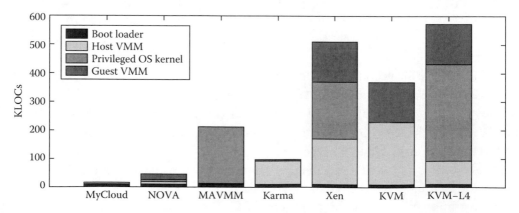

FIGURE 20.8 TCB size comparison of some virtualization architectures. KLOCs, code lines of key components.

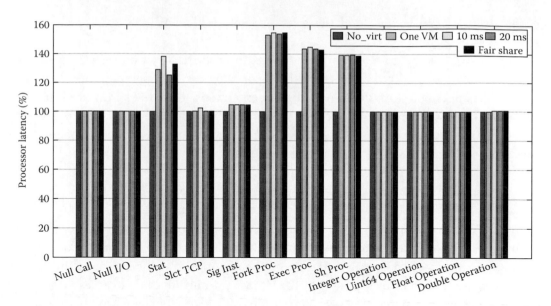

FIGURE 20.9 CPU latency measurements, measured by *lmbench*.

4. Run MyCloud with two VMs. The lightweight round-robin scheduler will be triggered by VMX CPU timer, and the scheduling interval is 20 ms, labeled as "20ms" in the figures.

5. Run MyCloud with two VMs. The scheduling algorithm will allow a busy VM to take more CPU time (95% CPU time) and assign an idle VM less CPU time (around 5% CPU time), labeled as "Fair Share" in the figures.

The results of CPU operations, 32-bit integers, 64-bit integers, float numbers, and doubles are shown in Figure 20.9. The enabling of two VMs slows down the performance by 2%, but the frequency of VM context switching does not impact the performance very much. Figure 20.9 also shows the performance for popular processes such as fork, exec, and sh. Please note the benchmark *lmbench* contains lots of context switches which have to be executed in the VMX root mode. The frequent nonroot/root mode transitions cause the performance reduction of "fork" and "exec" processes. However, in the real world, the applications in the guest VMs do not have so many context switches. Thus, the real performance of guest VMs in MyClound should be better than what we have in the experiments.

20.7 SECURITY ANALYSIS

For the privacy protection interface, because malicious system administrators are deprived of the privileges to access users' privacy, they may try to hijack the hypercall and change the users' ACM when client VMs are modifying the ACM. MyCloud can defeat against this kind of attacks because VM identifiers are managed and checked by the VMM for each hypercall. Furthermore, because this is the only hypercall changing the ACM, the attack surface is very small. In MyCloud, the access control specified in Table 20.1 is precisely and strictly followed.

In terms of the VM-to-VMM attack surface, in any virtualization system, executions should be intercepted if they attempt to perform privileged operations. In MyCloud, VMEXIT happens on a privileged operation or exceptions. Thus, the VMM needs to interact with the VM frequently due to VMEXITs. In MyCloud design, TCB size is greatly reduced by excluding the complicated drivers, management programs, and complex scheduling codes. The control VM is put into the nonroot mode.

Currently, the TCB of MyCloud is quite small (~5.8K LOCs in our prototype) and can be easily verified (recent work has shown the capability to verify ~8.7K LOCs VMM [43]). As long as the TCB is secure, the privacy protection is guaranteed.

When VM-to-VM attacks are considered, the security of MyCloud TCB ensures the enforcement of VM isolation. Thus, many VM-to-VM attacks are immunized. If a VM attempts to access memory pages that do not belong to it, it will be trapped through an EPT violation exception and handled by the VMM. The only interface to access other VM's space is through a hypercall. In such a situation, MyCloud will check whether the access is authorized by the pages' owner or not. In this way, privacy breaching through memory access can be prevented.

Some may concern that if a VM can launch VM-to-VM DoS attacks by causing a lot of unauthorized memory accesses. This attack forces the VMM to process VMEXITs frequently and takes CPU time slices away from the other VMs. Due to this concern, we provide a simple timer-based round-robin algorithm to protect against DoS attacks. The availability is always guaranteed by round-robin algorithm because time slices are fixed for each VM. Alternatively, MyCloud can defend against it by keeping statistics of VMEXITs (e.g., a large number of unauthorized memory access with a time period) and quarantining such VMs.

In MyCloud design, the cloud provider owns only the control VM and indirectly manages cloud resource allocation through the interface provided by the VMM. Note that cloud management tools also rely on the same set of interfaces provided by the VMM. Any resource allocation change requested by the control VM will be checked and handled by the VMM. In this way, the cloud provider cannot stealthily manipulate the users' secrets. Moreover, the control VM is not more privileged than any guest VM. Even if the control VM is compromised or exploited by inside attackers or malicious codes, the access toward the resources allocated to guest VMs will be intercepted by MyCloud. Thus, insider attacks can be eliminated.

20.8 DISCUSSION

Because a VM is usually attached to virtual or physical disks, anything stored in those disks can be accessed without the control of the VM. Thus, it is the user's responsibility to encrypt sensitive data when the data needs to be stored into any storage devices. Due to the same reason, a user should disable OS swap file or use encrypted swap files against attacks to the data on the storage devices. A VM's network traffic should be treated in the same way. Because the cloud provider can always inspect user's traffic through an intrusion detection system or network management software, the users should protect their network traffic through encryption if they have privacy concerns.

In MyCloud design, we provided mechanisms for low-level access control, but we do not try to provide policies, such as which part of VM space should be protected. We believe that the policy should be determined by the cloud provider's SLA and the clients.

For example, it will benefit the clients if the clients agree to grant access to the OS critical data structures to protect the VM from malicious codes. By this way, the cloud provider can periodically scan the VM's critical data structures to make sure it is not compromised and malicious code free. However, such efforts are related to the previous problems—how to determine the exact boundary of protection or how we are certain that we are not over-protecting or underprotecting our sensitive data. We will consider those problems in our future research.

In MyCloud design, any type of physical attacks, including SMM attack, is not taken into consideration. SMRAM and SMM registers are assumed to be protected and set up properly. However, in order to tamper with the SMM-based attacks, we are designing a specific BIOS for MyCloud based on SeaBIOS and coreboot. The new BIOS can not only load hypervisor correctly but also lock the SMRAM by setting the *D_LOCK* bit on the chipset. Additionally, we remove the redundant codes for booting and initializing processes, further reducing the size of TCB.

The integrity of MyCloud platform can be protected in several steps. During the boot procedure, SRTM based on TPM can be used. Later on, DRTM such as Intel TXT/MLE technology can be used to verify the integrity of platform. In order to allow remote users to attest the integrity of the platform, MyCloud implements a simple key management mechanism such as CloudVisor [10]. When users create a new VM, they encrypt the VM key (*KVM*) and the VM image by a public key of TPM (*KAIK* [*KVM*|VM imange}) so that only MyCloud can decrypt and verify the VM key. If the VM key is approved, MyCloud will store it in hypervisor' memory space in order to ensure that the cloud provider cannot modify the VM key. Then, MyCloud will send the encrypted hash value of VM image by using the VM key (*KVM* {*Hash*(VM image)} to remote users. Hence, the remote users can authenticate the integrity of cloud platform.

20.9 NEXT STEP IN FUTURE: AGILE CLOUD WITH PRIVACY PROTECTION

Existing technology does not allow fast deployment and configuration of cloud platforms. Thus, we proposed an architecture shown in Figure 20.10. The architecture is called A-Cloud for "agile" cloud.

In the architecture, the software stack shows a logical structure. It is not strictly mapped from the ring structure of x86 architecture. In the proposed architecture, the host VMM (1) provides the virtual BIOS to virtual devices for guest VMM (KVM and Xen in the figure, can also be others); (2) isolates the guest hypervisor and resource managers, for example, the file system manager and the resource allocator; (3) handles VMEXITs; (4) enables "micro-reboot" that can be implemented in the scheduler part; and (5) supports the platform-wide ACM. The guest VMM can be either type I (like Xen) or type II (like KVM) VMMs. It initializes and manages the guest VMs on its own platform.

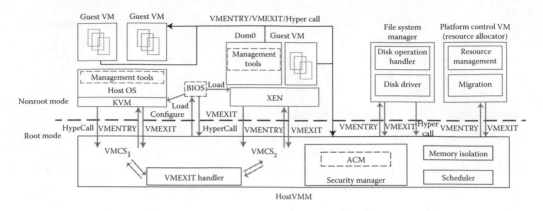

FIGURE 20.10   A-cloud virtualization architecture.

The file system manager provides file systems to guest VMMs and guest VMs, stores the VM images, and provides disk drivers. The resource allocator, also denoted the "platform control VM," manages resources (like memory, disk, and device) and migration of VMs. Note that the file system manager is not part of the control VM in order to protect the platform in case the platform control VM is compromised.

Different from the existing nested architectures, such as IBM Turtle [12] and CloudVisor [10], our host VMM is not a fully functional hypervisor or just a simple filtering and forwarding component for VMEXITs. It is also different from our previous work, MyCloud [7] that does not support the nested architecture and has limit functionalities. The key innovation is the carefully designed separation of privileges among system components and the built-in privacy protection in the virtualization platform.

The security manager has both platform's and user's ACMs and checks the results of resource management against the ACMs. This design supports the separation of resource management and security management in order to reduce the TCB size of the platform. In our design, only software components in the root mode belong to the TCB.

The platform control VM determines if an incoming VM can be supported by an existing guest hypervisor and virtual devices. If not, the platform control VM will boot/reconfigure a guest hypervisor automatically to meet the VM-running requirements. Note that if the security and resources requirements of a VM cannot be satisfied by the host hypervisor regardless configuration, a discovery procedure will be initiated to find a match in the cloud.

The proposed architecture is mainly to address the fast switching between type I and type II cloud platforms while providing privacy protection built in the cloud platform. We are developing the platform and will report our progress in future publications.

20.10 SUMMARY

In this chapter, we described the privacy protection problem in cloud computing. We formally described the privacy protection problem and discussed the solutions through architectural designs. As an example, we described a cloud computing platform, MyCloud that protects the user's privacy against cloud administrators. The core design of MyCloud is to deprivilege the control VM and remove the control VM from the TCB of the cloud platform. At the same time, MyCloud enables users to set up an ACM in the VMM to protect the user's space. Compared with solutions using encryptions, architectual designs have much less computing costs while enabling arbitrary processings.

ACKNOWLEDGMENTS

Wanyu Zang and Meng Yu were partially supported by the National Science Foundation (NSF) CNS-1422355. Meng Yu was partially supported by the NSF CNS-1100221 and NSF IIP-1342664. Peng Liu was partially supported by the NSF CNS-0905131, the NSF CNS-1422594, Air Force Office of Scientific Research (AFOSR) W911NF1210055, and Army Research Office (ARO) W911NF-09-1-0525 (MURI).

REFERENCES

1. Thibodeau, P. Snowden revelations may cost U.S. cloud providers billions, says study. http://www.computerworld.com/s/article/9241489/Snowden_revelations_may_cost_U.S._cloud_providers_billions_says_study?source=rss_keyword_edpicks (August 2013).
2. Gentry, C. A fully homomorphic encryption scheme. PhD thesis, Stanford University, Stanford, CA. crypto.stanford.edu/craig (2009).
3. Chen, Y.Y., Jamkhedkar, P.A., Lee, R.B. A software-hardware architecture for self-protecting data. In *19th ACM Conference on Computer and Communications Security*. Raleigh, NC (October 16–18, 2012).
4. Lie, D., Thekkath, C., Mitchell, M., Lincoln, P., Boneh, D., Mitchell, J., Horowitz, M. Architectural support for copy and tamper resistant software. *SIGPLAN Not.* **35**(11) (November 2000): 168–177
5. Chen, X., Garfinkel, T., Lewis, E.C., Subrahmanyam, P, Waldspurger, C.A., Boneh, D., Dwoskin, J., Ports, D.R. Overshadow: A virtualization-based approach to retrofitting protection in commodity operating systems. In *ASPLOS XIII: Proceedings of the 13th International Conference on Architectural Support for Programming Languages and Operating Systems*. ACM: New York (2008) 2–13.
6. Butt, S., Lagar-Cavilla, H.A., Srivastava, A., Ganapathy, V. Self-service cloud computing. In *Proceedings of the 2012 ACM Conference on Computer and Communications Security*. ACM: New York (2012) 253–264.
7. Li, M., Zang, W., Bai, K., Yu, M., Liu, P. Mycloud—Supporting user-configured privacy protection in cloud computing. In *Annual Computer Security Applications Conference*. New Orleans, LA (December 2013).
8. Pan, W., Zhang, Y., Yu, M., Jing, J. Improving virtualization security by splitting hypervisor into smaller components. In Cuppens-Boulahia, N., Cuppens, F., Garcia-Alfaro, J., eds. *Data and Applications Security and Privacy XXVI*. Volume 7371 of *Lecture Notes in Computer Science*. Springer: Berlin, Germany (2012) 298–313.
9. Murray, D., Milos, G., Hand, S. Improving xen security through disaggregation. In *Proceedings of the Fourth ACM SIGPLAN/SIGOPS International Conference on Virtual Execution Environments*. ACM: New York (2008) 151–160.
10. Zhang, F., Chen, J., Chen, H., Zang, B. Cloudvisor: Retrofitting protection of virtual machines in multi-tenant cloud with nested virtualization. In *Proceedings of the Twenty-Third ACM Symposium on Operating Systems Principles*. ACM: New York (2011) 203–216.
11. Williams, D., Jamjoom, H., Weatherspoon, H. *The Xen-Blanket: Virtualize Once, Run Everywhere*. ACM EuroSys (2012).

12. Ben-Yehuda, M., Day, M., Dubitzky, Z., Factor, M., Har'El, N., Gordon, A., Liguori, A., Wasserman, O., Yassour, B. The turtles project: Design and implementation of nested virtualization. In *Proceedings of the 9th USENIX Conference on Operating Systems Design and Implementation*. USENIX Association (2010) 1–6.

13. Kauer, B., Verissimo, P., Bessani, A. Recursive virtual machines for advanced security mechanisms. In *IEEE/IFIP 41st International Conference on Dependable Systems and Networks Workshops*. IEEE (2011) 117–122.

14. Chuang, I.H., Li, S.H., Huang, K.C., Kuo, Y.H. An effective privacy protection scheme for cloud computing. In *13th International Conference on Advanced Communication Technology* (February 2011) 260–265.

15. Steinberg, U., Kauer, B. Nova: A microhypervisor-based secure virtualization architecture. In *Proceedings of the 5th European Conference on Computer Systems*. ACM: New York (2010) 209–222.

16. Heiser, G., Uhlig, V., LeVasseur, J. Are virtual-machine monitors microkernels done right? *SIGOPS Oper. Syst. Rev.* **40**(1) (January 2006) 95–99.

17. Klein, G., Elphinstone, K., Heiser, G., Andronick, J., Cock, D., Derrin, P., Elkaduwe, D., Engelhardt, K., Kolanski, R., Norrish, M., Sewell, T., Tuch, H., Winwood, S. seL4: Formal verification of an OS kernel. In *Proceedings of the ACM SIGOPS 22nd Symposium on Operating Systems Principles*. ACM: New York (2009) 207–220.

18. Nguyen, A., Schear, N., Jung, H., Godiyal, A., King, S., Nguyen, H. MAVMM: Lightweight and purpose built VMM for malware analysis. In *Annual Computer Security Applications Conference*, 2009. IEEE (2009) 441–450.

19. McCune, J., Li, Y., Qu, N., Zhou, Z., Datta, A., Gligor, V., Perrig, A. TrustVisor: Efficient TCB reduction and attestation. In *2010 IEEE Symposium on Security and Privacy (SP)*. IEEE (2010) 143–158.

20. Intel Inc. *Intel® 64 and IA-32 Architectures Software Developer Manuals* (2009).

21. Intel Coperation. *Intel® Trusted Execution Technology* (2011).

22. Azab, A., Ning, P., Zhang, X. SICE: A hardware-level strongly isolated computing environment for ×86 multi-core platforms. In *Proceedings of the 18th ACM Conference on Computer and Communications Security*. ACM: New York (2011) 375–388.

23. McCune, J.M., Parno, B.J., Perrig, A., Reiter, M.K., Isozaki, H. Flicker: An execution infrastructure for TCB minimization. *SIGOPS Oper. Syst. Rev.* **42**(4) (April 2008) 315–328.

24. Keller, E., Szefer, J., Rexford, J., Lee, R. NoHype: Virtualized cloud infrastructure without the virtualization. In *ACM SIGARCH Computer Architecture News*. Vol. 38. ACM: New York (2010) 350–361.

25. Szefer, J., Keller, E., Lee, R., Rexford, J. Eliminating the hypervisor attack surface for a more secure cloud. In *Proceedings of the 18th ACM Conference on Computer and Communications Security*. ACM: New York (2011) 401–412.

26. Biederman, E. Kernel korner: About LinuxBIOS. *Linux J.* **2001**(92) (December 2001) 7–.

27. Bleikertz, S., Kurmus, A., Nagy, Z.A., Schunter, M. Secure cloud maintenance: Protecting workloads against insider attacks. In *Proceedings of the 7th ACM Symposium on Information, Computer and Communications Security*. ACM: New York (2012) 83–84.

28. Song, D., Shi, E., Fischer, I., Shankar, U. Cloud data protection for the masses. *Computer* **45**(1) (2012) 39–45.

29. Popek, G.J., Goldberg, R.P. Formal requirements for virtualizable third generation architectures. *Commun. ACM* **17**(7) (July 1974) 412–421.

30. Belpaire, G., Hsu, N.T. Formal properties of recursive virtual machine architectures. In *Proceedings of the Fifth ACM Symposium on Operating Systems Principles*. ACM: New York (1975) 89–96.

31. Belpaire, G., Hsu, N.T. Formal properties of recursive virtual machine architectures. *SIGOPS Oper. Syst. Rev.* **9**(5) (November 1975) 89–96.

32. Wang, Z., Lee, R.B. New cache designs for thwarting software cache-based side channel attacks. In *Proceedings of the 34th Annual International Symposium on Computer Architecture.* ACM: New York (2007) 494–505.

33. Halfond, W.G.J., Orso, A., Manolios, P. Using positive tainting and syntax-aware evaluation to counter SQL injection attacks. In *SIGSOFT '06/FSE-14: Proceedings of the 14th ACM SIGSOFT International Symposium on Foundations of Software Engineering.* ACM: New York (2006) 175–185.

34. Haldar, V., Chandra, D., Franz, M. Dynamic taint propagation for java. In *21st Annual Computer Security Applications Conference* (December 5–9, 2005) 9pp.

35. Luk, C.K., Cohn, R.S., Muth, R., Patil, H., Klauser, A., Lowney, P.G., Wallace, S., Reddi, V.J., Hazelwood, K.M. Pin: Building customized program analysis tools with dynamic instrumentation. In *PLDI* (2005) 190–200.

36. Pfoh, J., Schneider, C., Eckert, C. A formal model for virtual machine introspection. In: *VMSec '09: Proceedings of the 1st ACM Workshop on Virtual Machine Security.* ACM: New York (2009) 1–10.

37. Anderson, R., Kuhn, M. Tamper resistance—A cautionary note. In *Proceedings of the Second Usenix Workshop on Electronic Commerce.* Volume 2. (1996) 1–11.

38. Anderson, R., Kuhn, M. Tamper resistance: A cautionary note. In *Proceedings of the 2nd Conference on Proceedings of the Second USENIX Workshop on Electronic Commerce.* Volume 2. USENIX Association: Berkeley, CA (1996) 1–1.

39. Wojtczuk, R., Rutkowska, J. Attacking SMM memory via Intel CPU cache poisoning. In *Invisible Things Lab* (2009).

40. Tomlinson, A. Introduction to the TPM. In *Smart Cards, Tokens, Security and Applications* (2008) 155–172.

41. Garfinkel, T., Pfaff, B., Chow, J., Rosenblum, M., Boneh, D. Terra: A virtual machine-based platform for trusted computing. In *ACM SIGOPS Operating Systems Review.* Volume 37. ACM: New York (2003) 193–206.

42. Singaravelu, L., Pu, C., Härtig, H., Helmuth, C. Reducing TCB complexity for security-sensitive applications: Three case studies. *SIGOPS Oper. Syst. Rev.* **40**(4) (April 2006) 161–174.

43. Klein, G., Elphinstone, K., Heiser, G., Andronick, J., Cock, D., Derrin, P., Elkaduwe, D., Engelhardt, K., Kolanski, R., Norrish, M., Sewell, T., Tuch, H., Winwood, S. seL4: Formal verification of an OS kernel. In *Proceedings of the ACM SIGOPS 22nd Symposium on Operating Systems Principles.* ACM: New York (2009) 207–220.

44. Jhala, R., Majumdar, R. Software model checking. *ACM Comput. Surv.* **41**(4) (October 2009) 21:1–21:54.

45. Advanced Micro Devices. *AMD64 Architecture Programmer's Manual Volume 2: System Programming* (December 2011).

46. Intel Corporation. *Intel® Virtualization Technology Specification for Directed I/O Specification.* www.intel.com/technology/vt/.

47. Advanced Micro Devices. *AMD I/O Virtualization Technology (IOMMU) Specification* (February 2009).

48. Intel Corporation. *Intel® PCI-SIG SR-IOV Primer: An Introduction to SR-IOV Technology* (January 2011).

49. Meth, K.Z., Satran, J. Design of the iSCSI protocol. In *Proceedings of the 20th IEEE/11th NASA Goddard Conference on Mass Storage Systems and Technologies.* IEEE Computer Society: Washington, DC (2003) 116–.

V

Appendices

Appendix A: List of Top Private Cloud Computing Security

Implementation and Deployment Companies

Company	URL	Security Category
1. Abiquo	http://www.abiquo.com/	Cloud management
2. AccelOps	http://www.accelops.com/	Data center
3. Akamai	https://www.akamai.com/	Infrastructure
4. Amazon Web Services	http://aws.amazon.com/	Cloud provider
5. Apigee	http://www.apigee.com/	Infrastructure
6. AppDynamics	http://www.appdynamics.com/	Cloud management
7. Appistry	http://www.appistry.com/	Platform
8. Apple	http://www.apple.com/	Platform
9. Apprenda	http://apprenda.com/platform/	Platform
10. ARM	http://www.arm.com/	Data center
11. Aryaka	http://www.aryaka.com/	Infrastructure
12. AT&T	http://www.att.com/	Infrastructure
13. Barracuda Networks	https://www.barracuda.com/	Security
14. Bluelock	http://www.bluelock.com/	Infrastructure
15. Boundary	http://www.boundary.com/	Infrastructure
16. Box	https://www.box.com/	Storage
17. CA Technologies	http://www.ca.com/us/default.aspx	Security
18. Calxeda	http://www.calxeda.com	Data center
19. Caringo	http://www.caringo.com/	Storage
20. China Telecom	http://en.chinatelecom.com.cn/	Cloud provider
21. Cisco Systems	http://www.cisco.com/	Infrastructure
22. Citrix Systems	http://www.citrix.com/	Infrastructure
23. Cloud9 Analytics	http://www.cloud9analytics.com/	SaaS
24. Cloudera	http://www.cloudera.com/content/cloudera/en/home.html	Big data storage
25. CloudPassage	https://www.cloudpassage.com/	Security
26. CloudScaling	http://www.cloudscaling.com/	Infrastructure

Company	URL	Security Category
27. CloudShare	http://www.cloudshare.com/	SaaS
28. CloudSwitch	http://www.cloudbook.net/community/ companies/cloudswitch-inc	Infrastructure
29. Couchbase	http://www.couchbase.com/	Big data
30. Dell	http://www.dell.com/	Data center
31. Delphix	http://www.delphix.com/	Virtualization
32. DotCloud	https://www.dotcloud.com/	Cloud provider
33. Dropbox	https://www.dropbox.com	Storage
34. Egnyte	http://www.egnyte.com/	Storage
35. Embrane	http://support.embrane.com/	Infrastructure
36. EMC	http://www.emc.com	Storage
37. Engine Yard	https://www.engineyard.com/	Platform
38. Eucalyptus Systems	https://www.eucalyptus.com/	Cloud provider
39. Evernote	https://evernote.com/	Storage
40. Facebook	http://www.facebook.com	Data center
41. Flexiant	http://www.flexiant.com	Platform
42. FluidInfo	http://www.fluidinfo.com	Big data
43. Fusion IO	http://www.fusionio.com/	Storage
44. GigaSpaces	http://www.gigaspaces.com/	Platform
45. GoGrid	https://www.datapipe.com/gogrid/	Cloud provider
46. Google	https://www.google.com/?gws_rd=ssl	Cloud provider
47. Green Revolution Cooling	http://www.grcooling.com/	Data center
48. Heroku	https://www.heroku.com/	Platform
49. Hewlett-Packard	http://www.hp.com/country/us/en/uc/ welcome.html	Cloud provider
50. Hubspan	http://www.hubspan.org/	Platform
51. IBM	http://www.ibm.com/us/en/	Cloud provider
52. Intel	http://www.intel.com/content/www/us/en/ homepage.html	Data center
53. Joyent	https://www.joyent.com/	Cloud provider
54. Juniper	http://www.juniper.net/us/en/	Infrastructure
55. Kaavo	http://www.kaavo.com/	Cloud management
56. Keynote Systems	http://www.keynote.com/	SaaS
57. Layered Technologies	http://layeredtechnologies.net/	Data center
58. LiveOps	http://www.liveops.com/	Platform
59. LogicWorks	http://www.logicworks.net/	Data center
60. LongJump	https://na.longjump.com/networking/Service	Platform
61. Marketo	http://www.marketo.com	SaaS
62. McAfee	http://www.McAfee.com	Security
63. Mezeo	http://www.mezeo.co.za/contact-us	Storage
64. Microsoft	http://www.microsoft.com	Cloud provider
65. MongoDB Inc.	https://www.mongodb.com/	Big data
66. Nasuni	http://www.nasuni.com	Storage
67. NetSuite	http://www.netsuite.com	SaaS
68. New Relic	https://newrelic.com/	Cloud provider

Company	URL	Security Category
69. Nicira	http://www.vmware.com	Infrastructure
70. Nimbula	http://www.oracle.com	Cloud provider
71. Nutanix	http://www.nutanix.com	Storage
72. OpenStack	http://www.openstack.org	Platform
73. OpSource	http://www.opsource.com	Data center
74. Oracle	http://www.oracle.com	Cloud provider
75. OS33	http://os33.com/	Platform
76. Panda Security	http:www.pandasecurity.com	Security
77. Panzura	http://panzura.com/	Storage
78. Ping Identity	https://www.pingidentity.com	Security
79. Puppet Labs	http://puppetlabs.com	Cloud management
80. Qualys	http://www.qualys.com	Security
81. Rackspace	http://www.rackspace.com	Cloud provider
82. RainStor	http://rainstor.com	Big data storage
83. Red Hat	http://www.redhat.com	Data center
84. RightScale	http://www.rightscale.com	Cloud provider
85. SafeNet	http://www.safenet-inc.com	Security
86. Salesforce.com	http://www.salesforce.com	Big data storage
87. SAP	http://www.sap.com	Enterprise software
88. SeaMicro	http://www.seamicro.com	Data center
89. Sentilla	http://www.ericsson.com	Data center
90. Skytap	http://www.skytap.com	Platform
91. SOASTA	http://www.soasta.com	SaaS
92. Symantec	http://www.symantec.com	Security
93. SynapSense	http://www.synapsense.com	Data center
94. Tidemark	http://tidemark.com	Performance management
95. Trend Micro	http://www.TrendMicro.com	Security
96. Vembu Technologies	http://www.vembu.com	Storage
97. Verizon	http://www.verizonwireless.com	Cloud provider
98. Virtustream Inc.	http://www.virtustream.com/	Cloud provider
99. Vmware	http://www.vmware.com	Data center
100. Webroot	http://www.webroot.com	Security
101. Websense	http://www.websense.com	Security
102. Workday	http://www.workday.com	SaaS
103 Zendesk	http://www.zendesk.com	SaaS
104. Zetta	http://www.zetta.net	Storage
105. Zeus Technology	http://www.riverbed.com	Infrastructure
106. Zimory	http://www.zimory.com	Infrastructure
107. Zuora	http://www.zuora.com	SaaS

Appendix B: List of Private Cloud Computing Security

Products and Services

Security Product/Service	Company	Location	Description
Agathon Dedicated Hosting	Agathon Group	https://www.agathongroup.com/	Storage and managed hosting: This service features security, proximity badge access, climate control, power conditioning, and so on.
AIT Web Hosting	AIT, Inc.	https://www.ait.com/	Managed hosting: Includes dedicated and clustered servers, security products as well as custom e-commerce, and web hosting solutions.
Akamai Web Application Accelerator	Akamai Technologies, Inc.	https://www.akamai.com/	Operations software and services: Includes capabilities oriented for business or extranet applications running in the cloud, such as advanced access control rules integrated within complex firewall access policies, and the ability for SaaS application vendors to provision and manage on an application-by-application and a user-by-user basis.
Network Management Service	Allied Technology Group	http://www.alliedtechgroup.com/	Cloud enablers consultants: Offers full IT and network support for cloud computing, to network security and management.
Cloud Security API	Altor Networks	http://www.juniper.net/us/en/products-services/security/	Security resources: To meet the security requirements of both public and private cloud computing initiatives, this interface allows full automation of security management within the virtual data center.
Altor Virtual Firewall	Altor Networks	http://www.juniper.net/us/en/products-services/security/	Security resources: A software security appliance that runs in a virtualized environment and enforces security policy on a per-virtual machine basis.

Security Product/ Service	Company	Location	Description
Amazon VPC/ Virtual Private Cloud	Amazon.com, Inc.	http://aws.amazon.com/	Infrastructure as a service: A secure and seamless bridge between a company's existing IT infrastructure and the Amazon Web Services (AWS) cloud.
Message Sniffer	AppRiver	http://www.appriver.com/	Security resources: An e-mail scanning engine that captures spam when implemented in a managed environment.
AppRiver	AppRiver	http://www.appriver.com/	Security resources: A managed services provider specializing in secure messaging solutions.
SecureTide	AppRiver	http://www.appriver.com/	Security resources: Prevents spam, phishing, viruses, and other Internet pollution from impacting an organizations infrastructure.
ArrowSphere	ArrowSphere	http://www.arrowsphere .net/	Consultants: Offers cloud services from providers within the areas of backup, security, unified communication, storage on demand, servers on demand, business applications, and communication and collaboration.
Hyperguard	Art of Defence GmbH	http://www.brocade.com/ en/products-services/ application-delivery-controllers/virtual-web-application-firewall.html	Security resources: An enterprise web application firewall with attack detection and protection functions that are freely configurable.
Hypersource	Art of Defence GmbH	http://www.brocade.com/ en/products-services/ application-delivery-controllers/virtual-web-application-firewall.html	Security resources: A source code analyzer that identifies and removes security-related vulnerabilities in web applications.
Hyperscan	Art of Defence GmbH	http://www.brocade.com/ en/products-services/ application-delivery-controllers/virtual-web-application-firewall.html	Security resources: A web application vulnerability scan server that scans web applications from the outside for security-related vulnerabilities.
Asankya's Application Delivery Network	Asankya, Inc.	http://www.dnsrsearch .com/index.php? origURL=http%3A// www.asankya .com/&r=&bc=	Network: An optimization service that enable a user to realize private network performance, security, and reliability while using the public Internet as a primary means of transit.
Aspera On-Demand for AWS	Aspera, Inc.	http://asperasoft.com/	Collaboration: Users have the freedom to transfer files at their full bandwidth capacity with highly valuable content being moved and stored reliably, in total security.

Security Product/ Service	Company	Location	Description
Synaptic Hosting Service	AT&T Hosting & Application	http://www.business.att .com/enterprise/ Portfolio/ application-services/	Infrastructure as a service: Provides a complete hosting package, including managed network, servers, security and storage, as well as a designated account support lead and a holistic service-level agreement.
Microsoft Exchange Hosting	Atlas Networks, LLC	http://www.atlasnetworks .us/	Office and communications: Reduces the total cost of ownership for a company's messaging infrastructure while increasing reliability, security, and scalability.
InterGuard	Awareness Technologies	http://www. awarenesstechnologies .com/	Security resources: An ultra light desktop agent managed through the cloud that delivers 360° protection from an entire range of employee-based internal threats.
Backblaze	Backblaze, Inc.	https://www.backblaze .com/	Backup and disaster recovery: An online backup solution that encrypts and uploads all data to a secure datacenter.
Purewire Web Security Service	Barracuda Networks	https://www.barracuda .com/	Security resources: A cloud-based secure web gateway that protects users from malware, phishing, identity theft, and other harmful activity online.
BlueLock Virtual Cloud Professional	BlueLock, LLC	http://www.bluelock.com/	Infrastructure as a service: Offers a production environment with additional security features.
BlueLock Virtual Private Cloud	BlueLock, LLC	http://www.bluelock.com/	Infrastructure as a service: Wherever the cloud is located, it has its own dedicated capacity and security features.
Best VPS Hosting Company	Blurryhosting	http://www.blurryhosting .com/	Network: Hosting plans are fully customized and provide redundant storage space, security, and speed.
Cloud Security Services	Booz Allen Hamilton	http://www.boozallen .com/	Consultants: Provides certification and accreditation of cloud solutions, identity management, cloud segmentation, security audit, application and data obfuscation, and security integration.
Carpathia Cloud Orchestration	Carpathia Hosting, Inc.	http://carpathia.com/	Infrastructure as a service: A hybrid model that provides the security, availability, and reliability of a traditionally hosted environment paired with instant access to cloud computing and storage.
Catbird vSecurity Cloud Edition	Catbird Networks, Inc.	http://www2.catbird.com/	Security resources: Provides comprehensive, documented security, and compliance for cloud providers.
Data Center Solutions	CDI Southeast	http://www.cdillc.com/	Physical resources: Offers technology and services for consolidations, data center optimization, networking/security, storage, and virtualization.

Security Product/ Service	Company	Location	Description
End-User Computing Solutions	CDI Southeast	http://www.cdillc.com/	Operations software and services: Expertise in virtualization and security.
Hosted Web Security	CensorNet Ltd	https://www.censornet.com/	Security resources: A cloud-based web filtering solution for securing networks with multiple locations and remote, unsupervised, or roaming users.
CipherCloud	CipherCloud, Inc.	http://www.ciphercloud.com/	Security resources: Leverages strong encryption to protect sensitive data in real time before it is sent to the cloud.
XenApp	Citrix Systems, Inc.	http://www.citrix.com/	Cloud services management: Improves application management by centralizing applications in the data center, and controls and encrypts access to data and applications.
NetScaler	Citrix Systems, Inc.	http://www.citrix.com/	Operations software and services: A web application delivery controller that uses application accelerator methods such as HTTP compression and caching, thus ensuring application availability through advanced L4-7 load balancer and content switching methods, and increasing application security with an integrated application firewall.
Access Gateway	Citrix Systems, Inc.	http://www.citrix.com/	Operations software and services: Gives IT administrators a single point to manage access control and limit actions within sessions based on both the user identity and the endpoint device, providing better application security, data protection, and compliance management.
Hosted Desktop	ClevaGroup Limited	http://www.clevagroup.co.uk/	Desktop as a service: To securely access an entire Windows 8 and 10 desktop through an Internet-enabled Windows or non-Windows device, from anywhere.
CloudBuddy Personal	CloudBuddy	http://www.mycloudbuddy.com/	Desktop as a service: A free tool that creates an exploration interface for your virtual desktop on the cloud through data management, sharing, access, and security.
CloudFlare	CloudFlare, Inc.	https://www.cloudflare.com/	Security resources: Secures websites from spam and hacking attacks.
Wordpress Security Tool	CloudGuardian	http://www.leansecurity.com.au/	Security resources: Secures all WordPress websites, controls the admin access to the WordPress websites, ensures that the plugins are up to date and don't have any vulnerabilities, and monitors the WordPress version to reduce the risk of compromise.

Security Product/ Service	Company	Location	Description
Amazon AWS Security Tool	CloudGuardian	http://www.leansecurity .com.au/	Security resources: Makes sure the security groups are configured properly.
Cloudmark Desktop	Cloudmark, Inc.	http://www.cloudmark .com/en	Security resources: Provides protection against spam, phishing, and viruses for users of Microsoft Outlook, Outlook Express, Windows Mail for Vista, and Mozilla Thunderbird.
Cloudmark Sender Intelligence	Cloudmark, Inc.	http://www.cloudmark .com/en	Security resources: Uses real-time data from the Cloudmark Global Threat Network to create comprehensive sender profiles.
Cloudmark MobileAuthority	Cloudmark, Inc.	http://www.cloudmark .com/en	Security resources: Employs sender reputation data, content filtering technology, and environmental monitoring/analysis to ensure that mobile operators can protect their network and subscribers from evolving mobile messaging attacks and threats.
Cloudmark Gateway	Cloudmark, Inc.	http://www.cloudmark .com/en	Security resources: Provides protection at the network's perimeter. Cloudmark Gateway with features such as flexible policy management, advanced traffic shaping and intelligent IP/content filtering, a high-performance edge mail transfer agent, and integrates seamlessly with Cloudmark Authority and Cloudmark Sender Intelligence for a comprehensive messaging security solution.
CloudFilter	Cloudmark, Inc.	http://www.cloudmark .com/en	Security resources: Designed to release web hosting providers and service providers from the capital and administrative burden of managing e-mail security.
Cloudmark ActiveFilter for Mail Stores	Cloudmark, Inc.	http://www.cloudmark .com/en	Security resources: Enables detection of spam messages that have been delivered in the previous seconds or minutes.
Cloudmark Authority	Cloudmark, Inc.	http://www.cloudmark .com/en	Security resources: A message filtering solution that delivers antispam, anti-phishing and antivirus protection.
Halo SVM	CloudPassage, Inc.	https://www.cloudpassage .com/	Security resources: Addresses server vulnerability management needs with the scalability, speed, and elasticity needed for public, private, and hybrid infrastructure-as-a-service server environments.
Halo Firewall	CloudPassage, Inc.	https://www.cloudpassage .com/	Security resources: Allows users to build, deploy, and manage host-based firewall policies across their entire infrastructure-as-a-service cloud environment from a simple web-based interface.

Security Product/ Service	Company	Location	Description
AIMstor Information Security	Cofio Software, Inc.	http://www.cofio.com/	Security resources: Provides the ability to implement the level of control upon your data, whether it resides on laptops, desktops, file servers, application servers, or other support platforms.
CommGate Shield	CommGate Systems India Pvt Ltd	http://www.commgate.net/	Security resources: A highly secure Internet gateway firewall integrated with multiple security functions.
CommGate Enterprise Server	CommGate Systems India Pvt Ltd	http://www.commgate.net/	Physical resources: Delivers an integrated family of applications that simplifies Internet collaboration with e-mail and file-sharing, while consolidating the network and security systems at the network gateway.
CommGate Mail Xchange	CommGate Systems India Pvt Ltd	http://www.commgate.net/	Office and communications: A secure e-mail, contacts, group calendaring, and collaborative e-mail server solution based on the Zimbra Collaboration Server.
CSC Cloud Orchestration Services	Computer Sciences Corporation	http://www.csc.com/	Systems integrators: Provides automated arrangement, coordination, federation, management, security, and operation of private, public, and hybrid cloud computing environments, ensuring industry-specific compliance and auditing services.
Identity Management as a Service (IdMaaS)	Covisint LLC	http://www.covisint.com/	Security resources: Offers the tools to manage corporate employee access to resources and applications hosted outside of the company, such as benefits enrollment, pay stubs, corporate travel, and 401(k).
CryptoCard	CryptoCard, Inc.	http://www2.gemalto.com/ sas/index.html	Security resources: Reduces the risks associated with remote access and web-based processes through strong password security and increased compliance.
CryptoShield	CryptoCard, Inc.	http://www2.gemalto.com/ sas/index.html	Security resources: An authentication solution that consists of a suite of applications designed for implementing and operating strong passwords using a two-factor authentication, thus enabling password validation.
BlackShield ID	CryptoCard, Inc.	http://www2.gemalto.com/ sas/index.html	Security resources: A server-based strong authentication solution that identifies individuals before granting access to networks, data, and applications.

Security Product/ Service	Company	Location	Description
CryptoCard ICE	CryptoCard, Inc.	http://www2.gemalto.com/ sas/index.html	Security resources: Helps reduce the security risk during a business disruption by allowing staff to log in to a business network using a two-factor authentication rather than passwords which could leave your network open to hackers or ID thieves.
Crypto-Mas	CryptoCard, Inc.	http://www2.gemalto.com/ sas/index.html	Security resources: A global managed authentication service that leverages cloud-based security technologies and cloud computing to offer unrivalled availability and service levels.
AppGate Security Server	Cryptzone Group AB	https://www.cryptzone .com/	Security resources: Provides a security model for the perimeterless IT landscape; and, enables organizations to adopt a software defined perimeter approach for granular security control.

Appendix C: List of Private Cloud Computing Security

Compliance Standards

Type of Standard	Standard	Location	Description
Governance	ISO 38500—IT Governance	http://www.38500.org/	Not specific to private cloud computing but can be used by both private cloud service providers and private cloud service customers
Governance	COBIT	http://www.isaca.org/ COBIT/Pages/default .aspx	Created by the ISACA organization and provides a framework for IT governance and IT management and private cloud services
Governance	ITIL	http://www.itil-officialsite.com/	A set of practices for IT service management, which can be applied to the management of private cloud services
Governance	ISO 20000	http://en.wikipedia.org/ wiki/ISO/IEC_20000	An international standard for IT service management and private cloud services
Governance	SSAE 16	http://ssae16.com/	An audit standard that applies to service organizations, which can be applied to private cloud service providers
Risk and Compliance	HIPAA	http://www.hhs.gov/ocr/ privacy/	Relates to the handling of health-related information and private cloud services
Risk and Compliance	PCI-DSS	https://www. pcisecuritystandards. org/security_standards/	Relates to the security of payment card data and private cloud services
Risk and Compliance	FedRAMP	http://www.fedramp.gov	Provides a standardized approach to security assessment, authorization, and continuous monitoring for private cloud products and services
Risk and Compliance	FISMA	http://www.27000.org/	Places information security requirements on federal agencies and private cloud products and services
Risk and Compliance	ISO/IEC 27000-series	http://www.27000.org/	Relates to the security of ICT systems and private cloud products and services

Type of Standard	Standard	Location	Description
Risk and Compliance	ISO 27001	http://www.27000.org/	An advisory standard that applies to all types and sizes of organizations according to the particular private cloud information security risks they face
Risk and Compliance	ISO 27002	http://www.27000.org/	A collection of security controls that assumes that the design and/or operation of a private cloud service provider's information security management systems is consistent and compliant with the standard
Risk and Compliance	ISO 27017	http://www.27000.org/	Deals with the application of the ISO 27002 specification to the use and provision of private cloud services
Risk and Compliance	ISO 27018	http://www.27000.org/	Deals with the application of 27002 to the handling of personally identifiable information in private cloud computing
Audit Operational	SSAE 16	http://www.dmtf.org/standards/cadf	An attestation standard for private cloud services that have a significant impact on the financial statements of service customers
Audit Operational	DMTF	http://www.dmtf.org/standards/cadf	Supports the submission and retrieval of normative audit event data from private cloud service providers in the form of customized reports and logs that can be dynamically generated for private cloud service customers using their criteria
IETF	LDAP	http://tools.ietf.org/html/rfc4510	Widely used to provide access to directory servers, which include private cloud authentication and authorization services
OASIS	SAML 2.0 or higher	https://www.oasis-open.org/committees/tc_home.php?wg_abbrev=security	Used for the exchange of private cloud authentication and authorization data between security domains

Glossary

ACL: access control list

airframe: an open source private cloud computing platform targeted at organizations in the thinking stage of adopting a private cloud services model or evaluating options and alternatives for private cloud solutions

Amazon EC2: a commercial web service that lets customers rent computing resources from the Elastic Computer Cloud (EC2) private cloud

anything as a service: the growing diversity of services available over the Internet via private cloud computing as opposed to being provided locally, or on-premises

Apache Private CloudStack: an open source private cloud computing and infrastructure-as-a-service platform developed to help make creating, deploying, and managing private cloud services easier by providing a complete stack of features and components for private cloud environments

asynchronous javascript and XML (AJAX): a group of web development methods

authentication: a process of verifying the identity of a user, process, or device, often as a prerequisite to allowing access to resources in an information system

broad network access: capabilities are available over the network and accessed through standard mechanisms that promote use by heterogeneous thin or thick client platforms (mobile phones, laptops, and personal digital assistants)

certificate: a digital representation of information that at least identifies the certification authority issuing it, names or identifies its subscriber, contains the subscriber's public key, identifies its operational period, and is digitally signed by the certification authority issuing it

client: a machine or software application that accesses a private cloud over a network connection, perhaps on behalf of a subscriber

cloud application management for platforms (CAMP): a specification designed to ease management of applications across public and private cloud computing platforms

compliance: conformity in fulfilling official requirements

DBMS: database management system

desktop as a service: a form of virtual desktop infrastructure (VDI) in which the VDI is outsourced and handled by a third party

DMZ: demilitarized zone in network computing

DNS: domain name server

dynamic subsystem: a subsystem that is not continually present during the execution phase of an information system

enterprise application: describes applications that a business would use to assist the organization in solving enterprise problems

enterprise private cloud backup: solutions that typically add essential features such as archiving and disaster recovery to private cloud backup solutions

Eucalyptus: an open source cloud computing and infrastructure-as-a-service platform for enabling private clouds

FISMA: Federal Information Security Management Act

HTML: Hypertext Markup Language

HTTP: Hypertext Transfer Protocol

HTTPS: Hypertext Transfer Protocol Secure

hybrid private cloud: where the private cloud infrastructure is a composition of two or more clouds that remain unique entities but are bound together by a standardized or proprietary technology that enables data and application portability

hybrid private cloud storage: a combination of public cloud storage and private cloud storage where some critical data reside in the enterprise's private cloud, whereas other data are stored and accessible from a public cloud storage provider

IA-64: 64-Bit Intel Itanium architecture

IBM Private Cloud: a collection of enterprise-class technologies and services developed to help customers assess their private cloud readiness, develop adoption strategies, and identify business entry points for a private cloud environment

IBM Private CloudBurst: a solution from the IBM that is designed to provide resource monitoring, cost management, and services availability in a private cloud

IDS/IPS: intrusion detection systems/intrusion prevention systems

infrastructure as a service: a computer infrastructure, such as virtualization, being delivered as a service

internal private cloud: another name for a private cloud

IP: Internet protocol

iSCSI: Internet Small System Computer Interface

ISO: International Standards Organization

IT: information technology

ITL: Information Technology Laboratory

JVM: Java Virtual Machine

mobile private cloud storage: a form of private cloud storage that applies to storing an individual's mobile device data in the private cloud and providing the individual with access to the data from anywhere

multitenant: the phrase used to describe multiple customers using the same public cloud in private cloud computing

net-centric architecture: a complex system of systems composed of subsystems and services that are part of a continuously evolving, complex community of people, devices, information, and services interconnected by a network that enhances information sharing and collaboration

NFS: network file system

NIST: US National Institute of Standards and Technology

OMB: Office of Management and Budget

on-demand self-service: where a consumer can unilaterally provision computing capabilities, such as server time and network storage, as needed automatically without requiring human interaction with each service's provider

online backup: to back up data from your hard drive to a remote server or computer using a network connection

OpenStack Grizzly: the follow-up to the Folsom release of the OpenStack open source private cloud computing platform

OVF: open virtualization format

PaaS: platform as a service

PCAMP: Private Cloud Application Management for Platforms

PEM: privacy-enhanced mail

personal private cloud storage: a form of private cloud storage that applies to storing an individual's data in the private cloud and providing the individual with access to the data from anywhere

private cloud: the private cloud infrastructure is operated solely for an organization

private cloud application: a cloud application that describes a software application that is never installed on a local computer

private cloud backup: backs up data to a remote, private cloud-based server

private cloud backup service provider: a third-party entity that manages and distributes remote, private cloud-based data backup services and solutions to customers from a central data center

private cloud backup solutions: enables enterprises or individuals to store their data and computer files on the Internet using a storage service provider, rather than storing the data locally on a physical disk, such as a hard drive or tape backup

private cloud computing: a model for enabling on-demand network access to a shared pool of configurable IT capabilities/resources that can be rapidly provisioned and released with minimal management effort or service provider interaction

private cloud computing accounting software: an accounting software that is hosted on remote servers

Private Cloud Computing Reseller: a company that purchases hosting services from a private cloud server hosting or private cloud computing provider and then resells them to its own customers

private cloud database: a database accessible to clients from the private cloud and delivered to users on demand via the Internet from a private cloud database provider's servers

private cloud enablement: the process of making available one or more of the following services and infrastructures to create a public cloud computing environment: private cloud provider, client, and application

private cloud infrastructure as a service: where the consumer does not manage or control the underlying private cloud infrastructure, but has control over operating systems, storage, deployed applications, and possibly limited control of select networking components (host firewalls)

private cloud management: software and technologies designed for operating and monitoring the applications, data, and services residing in the private cloud

private cloud migration: the process of transitioning all or part of a company's data, applications, and services from on-site premises behind the firewall to the private cloud, where the information can be provided over the Internet on an on-demand basis

private cloud OS: a phrase frequently used in place of platform as a service to denote an association with private cloud computing

private cloud platform as a service: where the consumer does not manage or control the underlying private cloud infrastructure, including network, servers, operating systems, or storage, but has control over the deployed applications and possibly application hosting environment configurations

private cloud portability: the ability to move applications and its associated data between one cloud provider and another—or between public and private cloud environments

private cloud project: enables the IT infrastructure to become more capable of quickly adapting to continually evolving business needs and requirements

private cloud provider: an organization that provides private cloud services

private cloud provisioning: the deployment of a company's private cloud computing strategy, which typically first involves selecting which applications and services will reside in the private cloud and which will remain on-site behind the firewall or in the private cloud

private cloud security: where private cloud implementation aims to avoid many of the objections regarding private cloud computing security

private cloud server hosting: a type of hosting in which hosting services are made available to customers on demand via the Internet

private cloud software as a service: where the consumer does not manage or control the underlying private cloud infrastructure, including network, servers, operating systems, storage, or even individual application capabilities, with the possible exception of limited user-specific application configuration settings

private cloud storage: where the enterprise data and private cloud storage resources both reside within the enterprise's data center and behind the firewall

private cloud subscriber: a person or organization that is a customer of a private cloud

private cloud testing: load and performance testing conducted on the applications and services provided via private cloud computing, in order to ensure optimal performance and scalability under a wide variety of conditions

private community cloud: where the private cloud infrastructure is shared by several organizations and supports a specific community that has shared concerns

public key cryptography: an encryption method that uses a two-part key: a public key and a private key

public private cloud: where the private cloud infrastructure is made available to the general public or a large industry group and is owned by an organization selling private cloud services

public private cloud storage: a form of private cloud storage where the enterprise and the storage service provider are separate and the data are stored outside of the enterprise's data center

rapid elasticity: where capabilities can be rapidly and elastically provisioned, in some cases automatically, to quickly scale out and rapidly released to quickly scale in

Red Hat OpenShift: provides developers with a choice in languages, frameworks, and private clouds to build, test, run, and manage Java, Ruby, PHP, Perl, and Python applications

Red Hat private cloud computing: solutions for private clouds, hybrid clouds, and public clouds offered by Red Hat

Red Hat Private CloudForms: an infrastructure-as-a-service offering that builds upon a collection of more than 60 open source projects

resource pooling: where the provider's computing resources are pooled to serve multiple consumers using a multitenant model, with different physical and virtual resources dynamically assigned and reassigned according to consumer demand

service agreement: a legal document specifying the rules of the legal contract between the private cloud user and the private cloud provider

service-level agreement: a document stating the technical performance promises made by the private cloud provider, how disputes are to be discovered and handled, and any remedies for performance failures

software as a service (SaaS): a software delivery method that provides access to software and its functions remotely as a web-based service

software plus services: Microsoft's philosophy for complementing the software company's on-premises software offerings with private cloud-based remote computing software options

SP: special publication

SQL: Structured Query Language

SSL/TLS: Secure Socket Layer/Transport Layer Security

storage private cloud: the collection of multiple distributed and connected resources responsible for storing and managing data online in the private cloud

TCP: transmission control protocol

vertical private cloud computing: the phrase used to describe the optimization of private cloud computing and private cloud services for a particular vertical or specific use application

virtual machine (VM): an efficient, isolated duplicate of a real machine

virtualization: the simulation of the software and/or hardware upon which other software runs

VLAN: virtual local area network

VM: virtual machine

VMM: virtual machine monitor

VMware Private vCloud Connector: a tool that facilitates hybrid cloud computing for organizations

WSDL: Web Services Description Language

X.509: an ITU-T standard for a public key infrastructure

XML: Extensible Markup Language

Index

Note: Page numbers followed by f and t refer to figures and tables, respectively.